Joseph Haydn

AND THE CLASSICAL CHORAL TRADITION

Joseph Haydn
AND THE CLASSICAL
CHORAL TRADITION

LAWRENCE SCHENBECK

HINSHAW MUSIC
Chapel Hill, North Carolina

ISBN 0-937276-17-0

To Lynn Whitten, who brought me up in choral music

and to the memory of my father

CONTENTS

Preface and Acknowledgments *ix*

HISTORY

1 / CHURCH, STATE, AND ART IN 18TH-CENTURY AUSTRIA

2 / EARLY SACRED MUSIC

3 / OCCASIONAL MUSIC FOR THE ESTERHÁZYS AND OTHERS

4 / MASSES 1766-1782

5 / ORATORIOS 1767-1784; OPERA CHORUSES

6 / SMALLER SACRED WORKS AFTER 1766

7 / LATE SECULAR MUSIC

8 / LATE MASSES

9 / LATE ORATORIOS

PERFORMANCE

10 / PERFORMANCE PRACTICES

11 / GENERAL WORKLIST

12 / SPECIALIZED WORKLISTS

APPENDIX

Preface and Acknowledgements

Years ago, Walter Collins asked me why I had chosen Haydn for a major study in choral history and performance. For a number of very good reasons, I replied—Haydn's long life, his stylistic innovations, his fecundity. He was the major composer of choral music in the Classical era, playing a dominant role in the reinvention of the oratorio and Mass and contributing to countless other genres as well. A new and separate study devoted to his choral works was, if anything, long overdue.

This book is the result of that study. Written with the cooperation and guidance of the Research and Publications Committee of the American Choral Directors Association, it has necessarily been shaped by rather specific goals. A primary goal was to structure its design and content so that performing musicians, especially conductors choosing, studying, and preparing to perform choral music by Joseph Haydn, would find it useful. Thus the biographical and analytical material has been supplemented by *1)* a detailed essay on performance practices, *2)* a concise catalog of music that lists editions, instrumentations, timings, and other performance-related data, and *3)* various practical appendices.

A second goal was to create a guide to the Haydn literature that would aid further research on this music. For that reason, I included a comprehensive bibliography and documented all sources of information in the text. Homage must be paid to the scholars whose work informs so much of this little volume. If it were not for such pioneers as Carl Maria Brand, Irmgard Becker-Glauch, and H. C. Robbins Landon, also younger folk like James Dack and Bruce Mac Intyre, a compendium like this might not exist. It would at any rate be far slimmer and less helpful. I hope this book's careful documentation will inspire readers to consult the earlier work that was such a boon and beacon to me.

My third goal was more personal. It was to balance the practical and scholarly with something engaging that would offer, at times, a fresh view of Haydn's world and art. Whether I have succeeded in this will be judged differently by every reader. It may be that certain practices will lend the book an hauteur that was not intended. In discussing a time and place far removed from our own, I found it impossible to avoid foreign and unfamiliar terms and old spellings—thus *Capellmeister*, not *Kapellmeister*, and words like *Thurner-*

meister which have no real English equivalent. It was also difficult, and to my mind undesirable, to avoid theoretical and stylistic terms that some may find esoteric. Haydn's music is a sophisticated product of an era in which literacy and intellectual accomplishment conferred the sort of status reserved today for those who wear a certain kind of sneaker. For that reason, we may not always choose to discuss the *galant* characteristics of a Haydn Benedictus with our church choirs, or to outline sonata form in a Kyrie for our glee club. The trouble is that one cannot fully enter Haydn's world without knowing such things.

I must also confess to favoring earlier and lesser-known works with more space than some of their famous cousins received. Anyone who wants to know the basic data and the most important current research on, say, *The Creation* can find it here. But that person will also find relatively as much or more about the Göttweig *Missa brevis* or Haydn's first *Lauda Sion* setting. These works deserve more attention, especially from performers, and if they don't get it here, who will provide it?

You can still leaf past what doesn't interest you. The book is organized so that one may skip around without sacrificing basic intelligibility. The first chapter includes an overview of Austrian history and culture to Haydn's time, ending with a summary of his childhood and early choral experiences. Important as this material is, no reader will suffer greatly by postponing its ingestion in favor of more urgent matters. Likewise, the chapters on various choral genres can stand alone fairly well as sources of information. It would be less wise to dip in and out of the performance-practices essay, though; too much of the embroidery there only makes sense when seen as part of the tapestry. Incidentally, performance-practice data specific to an individual work is usually embedded in the historical narrative for that work, not in Chapter 10 itself.

I am deeply grateful to a number of people who helped to make this study possible and as good as it is. First of all, the official readers on the ACDA Research and Publications Committee provided steady support and assistance with a broad range of issues. They were Richard Cox, Alfred Mann, and R. Lynn Whitten. Walter S. Collins coordinated their efforts and provided moral support of his own; later Ray Robinson headed up the team. Nicholas Temperley and James Dack also made useful suggestions, and Stewart Carter graciously gave the performance-practices essay a final close reading. Whatever mistakes and omissions remain are my work, not theirs.

A grant from the National Endowment for the Humanities enabled me to study manuscripts and other materials in Austria in the Spring of 1989. The institutions I visted are listed below. I was also able to visit performance sites at that time, including St. Stephen's Cathedral, Vienna's Augustinerkirche, the pilgrimage church at Mariazell, and the major Haydn churches in Eisenstadt.

My home base for most of this research was the Staley Library at Millikin University in Decatur, Illinois, where Carol Batterham, Tschera Connell, and Marjorie Wille provided service above and beyond, etc., on many occasions. In the book's final stages, I relied upon the collections and assistance of the Robert W. Woodruff Library of the Atlanta University

Center (Joseph Troutman), the Pullen Library of Georgia State University (Ralph Russell), and the Woodruff Library at Emory University. A number of other libraries also made materials and services available: University of Colorado at Boulder (Karl Kroeger), University of Illinois at Champaign-Urbana, BBC Music Library (Michael White) in London, the Staatsbibliothek (Joachim Jaenecke) in Berlin, and in Vienna the Austrian National Library (Günter Brosche) and the Gesellschaft der Musikfreunde (Otto Biba). The Benedictine Monasteries of Lambach (Herbert Nöbauer, Stiftsorganist), Kremsmünster (Pr. Alfons Mandorfer), Melk (Pr. Bruno Brandstetter), and Göttweig (Pr. Gregor M. Lechner, Art Collection) provided generous access to their collections of eighteenth- and early nineteenth-century performance materials and equally generous Austrian hospitality.

I would also like to thank the following persons for providing microfilms, dissertations, pre-publication editions, or other materials: Dennis Shrock, James Dack, H. C. Robbins Landon, the Berlin Staatsbibliothek (Preussischer Kulturbesitz, Musikabteilung), Doblinger Verlag (Herbert Vogg), Mark Foster Music Co. (Mark Junkert, then Carla Hennes), Carus Verlag (Günter Grauling), Foreign Music Distributors (Robert Walls and George Sturm), and Broude Brothers (Ronald Broude). Permission to reprint copyrighted material from a number of sources was immensely helpful and I am grateful to all those who gave it, including the Indiana University Press, A. Peter Brown, Neal Zaslaw, Stanley Sadie, H. C. Robbins Landon, and the music publishers Carus, Henle, Broude Brothers, and Doblinger. Specific acknowledgements of individual items are made in the text, usually in proximity to the item.

Thanks also to the staff at Hinshaw Music for their help as this book found its way to press. Don Hinshaw's unwavering enthusiasm was just one more example of his lifelong concern for furthering the choral art. I will always remember Leonard Van Ness's patience and assistance in the book's early stages, not to mention Lee Thomas's positive attitude whenever we encountered what seemed to be one more insurmountable obstacle.

My son David edited the index, even though it distracted from karate practice, and my daughter Cathy helped with some of the research tasks. I have noticed in reading acknowledgements that the author's spouse always seems to be mentioned last. Now I finally understand just how unfair that is. My wife Lyn was my greatest supporter and most steadfast ally; she also contributed materially to the project with music engraving, proofreading, and persistent attention to business details. I will be grateful to her for that, and for much more, for the rest of my life.

Spelman College
Atlanta, Georgia
4 July 1995

HISTORY

1

CHURCH, STATE, AND ART IN EIGHTEENTH-CENTURY AUSTRIA

THE HABSBURGS AND THE COUNTER-REFORMATION

> I am descended from a long line of Christian Emperors of this noble German nation, and of the Catholic kings of Spain, the archdukes of Austria and the dukes of Burgundy. All were faithful to the death to the Church of Rome, and they defended the Catholic Church and the honor of God.
>
> I have resolved to follow in their steps. A single monk who goes counter to all Christianity for a thousand years must be wrong. Therefore I am resolved to stake my lands, my friends, my body, my blood, my life and my soul in pledge for this cause.[1]

These words of young Charles V, spoken as he placed Martin Luther under the ban of Empire, could as easily have come 200 years later from Charles VI, Holy Roman Emperor during Joseph Haydn's childhood. The latter Charles also saw his throne as a sacred trust, his political mission as divinely ordered. He was the last member of his family to live in the hope of uniting the civilized world under one church and one ruler.

It could be said that the Habsburgs forged Austrian society and culture from their very dreams. As part of their role, they assumed leadership for more than two centuries in the patronage of Austrian church music, creating the spiritual and artistic world in which Joseph Haydn was born, was educated, and worked. If we are fully to understand Haydn's early church music, we must also know the Habsburg world-view that shaped it.

Not every Habsburg was as fervent a supporter of the Church in Rome as Charles V. Lutheranism had made strong inroads in Vienna and its environs, reaching even many

---

[1] Charles V's opening remarks at the Diet of Worms, quoted in Crankshaw *Habsburgs*, 65.

members of the nobility. Emperor Maximilian II (r. 1564-1576), one of the more independent intellects in his family, had actually refused the last rites and admitted no clergy to his bedside: "My priest is in heaven," he said.[2]

Maximilian's death unleashed the full force of the Counter-Reformation on Austria. The highly disciplined, fanatical Society of Jesus had been responsible for educating Maximilian's son Rudolph in Spain. When Rudolph assumed the throne, the Jesuits gained virtually complete control over the intellectual life of a great nation, a control they would retain for almost two hundred years.

A slow but steady erosion of Protestant rights and privileges began. As the Habsburg bureaucracy increased its hold on local government, education, customs barriers, and the like, Protestants saw their livelihoods diminish together with their religious freedom. Under Ferdinand II (r. 1619-1637), the wholesale expulsion of Protestants from imperial soil began in earnest. One of Ferdinand's first acts in Styria was to force the evacuation of over half of its people because they were not members of the true Church. Faithful Catholic subjects were imported to take the place of those hauled away. Old churches were restored to the Catholics, and the new churches and schools built by the Protestants were pulled down. Jesuit colleges were established at Graz and Bruck-an-der-Mur.[3]

An exodus of Protestants continued throughout the Thirty Years' War (1618-1648). Viennese municipal records show that in one year alone over a thousand families, including many of the most skilled and prosperous, paid an exit tax and left. According to Austrian scholar E. H. Buschbeck, "The number of those who preferred emigration to recantation was enormous, and it was the staunchest and most upright elements who chose exile rather than submission. Austria has probably never quite repaired this loss; it has left deep and permanent marks on her character."[4]

By Haydn's time, the country was again steadfastly Catholic, but its Catholicism had been left with special qualities. That was due partly to the proximity of Italy and partly to the lingering effects of the Counter-Reformation. Running through all the descriptions we read of civic holy days, feasts, and pilgrimages sponsored by various "brotherhoods" is the sense of an infra-religion for the people and by the people, an accumulation of activities that strove to fill the emotional void remaining after Protestantism fled. The Jesuits may have controlled Vienna's intellectual life and, through their institutions, shaped the minds of its future leaders. But beneath people's compliant behavior lay defiance; at the very least they harbored a desire to add immediate, sensible gratification to their religious lives. Ilsa Barea, a wise and subtle observer of Viennese history, detected the essence of this attitude in the writings of Abraham a Sancta Clara, an Augustinian friar who came to Vienna in 1662:

---

[2] Crankshaw *Habsburgs*, 94-98.

[3] Crankshaw *Habsburgs*, 100-105, 111.

[4] Buschbeck *Austria*, 68.

What I have read of [Abraham's] works has left me with the vivid impression that among the ordinary Viennese at the end of the seventeenth century there were two tendencies at work which defied their spiritual advisers. One was an almost pagan enjoyment of every sensual pleasure, whether food or fine music, a Punch-and-Judy show, the spectacle of a religious procession, or the game of love. It was an attitude of "let us eat, drink and be merry, for tomorrow we die" with a vengeance. The burden of individual responsibility before God and one's own conscience, which Protestant teachers had laid on the shoulders of their pupils, had been lifted from the Viennese; it was as if they had been glad to surrender all responsibility for their consciences to the new instructors. . . .

The other tendency was a sly distrust of all authority and all heroics, so strong that it bordered on anarchism. Behind it lay not only the experiences of three or four generations with a succession of lip-servers, turncoats and spurious converts, but the much older legacy of the border fortress: a familiarity with civic muddle, military blunders, weakness of rulers, with camp-followers and racketeers, half-victories, half-defeats, and with the willy-nilly toughness of those not important, rich or lucky enough to get away from dangers.[5]

One could say—if we may leap forward to Haydn for a moment—that evidence of this second, antiheroic tendency is present in his choral music of the last Viennese period. The "Nelson" Mass seems, at root, more concerned with war's ravages and dangers than with its heroes. None of *Fidelio*'s idealism burns through its pages. On the other hand, a tendency to hedonism is abundantly evident in most of the other Haydn Masses. That tendency has so often been a focal point in modern criticism of Classical sacred music that it has become an analytical cliché.

The Viennese endured a great plague and a Turkish siege at the end of the seventeenth century, but neither event intensified their religious faith or purged it of indulgent elements. For the common citizen, the true memorial to the Great Plague was that enduring song "Ach, du lieber Augustin" about a rascally piper who tumbled, dead drunk, into a pit filled with plague corpses and yet survived to drink and pipe again. As for the Turkish invasion, people memorialized it in true Viennese fashion by introducing coffee and butter crescents to the taverns.

Thus a considerable moral price seems to have been paid for those lovely Baroque pilgrimage churches dotting the hillsides of Austria and southern Germany. And we shall see that the sacred music of Joseph Haydn, which fits so well in those elaborate, gilded interiors, nevertheless contains more than a little *Volkstümlichkeit*—the hearty, irrepressible vitality of a people who managed to withstand centuries of Jesuit "edification."

---

[5] Barea *Vienna*, 55-56.

CHARLES VI AND THE ARTS OF THE BAROQUE CHURCH

The young Haydn was most directly affected by the Habsburg dynasty in the persons of Charles VI and Maria Theresa. Charles's regressive administration, so disastrous for Austria in political and economic terms, proved on the other hand to be the last brilliant flowering of the Baroque aesthetic in central Europe.

Charles had been made King of Spain in 1706 when his brother Joseph I was crowned Emperor. He became Emperor himself in 1711 when Joseph died of smallpox. Soon after Charles's coronation a plague epidemic broke out in Vienna, and, as a thank-offering for its eradication, he vowed to build a church dedicated to his name-day Saint, Charles Borromeo. The Karlskirche became Vienna's most impressive Baroque church, a symbol of Charles's fondest spiritual and political ideals.

Those ideals consisted mainly of resurrecting the Holy Roman Empire that Charlemagne had known, an occidental power united by one faith under one ruler. But the resistance of the wider European community, coupled with his own bungling, denied Charles any hope of realizing his dream. By the time of his death, the empire teetered at the edge of ruin. The only bright spots in his legacy were the glittering palaces and churches going up in Vienna and the great musical tradition he had fostered at court. Both efforts were among the final outbursts of Counter-Reformation zeal, splendid displays of the Church Militant's strength and will.[6]

Charles's father Leopold had set the Viennese building boom into motion. He was aided immensely by the emergence of a group of native architects—chief among them Bernhard Fischer von Erlach, Lukas von Hildebrandt, and Jacob Prandauer—who combined Baroque Italian felicity of style with Gothic seriousness, giving both new force. Much the same process would occur in Austrian music, but there the stylistic fusion would necessarily take much longer to bear its finest fruit.

Fischer von Erlach designed the Karlskirche. No less an intellect than Gottfried Wilhelm Leibniz acted as advisor to the project, attempting to add the heft of empire to the already intricate symbolism of the church's ornamental features. At least one modern commentary stresses the uneasiness of that combination:

> The church is compact and looks vaster than it is. Fischer gave it aloof grandeur and bizarre exuberance, classical simplicity and dramatic flamboyance in an odd blending of forms. Behind a severe portico, looking like the entrance to a Roman temple, soars an oval dome whose copper roofing has turned a soft green. The portico is flanked by two free-standing columns decorated with spiral bas-reliefs. They recall minarets or triumphal columns of ancient Rome. More reconditely, as part of the complex programme of allusions, they were supposed to recall the Pillars of Hercules which are Spain's gate to the New World. All served the triumph

---

[6] Riedel *Hofe Karls VI*, 9.

of the Emperor, who saw himself as the protector of the Church Triumphant. . . .
To make the message clearer, the two columns are topped by the imperial crown
of which the Cross is only part and apex; the dome is crowned by a globe and
Cross, symbols of the universal empire and the universal church. . . . The whole of
the Karlskirche is a stage [for] the glitter and colour of ecclesiastic displays, unexpectedly chill and rational inside despite the gilt-stucco outburst of the altar and
Rottmayr's immense frescoes. . . . It has never been a place for simple souls at
prayer.[7]

Whatever their effect today, such Baroque churches have often been recognized as visual counterparts to the sacred musical creations of Haydn and Mozart. Their depiction,
within a relatively modest space, of miracles, saints' lives, and heaven itself, together with
the intricate ornamentation applied to their every surface, presents obvious if somewhat
superficial parallels to mid-eighteenth-century musical style.

Some critics have seen still deeper connections. Hans Sedlmayr called the architectural
style of Fischer von Erlach a *Reichsstil* (empire style) because of its obvious ties to the political ideals of the Holy Roman Empire: the emperors and their allies employed the de-
signers and artisans; the new style, based on a synthesis of Italian, French, and indigenous
traditions, evolved parallel to the house of Habsburg's struggle for hegemony in Europe;
and the spiritual/artistic program of almost all the representational artwork served to glorify the imperial family and allegorize its central beliefs.[8] Similar criteria can be applied successfully to much of the music created for the court. Many operas, serenades, and cantatas
were composed especially for feast days in the Emperor's family or to solemnize political
events. In such works, apotheosis and allegory flourished.

It is more difficult to determine a relationship between the imperial "cult of ideals" and
style in church music, with its prescribed texts and definite liturgical functions. But no one
can deny that the churchly musical culture of the time was in essence a courtly culture. The
dominance of the Emperor and his circle in Viennese church music must stand as de facto
evidence of a symbiotic pact between the court's needs and the Church's accommodating
nature. In the epoch between the Council of Trent[9] and the papal encyclical *Annus qui*
(1749), music was an integral feature of courtly church solemnities, so the influence of the
court's ideals was to be expected; our discussion of Fux and Caldara in this chapter hints at
that. For Haydn it is easy to trace such influence in the cantatas and Masses written for the

---

[7] Barea *Vienna*, 73-74.

[8] Sedlmayr "Reichsstil," 126ff.

[9] From 1545 to 1563 a Council was held intermittently at Trent in northern Italy to determine ways to purge the
Church of abuses and dereliction. See Jungmann *Mass* 1, 127-141, for a discussion of the Council's deliberations
on the liturgy of the Mass; François Lesure, "France in the Sixteenth Century (1520-1610)," 250-251, and Henry
Coates and Gerald Abraham, "The Perfection of the *A Cappella* Style," 317-318, both in *NOH* 4, succinctly summarize the effects of the Council's deliberations on church music.

Esterházys. That family was able, in fact, to maintain the *Reichsstil* long after the Habsburgs themselves had abandoned it.

It is important not to think of such courtly influence as purely negative or as mere secularization. Rather, it represents the sentiment that only the highest—and most contemporary, most readily communicative—form of art was worthy of functioning in the service of God. The doctrine of divine right implied that the musical style representative of society's leading order, the nobility, should also be perceived as the most vital for veneration of the Deity. In the collective breakdown of the aristocratic order at the beginning of the nineteenth century, this essentially medieval view of humankind finally changed, and a new attitude toward music in worship also came slowly into being.[10] Meanwhile, even the most outwardly political of the Habsburg churchly ceremonies could be seen as worldly, yet theocentric, since the imperial family's role in the kingdom had been fixed in heaven, and every form of art on display was centered in the service of God and the Church Triumphant.[11]

COURTLY AND CHURCHLY CEREMONIAL

Public worship held a central position in the ceremonial life of the Habsburg court. This was especially due, in the years following the Counter-Reformation, to its desire to display the united power and prestige of Church and Empire in every possible way. The Emperor was the only layman permitted to wear the bishop's mitre; whenever a new ruler was garbed at coronation with those ancient robes so like the pontiff's vestments, the divine sanction of imperial office was given the strongest possible visible expression.[12]

One of the most striking features of court ceremonial was the group of public Masses in which the entire court apparatus took part and which, especially in the larger churches, was open to everyone. The Emperor presided over these Masses as if he were a medieval pope in the midst of his people. Several churches in Vienna, including St. Stephen's, were established as stations in a yearly cycle of such celebrations; impressive traditions and rituals became associated with them over the course of the years. At these affairs, the choirboy Haydn (see below) had ample opportunity to witness the full panoply of imperial ceremony.[13]

---

[10] Fellerer *Soziologie*, 26.

[11] See also Ursprung *Kirchenmusik*, 219ff.

[12] Riedel *Hofe Karls VI*, 24.

[13] Riedel *Hofe Karls VI*, 25. Riedel gives a list of these *Pontifikalamten* and ceremonial details on 45-46. See Pohl *Haydn 1*, 52-53, on festival observances and esp. details of Holy Week ceremonial. Mac Intyre *Mass*, 571-575 (Appendix A), supplies a calendar of the liturgical year in Vienna *ca.* 1750.

An entire group of public services also grew out of the special devotions and interests of the house of Habsburg. These so-called *Pietas Austriaca* were generally created, or revived, as incentives to spiritual renewal during the Counter-Reformation. For Haydn scholars, two subcategories of this group hold special interest: the *Pietas Eucharista*, or veneration of the Eucharist, and the adoration of the Blessed Virgin Mary.

The Pietas Eucharista originated with Rudolph, in whose lifetime the revival of the Feast of Corpus Christi fell. Spurred on by the Council of Trent and reacting to Protestant disavowal of the Real Presence of Christ in the eucharistic meal, Rudolph had striven to renew the veneration of the sacraments by means of this Feast. Ferdinand II later placed it at the center of religious life and clothed it in all possible Baroque pomp. After the suppression of the Protestant Landowners Revolt in 1622, he caused a Corpus Christi procession to be celebrated for the first time by the entire court and city. Every year from then on, under the combined leadership of the Toisonritter,[14] the assembled clerics, the university faculty, and the magistrates, the procession would start from St. Stephen's and could be seen winding through the principal streets and squares of the Inner City.[15]

> Once the custom of carrying the Host in procession began, it rapidly spread and developed into a most splendid affair. All over Europe it was treated as a veritable triumph of Christ the King. The whole community from highest to lowest took part enthusiastically in this manifestation of faith and devotion. It was not confined to the church building or even to the churchyard but wended its way through the town and even into the open country. In Germany and Austria it became associated with the processions for good weather, which explains the practice of celebratory benediction four times en route, given towards corners of the earth.[16]

Haydn wrote at least two settings of music for such Corpus Christi processions,[17] and when we examine them, their combination of ardor and popular style clearly indicate the central place these processions held in ordinary believers' hearts.

---

[14] The Knights of the Golden Fleece. This order was part of the Burgundian heritage of the house of Habsburg. A *Toison-Gottesdienst* (literally, Service of the Fleece) held the highest ranking of any churchly ceremony and was usually celebrated at High Mass and First Vespers of all high Feasts of Our Lord, Our Lady, and the Apostles whenever the Emperor was in residence in Vienna. On Easter Sunday, Corpus Christi, and the Feasts of the Immaculate Conception and St. Stephen, these observances took place at the cathedral with all the knights attendant; otherwise they were held in the Hofburgkapelle, St. Augustine's, or one of the other Viennese churches.

[15] Riedel *Hofe Karls VI*, 25-27. A prominent feature of many such processions was the swearing of an oath by the city fathers, reaffirming their belief in whatever church doctrine was being celebrated. The oath had the special benefit in earlier times of assuring that no Protestant individualism had survived to taint the political system.

[16] W. J. O'Shea, "Corpus Christi," *New Catholic* 4, 347.

[17] See the Catalog discussions of XXIIIc:4 and 5 (both titled *Lauda Sion* in the *New Grove* worklist), and our discussions of the individual works in Chapters Two and Six.

Strongest of the Pietas Austriaca, stronger even than the Corpus Christi observances, was the Adoration of the Mother of God. No more the "mother of sorrows" of the Gothic era, the Mary of the Counter-Reformation had become Maria the Queen, the warrior in all of God's battles, patroness of godly men in their struggle against heretics and unbelievers. Many churches and chapels built after the Battle of the White Mountain (1620) were named Maria de Victoria. After other victorious battles, new feasts of Mary were established—for example, the Rosenkranzfest following the sea battle at Lepanto (1571), which Prince Eugene extended to the entire church after the battle at Peterwardein (1716).[18] In this context, Joseph Haydn's lifelong attachment to the Virgin can be viewed as having a (conservative) political aspect as well as a religious one. And his Masses, many of which bear outright dedications to the B. V. M. or else commemorate specific courtly/historical events, are perceptible outgrowths of the memorializing tendency fostered by the Habsburgs.

CHRISTIAN WORSHIP IN YOUNG JOSEPH HAYDN'S TIME

As noted above, the imperial court had more than a little influence on church music in Austria as a whole, and the Habsburgs' propensity for a splendid and pleasant music at worship was enthusiastically taken up by their subjects. Not only did the increasingly operatic style of church music provide the magnificence needed at court, it also spoke directly to the feelings of many a citizen. The residents of Vienna continually flocked to public Masses, Vespers, litanies, miscellaneous devotions, and processions or went on pilgrimages to various outlying churches.[19] Music-making was an integral part of most of these activities. Of his visit in 1781, the Berliner Friedrich Nicolai wrote: "I heard much church music [in Vienna], for still at that time Masses were constantly performed with music; and because the starting time for each church was different, I could certainly hear the music for three or four Masses on Sundays or holidays."[20] Concerted music was used for civic occasions as well, although perhaps one could more accurately say that church ritual often served to celebrate temporal events. For special happenings, equally special music was often provided.[21] Choruses accompanied by wind instruments were a feature of many proces-

---

[18] Riedel Hofe Karls VI, 28.

[19] See Mac Intyre Mass, 13-17. The present narrative relies heavily on Mac Intyre's excellently marshalled summary of church music activities in eighteenth-century Vienna.

[20] Nicolai Beschreibung 4, 544 (10. Abschnitt: "Von der Musik in Wien").

[21] Landon HCW 1, 54-55, mentions several such occasions in Hainburg during Haydn's childhood; for Vienna, Mac Intyre cites a Festmesse composed in 1773 by Leopold Hofmann in honor of Joseph Hörl's election as Bürgermeister (Mac Intyre Mass, 14). Our readers may also be familiar with the similar experiences in Leipzig of J. S. Bach, whose Cantata BWV 119, Preise, Jerusalem, den Herrn, commemorates the inauguration of a new town council.

sions; numerous private ceremonies, pilgrimages, and nearby monastic establishments also required music in prodigious amounts. It has been said that the churches were the earliest concert halls in Vienna; one author has even referred to the development of "church concerts with liturgical accompaniment."[22] Undoubtedly the cost and questionable propriety of such practices were factors leading to Joseph II's ecclesiastical reforms of 1783.[23]

Regardless of the extent to which music sometimes may have overshadowed other considerations in the service, we must remember that performances of sacred choral music in Vienna took place only as part of the liturgy. By and large one did not expect to hear such music at a public concert.[24] Accordingly, it helps to consider the sacred works of Haydn and other Viennese Classic composers from a liturgical standpoint, for their main function was to inspire worshipers' devotion.

Then as now, Mass was the central institution of religious practice for Roman Catholics. It was (is) divided into two sections. The Synaxis, or Mass of the Catechumens, begins the service and consists of prayers, songs of praise, and instruction in Christian beliefs. The second, but more important, part of Mass is the Eucharist, or Mass of the Faithful, in which the Last Supper of Christ and his disciples is reenacted as a reminder of Christ's offering to all believers. When the words of consecration are spoken over the elements of bread and wine, Christ and his sacrifice become present again.[25]

The actual celebration of Mass in Haydn's time was an experience far removed from that of today. For the Catholic in the 1750s, the dominant historical force behind common worship was not Vatican II but the Counter-Reformation. Several trends beginning shortly after the Council of Trent had the effect of removing congregants from active participation in the service. First, the Missal of Pius V, issued in 1570, forced a uniform liturgy upon Catholics throughout the world. While it was meant to curb abuses that had arisen in various localities, it also managed to squelch much of the experimentation and use of indigenous customs that had preserved vitality in the Church and provided new forms of expression since Christianity's earliest days. Local practices continued to be a part of many Masses, of course, but now they stood more or less apart from the core of prescribed liturgy—and could no longer enrich or renew it.[26] Jungmann speaks eloquently of the quandary this produced:

---

[22] Ursprung *Kirchenmusik*, 219.

[23] See Chapter 4.

[24] Although that would have been possible in Paris or London. See Mozart's letter to his father regarding a Paris *concert spirituel* performance of the Holzbauer/Mozart *Miserere*; Anderson *Letters of Mozart* 2, 521 (L. 300a). Haydn's *Stabat Mater* (XX*bis*) also received performances at these Parisian concerts. See Chapter 5.

[25] Five texts commonly referred to as the Ordinary were the parts of the Mass most frequently given musical settings by eighteenth-century musicians. Of these, the Kyrie, Gloria, and Credo are part of the Synaxis; the Sanctus-Benedictus and Agnus Dei are part of the Eucharist.

[26] See Jungmann *Mass* 1, 127-141.

> The liturgy of the Mass [stood] before the faithful in all its splendor, but it [was] a splendor whose greatness [was] self-contained and whose arrangement [was] as immutable as it [was] puzzling. . . . Indeed, the Mass was actually treated as self-contained even where it appeared in its festive form and where a Baroque culture could share with it its own riches. . . . Music spread its gorgeous mantle over the whole Mass, so that other details of the rite scarcely had any significance. . . . Church music, which had fallen more and more into the hands of laymen, forgot that it was meant to subserve the liturgical action. As a result of this, the music often fitted very poorly into the liturgical setting. . . . On the other side, the celebrant often tried to continue with the offertory even while the choir was still singing the Credo. . . .
>
> The place taken by the choir corresponds to this new situation—not in the *choir* from which it derives its name, but far away, on the boundary between the world and the church, in the organ-loft.[27]

This distancing was fed by two other phenomena. The Church's clash with Protestantism had caused it to stress the Real Presence as the central feature of the Eucharist and to neglect most of its other aspects. Any notion that the faithful had a part to play, that they should co-offer with the priest, was thrust aside by a continual emphasis upon Christ's offering. Once Luther had denied the exclusivity of the priesthood, the Roman Church reacted with a deeper disinclination to link priest and people; instead, Catholic ritual used every opportunity to underscore the distinctive and separate role of the celebrant. It was hardly necessary. Even at that time, few Catholics could understand liturgical Latin. Rome continued to take the stand that the Latin prayers of the Mass were not to be given to the faithful in any way, certainly not made known in the vernacular. The fundamental assumption was that, as Jungmann put it, "the faithful would reverence the liturgy of the Mass more if the veil of mystery were kept around it. The old idea of the canon as a sanctuary which only the priest could enter thus survived and was in fact extended to the whole Mass."[28]

For those reasons, it is not surprising that the general practice of the Church was remarkably congruent with the atmosphere encouraged in court ceremonies (see above). Glorious music; beautiful paintings, architecture, statuary, stained glass, icons and relics; and every possible accouterment of ceremony—robes, candles, bells, incense, processions—were relied upon to communicate the power of God even as they did the power of the Emperor. They served as a substitute for active participation, conveying an emotional message that the average congregant was otherwise unable to receive in the service.

---

[27] Jungmann *Mass* 1, 148-149.

[28] Jungmann *Mass* 1, 143-144.

MUSIC AT WORSHIP

Although Mass was the center of Catholic worship experience, other services—of which there were many—followed more or less the same prescription for beauty and mystery.[29] Concerns were often voiced about the true purpose of music in the church and the proper characteristics of sacred style. Regarding purpose, theorists found themselves in remarkable agreement. Church music, Fux reminded his students in *Gradus ad Parnassum* (1725), exists in order "to arouse prayerful devotion during a service."[30] In a *Critischer Musicus* article of 15 October 1737, J. A. Scheibe wrote, "The chief purpose of church music is principally to edify the listeners, to encourage their prayer so as to thereby awaken in them a quiet and holy reverence before God's presence."[31] His feelings were echoed by Mattheson, Quantz, Koch, and others.[32] As to how this reverence was to be awakened, opinions diverged.

In a treatise of 1649, Marco Scacchi had first distinguished among three musical styles: church, chamber, and theatre.[33] Eighteenth-century theorists continued to support those divisions, and composers endeavored to employ them appropriately. Nevertheless the number and variety of church services, along with other social trends, created manifold possibilities for mixing and confusing styles. By 1800 or so, "church style" would merely denote learned polyphony, and treatises would freely acknowledge that the music actually heard in sanctuaries was heavily influenced by the theatre and concert hall.[34]

As for church style during Haydn's early professional life, one could find two poles of opinion; they are aptly expressed below by Charles Burney and Johann Mattheson. Burney, writing in the early 1770s, held out for the *a cappella* tradition:

> I do not call every modern oratorio, mass or motet, *church music*; as the same compositions to different words would do equally, indeed often better, for the stage. But by *Musica di Chiesa*, properly so called, I mean grave and scientific compositions for voices only, of which the excellence consists more in good har-

---

[29] Mac Intyre *Mass*, 17-18, and Riedel, "Liturgie und Kirchenmusik," 126-131, summarize the ways in which both instrumental and vocal music were employed in Viennese churches at the time.

[30] Fux *Gradus* (3), 182, 192.

[31] Scheibe *Critischer*, 161.

[32] Summary in Mac Intyre *Mass*, 50-51.

[33] Scacchi *Discorso*. See R. J. Pascall, "Style," *New Grove* 8, 320ff; and Bukofzer *Baroque*, 4ff., for later developments.

[34] Koch *Lexikon*, "Styl, Schreibart," col. 1450-1451. Ratner *Classic Music*, 172-180, discusses the influence of *galant* style on *alla breve* church music (as in the learned style).

mony, learned modulation, and fugues upon ingenious and sober subjects, than in light airs and turbulent accompaniments.[35]

Not surprisingly, he found the music of Georg von Reutter the Younger, Haydn's early teacher, to be "without taste or invention" and judged a *Te Deum* performance he heard at St. Stephen's as having "great noise and little meaning."[36]

Johann Mattheson was not afraid, however, to include "madrigal [i.e., cantata] style" and "instrumental style" among the compositional manners one might effectively use in the worship service.[37] Moreover he defended—in measured words—the necessity of delight:

> One should not . . . indiscriminately abandon all vivacity in the sacred service, especially since the style of writing under discussion often naturally requires more joyousness and cheerfulness than any other, namely according to the subject and circumstance giving occasion for it. . . . Idleness, indolence, and impotence are not seriousness, magnificence, nobility and majesty. Joy does not contradict serious; for then all mirth would have to consist of jesting. A cheerful disposition is best disposed for devotion; where such is not to be done mechanically or simply in a trance. Only the appropriate discretion and moderation with the joyful sounds of the clarino trumpets, trombones, violins, flutes, etc., must never be lost sight of, nor be to the slightest detriment of the familiar commandment, which says: *Be joyous, yet in fear of God.*[38]

Elsewhere Mattheson had baldly claimed for church music the same goals as for opera, "namely that the sentiments of the audience should be moved either to love, to pity, or to joy."[39]

The Church failed to see it quite that way. A long series of decrees going as far back as the Council of Trent attempted to curb theatrical elements in the music of the service.[40] In 1749 the papal encyclical *Annus qui* forbade not only the vocal elements of theatre style, such as "the solo, the duet, the trio, etc.," but also "*timpani*, hunting horns, trumpets, oboes, flutes, *Salteri*, mandolins, and, in general, all instruments which are theatrical in character." Figured music, including instrumental accompaniment, would be permitted only if it were "of such nature as to arouse among the faithful, sentiments of piety and de-

---

[35] Burney *State* 1, 334.

[36] Burney *State* 1, 361.

[37] Mattheson *Capellmeister* (2), 196-210, 220-221 (pt. 1, ch. 10, §§ 34-69, 99-101).

[38] Mattheson *Capellmeister* (2), 209 (pt. 1, ch. 10, §67).

[39] Reply to Joachim Meyer's *Unvorgreifliche Gedanken über die neulich eingerissene theatralische Kirchenmusik. . .* (1726), quoted in Müller *Hasse*, 25.

[40] The Tridentine "rules for sacred music" specify only that music with a "sensuous or impure character" must be avoided. But see the Decree by the Sacra Visita Apostolica of 1665 ("To sing with a solo voice, whether high or low, a hymn or a motet, in whole or in large, is forbidden.") and other documents in *White List*, 3-5.

votion and to uplift the soul toward God." The text was to be set so that its words were "perfectly and clearly intelligible."[41]

We may justifiably wonder whether this encyclical enjoyed any support at all in music-loving Vienna. At most it seems to have influenced a 1753 decree from the Archepiscopal Consistory that forbade trumpets and timpani in services and processions; a month later, an imperial *Hofreskript* (court document) apparently placed the entire Habsburg empire under the same ban.[42] This decree may only have applied to certain usages, however:

> [What the *Hofreskript*] meant were *intradas* by trumpet choirs (sometimes even doubled) which played on high feasts at the beginning and end of High Mass as well as after the Gospel; also in a Te Deum they played before its beginning, before the verse "Te ergo quaesumus" (at genuflection), and at the end, and also between verses of the processional litany. The use of obbligato trumpet parts for concerted church music was not affected, as proven by contemporary performance remarks and directories.[43]

In any case the prohibition seems to have been difficult to enforce. Outside Vienna it may have been widely ignored; within the city the ban was unofficially lifted after 1767, when fanfares were desired at a thanksgiving service for the recovery of Maria Theresa from illness.[44]

We shall see that, of Joseph Haydn's post-1750 concerted Masses, only one lacks trumpets and drums. In fact, Haydn seems to have opted from the very beginning for the theatrical side in the debate. His first two Masses (c. 1749) feature shamelessly operatic vocal and instrumental style, and their texts are not always as "perfectly and clearly intelligible" as *Annus qui* would have liked. In those and many other ways, Haydn's early sacred music fully embraced the contemporary Austrian style. Considering his musical upbringing, it could hardly have been otherwise.

HAYDN AS CHOIRBOY

Joining the choir at St. Stephen's Cathedral in Vienna probably changed Joseph Haydn's life forever. Self-made man and largely self-made musician, Haydn nevertheless always acknowledged his professional beginnings—roots thrust deeply into the soil of the

---

[41] All quotations from the summary of *Annus qui*'s musical regulations in *White List*, 5.

[42] See Mac Intyre *Mass*, 43, and esp. 690 n. 90-91 citing Biba, Riedel, Unverricht et al. Text of the *Hofreskript* in Brand *Messen, 189*.

[43] Riedel "Liturgie," 123.

[44] Fellerer "Liturgical Basis," 165.

Church and its music. Had it not been for eighteenth-century Austrian churches and their *Capellen*, he conceivably might never have become a musician at all.

Very little in Haydn's early years at home marked him as precocious. His father Mathias, a wheelwright in the Lower Austrian village of Rohrau, could play the harp a bit and liked to practice after work. We are told by G. A. Griesinger, one of Haydn's earliest biographers, that Mathias had a "good tenor voice, and his wife, Anne Marie, used to sing to the harp." As for their eldest son, "The melodies of these songs were so deeply stamped in Joseph Haydn's memory that he could still recall them in advanced old age."[45]

Haydn's first opportunity for formal training in music came when he left for Hainburg to become a choirboy:

> One day the headmaster from the neighboring town of Hainburg, a distant relative of the Haydn family, came to Rohrau. Meister Mathias and his wife gave their usual little concert, and five-year-old Joseph sat near his parents and sawed at his left arm with a stick, as if he were accompanying on the violin. It astonished the schoolteacher that the boy observed the time so correctly. He inferred from this a natural talent for music and advised the parents to send their Sepperl (an Austrian diminutive for Joseph) to Hainburg so that he might be set to the acquisition of an art that in time would unfailingly open to him the prospect "of becoming a clergyman." The parents, ardent admirers of the clergy, joyfully seized this proposal, and in his sixth year Joseph Haydn went to the headmaster in Hainburg. Here he received instruction in reading and writing, in catechism, in singing, and in almost all wind and string instruments, even in the timpani. "I shall owe it to this man even in my grave," Haydn oftentimes said, "that he set me to so many different things, although I received in the process more thrashings than food."[46]

This headmaster, Johann Mathias Franck, provided Haydn's first contact with the worlds of church and choral music. Franck was about fifty when he took charge of his younger cousin's education. He had served at Hainburg since 1732; Haydn moved into his home in 1737 or 1738. The household included Franck's second wife Juliana, two other children (a third was born in 1739), and the two preceptors who assisted Franck as schoolmaster. On the ground floor a beer house flourished, and elsewhere in the same building seventy or eighty children attended the school itself, arriving at seven a. m. and leaving at three in the afternoon. Breaks were observed for daily Mass and lunch.[47]

---

[45] Griesinger *Notizen* (3), 9.

[46] Griesinger *Notizen* (3), 9.

[47] Franck was also the village sacristan. In that capacity, he shouldered a bewildering list of responsibilities including the church's clock and its bells. The bells were to be rung "not only in winter but also in summer at seven o'clock in the morning, as well as noontime with the bells of middle size, and with the great bells for prayer service." For thunderstorms, when bells were rung continually in warning, Franck was provided with two assistant bell-ringers. He received extra pay for winding the clock. Landon *HCW* 1, 51.

Being both town *Schulrektor* and *Chorregent* of the Church of SS. Philip and James, Franck was charged with teaching the boys music in addition to the usual subjects. He saw that they attended church at least four times a week, that they behaved themselves properly there, and that the stronger singers among them performed "on ordinary Sundays and Holy Days"—as per Hainburg's *Instruction für den Schulmeister oder Rectore* of 1734— "Masses with four vocal parts, viz. bass, tenor, alto and discant with two violins." For great feast days and the first Sunday of the month Franck would also have "trumpets and kettle-drums and hunting horns together with Violon [double bass] and Passetl ['cello]." The choir's repertory consisted of works by a few local masters or by such prominent court composers as J. J. Fux, Antonio Caldara, and the Reutters, *père et fils.*[48]

ST. STEPHEN'S

Although Haydn's experience in Hainburg may have marked his first steps in the wider world of music, his true commencement as a musician took place in Vienna, where he journeyed in 1740 to join the choir at St. Stephen's Cathedral. There he encountered not only more proficient music-making, but also the magnificence and cosmopolitan variety of a great European capital in its ascendance. Vienna was the commercial, political, and cultural center of Austria, a fact which probably counted for little with the eight-year-old "new boy" in the Stephansdom Capelle.

> Haydn . . . had been some three years in Hainburg when the Court Capellmeister Reutter, of Vienna, director of music at St. Stephen's Cathedral, visited his friend the dean [the Parish Priest Anton Johann Palmb] in Hainburg. Reutter told the dean that his older choirboys, whose voices were beginning to break, would be useless to him, and that he had to replace them with younger subjects. The dean proposed the eight-year-old Haydn, and he and the schoolmaster were called at once. The poorly nourished Sepperl cast longing glances at the cherries that were sitting on the dean's table. Reutter tossed a few handfuls into his hat, and seemed well pleased with the Latin and Italian strophes that Haydn had to sing. "Can you also make a trill?" asked Reutter. "No," said Haydn, "for not even my cousin [i.e., Franck] can do that." This answer greatly embarrassed the schoolteacher, and Reutter laughed uproariously. He demonstrated the mechanical principles of trilling, Haydn imitated him, and at the third attempt succeeded. "You shall stay with me," said Reutter. The departure from Hainburg soon followed, and Haydn came

---

[48] Our discussion of Hainburg and Johann Franck is drawn from Landon *HCW* 1, 51-55. Landon's principal sources were Maurer, *Geschichte der landesfürstlichen Stadt Hainburg* (Vienna, 1894), and E. F. Schmid, *Joseph Haydn . . .* (Kassel, 1934), esp. 89ff.

as a pupil to the Choir School at St. Stephen's Cathedral in Vienna, where he stayed until his sixteenth year.[49]

This Georg Reutter the Younger was an extremely busy man. In 1731 he had gained his first appointment, as court composer, and almost at once had become prominent as a supplier of operas and oratorios to Charles VI and his circle. Between 1731 and 1740, thirty-eight of his operas were performed, making him the most prolific of the Viennese court composers after his teacher Caldara. He also wrote a great deal of church music and managed to garner an unprecedented number of appointments in the years that followed; by 1756 he was both first and second Capellmeister at court as well as at St. Stephen's. All this activity evidently caused him to neglect his responsibilities at the cathedral; the city council complained that he was not often seen there. Historians have criticized him for largely failing to discern Joseph Haydn's creative talent or take significant steps to foster it.

> No instruction in music theory was undertaken in the Choir School, and Haydn remembered receiving only two lessons in this from the excellent Reutter. But Reutter did encourage him to make whatever variations he liked on the motets and Salves that he had to sing through in the church, and this practice early led him to ideas of his own which Reutter corrected. . . . Stimulated by his imagination, he even ventured into composition for eight and sixteen parts. "I used to think then that it was all right if only the paper were pretty full. Reutter laughed at my immature output, at measures that no throat and no instrument could have executed, and he scolded me for composing for sixteen parts before I even understood two-part setting."[50]

In Reutter's defense it must be said that he was under no obligation to provide even the most meager theoretical instruction or compositional advice. And Haydn was by all accounts a late bloomer. His brother Michael even managed to outshine him by the time both were members of the cathedral choir.[51] Perhaps posterity should be grateful that Reutter's influence on the young Joseph was limited largely to the works that the choirboy

---

[49] Griesinger *Notizen* (3), 9-10. Careful readers will notice that, since Haydn was dismissed from St. Stephen's *Cantorei* no earlier than 1749 (see text following), he would have been nearly eighteen.

[50] Griesinger *Notizen* (3), 10. This is the most detailed early account of Haydn's tutelage. Other authorities, from Dies through Geiringer, have cited rather less attention to the fledgling composer from Reutter. Cf. Landon *HCW* 1, 42-43, 49; Geiringer *Haydn*, 19-20.

[51] Dies *Nachrichten* (3), 88. "The Empress [Maria Theresa] had already let it be said in jest to Capellmeister Reutter, 'Joseph Haydn doesn't sing any more; he crows.' So Reutter had to replace Joseph with another soprano for the ceremony [at Klosterneuburg in honor of St. Leopold]. His choice fell upon Joseph's brother, Michael. The latter sang so beautifully that the Empress had him called before her and presented him with twenty-four ducats." Landon *HCW* 1, 59, placed this occasion on 15 November 1748, noting that both Vespers and High Mass were celebrated with the Court in attendance. *Leopoldi-Tag*, commemorating the patron saint of Lower Austria, is "still celebrated with great style at Klosterneuburg Abbey."

heard at the cathedral. In spite of his experience and the ease with which he wrote, Reutter was a musician of limited creative gifts.[52]

It was nevertheless Haydn's unalloyed good fortune to have entered court service while the impact of four great patron-emperors—Ferdinand III, Leopold I, Joseph I, and Charles VI—was still strongly felt. Under these four successive monarchs (regnant 1637-1740) a brilliant era in Viennese music had flourished. Being practiced musicians as well as patrons, they had used their informed authority to bring the finest composers and the most elevated of musical styles to court in rich series of opera, oratorio, and churchly performances. Although the Capelle declined dramatically under Maria Theresa (r. 1740-1765) and "the excellent Reutter," Haydn came to Vienna and to St. Stephen's Cathedral in the last days of Charles VI's reign, and he encountered not only a mighty edifice, one of the glories of the Inner City's architecture, but also a celebrated musical establishment.

Let us first consider the church: St. Stephen's began as a *Pfarrkirche* or parish church in the twelfth century and, as with many great European cathedrals, its completion had been a slow process reflected in the mingled Gothic and Romanesque styles of the Stephansdom as the eighteenth-century Viennese knew it. Unlike its Salzburg counterpart, the cathedral in Vienna was not subjected to a Baroque transformation; even its interior was largely spared the effects of remodeling. Whatever Baroque furnishings were added in the seventeenth and eighteenth centuries—altar, epitaphs, pews, oratory, organ—had minimal formal effect, given the scale of the room, and so were easily able to become a part of things without intruding. On the Epistle side was situated the Emperor's oratory, and opposite it on the Evangelist side the music loft and the small organ. Here stood, at high feasts and exceptional occasions, the Emperor's Court Capelle, often bolstered with cathedral musicians.[53]

This was the building in which Haydn now prayed, studied, and sang. Even today, visitors crossing the threshold of St. Stephen's are astonished by the interior. Its vast and shadowy vault seems to go on forever. From the great tower of the cathedral, one can see to the west the green slopes of the Vienna woods and, rising eastward, a Hungarian plain perpetually clouded in mists. But within St. Stephen's walls, it is possible to experience something yet more enormous, akin perhaps to medieval faith: a sensation of being at once humbled and lovingly embraced.[54]

St. Stephen's was still the parish church for many people in its vicinity; nonetheless it was also a bustling urban institution and, next to the great Hofburgkapelle (the princely

---

[52] Eva Badura-Skoda, "Reutter, (Johann Adam Joseph Karl) Georg (von)(ii)," *New Grove* 15, 772-774. Our discussion is drawn from Badura-Skoda and from Stolbrock "Reutter."

[53] Riedel *Hofe Karls VI*, 44.

[54] Burney, Anglican to the core, was rather less impressed: "The church is a dark, dirty, and dismal old Gothic building, though richly ornamented; in it are hung all the trophies of war, taken from the Turks and other enemies of the house of Austria, for more than a century past, which gives it very much the appearance of an old wardrobe." Burney *State* 1, 239-240.

chapel) and the Augustinerkirche, the house of worship most frequented by the imperial court.[55] Haydn soon found himself in the midst of an endless series of church services and ceremonies requiring music—Masses both festive (*solemnis*) and short (*brevis*), Vespers, funerals, Te Deums, traditional *rorate* ceremonies for Advent, and, of course, the processions so beloved of the Viennese. Because of Reutter's connections at court, Haydn and the other choirboys also participated at times in private academies, outdoor performances, and even Latin dramas given by the Jesuits.[56] Dies, another of Haydn's early biographers, emphasized the refreshments that were bestowed upon the always-famished Haydn at these events: because of Reutter's stinginess with provisions in the *Capellhaus*, Joseph became "seized with an incredible love for academies."[57] From a musical point of view, the outings gave the young musician an important opportunity to hear secular music too.

A brief description of some of the young Haydn's experiences at the cathedral may be of interest. Almost immediately upon his arrival in Vienna, he was witness to a singular commemoration—the huge Requiem service at St. Stephen's for Charles VI, who had died on October 20 of 1741. The Emperor was buried in the Capuchin's Crypt on the Neue Markt, but his heart was deposited in the Augustinerkirche and, as was customary, the cathedral received his entrails in a silver container.

Perhaps Haydn was affected in a more personal way by the deaths of two musicians for whom the cathedral provided Requiems. On February 13, 1741, Johann Joseph Fux, Imperial Court Capellmeister and great master of counterpoint, died and was buried beside his wife's grave after a solemn service at St. Stephen's. On July 28, Antonio Vivaldi, who may have come to Vienna in hopes of gaining imperial patronage, was buried in the cemetery of the Bürgerspital; no elevated observance marked his passing. His biographer Alan Kendall, noting the extreme poverty in which Vivaldi spent his final months, reckoned that the outlay for the funeral entitled him only to six pall-bearers, six choirboys, and "the *Kleingeläut* or pauper's peal of bells, which . . . cost [but] two florins and thirty-six kreuzer."[58] Haydn was undoubtedly among those six choirboys.

Of course Haydn would have been present too at happier occasions: in Pressburg at the coronation of Maria Theresa, and at the joyful celebrations of the births of Joseph, heir to the throne (1741), and Leopold, the next in line (1747). Another time for grand Catholic ceremony, possibly the last which Haydn saw as a choirboy, was the jubilee of Cardinal

---

[55] It had attained cathedral status in 1469 at the behest of Friedrich III and had more recently been made an archbishopric under Charles VI's sponsorship. The cathedral had, for this and other reasons, become an important "station" in the yearly cycle of public Mass celebrations begun by Emperor Ferdinand II in the 1620s (see text above).

[56] See Geiringer *Haydn*, 21-22, which provides brief details of a Reutter Latin drama on the Emperor Constantine, performed by a cast of two hundred, and also music in honor of St. John, given from brilliantly illuminated boats floating on the Danube Canal.

[57] Dies *Nachrichten* (3), 87.

[58] Kendall *Vivaldi*, 93.

Archbishop Sigismund Count Kollonicz in October 1749.[59] The day began with the ringing of church bells all over Vienna:

> An enormous procession of clergy and dignitaries marched solemnly into the cathedral, which was lighted by myriads of candles. Archbishops, bishops and prelates assisted at High Mass, all dressed in the most ornate robes and carrying gorgeous wreaths on their arms. Cardinal Kollonicz's wreath was of pure gold, a present from the Empress Maria Theresa, and the chalice he used was adorned by a magnificent wreath wrought in silver, a gift from the Queen of Portugal. Members of the imperial family were carried to the building in golden sedan chairs and accompanied by the knights of the Golden Fleece, the ambassadors, and the high nobility, all resplendent in robes of gold and silver encrusted with precious stones.[60]

MUSIC AT ST. STEPHEN'S

The cathedral supported at this time six boy choristers and approximately thirty other musicians, not all of whom could have been considered full-time employees. Apart from the boys, nine other singers and three *Extra-Vocalisten* comprised the choir. The instrumentalists were mainly string players (eleven, counting *Accessisten* and private substitutes), although the rolls listed one "cornet" and one bassoonist. Organist Anton Reckh was also a composer and accordingly received extra pay. For trumpets, trombones, and timpani, St. Stephen's relied upon the services of the Imperial Trumpeters and the *Thurnermeister*[61] with his apprentices. The full orchestra would have been used for solemn Mass on feast days and special occasions. At all other times—that is to say, during normal weeks and during Advent—a short Mass would have been celebrated using the *Missa brevis*, with its telescoped Gloria and Credo texts and customary reduced accompaniment of two violins and basso continuo—the "Viennese church trio."[62]

---

[59] Primary source: *Wiener Diarium* 86/87, 1749. Pohl *Haydn* 1 (75-77) takes two-thirds of a page just to list—mostly by group—the members of the great procession and the order of march.

[60] Geiringer *Haydn*, 21-22.

[61] In most Austrian municipalities, the Thurnermeister and his journeymen were trumpeters and tympanists, descendants of the watchtower heralds who welcomed (warned of) visitors, sounded the hours, and otherwise provided ceremonial music for the city. We are told that in Haydn's time, the tradition of high brass playing was slowly dying out; in Eisenstadt, for example, the Thurnerei "gradually came to be primarily string players (violins and a double bass), supplying dance music for the town's official functions." Landon *HCW* 1, 342. See also Chapter 4, on the Eisenstadt Capella's use of Thurnerei.

[62] So called because that instrumental combination was a commonplace in the region's sacred music. The basso continuo generally employed organ, double bass, and possibly cello or bassoon. See our discussion above of the

In addition to the principal Capelle, a smaller group independent of the first was supported by a trust fund. This was the *Music-Capelle beim Marianischen Gnadenbild* (literally the "Chapel Music for the Miraculous Image of Mary"), consisting of three boys, three men (alto-tenor-bass), a church trio, and wind instruments (two cornets, one bassoon and three trombones, augmented when necessary by members of the Imperial Orchestra or the Thurnermeister—we assume that the Gnadenbild choristers were augmented on such occasions as well). Its Capellmeister (at first Georg Reutter; from 1743 Ferdinand Schmidt) received 300 florins of the 2,800-fl. yearly budget outright, another 50 fl. "adjutum" and 600 fl. to feed and train the boys. On virtually every day of the year, they provided a sung Mass at 11 a.m. and the Laurentian Litany at 5 p.m., also with music.[63] Robbins Landon speculated that the *Missa brevis Rorate coeli desuper* attributed to Haydn was composed for this Gnadenbild Capelle at some point very early in his career.[64]

It was also possible for the cathedral complement to join the Court Capelle on special occasions, and that stellar assembly, with its operatic soloists, choir of twenty-seven, and forty-eight instrumentalists,[65] made possible the performance of almost any work. The chronicles inform us of solemnities in which the *Te Deum* required two and sometimes three choirs of trumpets and timpani.[66]

HAYDN'S ARTISTIC ANCESTORS

Although Haydn's immediate influences in the style of his early church music were undoubtedly those around him—Reutter, Jr., and later Porpora—he could also draw upon the achievements of the preceding generation of composers at the court of Charles VI. Johann Joseph Fux (ca. 1660-1741) and Antonio Caldara (1670-1736) were the principal figures in this group; both were firmly anchored in the High Baroque tradition.

Capellmeister Fux was still in charge of the Imperial Court Music when the eight-year-old Haydn entered the choir at St. Stephen's. A close relationship existed between the

---

church music in Hainburg and the discussion of orchestral texture in Austrian church works in Part Two of this book.

[63] Both services had been established in veneration of the Maria-Pötsch-Bild (Gnadenbild), a portrait of the Blessed Virgin that had originated in the Hungarian village of Pötsch. According to several witnesses, the painting had shed real tears on November 4, 1696, and came to be considered miraculous. It was brought from Pötsch to Vienna and, after being displayed at the Favorita, St. Augustin's, and various other churches, was ultimately installed in a silver tabernacle at the high altar of St. Stephen's in 1697. The anniversaries of the miracle and the picture's installation at the Stephansdom were commonly celebrated with a "Pontifical" Mass in the presence of the Emperor. Riedel *Hofe Karls VI*, 45.

[64] Landon *HCW* 1, 56. On cathedral activities during Haydn's decade there, the most complete source (and the origin of virtually all the information above) is still Pohl *Haydn* 1, 27-78.

[65] Described more fully in Chapter 10.

[66] Pohl *Haydn* 1, 52. See the description of a Fux *Te Deum* for double choir and orchestra below.

principal court musicians and the cathedral: Fux's *Singfundamente* assisted in the training of the choirboys, and his Masses and Vespers remained an important part of the choir's repertory for many years.[67] Although he composed numerous concerted works, his special mission was to carry on the sixteenth-century style of church music, codifying its procedures in his archetypal treatise *Gradus ad Parnassum*.[68] He also created sacred works in this *stile antico*, striving for the purity, detachment, and quiet virtuosity that he had discovered in the *a cappella* music of Palestrina. Haydn would seldom utilize *stile antico* for his own sacred music.[69] We know, however, that very early in his career he obtained a copy of *Gradus*, read it, and reread it, making marginal notes over a period of many years and relying heavily on it in his own composition teaching.[70]

Antonio Caldara, who was until his death in 1736 the Vice-Capellmeister at the court of Charles VI, carried the contemporary Neapolitan manner in church music to a similar high level of achievement. In Caldara's music we encounter the same lively, popular-sounding melodies, the same concision and balance, the same alternation of Italian verve and *dolcezza* that are so often appealing in Haydn's scores. Haydn was eventually to bring a more advanced structural command to his writing, allowing for the emergence of longer, more complex, and more expressively varied compositions. Still, he would have been fortunate in his early career to have had at hand as much of Caldara's music—lucid, tasteful, skilled, but scarcely unfeeling—as of Reutter's.[71]

A glance at representative works by these two composers will better reveal their relative strengths and weaknesses while providing a concise view of the sacred-music horizon in Austria *circa* 1725.

---

[67] Careful records of performance dates were entered on the covers of the original partbooks for many of Fux's sacred works. The *Missa brevis solennitatis* composed in 1740, for example, was heard nineteen times between June 10, 1741 and May 1, 1750. Fux's *Missa Preces tibi Domine laudis offerimus* received sixty-three performances between 1720 and 1752; his biographer notes further, "Bis 1740 jährlich 3-4 Mal gewöhnlich." See Köchel *Fux*, Beilage X (Thematisches Verzeichniss), 10ff. As late as 1772, Burney wrote of hearing, "in the cathedral, some admirable old music composed by Fux, not very well performed, indeed, as to singing or accompaniments." Burney *State* 1, 244.

[68] Vienna, 1725. See Fux *Gradus* for information on facsimiles, modern editions, and excerpts.

[69] We are more apt, in fact, to encounter the influence of Fuxian counterpoint in Haydn's instrumental works. See, for example, his Symphony No. 3 (I:3), the finale of which is very plainly set in Fux's third species: cantus-firmus-like whole notes are played off against a steady succession of quarter notes. Haydn's few surviving choral works in *stile antico* include the incomplete *Missa Sunt bona mixta malis*, the second of the four *Hymnus de Venerabili* (*Lauda* 1) of c. 1767, and the late motet *Non nobis Domine*.

[70] See Mann "Critic" for a detailed study of Haydn's use of *Gradus*.

[71] Haydn acquired at least two manuscript scores of Caldara's Masses later in life. His copyist Elssler's catalog of Haydn's music library, prepared in 1804-1805, lists "2. Messen in der Partitur manuscript gebunden" as item no. 213 of the "geschrieben musicalien." A later catalog prepared for the Vienna City Magistry (and copied, with annotations, by Ignaz Sauer and Joseph Eybler for the Court) after Haydn's death specifies that these are "noch eigenhändiger" [autographs] and that "die erste am 14. Juny 1717 und die zweyte am 5<u>ten</u> Juny 1718 in Wien geschrieben worden sey." Landon *HCW* 5 reprints both catalogs in full, 299-320 and 391-404.

What the eighteenth century called *stile antico* often bore scant resemblance to Pal-estrina. At the dawn of the Baroque age, the floodtide of *secunda prattica* music had oblit-erated musicians' taste for Renaissance modal polyphony. Even those sixteenth-century works which survived were usually refitted with basso continuo, orchestral accompaniment, and *ficta* to suit the new aesthetic. At first, composers troubled themselves to keep only certain features of classic polyphony: canon, cantus firmus, scalewise melodic motion. After about 1650, some, like Giacomo Carissimi (1605-1674), showed a deeper interest in the principles of Renaissance music; nevertheless they combined those principles with contem-porary operatic practices to create their own viable church styles.

In the era that followed, encompassing the careers of Alessandro Scarlatti (1660-1725), Antonio Lotti (1667-1740), Leonardo Leo (1694-1744), Francesco Durante (1684-1755), Padre Martini (1706-1784), Fux, Georg Wagenseil (1715-1777), the Haydns, and many others, the most notable characteristic of the use of *stile antico* was the very personal view—albeit heavily influenced by nationality and "school"—that each composer brought to it. In general, Renaissance concepts of melody and tactus had long since given way to period structure and a metric framework. Harmonic considerations weighed heavily, as for example in the treatment of melismas, which now often lost their purely melodic signifi-cance by being doubled in thirds, sixths, or tenths by other voices. Such linkage markedly diminished the independence of the several lines in a composition; sometimes it engen-dered a kind of quasi-polyphony in which the leading voice and accompanying voices were none too subtly managed. As with the widespread use of dissonance and chromaticism (*vide* Lotti, Durante), these declamatory techniques stemmed from the Baroque desire to highlight text and affect.[72]

Within the context of such practices, Fux's church works in the old style strike a con-servative, carefully ordered pose. Perhaps at the expense of variety and expressiveness, he avoided much of the chromaticism and declamatory fervor that infected his Italian col-leagues. His music is nearly always dignified, appropriate, and skillfully crafted. At the end of the chapter are given, as Examples 1.1 and 1.2, a typical contrapuntal exposition and a section in Netherlandish "familiar style" from the Sanctus of his *Missa Quadragesimalis*.[73]

Fux could also apply his contrapuntal skills to church music in the *stilus mixtus*, a man-ner that combined homophonic *galant* sections with contrapuntal concerted ones, diluting both styles in the process.[74] As shown in Example 1.3, from the *Missa* in C, KV 46,[75] he did not always handle such combinations felicitously. Here, the agreeable and regular sub-

---

[72] Fellerer "Altklassische Polyphonie."

[73] In *Denkmäler der Tonkunst in Österreich* 1/1, ed. J. E. Habert and G. A. Glossner (Vienna, 1894), 89-111.

[74] Cf. Fux's own warnings about this style in *Gradus* (3), 182, 192; along with earlier theorists, he preferred to think of the style as one that mixed concerted sections with polyphonic *a cappella* sections. By the mid-1700s such definitions were no longer accurate.

[75] Practical edition by Wolfgang Fürlinger (Hänssler-Verlag HE 10.275, 1977).

ject has been only too obviously constructed for the sole purpose of contrapuntal use—it seems devoid of intrinsic melodic or rhythmic vitality. Furthermore, the desire for a pleasing flow of thirds, etc., within a simple harmonic framework appears to have blocked any opportunities to develop interesting variations (i.e., counterpoint!) as the passage moves along.[76]

Perhaps Fux was most successful with concerted music when he turned to works in the colossal-Baroque manner, which had never really gone out of fashion.[77] In a piece like the *Te Deum* E 37,[78] his straightforward, simple themes sound grand and broadly hewn; they seem fashioned expressly to fill vast spaces, and to do so with just the right proportions of antiphony and activity (see Ex. 1.4a). This is music that can become great once it sounds within a great church.

As Example 1.4b for four solo basses makes clear, Fux was capable of setting himself formidable contrapuntal challenges even in florid Baroque music. This excerpt's rhythmic structure, incidentally, is the same as that of the opening theme in Joseph Haydn's second *Te Deum* setting. Haydn, who possessed the autograph score of this work,[79] undoubtedly drew inspiration from the agile, exuberant manipulation of materials in sections such as this. Likewise he must have appreciated the prowess in Fux's combination of a long rising line and a series of arpeggiated *parlando* statements ("non confundar") in the finale (Example 1.4c).

Turning now to Antonio Caldara and his *Missa* in G,[80] we find that commonplace of Italian Baroque church music: the Kyrie set as a *sinfonia*-like Allegro.[81] Caldara's movement, however, with its reduced scoring and the simpler contours of its melodies, may reflect a more *galant* viewpoint (and the environment of the Viennese court): coloratura is carefully avoided, and a certain squareness dominates the melodic design (Ex. 1.5). Indeed, apart from its Baroque phrase constructions—especially a reliance on sequential ac-

---

[76] The *Gradus* has been criticized for encouraging just such stodginess. See Arnold "Haydn's Counterpoint," 52-54.

[77] And almost never did—witness C. P. E. Bach's massive *Heilig ist Gott* of 1779, scored for alto solo, two choirs, and two orchestras each having 3 trumpets, 2 oboes, bassoon, timpani, and strings with continuo. Haydn owned a score of this work, evidence of his strong and continuing interest in Bach's music.

[78] In Johann Joseph Fux, *Sämtliche Werke* 2/1, "presented" [*vorgelegt*] by István Kecskeméti. Hellmut Federhofer, gen. ed. Johann-Joseph-Fux-Gesellschaft, Graz (Kassel and New York, 1963).

[79] Landon *HCW* 5, 402; in the Sauer-Eybler catalog (see fn. 28) is listed "558. Te Deum Laudamus für ein wohlbesetztes Kirchenchor in lat. Sprache, Partitur." Also, as It. 548, "Fux. Messa canonica a Capella tutta in canone con qualche diversita particolare. rar!"

[80] Practical edition by Wolfgang Fürlinger (*Die Kantate* 208; Hänssler HE 10.208, 1964)

[81] Cf. Handel's *Dixit Dominus* (*c.* 1707-1710) or Alessandro Scarlatti's "St. Cecilia" Mass of 1720. Strong traditional forces governed this practice: in seventeenth- and early-eighteenth-century north Italian Masses, a separate *sinfonia* commonly preceded the Kyrie and sometimes other movements as well. This trait can also be found in Masses by Jommelli and Paisiello but less often in works by German or Austrian composers. See Mac Intyre *Mass*, 131, 716 n. 60, and 717 n. 12.

tivity—this *Missa* in G has features that we could as easily find in the later Masses of Mozart and Haydn.

This is a *Missa brevis;* the composer wastes no time in establishing its spirit and disposing of the first part of the text. In just ten measures, a fugato built on a sequence chain works around to a half-cadence on V of the relative minor. In six further measures, the movement ends; the same sequence (now in parallel sixths between alto and tenor) dissipates the tension and achieves a G-major cadence in as pleasing a manner as possible. To twentieth-century ears, the frankly celebrative mood of this movement may seem odd. One might charitably allow that it buoys up the text without quite crossing the border into frivolity, although those last six measures are certainly not for Puritans. To Italian or Austrian Catholics of the 1720s, such brisk style came as no surprise, and its effect was probably more neutral. People expected some liveliness as the music got under way, whether they were at theatre or church.

The more intimate "Christe," cast in a gently moving 3/4, melts any lingering traces of formality with its solo soprano and bass (a favored combination), introduced and supported by obbligato solo violins. The generally short phrases maintain *galant* simplicity, while the E-minor tonality and "pathetic" drop of a fifth in the "Christe" motive impart a portion of Italian sweetness at its most ingratiating. The "Kyrie" setting is then repeated, forming a miniature ABA.

Caldara's setting of the Credo (Ex. 1.6a and b) is a virtual guided tour of the techniques of vocal writing within the *Missa brevis* genre. Thanks to the composer's taste and skill, these seventy-eight measures serve as a model of what such a Mass could achieve, even in the most modest circumstances. A primary objective was shortness. This goal was specially emphasized in the wordy Gloria and Credo settings, sometimes to a ridiculous degree. To that end, it became customary to overlap parts of the text so that two or more sections might be sung at the same time.[82] Caldara managed his overlapping with the utmost discretion, accompanying it with changes of texture that continually enhance the brief span of music allotted. After four measures of straightforward homophonic declamation, the movement slides easily into "loosened" homophony[83] for five (!) bars, providing just enough counterpoint to maintain interest. A few exchanges between upper and lower voices follow (mm. 10-13); this introduces the text overlap, which continues in masterfully conceived solo passages. Notice with what care the smallest portion of text may be momentarily highlighted, simply by using a motive with a bit more identity than what sur-

---

[82] Cf. the settings of Gloria and Credo in Joseph Haydn's *"Little" Organ Mass* (XXII:7), which feature four simultaneous texts in their opening few bars. Michael Haydn must have felt that the proper spirit—not to mention musical consideration—was lacking in so perfunctory (31 m.) a Gloria setting. He made his own adaptation of it in 1795, "un poco più prolongato." See *JHW* XXIII/2, Anh. IV.

[83] Throughout this study, *loosened homophony* will refer to textures in which strict homophony is enlivened by the occasional rhythmic independence, imitation, or antiphonal deployment of individual or paired voices.

rounds it: "Deum de Deo," bass measures 16-17; "Lumen de lumine," measures 17-18.[84] In measures 19-27, the solo voices pyramid toward some restrained and contrapuntally delicate *fioritura* and then quickly reverse the process, giving to the bass the final words "descendit de coelis." Thus does Caldara marshal together the remaining text in this verbose first section of the Credo, all the while plotting a fit and lovely musical structure for it.

It had become traditional in Italian Credo settings to treat that portion of text describing Christ's earthly life in more intimate, expressive musical terms and at some length, even in a *Missa brevis*. Particularly in the Austrian Mass, we will often encounter this text's first few lines—"Et incarnatus est"—set as a cradle song of folk-like simplicity. In the *Missa* in G Caldara evokes the manger scene instantly, with simple means: *adagio* tempo, choral recitative (sung *piano*?), and subtle chromaticism (Ex. 1.6b). The well-worn motive[85] used imitatively for "ex Maria Virgine" varies texture while maintaining mood. A matter-of-fact "Crucifixus" (marked *Allegro* but not insensitive to the text) follows, providing a smooth transition to the rest of the movement.

One other portion of this Mass deserves attention: the Benedictus (Ex. 1.7). Here again we encounter a prototype for settings of this text throughout the Viennese Classic era. Intimacy is its hallmark. That may be as much due to the position of the Benedictus in the liturgy as anything else; it must follow the more extrovert Sanctus-Hosanna with no intervening ritual activity. For Classic composers, though, the musical need for contrast and repose suggested a turn to *Innigkeit*, an untranslatable word suggesting ardor, sincerity, closeness, cordiality, and more. Even though reduced scoring in the Benedictus can be traced back at least as far as Josquin, the dignified but accessible beauty of the typical Viennese Classic Benedictus suggested a new element in sacred music. Its solo voices and altogether intimate scale were perfectly suited to an age that delighted in things rational, domestic, and natural. We shall trace the descendants of this sort of movement with particular pleasure, for they seem to mirror the dawn of a more humane view of life itself.

Nor is the hint of courtly pomp which clings to this same Benedictus out of place. With its dotted rhythms and march-like flavor, it reveals another facet of the Austrian Mass that we will see in later works. Here Caldara may well be clothing the Deity in an earthly ruler's musical vestments, if not actually paying tribute to his own monarch. Or perhaps both intentions are present. The divine right of kings was still an article of faith in the Holy Roman Empire and, as we have seen, ceremonial reference to the emperor and his deeds went hand-in-glove with the use of secular musical materials in the house of God.[86]

---

[84] Cf. Joseph Haydn's setting in the *Heiligmesse* Credo mm. 31-34; Mozart's in the Credo of K. 427 mm. 59-62.

[85] Among many other cases, cf. J. S. Bach, "Et incarnatus est," *Symbolum Nicenum* BWV 232; Henry Purcell, *Jubilate* in D (mm. 205-212).

[86] Mac Intyre *Mass*, 716 n. 63 refers to an Albrechtsberger Benedictus (in his *Choralmesse*) based on Handel's "See the conqu'ring hero comes." Other overtly military settings include Joseph Haydn's *Mariazellermesse* Benedictus and esp. his *Nelsonmesse* Benedictus, which unsheaths the darkest side of that militarism.

The music of both Fux and Caldara was heard at St. Stephen's and elsewhere in Vienna long after their deaths; we can be sure that Haydn was familiar with it even as a choirboy.[87] He cannot have helped being more constantly aware, however, of the newer developments in church style as represented principally by Capellmeister Reutter. In addition he must have known something of the music of major figures outside Vienna, since music was quick to circulate in manuscript throughout the continent if it had merit. Thus it is unlikely that Johann Adolf Hasse (1699-1783) had escaped the young Haydn's attention.[88] Hasse was Capellmeister to the Saxon Court in Dresden from 1734 until 1764, when he removed to Vienna. It has been said that he represents as great a peak in Neapolitan church music as in Metastasian opera, "demonstrating the best characteristics of the school while often avoiding its greatest weaknesses."[89] Burney had high praise for his music, even when comparing it with the innovations of others: "Hasse may be regarded as the Raphael, and I have already called Gluck the Michael Angelo of living composers."[90]

Consequently we conclude this section by examining church music from Reutter and Hasse. Not the least of reasons for choosing these two composers is the simple availability of their scores. For many other Viennese composers of the same generation—Monn, Wagenseil, Tuma, Bonno, Predieri among them[91]—scholarly editions of choral church music (or at least serviceable dissertations, in English) have not yet appeared.[92]

Georg Reutter, Jr.'s *Missa Sancti Caroli* (1734)[93] is what might be called a "cantata" or, preferably, a "number" Mass.[94] In such works, the text is customarily broken up into shorter segments, each of which is given a separate musical setting. Thus maximum length

---

[87] Regarding Fux, see fn. 69; for Caldara, see Roche "Caldara," which discusses the Mass in G and two other works.

[88] Years later, Haydn sent a copy of his *Stabat Mater* to Hasse and treasured the favorable comments he received from the aged master. See Landon *HCW* 2, 144.

[89] Edward Olleson, "Church Music and Oratorio," *NOH* 7, 291.

[90] Burney *State* 1, 353-354.

[91] For Mathias Georg Monn (1717-1750) and Georg Wagenseil (1715-1777), see Philipp "Messenkomposition." For Franz Tuma (1704-1774), see Vogg "Tuma." For Giuseppe Bonno (1711-1788), see Schienerl "Bonno." For Luca Antonio Predieri (1688-1767), see Freunschlag "Predieri."

[92] An important step toward understanding these masters' collective and individual contributions to the sacred-music genre was taken with the publication of Bruce C. Mac Intyre's *The Viennese Concerted Mass of the Early Classic Period*. Within its 764 pages are sketched the musical portraits of a host of significant composers. Mac Intyre's work has helped immensely in clearing a path for future scholars in this area.

[93] Literally, the *Mass of Saint Charles*. Critical edition by P. Norbert Hofer in *Denkmäler der Tonkunst in Österreich* 88 (Vienna, 1953), 1-57.

[94] Robbins Landon, Olleson, and others called such works "cantata" Masses; their obvious referent is the Mass in B Minor BWV 232 of the great cantata composer J. S. Bach. However, this convenient modern term is misleading, because such Masses lack recitative-aria pairs, continuous narrative, and other style features of the Baroque cantata. F. W. Riedel and B. Mac Intyre have suggested the name "number" Mass, which is adopted herein. See Mac Intyre *Mass*, 5.

and variety contribute to a sense of unrestrained splendor, and the patron can be assured that his Saint's Day—or perhaps his niece's wedding—will be accorded its proper significance. This work is scored for an expanded, but not unusual, complement of two *clarini*, alto trombone, timpani, two violins, and continuo. To give an idea of its overall structure, the movements of the Kyrie and Gloria have been listed below, together with their meters, tempi, keys, and performing forces (assuming continuo throughout).

Kyrie				
Kyrie	C	Allegro	C	Tutti
Christe	3/8	Un poco Andante	F	SB duet, vlns
Kyrie	C	Andante (fugue)	C	Tutti
Gloria				
Gloria in excelsis	C	Allegro un poco—C	Tutti	
Laudamus te	C	Andante	a	S solo, vlns
Gratias agimus tibi	C	Un poco Andante	d	A solo, trmb
Domine Deus	C	Andante	B♭	TB duet, vlns
Qui tollis	C	Adagio	g →a	Choir
Quoniam	3/4	Allegretto	F	SA duet, vlns
Cum sancto spiritum	C	Adagio—(Allegro)C	Tutti	

Table 1.1: Disposition of Movements in Reutter *Missa Sancti Caroli*

In this Mass, as in most of Reutter's sacred music, the Neapolitan operatic manner steals a march on Austrian *Kirchenstil*. Reutter's most striking characteristics are *1)* scurrying violin passagework that can appear almost anywhere and *2)* choral homophony that is sometimes crudely executed and nearly always lacking in melodic interest. Both features are in evidence from the very opening bars of the Kyrie (Ex. 1.8).

First the homophony: any readers who have passed a first-year harmony course will notice the frequently awkward disposition of the choral lines in Ex. 1.8, including tenor below the bass (mm./beats 2/3, 8/3); tenor and bass unison or spaced at a third with upper voices more widely spread (mm./beats 8/2, 10/1-2, 11/1-3, 12/3 *et al.*); and crude doublings and spacings (mm./beats 10/3, 11/3). Similar roughness, including parallel fifths and octaves, has been discerned in Reutter's other sacred works.[95] Some of this was no doubt due to the haste with which Reutter had to work, but as much may have stemmed from his lack of real interest in church style.

As for the rushing string parts, "violins à la Reutter" do not seem out of place in a bustling Kyrie. But when they turn up in movements such as the Benedictus (Ex. 1.9),

---

[95] See Hofer "Beiden Reutter" and esp. Schenk "Göttweiger Rorate-Messe," 87-105. In discussing a work attributed both to Reutter and the young Haydn, Schenk summarizes Hofer's research with regard to this issue.

their presence is intrusive. No matter how diligently the vocal line attempts a sober, even majestic music, the *buffa*-like energy of the violin figures undoes that effort. Reutter is usually more successful in his less characteristic moments. The "Et incarnatus est" is pellucid and intimate in the manner of Caldara; the "Domine Deus, Rex coelestis" uses an aristocratic dotted motive to good, if familiar, effect. The final "Hosanna" fugue is as dull as anything Fux could have written.

Johann Adolf Hasse first absorbed the styles of contemporary opera and church music in Hamburg from 1714 to 1719, where he came under the influence of Reinhard Keiser (1674-1739) and Georg Philipp Telemann (1681-1767). Later he travelled in Italy, finally alighting in Naples. Not only was Naples a center for opera, but its churches were caught up in the city's musical life too, celebrating extended festivities called Octaves on the eight days following the feast of each church's patron saint. These festivals continued day and night, employing only the best vocal and instrumental music that could be had. Although Hasse appears not to have written any sacred works in Naples, the music-making of the Neapolitan churches clearly had a lifelong effect on his style.

While in Italy, Hasse studied briefly with Nicola Porpora (1686-1767). That arrangement was evidently unpleasant. He shortly thereafter became a pupil of Alessandro Scarlatti, whom he greatly admired. Porpora, to whom Haydn later apprenticed himself, never really forgave Hasse for his defection and caused him serious problems in Dresden.[96]

Hasse was summoned to Dresden in 1731, where he was made Royal Polish and Royal Saxon Capellmeister and developed a superb Capelle; his operatic activites meanwhile brought him fame throughout Europe.[97] Following the conversion of the Saxon court to Catholicism, the composer's immersion in modern Italian church style was turned to advantage in a brilliant succession of works for the newly erected Chiaveri chapel. The first of this series was a Mass in D Minor.[98] Written in 1751 for the chapel's dedication, it was praised as late as the early Romantic era, especially for its creative adaptation to the new building (which apparently suffered from a severely echoing acoustic).[99]

Like nearly all of Hasse's settings, this *Missa dedicationis templi* is a "number" Mass. Its thirteen contrasting movements converge in an arch form similar to that in many of Bach's vocal works (e.g., the Cantata BWV 4 or the *St. Matthew Passion*). Although Hasse's fame was built on his prowess as an opera composer, only five of the movements are solo pieces. But the opening choral statements of the Gloria (Ex. 1.10) show that Hasse was equally skilled at manipulating the stocks-in-trade of the Viennese Mass—homophonic text declamation and rapid violin figures.

---

[96] Wilson "Hasse" 1, 11-14.

[97] Wilson "Hasse" 1, 16, 19ff., 23.

[98] Described in one manuscript source as *Missa dedicationis templi* (Boston Public Library: No. 3 in M. 250.19).

[99] Wilson "Hasse" 1, 24-26.

Even without allowing for Hasse's need to simplify textures in the Dresden court chapel, we can consider this music effective. Its choral part-writing is judiciously planned yet exciting, and its contrasting instrumental lines have been thrown into strong relief. What is more, Hasse has built those lines upon one of the most apt and splendid rhetorical figures associated with the Gloria: ascending scales mimetic of the priest, who when singing the *incipit* raises his arms in joy.[100]

In the Benedictus of this Mass, binary aria form provides an often-encountered key plan for one of Hasse's motto arias. The binary aria was often used in the Viennese Classical Mass, including certain Haydn Masses. Its *Urform* of I → V ‖ X → I, originally derived from Baroque dance music, was used extensively for sonatas and arias in the first half of the eighteenth century and was eventually taken over as the tonal basis of sonata-allegro form.[101] Following an introductory orchestral ritornello, the first vocal strain modulates to a related key (usually V, vi, v, or III), which a short ritornello then affirms. The second vocal strain often begins with a transposed restatement of the first theme and then returns to the tonic key; a final ritornello closes the movement.

The music of Hasse's Benedictus, marked *Amorosetto*, is in the style most typical of the later Viennese Benedictus, marked not only by its binary structure, but also by its gentle pastoral qualities, 3/4 meter, and subdominant key. Here the pastoral feeling is reinforced by flutes doubling the violins and long melismas on parallel thirds and sixths for the singers.

When we encounter Haydn's longer aria forms, we see that structurally they resemble such movements. They show still more affinity with arias from Hasse operas. On the stage, Hasse was not bothered with special acoustic or liturgical considerations, so undoubtedly his style—classic in its own time—could emerge more freely there. A worthwhile stylistic comparison might therefore be made between arias such as the "Quoniam" of Haydn's *Cäcilienmesse* and the third-act "Si: correr voglio anch'io" in Hasse's *Ruggiero*.[102] Example 1.11 shows the opening measures of each.

Besides the strict matches of meter, tempo, and rhythmic character (e.g., the "drum" bass of each example), the excerpts are strikingly similar in their use of "heroic" melody figures (i.e., prominent leaps of a fourth in the head-motive, plus more widely spaced leaps elsewhere), contrasts of *forte* and *piano*, and general vocal display. Obviously Haydn felt the rhetoric of heroism could be used just as readily in a good sacred text as in *opera seria*. One might call this a liturgical *aria di bravura*.

---

[100] See W. Kirkendale "New Roads," 667-668. Beethoven uses a similar device in the Gloria of the *Missa Solemnis*. The subject of rhetorical figures in Classical choral music is discussed further in Chapters Two, Four, and Eight.

[101] See Dent "Italian Opera," esp. 270-273.

[102] *Ruggiero ovvero L'Eroica Gratitudine*, ed. Klaus Hortschansky. In *Concentus Musicus* I (Cologne, 1973) [aria, 373-379].

Table 1.1 compares the structural details of the Benedictus described above, Haydn's "Quoniam," and Hasse's "Si: correr." Note that in the second and third arias the opening ritornello introduces a short relief theme (B) in the dominant which may later appear also in tonic. The proportions of "Quoniam" and "Si: correr" are remarkably similar, the main difference being the expansion of the first strain and middle ritornello in "Si: correr" to accomodate additional florid vocalism (the coloratura even spills over into the ritornello).

Hasse's *Ruggiero* met a dismal fate when it was mounted at the same Habsburg festivity in Milan as the fifteen-year-old Wolfgang Mozart's *Ascanio in Alba*. His father Leopold wrote that the latter was "an extraordinary success. . . . It really distresses me very greatly, but Wolfgang's serenata has completely killed Hasse's opera."[103] Musical fashions changed quickly during the first twenty years after 1750. The young Haydn's struggle to master the elements of Italian style was quickly succeeded by a struggle to shape new musical procedures in the 1770s. His study of past masters like Fux, Caldara, and Hasse nevertheless continued, and he would incorporate their kind of craftsmanship into many works to come.

	Ritornello	*1st Strain*	*Ritornello*	*2nd Strain*	*Ritornello*
1751: Hasse,	A	A	A	A	A
Benedictus	I	I→V	V	ii→V	I
mm.	11	17	6	28	12
1766: Haydn,	A $^{(B)}$ A^1	A	A^1	A B	A^1 $^{(B)}$ A^1
Quoniam	I $^{(V)}$ I	I→V	V	V $^{(I)}$ X→I	I $^{(V)}$ I
mm.	18	20	5	33	13
1771: Hasse,	A $^{(B)}$ A^1	A	B A^1 B	A $^{(B)}$ A^1	B A^1
Si: correr (pt 1)	I $^{(V)}$ I	I→V	V→I	X $^{(I)}$ →I$^6_4$	I $^{(V)}$ I
mm.	18	28	12+	32	13
			(w/ singer)	(incl cadenza)	

Table 1.2: Binary Aria Forms in Hasse and Haydn

---

[103] Anderson *Letters of Mozart* 1, 296 (L. 148).

Example 1.1: Fux, *Missa Quadragesimalis*, Sanctus, mm. 1-8

Example 1.2: Fux, *Missa Quadragesimalis*, Sanctus, mm. 22-27

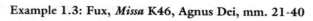

Example 1.3: Fux, *Missa* K46, Agnus Dei, mm. 21-40

Example 1.4a: Fux *Te Deum* E37, mm. 1-9

Example 1.4b: Fux, *Te Deum* E 37, mm. 274-276

Example 1.4c: Fux *Te Deum* E 37, mm. 551-554

Example 1.5: Caldara *Missa* in G, Kyrie, mm. 1-16

Example 1.6a: Caldara *Missa* in G, Credo, mm. 1-21

Example 1.6b: Caldara *Missa* in G, Credo, mm. 28-31

Example 1.7: Caldara *Missa* in G, Benedictus, mm. 1-7

Example 1.8: Reutter, *Missa Sancti Caroli*, Kyrie, mm. 1-10

Example 1.9: Reutter *Missa Sancti Caroli*, Benedictus, mm. 1-8

Example 1.10: Hasse *Missa* in D minor, Gloria, mm. 28-37

Example 1.11a: Haydn *Cäcilienmesse*, **Gloria, mm. 654-659**

Example 1.11b: Hasse *Ruggiero*, "Si: correr", mm. 18-23

2

EARLY SACRED MUSIC

THE SPANGLERS AND MARIANNA MARTINES

By 1749 or early 1750, Haydn's voice was no longer reliable, and he was dismissed from the *Cantorei* at St. Stephen's. By his own account, he

> then had to eke out a wretched existence for eight whole years, by teaching young pupils (many geniuses are ruined by their having to earn their daily bread, because they have no time to study). I experienced this, too, and would have never learnt what little I did, had I not, in my zeal for composition, composed well into the night; I wrote diligently, but not quite correctly, until at last I had the good fortune to learn the genuine fundamentals of composition from the celebrated Herr Porpora (who was at that time in Vienna).[1]

Biographers have traditionally painted a gloomy picture of the next few years in Haydn's life. Undoubtedly Haydn suffered some deprivations during this time, but he was not without protectors and champions. New studies have shown that fairly soon after leaving St. Stephen's, Haydn was using his political skills to gain entrée to the Empress's court—at any rate, to its artistic doings. The 1773 autobiography of Marianna Martines, undoubtedly the most celebrated of Haydn's "young pupils," indicates that she began studying with him in 1751. Martines' respected benefactor the court poet Metastasio could have gotten her any of a number of established tutors; that he allowed her to stay with Haydn for three years speaks as well for the young man's standing at court as it does for his talent. Metastasio was one of Haydn's fellow residents at the Michaelerhaus, and

---

[1] Haydn, autobiographical note; complete in Landon *HCW* 2, 397-399.

that may account for their initial meeting. Still, this Metastasio connection and Haydn's later association with Porpora are evidence of his early success in musical circles.[2]

Aside from his taking pupils and eventually studying with Porpora, we can establish few other guideposts to Haydn's activities and artistic growth during that period. It is the least-well-documented point in his life. As many as five major sacred works and an interesting choral contrafactum can now be traced to these years: the *Missa Rorate coeli desuper*, the *Missa brevis a due Soprani*, a *Lauda Sion* (*Hymnus/Motetto de venerabili Sacramento*), an *Ave Regina* in A, a *Salve Regina* in E, and the chorus *Sit laus plena*. Haydn may well have composed more.[3] Indeed, only in the past thirty years have pioneering scholars added some of the above works to the Haydn canon. But the circumstances that occasioned these pieces are not always known, and attempts to divine their stylistic ancestry sometimes amount to genteel snark hunting. It seems prudent not to overplay the achievements of these early works or to pretend a heritage for them which their maker himself may hardly have acknowledged. Thus the following account must be speculative in connecting some events with the early choral music and ambivalent when discussing possible influences.

During his first few months outside the cathedral, Haydn found the friendship of Johann Michael Spangler and his family extremely important. Spangler, a singer at the Church of St. Michael and a private teacher, was no more than a nodding acquaintance. But legend has it that when he saw the young man wandering through Vienna's chilly streets, Spangler invited him to share lodging with his own family. Haydn gratefully accepted. With a roof over his head and the food purchased from his first meagre earnings as a freelancer, his worries about immediate survival could cease.

---

[2] Brown "Marianna Martines"; the court copyist Gegenbauer is mentioned as another possible connection at court (70n.). As an adult, Martines became known as a composer in many genres, including sacred choral music; see Mac Intyre *Mass*, 80-82.

[3] This accounting passes over obvious apocrypha and/or youthful exercises like the twelve-voice *Salve Regina* mentioned in Dies [(3), 87]. As for spurious and misattributed works of this period or any other in Haydn's life, it is beyond the scope of the present study to make a detailed report or even a serious listing—there are far too many such pieces. Perhaps the following remarks by Robbins Landon, excerpted from his own lengthy but also incomplete account, will give the reader fair warning: "In the case of the sacred music . . . Hoboken's Catalogue (vol. II) has included as genuine many works which are probably or certainly spurious." Landon went on to list and summarily discuss a number of works, including two better-known examples: "The *Mottetto de Tempore* 'Super flumina Babylonis' is a work by J. B. Vanhal (Becker-Glauch ["Neue Forschungen"], 169). . . . Of the Marian Antiphons, many of those listed as genuine by Hoboken must, we believe, be eliminated. We emphatically do not concur with Frau Dr. Becker-Glauch in considering the weak and (as far as sources are concerned) poorly represented *Salve Regina* in E flat (XXIIIb:4) to be a work of Haydn's." Landon *HCW* 1, 157. To Landon's list we must add his own 1960 edition of the *Litaniae de Beata Maria Virgine* in C (XXIIIc:C2; probably by Heyda). Also: the Requiem edited in the 1920s by E. F. Schmid under Haydn's name has turned out to be the work of a minor composer; a cantata published in 1970 as *Die Erwählung eines Kapellmeisters* (XXIVa:11*) is not based on authentic manuscripts. For a general introduction to problems of authenticity, see Geiringer *Haydn*, 195-203; on the choral music, see also Becker-Glauch "Neue Forschungen," esp. 168-169; also Mac Intyre "Doubtful." The most reliable short guide to Haydn's works, real and imagined, is the worklist by Georg Feder in Larsen *New Grove Haydn*.

To make ends meet, Haydn "played for money in serenades and in the orchestras" and was engaged as a freelancer at various churches:

> [He] was first violinist for the Brothers of Mercy in the Leopoldstadt, at sixty gulden a year. Here he had to be in the church at eight o'clock in the morning on Sundays and feast days. At ten o'clock he played the organ in the chapel of Count Haugwitz, and at eleven o'clock he sang at St. Stephen's. He was paid seventeen kreuzers for each service.[4]

No doubt such experiences deepened his practical knowledge of church style, especially from the instrumental point of view. When his situation improved a little in the next few months, Haydn was able to move into his own miserable garret in the old Michaelerhaus near the Church. And just in time, too, for in September of 1750 the Spanglers added another baby to their already-overcrowded quarters.[5]

This child was Maria Magdalena Spangler and, because she figures prominently in the records of an early choral work, we depart for a moment from strict chronology to introduce her. At the Benedictine Priory of Mariazell, an entry on the cover of a manuscript of Haydn's *Ave Regina* in A (XXIIIb:3) notes that the manuscript's owner received it in 1763 from a tenor at St. Michael's Church in Vienna. In all probability, that was Johann Michael Spangler. The note goes on to praise Spangler's eleven-year-old daughter, who sang the *Ave Regina* beautifully: that was Maria. Irmgard Becker-Glauch, whose source studies have established this work's authenticity, reasoned that since Maria was born in 1750, the famous performance of the *Ave Regina* must have taken place in 1761 or 1762. Six years later Haydn was to engage this same Maria (now called Magdalena) Spangler for the Esterházy court music. First appearing as Grilletta in Haydn's *Lo speziale* (1768), she went on to sing demanding roles in *Le pescatrici* (1770), *L'infedeltà delusa* (1773), and *L'incontro improvviso* (1775).[6] She was also the soprano soloist when *Il ritorno di Tobia* was first performed in 1775.[7]

Besides the early Masses and other sacred choral music, Haydn in the 1750s wrote serenades, quartet-divertimenti, some keyboard sonatas, string trios, and dance music.[8] Since the young composer was still finding his way into these forms' varied idioms and manners, we cannot expect to find many remarkable stylistic correspondences between Haydn's early instrumental works and his early choral music. That kind of synthesis shines through properly in Haydn's more mature efforts. But it is worth noting overall that the

---

[4] Greisinger (3), 11, 14; presumably Haydn had gotten through his voice change by this time and was engaged at the cathedral on the tenor part.

[5] Geiringer *Haydn*, 27-28; see also Larsen *New Grove Haydn*, 6-7.

[6] See Becker-Glauch "*Ave Regina*," 71, and Landon *HCW* 2, 48.

[7] Landon *HCW* 2, 215: "Sara: Magdalena Friberth (from the *Capelle*)."

[8] Landon *HCW* 1, 77; special reference is made to the Serenade (II:2) and the "Seitenstetten" Minuets (IX:1).

cheerful *galant* simplicity of his first *Lauda Sion* (see below) has many cousins in these string trios, sonatas, and quartets. Major keys and "popular" melodies abound; within a work, the same key gets used for most movements. The sonatas usually include a minuet, and many of the early quartets have two.[9]

Haydn was also working assiduously to fill the gaps in his musical education, poring over Fux's *Gradus ad Parnassum*, Mattheson's *der vollkommene Capellmeister*, and Kellner's *Unterricht im Generalbass*. One can get a notion of how steady and thorough was Haydn's study of these books by perusing their margins, which he filled with annotations over the course of his life.[10] He may also have become acquainted with C. P. E. Bach's *Versuch* (the first part appeared in 1753), although it appears that his most intense involvement with Bach's music did not take place until the 1760s.[11] Incidentally, Michael Haydn was now finishing up his own days at St. Stephen's. From 1753 to '54 he would attend the Jesuit Seminary in Vienna, which gave his early career a considerable boost. Musically Michael may also have been ahead of his brother at this point: Robbins Landon wrote that his *Missa in honorem. sanctissimae Trinitatis* of 1754 "by far outshines the attractive but modest *Missae breves* in F and G of [Joseph's] youth."[12]

HAYDN'S FIRST MASSES

Both the *Missa Rorate coeli desuper* (XXII:3)[13] and the *Missa brevis* in F (XXII:1) were probably composed around the time of Haydn's departure from St. Stephen's. Since we have no clues as to their use in his life other than a date of composition—1749—for the F-Major Mass, they may as well serve here to introduce readers to Haydn's early choral church music.

In May of 1957 H. C. Robbins Landon astounded the musicological world by announcing his discovery of the long-lost Haydn *Missa Rorate coeli desuper* at the Abbey of Göttweig in Lower Austria. The work was performed in July and appeared in print later the same year. Almost as quickly, its authenticity was challenged, principally by Erich Schenk, who made a case for Reutter as composer. Hoboken and Larsen eventually joined

---

[9] See the keyboard sonatas XVI:1, 2, and 4; the keyboard trios XV:C1 and 37; and the quartets "Op. 1" and "Op. 2," which are really five-movement *divertimenti*.

[10] Geiringer *Haydn*, 29-30. Haydn's collection included one devoted entirely to church music, Münster's *Scala Jacob* (see Bibliography).

[11] Brown "Influence," 161-163.

[12] Landon HCW 1, 78.

[13] Hoboken regarded the *Missa Rorate coeli desuper* that Robbins Landon discovered (see following text) as inauthentic and assigned it a separate index number (XXII: ii, 73). To avoid superficial confusion, the present study uses the Haydn (i.e., authentic) number in all references to this *Missa*, whether they indicate the work presently known or some "once and future" setting.

in refusing to accept the work as Haydn's; in contrast, Becker-Glauch and Geiringer also regarded it as authentic.[14] Since the dispute has never really been settled, we will summarize below the main arguments for and against Landon's 1957 discovery (hereafter referred to as the Göttweig Mass).[15]

For: 1) Around 1805 Haydn entered the incipit for a "Missa Rorate coeli desuper/in g" in his *Entwurf-Katalog* (*EK*), a scrupulous record of his own works that he had begun keeping in 1765 (Ex. 2.1a). His copyist Johann Elssler made a longer entry for the same Mass in the so-called *Haydn-Verzeichnis* (*HV*)[16] of 1805 (Ex. 2.1b), although the added notes do not quite agree with the opening theme found in the Göttweig Mass (Ex. 2.1c).[17]

Example 2.1: *Missa Rorate coeli* incipits

2) The manuscript parts discovered by Landon at Göttweig Abbey are marked "Missa . . . Del Sig[re] Josepho Hayden," with the last two words scratched out. Presumably this cancellation occurred in the early nineteenth century when the Mass was no longer familiar to musicians. It was then listed in the Göttweig catalogue as an unknown work.

3) Although in various manuscript copies the Göttweig Mass is attributed to Reutter or to Ferdinand Arbesser (c.1719-1794; Reutter's organist), none of those copies are located in places geographically close to Vienna. This supports the idea that Viennese copyists decided to market an early Haydn work under the names of better-known composers—not an uncommon practice. Haydn's organ concertos and his *Missa brevis* in F were also attributed to other composers, and after Haydn became famous, the works of others were sold with his name attached.

---

[14] See the short bibliography appended to the entry for this work in Chapter 11.

[15] The arguments for authenticity are based largely on Landon *HCW* 1, 139-143; arguments against are taken from Schenk "Göttweiger Rorate-Messe."

[16] See Landon *HCW* 5, 294-295 for a brief description of *EK, HV*, and other catalogues.

[17] Haydn also misquoted in *EK* the bass incipit for the *Kleine Orgelmesse*, presumably because of faulty memory; Elssler corrected it for him in *HV*. Landon cited this further instance of misquotation in order to bolster the notion that differences between the *EK, HV*, and Göttweig incipits could be attributed to memory lapses on Haydn's part. The situations are not exactly parallel, however, and any attempt to use one in support of the other must be regarded with caution. Cf. Landon *HCW* 1, 141-142, and Larsen *HHV*, 210-214.

4) The Göttweig parts contain many mistakes in partwriting as well as other compositional crudities, all of which would point to the young Haydn as composer rather than the more experienced Reutter or Arbesser.[18] On the other hand, the Mass's Reutterian elements can be considered merely the obvious influences of a master upon his pupil's first efforts.[19]

Against: 1) The *EK* entry is the only direct evidence of Haydn's authorship, and it must be regarded with suspicion. Haydn made it after his trips to England, when his memory of the events of fifty years earlier was no longer as clear as it might have been. Furthermore, the longer incipit in the *HV* is not merely an extension or variant, it implies a theme-type with a wholly different harmonic and motivic character than that of the Göttweig Mass. The theme-type as found in the Göttweig Mass is, however, prominent in many of Reutter's other works.

2) Since Landon's discovery, a number of other manuscript sources and catalog listings of the Göttweig Mass have come to light. The total number of attributions is now: *a)* for Reutter, five sources, incl. two catalogues and three sets of parts; *b)* for Arbesser, one catalogue and two sets of parts; *c)* for Haydn, the listings in *EK*, *HV*, and Fuchs's *Thematisches Verzeichnis* of 1839 (probably taken over from the earlier catalogues) plus—only—the Göttweig parts. Not only is the work more widely attributed to Reutter than first thought, but its style is so characteristic of that composer that no one had ever questioned the attribution. On the contrary: the experienced Reutter scholar P. Norbert Hofer listed the Göttweig Mass as No. 22 in his reliable thematic catalog and repeatedly cited it as a paradigm of Reutter's *Missa brevis* style.[20]

3) The compositional crudities cited as evidence of the young Haydn's hand are in fact highly characteristic of Reutter; numerous examples can be found in the older man's work of what Hofer termed "an amateurish impression" stemming from "many mistakes in the parts." Perhaps the most telling evidence of Landon's stylistic misapprehension in this regard lies in his 1957 edition of the Göttweig Mass. According to Schenk, Landon's lack of familiarity with the typical roughness of Reutter's voice leading caused him to ascribe many of the "mistakes" in the Göttweig parts to copyists' errors and to "correct" them in his edition. Collation of all the manuscript sources has demonstrated, however, that most of those "mistakes" were intended by the composer.

---

[18] See Haydn's remark from 1776, "I wrote diligently, but not quite correctly," in a letter to Leonore Lechner; Landon *HCW* 2, 398.

[19] Here and later, Griesinger's comment about Haydn's early training might be borne in mind: "Reutter did encourage him to make whatever variations he liked on the motets and *Salves* that he had to sing through in the church, and this practice early led him to ideas of his own which Reutter corrected." Griesinger *Notizen* (3), 10. One could assume that Haydn, in the case of the *Missa Rorate coeli desuper*, was making "variations" on a plainchant motive (see text following); he might, however, have been paraphrasing one of Reutter's pieces!

[20] "Beiden Reutter," Thematisches Katalogue; see also Schenk "Göttweiger Rorate-Messe," 98.

Conclusion: The question is unlikely to be resolved soon. Recently, Arbesser has been suggested as the most likely author, based on stylistic criteria.[21] Two of his works, the *Missa Nubes pluant justum* and a Mass in G (known in its Göttweig source as *Missa Rorate coeli*), share several important features with the present Mass. In addition, the *Missa Nubes* has the distinction of being attributed to Reutter in a number of catalogues or copies.[22] Thus the argument that Viennese copyists passed off the Göttweig Mass as that of a better-known composer may now be given a new interpretation.

More detailed scrutiny of Reutter, Arbesser, and others has made scholars aware that many stylistic traits previously associated with one musician may actually have been the common coin of church composers in Vienna. Whether or not the Göttweig Mass is Haydn's *Missa*, the influence of his teachers is obviously strong. Little of Haydn's subsequent style can be discerned.[23] In a later work, the question of authenticity might be more significant; there our views of influence and stylistic evolution could be significantly altered by putting something new into the known framework of the composer's output. But acceptance of this little piece will provide us with few fresh insights; rejection would deprive us of fewer still. Performers will have to evaluate the Göttweig Mass on the basis of its musical substance, not its uncertain pedigree.

The title *Missa Rorate coeli desuper* comes from the first phrase of Isaiah 45:8: "Drop down, ye heavens, from above, and let the skies pour down righteousness: let the earth open, and let them bring forth salvation, and let righteousness spring up together; I the Lord have created it." This beautiful prophetic verse appears in the course of both the Saturday (Ember Week) and Sunday (4th Advent) services of the week before Christmas. At Sunday Mass, it serves as Introit (see below).

The Saturday Mass is an Advent tradition in German-speaking countries and is often referred to as a *Rorate* Mass.[24] When Mass was sung at the Saturday service, the Credo was not included; conversely, on an Advent Sunday the Credo would be heard, but not the Gloria. The composer of the present Mass had provided for both possibilities by setting a complete Ordinary.

Advent is a penitential season, and the music written for it is usually modest in scale. The Göttweig Mass's lack of vocal solos, its scoring for church trio, and its length of less

---

[21] Mac Intyre *Mass*, 59.

[22] Mac Intyre *Mass*, 593.

[23] Runestad summarized these differences concisely: "Even compared with other Haydn missa brevis settings the shortness of the Rorate is startling. . . . It uses no soli. The only independent instrumental sections in the entire work are the [2- and 3-measure] introductions. . . . There are no fugues, fugal passages or contrapuntal sections; the chorus texture is pervasively homophonic to the extent that all voice parts have exactly the same rhythms throughout in the Benedictus and Agnus Dei." He further cited the work's extreme polytextuality and its reliance on the tonic key for every movement; "Masses," 125-126.

[24] Landon *HCW* 1, 142, mentions a "substantial 'Rorate' music literature of the period." Haydn and the Esterházy Capelle participated in *Rorate* Masses yearly; see Chapter 3.

than ninety measures are therefore quite appropriate. This Mass is in fact the shortest of all the short Masses associated with Joseph Haydn.[25] It is just half the length of the most brief *Missa brevis* documented in Mac Intyre's survey: the Arbesser (!) *Missa Nubes pluant justum*, 199 measures long and named for the words ("let the skies pour down righteousness") in Isaiah 45 that follow "Rorate coeli . . ."[26] Both works were probably intended as *Rorate* Masses.

Much of the thematic material for the Göttweig Mass derives from a portion (bracketed in Ex. 2.2) of the Gregorian Introit for the Fourth Sunday of Advent. This derivation is most clearly felt in the Kyrie (see Ex. 2.1c). Schenk has pointed out that Kyries in *Rorate* Masses by Reutter and Arbesser exhibit the same melodic impulse in their opening bars and that the basic design of this type of Gregorian motive—ascending stepwise motion capped with the leap of a third—was echoed in a much-loved eighteenth-century theme type, used for everything from Fuxian exercises to pre-Classic minuets.[27] What is especially interesting about the motive's employment in the present Mass is its appearance not only in the Kyrie but again in the Credo and in the Gloria, where it is inverted (which is rhetorically fitting, given the text "et in terra pax"). The Gloria of Arbesser's *Rorate* Mass also brings back the Gregorian motive, but in original form.[28]

Example 2.2: Gregorian Introit *Rorate caeli desuper*

In every movement save the Agnus, Reutterian violin passagework is much in evidence. Identification of the principal violin motive is very strongly felt between Kyrie and Gloria

---

[25] Cf. XXII: 1, 6, and 7.

[26] Mac Intyre *Mass*, esp. Appendix C, 593.

[27] Schenk "Göttweiger Rorate-Messe," 99-101; specific reference is made to a Reutter "Rorate" Mass in F of 1753 and an Arbesser MS at Göttweig known as the "Missa Rorate Coeli," again from 1753.

[28] Landon recognized further permutations of the chant fragment; see *HCW* 1, 143-144.

(cf. Ex. 2.1c and 2.3); the same motive reappears briefly in the "Pleni sunt coeli. . . . Osanna" and "Osanna" portions of the Sanctus and Agnus Dei. In the Credo and Bene-dictus, the passagework remains active but is less clearly related to the principal motive.

The Gloria is remarkably curt. As we have seen, a certain amount of text overlap can be expected in the *brevis* style, yet one can hardly help feeling that it is overdone here. From beginning to end—a scant eight-and-a-quarter bars—each section of the choir furiously gives out a different section of text, dispensing with the entire movement in less than a minute. Example 2.3 shows two typical measures (one quarter of the piece). It cannot have edified the faithful overmuch.

Example 2.3: Göttweig Mass, Gloria, mm. 3-4

The Sanctus, with its opening short fugato, and the Benedictus, with its triplets in the violins and an opening ritornello taken over by the choir, are both typical of Austrian Masses of the time and especially typical of Reutter's settings.[29]

A less commonly encountered solution to one of the compositional problems of the Viennese Mass can be seen in the Agnus Dei, a single-movement Adagio with no change of tempo, meter, or texture for the "Dona nobis pacem." Viennese composers generally preferred using the Dona to introduce lighter, faster music, bringing the Mass to a close in the lively manner of an operatic finale. Here the only change at that point is a dramatic drop to *piano* and G minor, both of which continue to the warm, dignified plagal cadence of the final two bars. Readers will want to compare this Agnus (Ex. 2.5a) with similarly quiet settings in the *Missa Sancti Nicolai* (XXII:6) and the *Kleine Orgelmesse* (XXII:7).[30] In the *Nicolai* Agnus the pastoral 6/4 music of Haydn's Kyrie is reprised—a common de-vice in Viennese Masses, but one that works especially well in this case. The Agnus of the *Kleine Orgelmesse* (Ex. 2.4) also contains pastoral elements (parallel thirds in both strings

---

[29] Schenk "Göttweiger Rorate-Messe," 98.

[30] One other atypical Dona needs to be mentioned: the quiet 3/4 setting in Arbesser's previously cited *Missa Nubes pluant justum*; see Mac Intyre *Mass*, 559.

and voices) and cleverly mimics a plagal cadence in its closing measures by using a two-note motive moving downward from I to V (*quasi* IV → I).

Much has been made of the deficient partwriting, etc., in the Göttweig Mass, especially in connection with the question of its ancestry. Space permits the quotation of only three examples. Example 2.5a shows the close of the Agnus, with its strong and simple final cadence and some curious choral voicings in measure 19. An egregious excerpt from the Credo (Ex. 2.5b) shows a tritone approached by skipwise similar motion in bass and alto voices as part of the polytextual "Et resurrexit." Finally, Example 2.5c offers two chords from the Agnus that wish they were three—the sort of underachieving progression, or overambitious escape tone, that still crops up on freshman harmony papers.

With the F-Major Mass of 1749, we are on firmer ground regarding authenticity. Happily, it is also a work that both echoes the venerable Caldarean tradition and sounds the first few, true notes of Haydn's own later style. Haydn himself was the rediscoverer of this youthful effort in 1805, when he turned up a copy of the work at the Servite Monastery at Rossau. Dies chronicled the old man's reaction in his *Biographical Accounts*:

> The recovery of this child, lost fifty-two years before, gave the parent great joy. He examined it attentively, conducted an investigation, perceived it was not unworthy of him, and determined to dress it in modern clothes.
> "What specially pleases me in this little work," said Haydn, "is the melody, and a certain youthful fire, and this stirs me to write down several measures a day in order to provide the voices with a wind-instrument accompaniment."[31]

Stylistically and also in terms of authenticity, the expanded wind accompaniment is controversial; it is seldom used today. The original orchestration serves this Mass's delicate music quite well—no "modern clothes" were really necessary.[32]

Like the Göttweig Mass, the F-Major Mass is scored for mixed chorus and church trio. Special interest lies in the two solo soprano parts: they inevitably call to mind young Joseph and his brother Michael, the twin stars in St. Stephen's vocal firmament around the time this Mass was composed. From their very first appearance in the Kyrie, these duet passages signal a regard for Italian elegance that is the most progressive aspect of the work. By contrast, the string writing still seems cluttered in the Reutter way—note the varied rhythms of the first two measures, given as Example 2.6.

Fortunately, Haydn's more transparent scoring in the duet sections enables their intimate beauty to shine forth without strain. The effect is of a Baroque concerto grosso, and in fact the structure of the Kyrie emphasizes that idea; the opening ritornello of measures

---

[31] Dies *Nachrichten* (3), 117.

[32] Some authorities doubt that Haydn did more than supervise the wind arrangement's completion by others; see Landon *HCW* 1, 145-146. Denis McCaldin made an extensive musical analysis of that version, claiming (not always successfully, we feel) that it reflects Haydn's wide experience as a symphonic composer, especially in the areas of doubling and rhythmic punctuation. See McCaldin "First."

1-2 returns in modified form at the "Christe" and again more directly at the final "Kyrie." It is also possible to find in this Kyrie—like that of the Göttweig Mass—a two-reprise tonal structure (‖: I → V :‖: X → I :‖) hinting at the great symphonic sonata-forms of the later Masses.[33]

As we would expect, the Gloria features a telescoped text. But it is handled here with much more care than in the *Rorate* Mass; overlapping is delayed until measure 9 and then echoes the text's parallel constructions with an imitative texture (Ex. 2.7).

Carl Maria Brand emphasized that, of the twelve fully authenticated Masses, only this one has no fugues. In his eyes, the "enlivened declamation" of this section and of similar spots in the Credo ("et resurrexit") and Sanctus ("gloria tua," "hosanna") was a beacon shining toward Haydn's future development of choral polyphony.[34]

The two sopranos have little to do in the first two-thirds of the Gloria, but they virtually take over the final ten measures with a splendid cadenza-like coda on "amen." This entire coda is repeated at the end of the Credo; we quote it as Example 2.8. With a touch of hyperbole, Robbins Landon called this repetition of the "amen" passage an "astonishing formal operation. . . . It is perhaps naive but it is also a stroke of genius (the two not being, and certainly not in Haydn, mutually exclusive)."[35] Astonishing or not, it is certainly early evidence of a lively and unconventional mind.

The repeated "amen" is more than merely a charming means of unifying the two movements, however. A larger plan is involved. As we have seen, Viennese composers commonly reused the material of the Kyrie for the Agnus at the end of a Viennese Mass, and in this Haydn followed suit. His Dona here is identical to his Kyrie, making the very beginning and very end of the setting the same. Given that most striking symmetry, we can go further and regard the "amen" codas of the Gloria and Credo as landmarks enhancing this balance from within. Thus all three macro-segments of the Ordinary are linked in an arch form of unifying devices. Such planning hardly qualifies as naiveté.

Aside from the "amen," the Credo is divided into the three traditional sections: "Patrem omnipotentem," "Et incarnatus est," and "Et resurrexit."[36] The two sopranos are absent until their burst of *fioritura* at the end. Haydn disposed of the first section in less than seven measures of loosened choral homophony and overlapped text, neglecting, in fact, to set the words "Et in unum Dominum Jesum Christum, Filium Dei unigenitum." This sort of omission should not be construed as deliberate doctrinal revision by a rebellious composer. It was fairly common for eighteenth-century musicians to repeat, rear-

---

[33] See Dack "Origins," 131.

[34] Brand *Messen*, 10-11.

[35] Landon *HCW* 1, 146-147.

[36] The first phrase is, as in the Gloria, intoned by the celebrant; see Chapter 10. The Credo of Caldara's Mass in G is discussed in Chapter 1, providing further insights and an interesting comparison with this work.

range, or even omit portions of the Mass text for musical reasons.[37] There may simply not have been room for those words within Haydn's musical plan. We should probably be thankful for the omission if it helped make this section even marginally more intelligible than its counterparts in the Göttweig or "Little Organ" Masses. Textwise, all three settings tend toward babel. The "Et incarnatus est" is handled sensitively, especially the Crucifixion scene (Ex. 2.9). "Et resurrexit" and the rest of the Credo text spring to life with the polyphonic touches previously mentioned.

The Sanctus is a two-part structure, slow-fast, with the latter section introducing "Pleni sunt coeli." This makes it formally similar to most other Viennese Classic settings, including the Göttweig Sanctus and those in many later Haydn Masses.[38] A Viennese Sanctus tended to be short, as is this one, because silence had to reign during the consecration and elevation of the Host.[39] The roles of the two sopranos are reduced here but not eliminated; a plagal cadence ends the movement.

Haydn's Benedictus also follows Italo-Austrian tradition. The two sopranos have full sway, their operatic binary aria introduced with a refulgent fourteen-measure ritornello. Rhythmic unity is provided by the syncopations of the violin parts, a feature common to both Italian opera and contemporary Viennese church style. To end, the movement repeats the Sanctus's choral "Hosanna," also a common practice.

In his Agnus, Haydn also maintained Viennese tradition. An Agnus was usually the shortest part of the Mass, with composers relying upon formal stereotypes and music heard earlier.[40] Here the teenage master took just twelve measures of solemn choral homophony—an invocation of the Lamb of God—to bring the music from D minor around to the dominant of F. Then, as mentioned above, he brought back the joyous music of the Kyrie for the "Dona nobis pacem" part of the text. The Agnus is skillfully done, and if the Dona seems more suited to an *opera buffa* finale, so be it. That was the style of the Mass in eighteenth-century Austria. Haydn's achievement in later years would lie not so much in a departure from these means as in an enrichment of their possibilities.

---

[37] See Mac Intyre *Mass*, 124-125. Of course, the encyclical *Annus qui* (1749) forbade any but the complete text. In Haydn's four late Masses, XXII:9-12, the words "Qui ex Patre Filioque procedit" are omitted for no discernible reason; perhaps he was working from a corrupt version of the text and, owing to his by-then extended neglect of sacred composition, did not spot the error.

[38] Mac Intyre *Mass*, 421.

[39] Jungmann *Mass*, 216-217.

[40] See Mac Intyre *Mass*, 479-481.

THE FIRST *LAUDA SION*

Haydn's connection with the beautiful Styrian village of Mariazell had begun even earlier than our account of Maria Spangler and the *Ave Regina* in A would indicate. In the
spring of 1750 he made his first pilgrimage to the miraculous shrine of the Virgin there.
The draining seventy-mile hike could take a week or more, yet it was a favorite of the Viennese. Haydn most likely traveled with a congenial group of fellow pilgrims. As Griesinger
described it,

> he had in his pocket several motets of his own composition and asked the Regens
> chori there for permission to take them into the church and sing them. This re-
> quest was denied him; but to achieve his purpose of gaining himself a hearing, he
> had recourse to trickery on the following day. He placed himself in the choir be-
> hind the boy who had the alto part to sing, and offered him a coin to give up his
> place to him. The boy did not dare to make the bargain, for fear of the director, so
> then Haydn reached quickly over the boy's head, seized the music on the desk,
> and sang to everybody's satisfaction. The Regens chori got together a collection of
> sixteen gulden and sent the hopeful youth back to Vienna with it.[41]

The "several motets" mentioned above may have included Haydn's first *Lauda Sion*
setting (XXIIIc:5), also titled *Mottetto I, II, III, IV de Venerabili Sacramento* or *Vier
"Hymnen de Venerabili."*[42] Since this *Lauda Sion* is easy to confuse with a later work also
entitled *Lauda Sion* (or *4 Responsoria de Venerabili*; XXIIIc:4; ca. 1768), we will refer to
them respectively as *Lauda* 1 and *Lauda* 2.

Like the *Missa Rorate coeli desuper* recovered in 1957, *Lauda* 1 was only recently
found, and as in the case of the former work, grounds for its authenticity are shaky.[43] An
entry on page 8 of the *EK* clearly refers to *Lauda* 2 by quoting the incipit from its bass
part. Another entry occurs on page 21, for a "Hymnus de Venerabili 1$^{\underline{mo}}$, 2$^{\underline{do}}$, 3, 4." but
with no incipit. That may be a reference to *Lauda* 1. The words have been scratched
through, however, and an entry for two keyboard sonatas, with their incipits, has been put
in their place. Perhaps Haydn, needing more room to enter sonatas and lacking an incipit
for the (other? earlier?) work, carelessly obliterated the only citation of it among his papers.

No autograph score exists. Becker-Glauch, who was the first to write about *Lauda* 1,
based her work on a manuscript copy found in the National Library at Budapest. In it, the
four hymns are attributed to "Haiden" or "Heyden"; no first name is given. At least the
works are not credited to *Michael* Haydn in any past or present catalogs of his works

---

[41] Griesinger *Notizen* (3), 11.

[42] By Landon (*HCW* 1, 147) and Hoboken (*Werkverzeichnis* 2, 162) respectively.

[43] See Becker-Glauch "Neue Forschungen," esp. 172-174, which details the provenance and significant stylistic
features of the work; the summary which follows in our text is based on Becker-Glauch's article unless otherwise
noted.

known to the Cologne Haydn-Institute. That does not rule out the possibility of a whole-sale misattribution.

Aside from the scratched-out entry in *EK* and the manuscript parts in Budapest, the case for accepting this as an early work of Haydn's is slim (although not nearly as fraught with problems as that of the Göttweig Mass). The parts originated in the Servite Monastery of Pest, so Becker-Glauch could cite Haydn's lifelong connections with that order. In speaking with Dies of his poverty-stricken Michaelerhaus years, Haydn had confessed that "Once [his] thoughts grew so gloomy, or more probably hunger plagued him so strongly, that he determined against all inclination to enter the Servite Order just to have enough to eat."[44] Like many of the stories Haydn pitched to his credulous early chroniclers, this reference to the Servites was probably a tongue-in-cheek variation on the truth, but we know from other sources that Haydn's association with the order was real and continuing. Brand mentions his "duties as organist with the Servites" without being more specific.[45] And it was at a Servite church/monastery in suburban Vienna that the score of Haydn's F-Major Mass turned up again in 1805; he also had himself carried there in 1807 and 1808 in search of a cure for his swollen legs.[46] So it is quite possible that parts for an early Haydn work could have found their way via the Servites to a monastery in Hungary.

As a final argument for their authenticity, Becker-Glauch cites these pieces' similarity to the early Masses: their musical substance points to a composer blessed with talent but lacking the proper schooling. Certainly we encounter here again the parallel octaves, etc., present in the Göttweig Mass and the Mass in F. Once more evident too is a peculiar disposition of the choral ranges in which tenor and alto parts lie quite low, the tenor occasionally crossing under the vocal bass. As a result either tenor and alto lines or alto and soprano are frequently at least an octave apart. This tendency may reflect a prevalent *galant* desire to make the upmost voice more prominent. We find its instrumental equivalent in Haydn's early string trios, where the second violin part lies low and occasionally crosses below the *basso*.[47] Robbins Landon commented on another "fingerprint" of the young Haydn present here: dotted patterns for the *clarini* in cadences and linking passages (as in *Sit laus plena*; cf. Ex. 2.12). The presence of such figures in *Sit laus plena* indicates that it is an early work; Haydn no longer used them in his symphonies for Count Morzin (Nos. 32 and 33; see below) or after he began to write for trumpets in 1774 (cf. Symphony No. 56).[48]

---

[44] Dies *Nachrichten* (3), 91.

[45] Brand *Messen*, 309.

[46] Dies *Nachrichten* (3), 240 n. 15.

[47] See esp. the trios V:1 and 2 (In *JHW* XI/1). Perhaps Haydn expected a keyboard player or bassist to double the violoncello part at the lower octave.

[48] Landon *HCW* 1, 153, 179.

Yet surely the most interesting aspect of *Lauda* 1 is its expansion of that sunny, popular quality first hinted at in the generalized Italianate style of the F-Major Mass. All four of these pieces (see Ex. 2.10) are in C major, 3/4 meter, and marked *Vivace;* all have the lively but simple "singing" theme type that Haydn used so fondly for his symphonic first movements in triple meter. Here, straightforward choral declamation and uncomplicated solo passages communicate the tune's message directly to the heart. Haydn also employed such a theme in the Kyries of the *Mariazellermesse* (1782) and *Heiligmesse* (1796)[49] and for his great hymn "Gott erhalte Franz den Kaiser."[50] All these works spring from the same vast well of feeling and folk sympathy in their creator.

This *Lauda Sion* is the first of Haydn's liturgical settings for the Feast of Corpus Christi; that holiday's happy Austrian traditions, outlined in Chapter 1, undoubtedly account for many of the stylistic features in *Lauda* 1.[51] The orchestra is comparatively large for a "small sacred work" and, in spite of its mainly accompanimental function, is often employed brilliantly. That all four movements are in the same key, meter, and tempo can be laid to the length of time that would have passed between each movement's performance during the great procession. Since each piece could have been performed in a different church to accommodate the four "stations,"[52] whatever desires the composer harbored for musical variety would easily have yielded in his planning to a (traditional?) festive unification of the sequence's verse settings.[53] Robbins Landon believed that custom also influenced the selection of verses set (1-3, 21, 22, 23) and the overall organization of each movement ([I] solos → choral tutti [I] →[V] ritornello → voices → ritornello → [I] voices).[54] It is a plan that owes more to Baroque style (use of orchestral ritornellos as framing elements) than to Classic (one looks in vain for a true recapitulation; at best the form resembles the early-Classic "sonata-binary").[55]

Haydn's possible use of the *Lauda Sion* plainchant is another link to tradition and to the Göttweig Mass as well. J. T. Berkenstock concluded that *Lauda* 1 contains widespread allusions to the original Gregorian melody; comparative examples are given in Example

---

[49] XXII:8 and 10, respectively; Haydn's skillful manipulation of the melody in the latter work made it an apotheosis of warmth, humor, and spiritual peace. See Chapter 7.

[50] In the first published reference to *Lauda* 1, Georg Feder hailed the fourth-movement motives that so joyfully call to mind "Gott erhalte"; "Quellen," 16.

[51] See Chapter 2.

[52] Owing to the organ accompaniment. But see Landon *HCW* 1, 148, which suggests possible outdoor performance for all but the first, at least in Budapest.

[53] But see below regarding the strong overall tendencies toward tonal unity, etc., in Haydn's early music.

[54] Landon *HCW* 1, 149, 153.

[55] Berkenstock "Smaller Sacred Compositions," 46-49, offers a detailed examination of form in these pieces; see also Newman *Sonata*, 143-147, for definitions and broader views of these procedures.

2.11.[56] The more obvious quotations (as in Ex. 2.11d and e) may exemplify the "variations" spoken of by Griesinger in his comments about Haydn's early training.[57] Certainly Haydn would have been thoroughly familiar with the *Lauda Sion* chant. A more likely notion (especially in the case of the less obvious "variations") is that, through contact from his earliest years on, Haydn had absorbed the essential melodic style of the Church's music and so could turn out a chant-like line as easily as he provided folk-like tunes for his symphonies.[58] Even as early as the *Missa Rorate coeli desuper* and this *Lauda Sion*, Haydn was drawing upon the common fund of Western melody and subjecting it to the motivic manipulation that would later be such a hallmark of his style.

KURZ AND *DER KRUMME TEUFEL*; PORPORA

The next vocal work Haydn composed was the comic opera *Der krumme Teufel* (*The Limping Devil*; XXIXb:1a). As we shall see, it had both an immediate impact and long-range influence on his choral style.

Outwardly the musical life of Vienna in the first half of the eighteenth century was encompassed by the court and the church. But a grass-roots development had also taken place, one that fused Italian and, to a lesser extent, French elements with a healthy measure of German folkishness. This was popular German theater, the old Viennese *Volkskomoedie* that, after 1712, finally found a respectable home in the Kärntnerthortheater. Readers may be aware that Mozart's *Die Zauberflöte* is a descendant of the same genre; its mixture of simple and operatic styles, its humor, and its reliance on fantasy and stage effects (*Maschineneffekten*) would have been familiar to any theatergoer of the 1750s. In addition to these elements, the typical Viennese comedy relied on improvised "bits," broad sexual and scatalogical jokes, and outright parodies of Italian arias (or even entire *intermezzi*).[59] The famous comedian J. J. F. von Kurz was a master producer, publicist, playwright, and star performer of such offerings—in every respect a worthy predecessor to Mozart's friend Emanuel Schikaneder.

Early accounts suggest that Haydn met Kurz (stage name Bernardon) in 1753 at the latest.[60] Records of theatrical performances at that time are sketchy, and it was not until

---

[56] Berkenstock "Smaller Sacred Compositions" 1, 40-43; 2, 4-7 (music examples).

[57] See n.19.

[58] Cf. Landon *Symphonies*, 262.

[59] Badura-Skoda "Comoedie-Arien," 59-61.

[60] Dies *Nachrichten* (3), 97-98, provides an amusing if well-embroidered story of their first meeting. He noted that "This opera was performed twice to great acclaim, and then was forbidden because of offensive remarks in the text." The "offensive remarks" referred to may have been barbs aimed at Giuseppe d'Afflisio, Italian rogue and swindler who was later director of the court opera. See Landon *HCW* 1, 77. Or they may have been run-of-the-mill "sexual licence and political lampoons" which Maria Theresa found offensive; *HCW* 2, 519-520.

1959 that documentation of a performance (the first?) of *Der krumme Teufel* was found: May 29, 1753, at the Kärntnerthortheater. The music has been entirely lost.[61]

Or perhaps not entirely—it has been argued that many of the songs in the anonymous collection *Teutsche Comoedie Arien*,[62] written for Kurz's plays in the 1750s, must have been composed by Haydn. His first effort with Bernardon and company being so successful, it is very likely that Haydn was kept on as a house composer for the troupe until they left Vienna.[63] The melodic style of those songs has turned up in some odd places, too: see the comments below on the orchestral introduction to Haydn's 1756 *Salve Regina*.

There is more. The opera itself was remounted ca. 1758 and again in 1770 as *Der neue krumme Teufel*. From these productions the libretti, at least, have survived. And Robbins Landon has suggested that the chorus *Sit laus plena* (XXIVa:*deest*) is an adaptation of a chorus from the opera.[64] This notion is based on good stylistic and historical evidence: the chorus has trumpets and drums, whereas Haydn had none at Esterháza on a regular basis until well into the 1770s. Moreover the dotted fanfare "fills" in the trumpet parts are found only in his very early works (see above) and not later. The combination of triplets and regular sixteenth-notes and the syncopated violin figures are also familiar from the first Masses—more violins à la Reutter.[65]

Though simple, the choral writing of *Sit laus* seems remarkably more assured than that of *Lauda* 1, which may not have been written much earlier.[66] A certain extroversion and reliance on primary colors help to make *Sit laus* an effective dramatic chorus. Perhaps the young Haydn found his temperament and skills better matched to the theatre than to the sanctuary at this point.

Luckily for Haydn, he would now encounter a person who could offer just what was most lacking in his creative palette—the craftsmanship and finish of the authentic Italian manner. Italian style was the primary model for musical study in the Vienna of the 1750s. Nicola Porpora was the Italian with whom Haydn would study—the only person who

---

[61] Landon *HCW* 1, 77.

[62] Critical edition: *Deutsche Komödienarien 1754-1758* in *DTÖ* 33, Bd. 64 (1926). Ed. R. Haas. *Deutsche Komödienarien 1754-1758*, 2. Teil, in *DTÖ* 121 (1971). Ed. Camillo Schoenbaum and Herbert Zeman.

[63] Haas "Stegreifkomödie," 1 ff., and esp. 54ff.

[64] Landon *HCW* 1, 170; the chorus, in MS parts by one of Haydn's pupils, was found at the Graz Diözesanarchiv. Based on attempts at matching the libretti texts to the *Sit laus* music, some of the possible sources are: Act II final chorus "Wahre Liebsucht alle Gänze" (1758 [and 1770?]); Act II chorus of wild men "Alle solt ihr itzt verderben" (1770 only); chorus "Ihr Betrüger! Ihr sollt sterben . . . " (1770 only). In the Graz MS., the chorus is preceded by a soprano-tenor duet, "Jam cordi," which likewise is a parody of the duet for two sopranos in Haydn's Esterházy Cantata "Destatevi, o miei fidi." See Landon *HCW* 1, 169-179.

[65] Landon *HCW* 1, 169-175.

[66] It is possible, but not likely, that the 1753 *krumme Teufel* lacked choruses entirely; even so the stylistic evidence in *Sit laus* places it closer to 1750 than 1760.

would ever give him formal training in composition. It was through Metastasio that Haydn became acquainted with the "now aged Capellmeister":

> Porpora gave voice lessons to the mistress of the Venetian ambassador, Correr, and since Porpora was too grand and too fond of his ease to accompany her on the fortepiano himself, he entrusted this business to our Giuseppe. "There was no lack of *Asino, Coglione, Birbante* [ass, cullion, rascal], and pokes in the ribs, but I put up with it all, for I profited greatly with Porpora in singing, in composition, and in the Italian language." Correr traveled in summer with the lady to the then much frequented baths at Mannersdorf, not far from Bruck. Porpora went there too in order to continue the lessons, and he took Haydn with him. For three months here Haydn acted as Porpora's servant, eating at Correr's servants' table and receiving six ducats a month. Here he sometimes had to accompany on the clavier for Porpora at a Prince von Hildburghausen's, in the presence of Gluck, Wagenseil, and other celebrated masters, and the approval of such connoisseurs was a special encouragement to him.[67]

So, in exchange for personal service, Porpora tutored Haydn in composition during this period. As Haydn accompanied Porpora's other lessons, his constant exposure to the Italian song style must also have led him toward more refined notions of vocal music.

AVE REGINA; SALVE REGINA IN E

We seldom catch specific Porporean elements in the Haydn works of this time, simply because Haydn's acquaintance with and use of the Italian manner was still embryonic. He got much of his initial experience with it at Porpora's side. Haydn was also coming into greater contact with the music of Bonno, Hasse, Gluck, and others; that must have made an equally profound impression on the young composer. For these reasons it would be presumptuous to speak of Porpora's individual style affecting the way in which Haydn interpreted Italian practices. Yet we have two works from the 1750s that show the general effect of Porpora's teaching: the *Ave Regina* in A (XXIIIb:3) and *Salve Regina* in E (XXIIIb:1).[68]

No autograph score of the *Ave Regina* exists, nor is the work entered in *EK* or *HV*. But scholars have long been aware of it and have generally been inclined to accept it as an authentic work by Haydn. Pohl mentioned it among the twenty-one works he listed as "Smaller Works of Church Music."[69] In the Haydn article for *MGG*, Larsen and Robbins

---

[67] Griesinger *Notizen* (3), 12; cf. Dies *Nachrichten* (3), 94.

[68] Mayeda "Porpora," esp. 48-57; Mayeda was evidently unaware of the *Ave Regina* in A, but uses the early *Salve Regina*—sometimes unconvincingly—for making comparisons with Porpora's general style.

[69] Pohl *Haydn* 2 [Anhang], 10f.

Landon counted it "among the sacred works the authenticity of which may be claimed with great probability."[70] Likewise Georg Feder placed it in the worklist of the *New Grove* "Haydn" without any remarks qualifying its origin.[71]

Eleven manuscript copies of this *Ave* have been uncovered so far. Of these eleven, eight supply Haydn's name in some form. Becker-Glauch applied what might be called the Michael Haydn test and found no reference to this composition in any of the numerous catalogues of his works.[72]

To a twentieth-century mind, the most curious aspect of these copies is their widespread substitution of one liturgical text for another. We have encountered contrafacta already in this study; it will be obvious to the reader before long that neither composers nor audiences were terribly fussy about such matters. In Viennese comedies, a familiar song or aria was often given new words for overtly humorous purposes. Likewise musicians felt little compunction about quoting, adapting, or stealing another composer's music if it suited their own needs.[73]

In six of the *Ave Regina* manuscripts, the Marian antiphon *Salve Regina, Mater misericordiae* is used as the text. In three manuscripts, *Ave Regina coelorum* is used. Both texts appear in the two remaining copies. Although the *Salve Regina* text appears more frequently, it is clear from a careful comparison of text underlay with melodic structure, musical accents, and the like that the *Ave* text fits better and is undoubtedly the original. The switch of texts must have come very soon in the work's dissemination, for even some of the earliest manuscripts carry the *Salve* text.

Why the change of texts? For the simplest of reasons, it would seem: the *Salve* text was apt to be used much more frequently. It was assigned by the reformed Breviary of Pius VI (1568) to be sung at the close of Vespers for the period beginning roughly with Trinity Sunday and ending before the first Sunday of Advent—a long stretch of time in the liturgical year. More significantly still, it was a favorite choice for the various special services held in Marian chapels or at the Marian altar which all the principal churches had.[74] The reworked *Ave*, like Haydn's two later *Salve* settings, was doubtless intended to be used primarily in the latter instance, following a long tradition of similar polyphonic and con-

---

[70] *MGG* 5, col. 1891.

[71] *New Grove* 8, 361; reprinted in Larsen *New Grove Haydn*, 124.

[72] Becker-Glauch "*Ave Regina*," 69-70; see also Becker-Glauch "Neue Forschungen," 175. All material in the present study regarding these manuscripts' provenance and condition is derived from Becker-Glauch's research.

[73] The most sophisticated form of this borrowing was the sort of thing Mozart did in alluding to Paisiello's *Barbiere di Siviglia* tunes in *Le nozze di Figaro* or quoting snatches from familiar operas in the last scene of *Don Giovanni*. Aside from the motivic use of folk or folk-like tunes, plainchant, etc. mentioned above, Haydn indulged in very little such quoting or adaptation; he seldom even quoted himself. See Feder "Similarities."

[74] The poem, probably by Aimar, Bishop of Le Puy, dates back to the eleventh century; its composition therefore coincides with the development of the Saturday votive Mass of the Virgin, for which it was universally adopted as an antiphon. See Michel Huglo, "Antiphon," in *New Grove* 1, 479-480; also Raby *History*, 225-227.

certed versions beginning with Dunstable and Ockeghem.[75] In contrast, the *Ave Regina* occupied no such favored position in either the regular liturgy or the special Marian services.[76]

Haydn's *Ave Regina* in A is divided into three movements, of which the first, a florid soprano solo, is the longest. Here the composer fully indulges his newfound Neapolitan manner. Diverse melodic ideas are set forth, each springing from the previous one to produce an unceasing stream of related motivic variation. To allow a sense of unhurried ease in working the material out, Haydn frequently calls up the Baroque devices of *Fortspinnung* (phrase extension) and sequence. Several opportunities for cadenzas are also provided. Although the orchestra is small, it is used well. Especially significant is the dramatic device of the orchestral unison (see Ex. 2.12a, mm. 29-30), which Haydn also employs as a key structural element in his concertos, keyboard trios, and quartets of the time.[77]

Becker-Glauch has described the structure of the first movement as "not a *da capo* aria, but a kind of recapitulation free of any schematicism."[78] Others have found proof here (and in similar parts of the E-major *Salve*) that Haydn soon "emancipated" himself from "constricting" formal patterns,[79] but that view probably confers too much sophistication upon Haydn at this point, while taking too little note of the *seria* forms' continuing influence. This movement, which contains ritornello features, elements of sonata structure, and a reminiscence of the motto aria (in the sharing of a motive between first ritornello and first soprano entrance), lies really no more than a few trills away from the Hassean binary-aria type discussed in Chapter 1 (cf. Tables 1.1 and 2.1). It reveals a young composer using old devices in his own ingenuous manner, within the modest scope of a concerted Marian antiphon. In later years, when he was faced with the need to construct imposing traditional arias in *Applausus* or *Il ritorno di Tobia*, Haydn returned at once to the "constrictions" of da capo form.

More significant, both for the sense of freedom it creates and from a structural standpoint, is Haydn's introduction of new material in the solo after the middle ritornello gets underway. Only about a third of the solo material in the dominant section can be traced to

---

[75] R. J. Snow, "Salve Regina," *New Catholic* 12, 1002.

[76] Cf. Reinhard G. Pauly with Charles H. Sherman, "Haydn, (Johann) Michael," in *New Grove* 8, 410; and Stanley Sadie, "(Johann Chrysostom) Wolfgang Amadeus Mozart," in *New Grove* 12, 726-727 for the related output of Michael Haydn and W. A. Mozart: Michael wrote 13 *Salves* and 7 *Regina coeli*, while Mozart (far less prolific in sacred music) also managed 2 *Regina coeli*. Neither is credited with an *Ave Regina*.

[77] See, for example, the keyboard trios XV:C1 and 37. In the first movement of the former, spirited unison passages articulate most of the major semicadences; in the latter's first movement, a 3/4 Adagio, the final cadence (and an ornate cadenza) is approached by a stirring series of unison 16th-note statements. Even one of the early keyboard sonatas (XVI:2) exhibits "orchestral" unison passages as part of its (North German? operatic?) rhetorical baggage—see below.

[78] "Ave Regina," 72.

[79] Landon *HCW* 1, 166.

the tonic section. That helps create a greater sense of return when the motto finally reappears in the closing ritornello.[80] Since Haydn has, however, already come back to the tonic (in m. 87) he must seek a further freshening here, and he accomplishes it with a charming, sly mode change at the moment of recapitulation (Ex. 2.12a, m. 103 ff.). Now *that* is the sort of detail which shows a youthful master at work.

The contrasting middle section of the *Ave Regina* is a lively bit of choral homophony surrounded by *rauschend* ("rustling") violins playing mostly in unison. Later the choir's declamation is loosened by imitative entries and the pleasant, regular clash of 4-3 suspensions. The young Haydn's choral voicing, with its low tenors and crossing men's parts, is still present, but we sense within it a deepening of skill.

Chorus and solo soprano alternate in the *adagio* final movement. The soprano, whose expressive cantilena begins with the *messa di voce* seen often in the music of Porpora and other Italians, is set off by broken chords played pizzicato by the strings; their presence lends a pronounced serenade-like character to the movement. Again Haydn uses his orchestral unison to break powerfully away from the serenade and usher in the first choral entrance (Ex. 2.12b); the figure appears again before the final choral statement. Another cadenza intervenes, and then a quiet plagal cadence ends the work.

To judge from the number of manuscripts extant, this *Ave Regina* was a favorite in the eighteenth-century sacred repertory (albeit often with a different text).[81] It is easy to see why. Haydn here mingled devotion with the sensuous pleasure of *bel canto* more successfully than in anything else he had written to this point. The fluid management of motives and tonal structure, the ease with which the clichés of florid song are handled, and the simple, yet fitting choral sections all point to a new command of the craft. They also tie this work to another, handled with still more skill and radiant with the same Italian beauty.

The *Salve Regina* in E (XXIIIb:1), from 1756, forms the climax of Haydn's apprenticeship in choral music. Biographical details from this time reveal a parallel rite of passage which the composer did not manage nearly so well. After his expulsion from the cathedral, Haydn had been befriended by a wigmaker named Johann Peter Keller (his younger brother Georg Ignaz was one of the violinists in St. Stephen's Capelle). The Keller family gave Haydn meals, saw that he was decently dressed, and otherwise made his early struggles in Vienna more tolerable. No doubt they saw a future husband for one of their two daughters in this ambitious and talented young man. Haydn did fall in love with the younger daughter, Theresa, but her parents had determined that she would enter a nunnery. In the Spring of 1755 she became a novice, and on May 12, 1756, she took her final solemn vows at the Convent Church. Years later Haydn recalled that he had written a concerto for the ceremony, probably one in C for organ (XVIII:1). At any rate when he found

---

[80] Berkenstock "Smaller Sacred Compositions," 67.

[81] It was even available commercially: a price of "3 f" (3 florins) can be seen on the Viennese copy owned by the Gesellschaft der Musikfreunde. Becker-Glauch "*Ave Regina*," 73.

that work among his papers he proceeded to date it "756." The original *Salve Regina* manuscript turned up at that time also, and Haydn readily applied the same date to it. Apparently he had preserved the autograph scores of these two early works for almost five decades; for him to do that, they must have held a special meaning indeed. It is possible that he conducted both works at the service in which Theresa took the veil.[82]

Neither score offers a hint of the emotional distress Haydn may have felt then, but that is hardly surprising. Joseph Haydn was no Berlioz, his Theresa no Harriet Smithson. What is more, the age in which they lived would have responded with confusion or distaste to personal confession masquerading as music, especially in a sacred work. The composer's task was to glorify God and to fashion, with all possible skill, something that would gratify the sense of hearing. This the E-Major *Salve Regina* does superbly well.

Its opening measures (Ex. 2.13) provide a striking example of Haydn's increased maturity. Not only are extreme contrasts of pitch and dynamics employed with assurance, they are also integrated into long, well-articulated formal units. To put it another way, the composer's continued reliance on concise and clearly defined motives is now allied with a new command of periodic/sectional structure: the motives cohere, they flow from one to the next with a natural sense of their relatedness and potential. One could say that Haydn's sense of what to do next has grown geometrically. Phrases are first balanced and then not merely spun out, but organically developed. Thus the immense leaps and dynamic shocks of measure 1 are followed by the more unified *cantabile* of measure 2 (its own inner balance beautifully shaped by falling and rising sixteenth-notes). But measure 3 cannily echoes both the melodic dualism of the first bar and the scalewise sixteenths of the second. As this synthesizing figure is carried forward into measure 4, Haydn adds just the right touch of harmonic tension—a secondary dominant launching the drive to the first major tonal articulation, V on the downbeat of measure 5. Yet he is hardly finished with these ideas. The following four measures use a ♪ ♫♩ motive derived from measure 3 and a return of the cadential material of measure 4 (itself derived from m. 2) to provide relief and then a full rounding-off to the orchestral introduction. The entrance of the soloist—in a very Neapolitan *messa di voce*—is smoothly overlapped with a repetition of the dramatic opening orchestral measure. Here as elsewhere, contrast and unity are skillfully interwoven. If we look ahead to the vocal solo proper, we shall find kernels of the orchestral introduction continuing on as the basis for much of the music. And Haydn later reworks the same melodic and harmonic elements to serve as orchestral mottoes in the third, fourth, and fifth movements. Performers may well intuit rather than recognize all of this design; one way or another, however, it imparts a sense of great strength.[83]

---

[82] Landon *HCW* 1, 81; Geiringer *Haydn*, 36-37. For a thorough study of the love affair, see Schmid "Jugendliebe."

[83] As well as having proved popular enough in Haydn's time to inspire theft. The orchestral introduction to an "Arie der Colombina" from *Leopoldl, der deutsche Robinson* (comedy by Heubel which appeared in Vienna "after Easter 1754" but before 1757) is quite similar thematically to the *Salve Regina* first-movement introduction. Ei-

In this first movement, the influence of Porpora and of the developing symphonic language of the North is easy to read and has prompted considerable comment.[84] We can see that Haydn is more adept in the florid solo style here than in the *Ave Regina*. But surely the most remarkable thing about these measures is their Olympian command of motivic and structural elements. Not a note is wasted, and not one is out of place. That the overall effect is of luminous beauty rather than careful craft is the ultimate tribute to Haydn's efforts.

Following the alternately grand and tender phrases of the first movement, Haydn propels the work forward with an athletic Allegro featuring the chorus. Within its declamatory texture, the sense of the text ("Ad te clamamus") is effectively underlined with brief suspended-ninth clashes. After a sudden *pianissimo* indication at measure 20 and four hushed measures of "exules filii Evae," the Allegro breaks off, however. What comes next (Ex. 2.14a) is Haydn's most thoroughgoing effort thus far in his sacred music to mirror the text in the music. Against an accompaniment stripped bare of musical interest, the soprano intones two brief phrases shaped to the words ("ad te suspiramus"). The mode has changed also, to minor, and as the solo continues with the text "gementes et flentes in hac lacrimarum valle," a chromatically descending sigh further emphasizes the suffering of earthly existence. The chorus (Ex. 2.14b) echoes this plaint to end the movement. In none of Haydn's earlier church works do we find the text expressed with such immediacy.[85]

As if to make amends for that flood of emotion, Haydn subjects the next two movements to more conventional treatment. The *allegro moderato* "Eja ergo advocata" is a *galant* soprano aria that presumably pleased the congregations of its time;[86] the short fourth movement, with its passionate choral homophony connecting the Baroque figures in the strings, may be more interesting today. Readers will find its character similar to that of the "Qui tollis" in Mozart's C-Minor Mass, K. 427.

To end, Haydn fashions an aria movement combining the popular theme type with the same thoughtful motivic development shown earlier. Soprano and chorus alternate in ex-

---

ther Haydn borrowed one of his own comedy-aria ritornelli to rework or (more likely) he or another composer knew good material when he heard it and so adapted the *Salve Regina* tune for the popular stage. See Badura-Skoda "Comoedie-Arien," 62-63.

[84] See Landon *HCW* 1, 160; Becker-Glauch "Kirchenmusik," 81; Brand *Messen*, 17-18.

[85] Becker-Glauch "Kirchenmusik," 83. Although both Becker-Glauch and Brand (*Messen*, 22) dismiss the motivic shaping of "vita, dulcedo" in this *Salve*'s first movement (mm. 31-34) as inconsequential, it can also be seen as a further, albeit minor example of Haydn's newly increased sensitivity to the text.

[86] In a lengthy study of Porpora's influence on the young Haydn, Akio Mayeda points to this movement as the first in the work to show the unmistakable impression of Haydn's mentor, citing the unison close of the violin prelude, its theme-type, and the shape of its codetta as being remarkably similar to those in Porporean aria preludes. Likewise the aria theme proper is echoed in arias by Porpora (and in later Haydn). Mayeda "Porpora," 54-56.

quisite supplications to the Virgin.[87] Before the work closes gently on a plagal cadence, the composer allows the soloist one last opportunity for a cadenza.

We have previously commented on a youthful lack of consistency in Haydn's style from form to form, a lack which can make cross-genre comparisons unsatisfying. But there are indeed some movements—seldom whole works—in his contemporaneous instrumental compositions that contain the same emotional richness and rhetorical command of this *Ave* and *Salve*. Among the early keyboard works, the second movement of the Sonata XVI:2, with its syncopations, unison passages, and sudden mood shifts, seems to stand apart from its more shallow companions. It would be a fair match for either the last movement of the *Ave* or the second movement of the *Salve*. And three early keyboard trios (XV:C1, 37, and 41) contain more than their share of similar expressive depth and variety. Haydn may have written these works for the lovely Countess Morzin (see below), who would have presided at the keyboard while the composer played the violin parts.[88] The presence of a woman seems once again to have spurred Haydn to his most personal, most mature utterance.

MARRIAGE

And what of Haydn's actual personal life at this point? That, too, reached a cadence of sorts with his marriage to another Keller daughter in November of 1760. Probably he was led into it out of a sense of obligation to the Keller family. Maria Anna Aloysia Keller has been described as "not good-looking, not pleasant, and not interested in music."[89] Her union with Joseph Haydn endured a lifetime but provided little happiness for either partner. Maria Anna took little interest in Haydn's burgeoning career, instead actively annoying him with her overgenerous support of the clergy. In return, the composer seems to have decided early on to look elsewhere for comfort. He later told Griesinger, "My wife was unable to bear children, and I was therefore less indifferent to the charms of other women."[90]

In 1759, Haydn received his first major appointment, as music director to Count Karl Joseph Franz Morzin. Morzin was a Bohemian nobleman who evidently squandered his fortune within a year or so of hiring Haydn. By that time, Haydn had been engaged by Prince Paul Anton Esterházy, the leading member of one of the richest and most powerful Hungarian noble families. Haydn was to spend the next thirty years of his life in the employ of the Esterházys; we shall encounter him next in that setting, tossing off a number of

---

[87] Brand noted the special sensitivity of mm. 6-8, in which the "coarse" bass-instruments absent themselves during the phrase "O dulcis virgo." *Messen*, 27-28.

[88] Landon *HCW* 1, 263.

[89] Geiringer *Haydn*, 37.

[90] Griesinger *Notizen* (3), 15.

choral masterpieces in between far more numerous other duties and works undertaken as Esterházy Capellmeister.

	Ritornello	1st Strain	Ritornello	2nd Strain	Ritornello
Ave 1st mvt	A	A B	A B	B (new mat.)	A
	I	I→V	V	V→X→I (I$^6_4$)	i I (I$^6_4$) I
mm.	20	24	30	27 (cad.)	34 (cad.)
Salve 1st mvt	A	(A) B	(A) (new mat.)	(A) B	A
	I	I→V	V v→I	I	I (I$^6_4$) I
mm.	8	19	15	7	12 (cad.)

Table 2.1: Binary Aria Forms in Haydn *Ave Regina*, *Salve Regina* in E

Example 2.4: Haydn *Kleine Orgelmesse*, Agnus Dei, mm. 62-73

Example 2.5a: Göttweig Mass, Agnus Dei, mm. 11-23

Example 2.5b: Göttweig Mass, Credo, m. 16

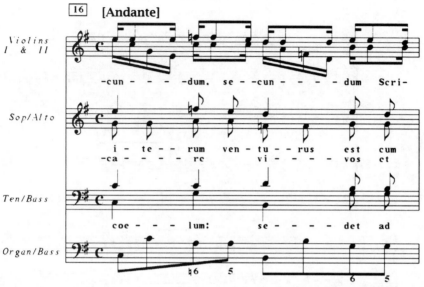

Example 2.5c: Göttweig Mass, Agnus Dei, mm. 3-4

Example 2.6: Haydn, *Missa* in F, Kyrie, mm. 1-8

Example 2.7: Haydn *Missa* in F, Gloria, mm. 9-14

Example 2.8: Haydn *Missa* in F, Gloria, mm. 19-29

Example 2.9: Haydn *Missa* in F, Credo, mm. 7-19

Example 2.10: Haydn *Lauda* 1, I, mm. 1-12

Example 2.11: *Lauda Sion* Hymn and Haydn's Use of It

a. Lauda Sion hymn v. 1

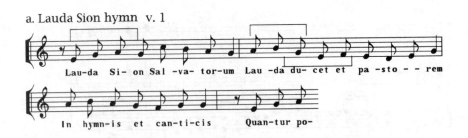

b. Haydn Lauda 1, I, mm. 1-4 sop

c. Haydn Lauda 1, I, mm. 19-22

d. Lauda Sion hymn, v. 19

e. Haydn Lauda 1, III, mm. 1-8 sop

Example 2.12a: Haydn *Ave Regina*, mm. 21-30, 95-106

Example 2.12b: Haydn *Ave Regina*, III, mm. 172-178

Example 2.13: Haydn *Salve Regina* in E, I, mm. 1-24

Example 2.14a: Haydn *Salve Regina* in E, II, mm. 24-33

Example 2.14b: Haydn *Salve Regina* in E, mm. 47-55

3

OCCASIONAL MUSIC FOR
THE ESTERHÁZYS AND OTHERS

EISENSTADT AND THE ESTERHÁZYS

One of the effects of the Counter-Reformation in Austria was the creation of a new class of nobility.[1] In their great endeavor to purge Protestants from the countryside, the Habsburgs had sought liegemen of unquestionable faith in Church and Empire, men whose armies could roll back the sea of doubt for another thousand years. Among the most valuable of those men was Nicolaus von Esterházy (1582-1645), to whom in 1622 a grateful Ferdinand II awarded the *Burgherrschaft* of Eisenstadt (i.e., the Castle and Lordship of the town). Nicolaus himself was made Count. Later the Castle was conferred as an hereditary estate to the family, which made a point of acquiring all the lands surrounding Eisenstadt as well. The town itself remained free, but it felt forever afterward the presence and potency of the Esterházys.

Like the rest of the area, Eisenstadt suffered from the Great Plague in 1679 and was heavily involved in the Turkish war of 1683, when it was forced into alliance with the Hungarian Protestant faction. Early in the eighteenth century, it suffered another invasion by Ferenc II, Prince Rákóczy, who saw an opportunity to strike while Austria was occupied with the War of the Spanish Succession. Imperial troops succeeded in driving back the rebels for good by 1709.

Once peace was more or less permanently restored, the Esterházy family could set about fostering the gentler arts and sciences, especially music. They also built or rebuilt various religious establishments in Eisenstadt; a number of these places are directly con-

---

[1] Regarding the Counter-Reformation in Austria, see Chapter 1. The following narrative is based on discussions of Esterházy family history in Landon *HCW* 1, 304-310, Tank *Studien*, 1-334, and Dack "Origins," 45-83.

nected with Haydn's choral works. After making a brief survey of the state of the Esterházy court music, we will explore those buildings.

MUSIC AT THE ESTERHÁZY COURT

From the very beginning of their rise to power, the Esterházys had collected musicians. By the end of the seventeenth century, a threefold division of the Esterházy Capelle could be seen: *1)* the *Feldmusiker*, wind players and drummers who accompanied the prince into battle or, when conditions were less favorable for war, played for parades, drills, and other military solemnities; *2)* the *Chormusiker*, a very small choir and orchestra that provided the concerted music at services in the Eisenstadt Castle Chapel; and *3)* the *Tafelmusiker*, which existed to furnish instrumental music at banquets and festivities and in the family's chambers.

By far the largest and most important of these groups in the 1680s was the Feldmusiker. But as the eighteenth century got underway, peace broke out in much of central Europe, and the role of that ensemble began to shrink. At the same time the Chormusiker became more prominent. Nicolaus's son Paul (1635-1715), whose pious construction work is noted below, was a professionally trained musician who saw that a series of fine choir directors was engaged for the newly-rebuilt Castle Chapel. His own *Harmonia coelestis*, a set of church music for all the feast days, was printed in 1711 and has been judged very attractive music, both the vocal writing and the rather full orchestrations.[2]

Paul's son Michael (1671-1721) was the first to succeed to the hereditary title of Prince after Charles VI bestowed it on the family. He was also a musician. In spite of his reputation for scaling down court expenditures from the often excessive levels maintained by his father, Michael seems to have encouraged the Chormusiker. It was he who firmly established the custom of having cantatas or operas performed to celebrate birthdays and namedays of the Prince and Princess. He also caused an annual Good Friday oratorio, often by a court composer, to be given.[3]

It seems hardly necessary to recount the exact numbers of the Chormusiker as it waxed and waned during this period. From the time of Prince Michael on, in spite of the in-

---

[2] See Landon *HCW* 1, 311; copies of the *Harmonia* can be found in the Esterházy Archives at Eisenstadt.

[3] In this connection we encounter the name of Wenzel Franz Zivilhofer, princely Capellmeister, who also wrote a cantata *Das wahre Ebenbild eines vollkommenen Fürsten* for Michael's birthday in 1715. Much of Zivilhofer's church music has survived in the Eisenstadt archives; after Haydn, Gregor Werner, and Franz Novotny (see text below), he was the most prominent of the eighteenth-century Esterházy church composers. Zivilhofer's 1715 cantata was evidently too complicated to be performed by the Eisenstadt Capelle; Landon tells us that "'certain *Comedianten*'" (i.e., Viennese singer-actors) were brought in to present it, thus helping establish a tradition with which Haydn had to cope during his own years of service. As part of the economy measures instituted by co-regent Princess Maria Octavia, Zivilhofer was dismissed in 1721. *HCW* 1, 311-312.

creased prominence they held, the church musicians never numbered more than three to five singers, two to four violinists, an organist, and a double-bass player. A bassoonist was usually available to double the continuo line, and sometimes other wind players could be had from the old Feldmusiker (or *Harmonie*, as it came to be called). We can assume also that visiting artists and children from the Castle school would on occasion augment the standing vocal forces. Still, it was not what could be called a robust choir.

The most positive step in the fortunes of the church music at Eisenstadt was the appointment of Gregor Joseph Werner (1693-1766) as Capellmeister in 1728. This was done by Princess Maria Octavia, who acted no doubt at the behest of her seventeen-year-old son Prince Paul Anton (1711-1762).[4] Werner's contribution to the Esterházy Capelle would lie not so much in building up the number of musicians (although new players were engaged, especially a number of winds) as in revitalizing the standards and style of music at court. Werner was himself a fine composer, leaving behind an abundance of Masses, Requiems, *Te Deums*, Vespers, Good Friday oratorios, and lesser church works, in addition to symphonies, concertos, and chamber music.[5] In general, his style reflects the learned manner of Fux (the 1720s, we will recall, were a time of vital activity for Fux and Caldara at the Imperial Court).

During Werner's early years as Capellmeister, Prince Paul Anton and his younger brother Nicolaus (1714-1790) studied with the Jesuits in Vienna, where they also learned music: Paul Anton the violin, flute, and lute, Nicolaus the gamba and violoncello. Paul Anton married and assumed his hereditary duties in 1734, but he was seldom in Eisenstadt. Instead he pursued a military career for some years and eventually rose to the rank of Field Marshal. Between campaigns he was able to serve as a minister to the Court of Naples, where his love of opera was fed mightily. By the time he returned home in the late 1750s to stay, Paul Anton had collected enormous trunksful of Italian music, so much so that he had to appoint a musician from the Burgtheater to catalog it all. Some of the other appointments he made—Carl Friberth, a fine Viennese tenor, and the soprano Anna Maria Scheffstoss—clearly signaled his intention to revive musical life at court and redirect it toward theatrical productions. The upshot was that when Haydn came aboard as Vice-Capellmeister in 1761, he found Werner's Capelle rather stronger than before, both in numbers and musicianship. Counting the new people, Werner could muster for the Chormusiker a choir of six or seven (which could be further augmented by the boy sopranos and altos from the chapel school), an organist, four to seven violinists, two cellists,

---

[4] He had succeeded to the title after the deaths of Michael and Michael's half-brother Joseph (his father). Until he came of age, his mother, Princess Maria Octavia, and a guardian, Count Georg Erdödy, acted as co-regents.

[5] See text following for a discussion of Werner's church music style; an interesting published example of his instrumental music is the *Symphonia da chiesa* edited by Imre Sulyok for Doblinger/Editio Musica (Diletto Musicale Nr. 315), Vienna/Budapest, 1969.

and a double bassist, plus (by drawing upon the Harmonie) a flutist, two oboists, two bassoonists, two *Waldhornisten*, and timpani.[6]

THE CHURCHES, CHAPELS, AND HALLS OF EISENSTADT

During the preceding century the Esterházys had not languished in other areas of patronage either, having seen to the construction of a number of impressive ecclesiastical buildings in Eisenstadt. The first wave of these consisted of the Franciscan Church and Monastery (in 1629), the Augustine Nunnery (in 1678), and the Baroque transformation of the Castle (1663-72). Part of this transformation was the opening of a chapel in the west wing; eventually Haydn and the Capelle would perform there on high feast days.[7] The second floor contained a great hall, its ceilings decorated with frescoes, its walls lined with portraits of Hungarian kings and generals. Haydn's orchestra would someday perform his symphonies and concertos in that room and, on occasion, vocal music. It was also used for banquets and festivities, again with the musicians in attendance.

Another institution that must be mentioned is the Hospital and Chapel of the Barmherzige Brüder (Brothers of Mercy), finished and dedicated in 1760 as one of the many charitable works of Prince Paul Anton. Haydn had been, as we have seen, first violinist for this same order in Vienna. In the winter of 1777-78 he composed the *Kleine Orgelmesse* for their chapel in Eisenstadt.

One last building in the neighborhood that would figure significantly in Haydn's music was the Bergkirche, which has a history stretching back to 1674. It was then that Count Paul built a chapel in Eisenstadt dedicated to St. Apollonia. In 1701, he decided to erect next to it a Mount Calvary Church containing an impressive Calvary scene (in German, *Kalvarienberg*) like the one he had visited near Maria Lanzendorf. Paul also saw to the Bergkirche's receiving, in 1711, a miraculous statue of the Virgin (it had come unscathed through the sacking and burning of Nagyhöflán during the rebellion and was later credited with other miracles). He planned to build a large pilgrimage church next door but finally erected a smaller Pantheon-shaped building, which became the second part of the "new" Bergkirche built from 1770 to 1777. This Mount Calvary Church witnessed the first performances of five of Haydn's last six Masses. Joseph Haydn is also buried there, his body lying in an elaborate white marble tomb in the crypt of the church. With that detail, we end our survey of Eisenstadt architecture and pick up Haydn where we left him—not only young and alive, but on his way to Eisenstadt to become a part of all this place and time.

---

[6] See Dack "Origins," 67-69; Landon *HCW* 1, 314-320; and Tank *Studien*, 339-340. All present slightly different accountings of the *Capelle*'s strength, which is to be expected given the flux in personnel which Paul Anton's ambitions (and Haydn's impending reorganization of the *Kammermusiker*) caused at this time.

[7] Haydn's presence was not required at the regular Sunday Masses in the chapel; when he was at Esterháza, as we shall see, it was not even possible.

HAYDN AND THE ESTERHÁZY PRINCES

With entry into the service of Prince Paul Anton, Haydn consummated his dramatic upward journey of the 1750s. In two years he had gone from freelance musician to house officer in a great court with a distinguished history of musical patronage. Having only recently served as valet to, and student of, Porpora, he was now expected to be a master: his contract of 1761 made him responsible for "everything [but the choir music], whenever there shall be a musical performance, and in all required for the same in general and in particular."[8] What is more important, he was soon to go from cosmopolitan if somewhat faceless Viennese composer to musical pioneer, something which his isolation in Eisenstadt (and later, Esterháza) would encourage. Of that experience, he later said,

> My Prince was content with all my works, I received approval, I could, as head of an orchestra, make experiments, observe what enhanced an effect, and what weakened it, thus improving, adding to, cutting away, and running risks. I was set apart from the world, there was nobody in my vicinity to confuse and annoy me in my course, and so I had to be original.[9]

From 1761 to 1766 Haydn served as Vice-Capellmeister for the Princes Esterházy (first Paul Anton and then Nicolaus), deferring to the aged Capellmeister Werner only where church music was concerned. After Werner's death in 1766, Haydn became Capellmeister in full to Prince Nicolaus, who had succeeded his brother upon the latter's death in 1762. Each succeeding year saw further growth in the musical activities at various noble households, especially at Nicolaus's favorite "summer" retreat, Esterháza. By the late 1770s, Haydn found himself the intendant of one of central Europe's busiest performing companies.

By and large Haydn's compositional activities from 1761 to 1782 reflect three stages of his life with the Esterházy court. In the very beginning, we find him composing mainly chamber works, concertos, and symphonies, as befit his job description. Apart from the so-called "Esterházy" cantatas, the first *Te Deum*, and some hymns, Haydn's politic deference to his colleague caused him to lay aside his own ambitions as a choral composer. But Joseph Haydn was a man who had been raised in the choir loft. It is not surprising that after Werner's death, a second-stage explosion of works came from the new Capellmeister including, within a half-dozen years, three or four Masses, a *Stabat Mater*, another *Salve Regina*, the giant *Applausus* cantata, and a number of lesser pieces. Each of them reveals a different facet of the creative expansion Haydn had embarked upon; each answers the tra-

---

[8] From the "Convention and Rules for Behaviour of the *Vice-Capel-Meister*" signed by Joseph Haydn on May 1, 1761. He was further admonished to "treat the musicians placed under him not overbearingly, but with mildness and leniency, modestly, quietly, and honestly." Full document translated in Landon *HCW* 1, 350-352.

[9] Griesinger *Notizen* (3), 17.

ditions of choral music with its own voice. Perhaps in this period the choral works do not echo the vanguard energies we find in the string quartets Op. 9, 17, and 20, but they are fully as expressive, rich, and diverse in musical elements as the contemporary symphonies. In a third stage after 1773, the flow of choral music ebbed along with the rest of Haydn's creative output; he was being forced to devote ever more time to the production of opera at Esterháza. Yet even this period produced major works, including the "Mariazell" and "'Little' Organ" Masses and the oratorio *Il ritorno di Tobia*. Only after 1783, with Joseph II's restrictions on church music, would the composer call a halt to new large-scale sacred choral pieces. It was a very fruitful twenty-one years.

THE ESTERHÁZY CANTATAS

If one could broadly characterize Haydn's pre-Esterházy choral music—a difficult task, given the surviving hodgepodge—one might speak of its being animated by a certain feminine principle. Perhaps something of the composer's sexual awakening, his first en- counters with the Jungian *anima*,[10] can be seen in these early church works. In Austria, the Corpus Christi observances are as much a celebration of Mother Earth as of the Body of Christ. Haydn seems to have responded most strongly to the holiday's terrestrial con- nections, to judge from *Lauda* 1. Its melodies and folkish *Gestalt* bring more to mind the warmth of late spring than the sentiments of St. Thomas's principled poem.

Still more referentially direct, of course, are the *Ave* and *Salve* settings. Outwardly they are supplications to Our Lady. But each phrase of the prayer comes clothed in the sensu- ous language of bel canto, its carnal associations immediately present along with the so- prano's tender *messa di voce*, the silvery elegance of her *fioritura*. Naturally we remember Maria Magdalena Spangler and Theresa Keller, whose ties to this music inevitably color it for us. But a much more significant datum is that the creative period climaxed in these two works was capped in Haydn's personal life by a marriage. Haydn's marriage was, in fact, doubly significant: it marked the culmination of his accelerating drive toward union with the feminine, manifested in the church works and in many private details; yet his lack of fulfillment within that marriage may have blocked his ability to draw fully upon the *an- ima* as a composer in the next few years.

---

[10] One of the archetypes that the pioneer of psychology C. G. Jung saw as primary shapers of human personality: "Every man carries within him the eternal image of the woman, not the image of this or that particular woman, but a definite feminine image. This image is fundamentally unconscious, an hereditary factor of primordial origin engraved in the living organic system of the man, an imprint or archetype of all the ancestral experiences of the fe- male, a deposit, as it were, of all the impressions ever made by woman. . . . Since this image is unconscious, it is always unconsciously projected upon the person of the beloved, and is one of the chief reasons for passionate at- traction or aversion." Jung, *The Development of Personality* (Princeton, 1970), 198.

For if one admits that the surviving vocal works of the late 1750s explore (unconsciously, to be sure) the feminine principle, one must equally concede a masculine, or at least anti-feminine, principle at work in Haydn's first Eisenstadt choral music, the so-called Esterházy cantatas and related sacred contrafacta of roughly 1762-65. The cantatas were written to celebrate Esterházy might and glory and especially the anniversaries and travels of the Prince. A fair proportion of the music is given over to *machismo* posturing, borrowed from opera seria but quite effective in this context. Elements brought in from Haydn's Viennese church music still shine forth, but the light they cast is of a different hue.

In fact Haydn seems to have developed a standard Esterházy courtly manner; it turns up in the 1760s scattered through a great deal of his music. The constellation of *1)* C major, *2)* strong dotted rhythms, *3)* Lombard (short-long) rhythms, and *4)* a basic orchestration consisting of oboes, horns, and strings, with bassoon doubling the *basso*, was so much a given at the time that it has been used to authenticate works of this period.[11] We can observe it in the opening movement of the C-Major Cello Concerto (VIIb:1) (Ex. 3.1) and in an aria from 1762's *Acide* (XXVIII:1) (Ex. 3.2).[12] If we then turn to a duet from the cantata *Destatevi, o miei fidi* (XXIVa:2), the resemblance is obvious (Ex. 3.3). Notice that Haydn almost manages a direct quote from the Cello Concerto's first ritornello.

The vocal lines of the duet are fiendishly difficult, especially in that the tenor is expected to match the soprano's coloratura at every turn. And this is not an exceptional requirement; a tenor aria from *Acide*, the ritornello of which was quoted above, is more daunting yet, full of trills, syncopes, and sixteenth-note triplets rising to a high C. Yet none of the virtuosity required in the arias and duets of these cantatas is frivolously employed; instead it is poured into carefully crafted forms—some conventional, some not—and it matches exquisitely the fulsome praise of its texts.

Three Esterházy cantatas survive: *Destatevi, o miei fidi* (XXIVa:2), *Da qual gioja improviso* (XXIVa:3), and *Qual dubbio omai* (XXIVa:4). Haydn listed six of these "Choruses" in the *EK*, including a *Vivan gl'illustri sposi* for Anton Esterházy's wedding, a *Dei clementi* celebrating Nicolaus's recovery from illness, and an *Al tuo arrivo felice* for Nicolaus's return from Paris.[13] The other three are not identified by occasion or title. It is tempting to assume they are the three works extant, but one cannot be sure; the ephemeral nature of

---

[11] See Landon *HCW* 1, 441ff., 464ff.; also Geiringer *Haydn*, 244-245.

[12] Concerto in C (VIIb:1) in *JHW* 3/2, *Acide* in *JHW* 25/1. See also the first movements of Haydn's Symphony No. 7 ("Le Midi") (*JHW* 1/3) and the interesting *Symphonia da chiesa* by Werner mentioned previously (n.5 above).

[13] Possibly the Prince's 1767 trip. See Feder's worklist in Larsen *New Grove Haydn*, 130.

such music augured poorly for its being carefully preserved or disseminated in original form.[14]

All three surviving works share certain features: *1)* Their texts laud the Prince's accomplishments, beneficence, and so forth, also making specific references to the occasion. The egregiously fawning Italian will seem quaint to modern ears; luckily the excellence of the musical settings more than compensates for it. *2)* Each work is relatively short (two to five movements) but opens with a long, richly orchestrated ritornello leading to a *recitativo accompagnato* for the soprano soloist. She informs the listeners—as if they didn't know!—of the reason for this musical celebration. *3)* In two of the works, the ritornello/recitative is followed by at least one extended aria or duet, usually a bravura vocal display. *4)* The cantata then ends with a slightly shorter *coro* more or less in the style of an operatic finale. It is technically more suited to an ensemble of soloists than to any but the smallest and most capable of choirs.

Destatevi, o miei fidi (XXIVa:2) was written for the name-day of Prince Nicolaus (December 6) in 1763. We may presume that it was performed at Eisenstadt Castle—in the great hall, not the chapel—by the combined forces of Vice-Capellmeister Haydn's newly reorganized Kammermusiker and Capellmeister Werner's Chormusiker. Personnel from Haydn's group would have included sopranos Barbara Fux and Anna Maria Scheffstoss, tenors Carl Friberth and Leopold Dichtler, three violins, a cello, two oboes, two bassoons, and four horns. From Werner's group, bass Melchior Griessler, alto Eleonora Jäger, tenor Joseph Dietzl, up to four more violins, and a contrabass could be had. Naturally some of the violinists would have played viola, and Haydn would have presided from the harpsichord.[15] Thus a fine band with a typical eighteenth-century balance was available.

Destatevi's five movements make it the longest of the three Italian cantatas. Anna Maria Scheffstoss, the more experienced of the two sopranos in the Capelle, probably sang the opening recitative and the soprano part in the fierce duet which follows (Ex. 3.3b). Her partner in that duet would have been Friberth, discussed below. Barbara Fux would have joined with Scheffstoss in the third movement, another duet, but this one an Allegretto in a quiet, relaxed vein. It must have provided the perfect means for Fux, whom Paul Anton engaged as an apprentice in 1757, to sing on an equal footing with Scheffstoss. Haydn later made Anna Maria Scheffstoss his Gasparina in *La canterina* (1766-7) and

---

[14] Undoubtedly a number of autograph scores and other manuscripts were destroyed in the two fires that ravaged Haydn's Eisenstadt home in 1768 and 1776. Also, we know that Haydn had either lost or given away the autographs of the three extant cantatas by 1804 or 1805, when Elssler drew up his catalog of Haydn works. Landon *HCW* 1, 494.

[15] Tank *Studien*, 489. Since Dietzl's primary role was Castle Schoolmaster, he may not have performed this difficult music with two professional tenors present; perhaps he essayed the bass line in the *coro* along with Griessler. Although Haydn wrote for the four horns almost as soon as he got them (Landon suggested those first works were a Cassatio in D (*deest*), the Symphony No. 13 in D, and the Symphony No. 72 in D), there is no reason to assume they were all present, doubling the parts, for this cantata.

chose her for the taxing soprano part in the *Stabat Mater* (1768). By comparison, Fux was to play Don Ettore (a supporting "trouser" role) in *La canterina* and go on to a number of parts in Haydn operas (e.g., Sandrina in *L'infedeltà delusa*) that suited her lighter voice.[16] Both sopranos had been trained toward a flexibility and range that many of today's singers would envy.

The fourth movement, the only real aria in the piece, is a stunner. The text at this point uses the raging sea as a metaphor for the fortunes of those who have not the security and joy of serving the Prince. Haydn seized upon that sea-image to create a heroic *Sturm und Drang* aria that quite overwhelms the comfortable succession of tributes previously trotted forth.[17] With plunging melodic line and turbulent accompaniment, the scene is set at once (Ex. 3.4). Things do not let up until a pause that abruptly halts the aria, bringing on the final chorus without a break. Was this a first warning of the experiments that colored so many of Haydn's works later in the decade?[18] A *da capo* chorus follows, depositing us back on familiar terrain—an operatic finale in 3/8 time—as the cantata ends.

Da qual gioia improviso (XXIVa:3) falls next in the chronology of these cantatas. It departs from the other two works in consisting only of the opening ritornello/recitative and a closing chorus. But the first movement is even more sumptuously scored than its predecessor, with two flutes and a separate bassoon part added. And the closing chorus introduces new formal intricacies, along with a solo harpsichord part for Haydn. Structurally it is a kind of double concerto, in which the voices are treated as one block and the harpsichord solo as another. A section of this movement is given as Example 3.5.

The indirect cause of this grand little piece was the coronation on April 3, 1764, of Joseph II as Holy Roman Emperor. Prince Nicolaus traveled to Frankfurt-am-Main to attend the festivities (the libretto refers to "that place where the Main washes its banks") and thence to Paris, where he toured Versailles. Upon his return to Eisenstadt he was greeted by Haydn and the Capelle with *Dal qual gioja*, perhaps with other works as well. Because it sheds some light on the new Prince, who was called "The Magnificent" and whose lavish court entertainments would involve Haydn for almost thirty years, we quote briefly from an account of the coronation festivities in Frankfurt. The young Goethe was witness to Nicolaus and his generosity there:

---

[16] Landon *HCW* 2, 48 (Fux), 54 (Scheffstoss). This is part of a summary list with details on each singer in the opera troupe at Eisenstadt and Esterháza from 1766 to 1790, 47-63; the same for the other theatrical personnel, 63-68, and the orchestra players, 70-82.

[17] Robbins Landon saw this as "the father of many D minor seascapes of this kind: 'Si obtrudat' from *Applausus* (1768), 'Varca il mar' from *Le pescatrici* (1769-70), 'Svanisce in un momento' (addition to *Il ritorno di Tobia*, 1784) and *The Storm* ('Madrigal,' 1792)." Landon *HCW* 1, 470.

[18] See the comments in Chapter 4 on Gluck's *Don Juan*, the so-called *Sturm und Drang* movement in music, and the nature of Haydn's experimental composition in the late 1760s and early 1770s.

PRINCE ESTERHAZY, the Bohemian envoy, was not tall, though well-formed, lively, and at the same time eminently decorous, without pride or coldness. . . .

This brilliant night [following the coronation] I purposed celebrating in a right hearty way; for I had agreed with Gretchen, and Pylades and his mistress, that we should meet somewhere at nightfall. The city was already resplendent at every end and corner. . . . We admired the various brilliant representations and the fairy-like structures of flame by which each ambassador strove to outshine the others. But Prince Esterhazy's arrangements surpassed all the rest. . . .

This eminent envoy, to honour the day, had quite passed over his own unfavourably situated quarters, and in their stead had caused the great esplanade of linden-trees in the Horsemarket to be decorated in the front with a portal illuminated with colours, and at the back with a still more magnificent prospect. The entire enclosure was marked by lamps. Between the trees stood pyramids and spheres of light, upon transparent pedestals; from one tree to another were stretched glittering garlands, on which floated suspended lights. In several places bread and sausages were distributed among the people, and there was no want of wine.[19]

Small wonder that this Nicolaus would return infused with the desire to create his own Versailles in Hungary or that two years later his Esterháza would be ready to accommodate both Prince and Capelle for the summer.

The Prince's name-day was celebrated in 1764 with the last of the three cantatas, *Qual dubbio omai* (XXIVa:4). Its three movements provide a classic synthesis of the elements so far encountered in these works. There is the opening ritornello/recitative, distinguished this time by its wit and rhythmic vitality, not to mention an ever more effective unification of motives: see the first ten bars' fresh-sounding shifts in dynamics and harmony (Ex. 3.6a), the rugged syncopation at measures 23-25 (Ex. 3.6b), and the clever device of smuggling the theme into the bass line and then brazening it forth in the final drive to the recitative (Ex. 3.6b, mm. 27-34).[20]

The soprano aria is no less lacking in vitality. In structure, it is a conventional da capo with the same sort of elaborate binary A seen in Hasse and later Haydn (Table 1.2) plus a shorter B section. The harpsichord soloist returns to offer further electricity to the movement, not only playing concerto-like passages during the ritornelli, but interacting with the soprano in a number of places. Each soloist is allotted a cadenza at the end of the A section. This harpsichord solo is more highly developed than the one in *Da qual gioja*, and the soprano work is of surpassing difficulty, ranging up to high C♯ with a brilliance only approached in the familiar opera repertory by Mozart's Queen-of-the-Night arias. Like

---

[19] Johann Wolfgang von Goethe, *Dichtung und Wahrheit*, translated by J. Oxenford as *The auto-biography of Goethe. Truth and Poetry: From my own Life.* London, 1848. Fifth Book, 147ff.

[20] Such motivic transference is also a feature of *Dal qual gioja*'s first movement (m. 15ff.), but here the motive is more interesting and its introduction into the bass handled with more finesse.

them, there is a somewhat icy quality to this music. The piece is perfectly suited to its purpose, but one suspects Haydn put less of his heart into it than he lent to the simplest of his works for the Virgin.

There is a brief *secco* recitative and then the final chorus, florid and attractive, with the vocal parts lying high enough to make a splendid impact (Ex. 3.7). It, too, is in da capo form with a short B section.

Questions have been raised about the librettist of the Esterházy cantatas. It could have been Girolamo le Bon, leader of a group of Italian "comedians" who first came to Eisenstadt from Pressburg in May of 1762. Bon and his family were engaged by Prince Nicolaus in July, he to direct scenic painting for the theatre, his wife (and perhaps their daughter?) to sing in the Capelle. Haydn wrote his first Italian opera, *La Marchesa Nespola*, for Bon's troupe, and they may have performed it together with the resident Eisenstadt singers that same summer.[21] If so, its success would account for the Prince's allowing Haydn to compose more vocal music in the immediate future. His patron was evidently so impressed with the new Vice-Capellmeister's prowess in Italian song, an unexpected bonus, that he raised Haydn's salary by fifty percent—his first official act concerning a member of the Capelle. So perhaps we owe these very cantatas and the first *Te Deum* to *La Marchesa Nespola*. And perhaps Bon wrote the libretti for the cantatas: he was capable, he was in the vicinity (i.e., Pressburg or Vienna), and he was known and trusted by Haydn and his Prince.[22]

Or perhaps it was Carl Friberth. Both Friberth and Leopold Dichtler had been associated with Bon's troupe, appearing in operas at Pressburg around 1759 or '60. Friberth, a man of many talents (he composed church music and arias), seems to have apprenticed with Bon at the wordsmith's craft. Later he contributed the excellent libretto for *L'incontro improvviso*. As a singer, his range extended to high C, and he was obviously capable of vocal athletics; Haydn used him for many leading operatic roles, also in the first performance of *Il ritorno di Tobia*.[23] He married Magdalena Spangler in 1769 and left the Prince's service in 1776.

---

[21] Tank (*Studien*, 453) gives a performance date of 1763, based in part on Feder's interpretation of the autograph date; that would have been after the troupe had departed and would cast doubt on the influence this work had on Prince Nicolaus vis-à-vis Haydn as vocal composer. See text following.

[22] Landon *HCW* 1, 370-372, 390.

[23] The *Jahrbuch der Tonkunst von Wien und Prag* of 1796 (p. 96, quoted in Landon *HCW* 1, 58) made these revealing comments about Friberth the singer: "His voice is supple, flowing and never empty, but has darkened by his having used it in too instrumental a fashion. In teaching for the voice he tries at all costs to protect it."

APPLAUSUS

A few years after the Esterházy cantatas were written, Haydn was asked to compose a similar work to honor the Abbot at Zwettl Monastery on the occasion of his fiftieth year in the priesthood. The resulting *Applausus* cantata of 1768 (XXIVa:6) is longer than the Esterházy cantatas but alike enough in style to warrant its discussion at this point.

Austrian monasteries in the eighteenth century often rivalled the princely courts in their practice and patronage of music.[24] The seeds of this unascetic attitude had been sown at the very beginnings of European civilization: only monastic life had offered young men of few means a more fulfilling life than soldiering or serfdom. Because, too, a succession of rulers (including the Habsburgs) had found it an advantage to ally themselves with the Church and its institutions, the governing class became accustomed to supporting the cloisters as centers for learning, artistic activity, and diplomacy.

With the rise of interest in Baroque art at the courts, concerted music became extremely fashionable in monastic circles as well. In some cases the *Regens chori* (i.e., monastery Capellmeister) became responsible for it in addition to the older round of chanted liturgical music; sometimes a separate *Regens chori figuralis* was appointed.

This person (and the other musicians) could be a "secular," brought in to assist with the establishment's music either on a regular basis or for special occasions. But it was not at all uncommon for the musicians to be members of the order. Many who had chosen the cloistered life came with musical backgrounds; a talented monk could also receive further training to prepare him for use to the house. Besides the *Regens chori*, the musicians of a monastic establishment might include a half-dozen boy sopranos from the choir school; an organist, usually an important personage in his own right who composed and played other instruments; a Thurnermeister, in charge of the wind players; and perhaps other professional singers and instrumentalists. For occasions demanding musical riches beyond the usual (e.g., the celebration of a churchly house's *Schutzheiligentag*, the feast of its patron saint), neighboring monasteries and churches sometimes honored each other by loaning musicians out. But evidence shows that this was more a courtesy than a needed kindness: at the richly endowed Abbey of Melk, for example, sufficient personnel and equipment were usually at hand to form a twenty-seven piece orchestra.[25]

---

[24] Among many studies of musical life in those monasteries, especially noteworthy are Kellner *Kremsmünster* and Freeman "Melk." We have drawn heavily from Freeman's dissertation to present the general summary that follows herein.

[25] The monasteries also harbored that occasional monk whose participation showed more enthusiasm than skill. Prior V. Waldmüller of Melk Abbey recorded the following in 1740: "I told Brother Caspar, who began some time ago to frequent the figural choir with [his] violin playing, not to go [there] at least on feast days, because he takes up the place of another musician. Because of his poor eyesight, he is inexperienced in rhythm, poorly understands this art, and confuses the others with his bad playing (this I have heard from both Father Marian, *Regens chori*, and Brother Lambert, a string player). In the meantime I gave him permission to attend [the choir] on ferial days." Quoted in Freeman "Melk," 113.

If the monks of Zwettl were perhaps not that well off, they nonetheless could be considered worthy performer-connoisseurs of practically any musical genre of their time. Anecdotal evidence from monastery chronicles bears witness to a common tradition of musical activity, ranging from lavish theatrical entertainments mounted for visiting dignitaries to the daily recreations of individuals in chamber music and song.[26]

Within this welter of activity, the *applausus* cantata or operetta was a familiar fixture. While its text treated in semi-dramatic allegory the sort of moral or theological issues that presumably concerned a religious community, its fashionably operatic music at the same time could delight that community's sophisticated tastes. Usually a resident scholar would concoct the libretto, using the most fulsome Latin available (or German, in which case the piece was termed a *Singgedicht*, literally a "sung poem"). The words were set in pairs of recitative and aria (duet, trio, etc.) culminating in a festive chorus, the whole seldom exceeding the length of a single opera-seria act. Da capo form was preferred for the arias and chorus.

As its name implies, the *applausus musicus* was used to honor a member of the order. Thus the chronicles from Melk show that *Regens chori* Gurtler composed an *applausus* given on January 13, 1746, in celebration of a new prelate's election; the visit of a provincial marshal in the early 1750s occasioned another such piece. Closer to Haydn's time, we can read of an *applausus* by J. G. Albrechtsberger (1736-1809) being produced at Säusenstein on July 18, 1762.[27] In 1767, the eleven-year-old Mozart contributed a *Singgedicht* entitled *Die Schuldigkeit des ersten Gebotes* ("The Obligation of the First Commandment"), K. 35, for the Archbishop's court in Salzburg. We shall comment further below on Mozart's piece, written within a year of his older colleague's effort for Zwettl.

Although Abbot Rainer Kollmann of Zwettl, the dedicatee of Haydn's applausus, made it known that he did not wish his *Professjubiläum* to become an elaborate affair, the monks nevertheless set aside 600 gulden in order to present him with a new set of porcelain, a portrait in oils, and a musical tribute. Haydn received 100 gulden. It is thought that Pater Johann Nepomuk Paul Werner, old Gregor's son, was responsible for the commission, since he was *Regens chori* at the Abbey until 1766.[28]

---

[26] For a description of operatic life at Kremsmünster, which included the latest works by Jommelli, Gluck, Piccini, and Salieri, see Kellner *Kremsmünster*, 543. Commenting on the dissemination of Haydn's music within the monasteries, Freeman notes that "by 1787 the [archives at Melk] could boast possession of exactly one-half of Haydn's entire symphonic production up to that year. . . . [Haydn's] works were purchased or studiously copied and performed at Melk from as early as the 1760s"; "Melk," 188-189. And (*vide* Landon *HCW* 1, 586-591) also at Göttweig, Lambach, St. Florian, and other houses from about 1762 on. It has long been held that some of Haydn's first twenty symphonies were intended for Austrian cloisters or for use in church services: see, for example, the charming Symphony No. 18 in *sonata da chiesa* style, of which Lambach Monastery possessed a copy, or the Symphony No. 32, a work as full of C-major pomp as many Austrian Masses of the time.

[27] Albrechtsberger was Capellmeister at St. Stephen's and briefly a teacher of Beethoven. See Freeman "Melk," 263ff., for a description of that performance.

[28] Becker-Glauch and Wiens "Vorwort" *Applausus*, vii-viii.

Abbot Kollmann's anniversary was celebrated on April 17, 1768, but Haydn's cantata was not performed until Sunday, May 15. Knowing he would not be present, Haydn sent the monastery a practical, detailed letter regarding the performance of the cantata at about the same time he sent the autograph score. The letter voiced Haydn's concerns about the fate of his music ("if I have perhaps not guessed the taste of these gentlemen, I am not to be blamed for it, for I know neither the persons nor the place") and went on to specify a number of areas in which performance problems were likely to occur. He made sure to offer solutions (and not a few stern warnings) to his unknown colleagues; altogether this document offers us an important look at Haydn's attitudes toward performance.[29]

The *Applausus* letter has, in fact, become better-known than the cantata. Considering their relative merits, it is hard to fault history's judgment. The letter is pithy, direct, and still helpful today. The cantata, although filled with beautiful parts, seems on the whole overlong and abstract. Its Latin text—in which the four Cardinal Virtues and a fifth Virtue, Theology, discuss the merits of monastic life—could hardly have engaged Haydn the innovator. He does manage to inject considerable variety into the accompagnato recitatives' instrumental interludes, and there is no lack of felicitous detail in the scoring of each aria. What is lacking, individually and collectively, is any dramatic impetus. Thus the numbers seem to spin their lovely phrases at considerable length and in the service of a sterile muse. Even the final chorus, one of Haydn's 3/4 Allegros, gives out a tempered festivity at best. The cantata gathered dust after its premiere at Zwettl;[30] modern conductors will be far more likely to revive the sacred contrafacta fashioned from its various numbers than the work itself. For that reason, we will defer detailed analysis of those numbers to the discussion on the contrafacta of the 1760s (below). It remains here only to compare Haydn's *applausus* briefly with other works in the genre while keeping an eye peeled for unique features.

The work's stylistic similarity to the Esterházy cantatas has already been mentioned. This is manifested particularly in the C-major pomp of the opening ritornello and the duet "Dictamina mea." Once again Haydn has written some fine music for the bass voice, here the *Sturm und Drang*-influenced "Si obtrudat" in D minor (!) and another vigorous aria in B$\flat$. The coloratura tenor is back again—were these creatures so readily available?—to deliver two very difficult numbers, one with a large harpsichord solo part, the other with an violin obbligato that echoes the vocalist's *fioritura*. As in *Qual dubbio* I, double cadenzas adorn both arias.

It is also useful to compare the Haydn *Applausus* with Mozart's *Die Schuldigkeit des ersten Gebotes*. Because Mozart's work is an early essay in a rigidly prescribed form, it is probably fairly representative of its genre. Haydn's work essentially consists of eight reci-

---

[29] The complete text of this letter is given in the Appendix.

[30] Robbins Landon believed that no performance was given between 1768 and 1958, when he supervised a revival for a BBC series entitled "The Unknown Haydn." Landon *HCW* 2, 236.

tative-aria pairs (the first "aria" a quartet, the third a duet, the last a chorus). Mozart's begins with a short, quick *sinfonia*[31] and proceeds through eight vocal numbers also, each introduced by at least one recitative. Whereas Haydn invariably employs *recitativo accompagnato*, Mozart appears to have saved orchestral accompaniment in the recitatives for especially dramatic moments. At these points, as in his settings of the arias, he varies the orchestration cleverly to correspond to the characters' emotional states. Thus the second aria, with its imagery of hunter and roaring lion, uses two solo horns with brief "hunting" motives; the third recitative paints the cries of the damned with fierce orchestral tuttis, shifting to softer, slower string accompaniment when the Christian's thoughts turn to "the knowledge of salvation."

Haydn, too, had taken care to employ cultivated variations in orchestral color. He knew that with *applausus* settings, diversions in the score could supply the interest so often lacking in the libretto. Besides the solo harpsichord and violin parts mentioned above, he used muted strings and divided viola parts to enrich the textures of several arias. His basic orchestra consisted of strings, bassoon, two oboes, two horns or trumpets, and timpani, the high trumpets and timpani adding characteristic verve to several numbers (see below). If Mozart's orchestrations seem still more imaginative—besides strings he calls for high trombone, pairs of flutes or oboes, bassoons, and horns, plus divided violas—that may be laid to a youthful enthusiasm for Baroque instrumental symbolism (flutes for pastoral moments, the trombone to evoke the priesthood, etc.) and his personal knowledge of the players at the Salzburg court.

What Wolfgang's *Singgedicht* lacks is a final chorus. Instead, its eighth number brings together three characters (Divine Mercy, Divine Justice, and The Christian Spirit) who vow to renew their struggle for lost souls. At least Haydn's libretto allowed him a triumphant choral note on which to end.[32]

---

[31] Haydn had directed that the first two movements of an "overture" (read *symphony*) be played before the opening ritornello of his applausus, which would take the place of the symphony's final Allegro. See the *Applausus* letter in the Appendix.

[32] The special circumstances in which Mozart created K. 35 have a great deal to do with this, of course. He had been asked to contribute only Act I of a Lenten sacred drama; Acts II and III were composed by Michael Haydn and Anton Cajetan Adlgasser (1727-1777) respectively, both men being connected with the Salzburg court at the time. So Mozart's work had to end at a point of dramatic tension, Worldly Spirit (a soprano) having momentarily seduced The Christian (a tenor) into dalliance with mundane pleasures. Each Act was performed separately in the Rittersaal of the Salzburg palace at intervals of a week, Mozart's on March 12, 1767. That performance by installments, together with the limitations on staging which the Rittersaal surely enforced, help position the work squarely in the camp of the *Singgedicht/applausus*, even though certain non-musical factors blur this categorization. See Gianturco *Mozart*, 24-32, from which we have drawn the information used in this discussion.

SOME SACRED CONTRAFACTA

Before sending off the autograph of *Applausus* to Zwettl,[33] Haydn made a copy to keep in Eisenstadt; he was understandably reluctant to consign any of his music to being used once and forgotten. Several adaptations of numbers from this work have since turned up (especially in Eisenstadt, at the Esterházy Church Music Archive and the Cathedral Church of St. Martin), and we can assume that these contrafacta were made with Haydn's approval even if he was not personally responsible for them. They will be discussed below, along with certain other sacred adaptations—to wit: *1)* contrafacta from *Applausus,* including *Dictamina mea* (B-G# B.6.b)[34] [with the *Alleluia* (XXIIIc:3)] and *O Jesu, te invocamus* (B-G# B.6.d); *2)* contrafacta from the Esterházy cantatas, including *Plausus honores date* and *Jam cordi* (XXIVa:2c) [with the chorus *Sit laus plena*]; and *3)* works assumed to be based on cantatas or operas written in the early 1760s but now lost, including *Quis stellae radius* [the "Motetto di Sancta Thecla"] (XXIIIa:4) and *O coelitum beati* (XXIIIa:G9). Although some of these pieces have yet to appear in modern performing editions, it seems likely that they will eventually find their way into the church and concert repertory, since they contain pleasant and (mostly) practicable music by a great composer.

The historical favorite among the *Applausus* contrafacta is *O Jesu, te invocamus,* an adaptation of the final chorus. Its popularity in Haydn's time is attested to by the number of manuscript copies that have come down to us, and by the printed score which Breitkopf & Härtel brought out in 1812.[35] Like the other "authentic" *Applausus* contrafacta, very few musical details of the original work had to be altered. For that reason the editors of the Haydn-Institut's *Applausus* were able to include *O Jesu* and other adaptations in the same volume simply by double-texting those movements.[36]

If we notice any immediate difference between this chorus and the Esterházy choruses of a few years earlier, it is that not a whiff of soloistic intricacy lingers here. Rather, Haydn seems to have been intent on producing short, elegant, rather stereotyped phrases (perhaps he was more anxious than usual to declaim the Latin properly for these fastidious monks); the lines are beautifully balanced if a bit pale, and faultlessly voiced to the point of slick-

---

[33] Signed with this chronogram: "HVNC APPLAVSVM FECIT IOSEPH HAIDN," doubtlessly to provide a pleasing puzzle for the learned monks (the acrostic adds up to 1768). Landon *HCW* 2, 145.

[34] Refers to index number assigned by Becker-Glauch in her thematic table of certain Haydn church works; see Becker-Glauch "Neue Forschungen," 237-241.

[35] This edition also supplied a second text, "Allmächtiger, Preis dir und Ehre!"

[36] *JHW* 27/2, 170 ff. In the same edition can be found *Quae res admiranda . . . Christus coeli atria, Dictamina mea, and Concertantes jugiter.* None of these contains choral music; the D-minor bass aria *Concertantes jugiter* is based on one of Haydn's inspired creations, however, and well worth examining. *Christus coeli atria* is an intricate solo quartet whose character would be lost if a choir attempted to sing it. *Resonant tympana,* a bass "motet" arranged from the aria "Non chymaeras somniatis," is mentioned by Pohl (*Haydn 2*, Anh., 10) and Geiringer ("Small Sacred Works," n.13; *Haydn*, 247), but was not considered an authentic contrafactum by the editors of the *JHW* volume, Becker-Glauch and Wiens. See "Vorwort" *Applausus*, ix.

ness. An initial homophony gives way to fugato texture, and that to invertible Italian thirds (see Ex. 3.8). The whole movement exemplifies what Larsen called "Midcentury style": a tendency toward the *galant*, toward easy, formulaic melodies and a weakening of harmonic tension.[37] It is the last glimpse of Haydn the bland cosmopolitan that we shall have, since his other post-1766 works show a rekindled desire to sing with his own voice.

The other outstanding contrafactum from *Applausus* is both more interesting and more problematic. To transform the splashy "Dictamina mea" duet into a sacred work, Haydn needed to change almost nothing; its allegorical Latin provided suitable thoughts already. But in most *Dictamina mea* manuscripts, Haydn's tiny *Alleluia* (XXIIIc:3) in G has been attached at the end, forming an Offertory-chorus pair. This cannot help but strike an odd note, not only because of the C-to-G key relationship of the two pieces but also due to their disparate scorings.[38] In the first movement, two horns have replaced the two oboes, two trumpets, and timpani of the original; the divided violas remain. The second movement is scored for strings only (with one viola line). Although there are soprano and alto soli in both movements, it is hard to escape the impression that the *Alleluia* originated elsewhere and was then cobbled, by hands unknown, onto the first piece.

But that may not be so: in his analysis of the *Alleluia*, J. T. Berkenstock argued convincingly that this chorus was intended to follow *Dictamina mea* in liturgical use, possibly at Epiphany Vespers.[39] Briefly, Berkenstock's argument has two points: first, it seems unlikely the *Alleluia* was ever an independent piece.[40] If it were, its fifty bars of *presto* 6/8 would last less than a minute. Moreover, the ascending triad motive with which it begins (see Ex. 3.9) is found in many Haydn choral works[41] and is commonly associated not with the beginning of an independent movement, but with commencement of a vigorous tempo after a slower, more contemplative section—exactly the case in the present pairing. Second, evidence from some early performance parts implies that the Offertory and chorus were used at Epiphany (January 6), possibly as a Gradual and Alleluia. That makes compositional sense if we view the text of *Dictamina mea* as an interpretation of the Epiphany message—enlightenment through teaching ("He who desires to be taught my precepts . . .

---

[37] Larsen "Observations," 124-129.

[38] Geiringer (*Haydn*, 247) has attempted to explain the key relationship by pointing out that the offertory dispenses with the original duet's da capo and ends in G, thus forming a bridge to the G-major chorus. That would be fine if it were true. As things stand, however, the overwhelming majority of *Dictamina* manuscripts do preserve the da capo in some way, so we are forced to search elsewhere for connections between these two movements.

[39] Berkenstock "Smaller Sacred Compositions," 142-148.

[40] Although we cannot doubt it is by Haydn; an autograph score exists which, through the dating of its paper, points to a composition date of 1768 or 1769 [!].

[41] See the "Pleni sunt coeli" or "Et resurrexit" motives in the *Grosse Orgelmesse*, first *Missa Cellensis*, *Missa Sancti Nicolai*, *Missa in Tempore Belli*, or *Harmoniemesse*.

let him approach this throne"). The opening of the *Alleluia* is also remarkably similar to the beginnings of certain chants for Epiphany Vespers.[42]

All that aside, matters of key and scoring remain to vex the tidy-minded. In this regard we can only point out that removing the oboes and timpani (hardly essential to the scoring in any case) and changing the trumpets to horns both tend to soften the pomp of this movement and bring it more in line with the simple *Alleluia*. And that awkward key relationship is echoed in at least one other authentic contrafactum, the beautiful *Quis stellae radius* examined below. Perhaps the best solution is simply to enjoy this forthright little chorus; its balanced ABA (with a complete recapitulation!) shows Haydn, free of form-hampering textual considerations, cleverly constructing a bagatelle for the New Year. When placed after the duet, its artless art seems epiphany indeed.

We turn now to the contrafacta based on Esterházy cantatas and early operas. Pride of place must go to two works whose originals have long since vanished: these are the so-called "Motetto di Sancta Thecla," *Quis stellae radius*, and the recently discovered *O coelitum beati*. Both pieces mate da capo arias for soprano with short choruses. Neither piece is of overwhelming difficulty, although a flexible soloist will be needed—one might wish for a Fux, if not a Scheffstoss.

The "Motetto di Sancta Thecla" acquired its nickname from Haydn's friend Carl Kraus, *Regens chori* at the Parish Church of St. Martin in Eisenstadt.[43] Kraus copied or otherwise acquired many of the composer's church works and may have made this adaptation, as we shall see, from a cantata since lost.[44] Neither the music nor the text shows much evidence of owing its inspiration to any *Commemoratio* for Saint Thecla, "Virgin and Martyr." Instead, Becker-Glauch masterfully pinpointed the origin of *Quis stellae radius* in a Latin cantata written for the entry of Prince Nicolaus into Eisenstadt—his first entry as Lord of the estate, on May 17, 1762.[45]

The literary theme for such a cantata would of necessity have mingled hope with grief, for the House of Esterházy had suffered twin tragedies that spring. First came the death of Prince Paul Anton on March 18; then on April 24 Princess Maria Octavia, the mother of

---

[42] Berkenstock cited the hymn *Illuminans, altissime* as found in the *Liber Vesperalis Mediolanensis* and two antiphons, that for the Magnificat *Orietur stella* and the *Benedictus Dominus* for second Vespers on the same day. We might add that such rising motives could be expected at Epiphany, whose Epistle mirrors such themes: "Arise, shine; for thy light is come. . . . And the Gentiles shall come to thy light, and kings to brightness of thy rising. . . . Lift up thine eyes round about, and see." (from Isaiah 60:1-6)

[43] The Martinskirche is one of the few Eisenstadt religious houses that does not owe its existence or present form to an Esterházy.

[44] The performance materials at St. Martin's include a bass part that Haydn himself signed, thereby establishing the authenticity of the work. Becker-Glauch hypothesized that the composer signed this part in 1765 or 1766 when he loaned the original cantata materials to Kraus for the adaptation. Becker-Glauch "Neue Forschungen," 182.

[45] Becker-Glauch "Neue Forschungen," 177-183. Becker-Glauch "Version" provides a shorter account, in English, of her scholarship on this work.

Paul Anton and Nicolaus, also passed away. The text of the soprano aria (which evidently underwent few changes) fitly refers to "monsters of the underworld [that] still angrily growl," but tells us to "worry not over these threats if God stands beside you," for "a pure spirit will uplift you when grief presses down." In musical terms, the aria's melody and moderated *fioritura* seem to breathe the same clement, consoling air (Ex. 3.10).

The 32-bar chorus moves to C major, giving Nicolaus his measure of welcome in more familiar terms. It seems less likely that the original text of this movement has survived; Example 3.11 provides two texts, one from the Eisenstadt manuscript and one from Budapest that seems to reflect the rhythms of the original music better.[46] We know this style of choral voicing, having encountered it in other of Haydn's earliest church works. The soprano line is often set well above the other voices; the tenor and bass are set so closely together that their parts occasionally cross.

Unlike the other cantatas and contrafacta, *Quis stellae radius* opens with a *secco* recitative. In order to make a proper beginning, Haydn probably played at least one symphonic movement ("overture") before this recitative, as he instructed the monks at Zwettl to do before the *Applausus* ("all you need to play is an Allegro and an Andante, for the opening ritornello takes the place of the final Allegro"). That could have been the overture-like Symphony No. 9, which ends with a Minuet and Trio. It has the additional benefit of being in C, so that a more rounded tonal form (C - F - C) emerges for the motet as a whole.[47]

No one is liable to come along with an erudite source story for *O coelitum beati*. Not only have the originals been lost, but one of the contrafactum manuscripts as well. We owe the existence of the work in its only present edition to Robbins Landon, who in the spring of 1983 discovered a complete manuscript in a Viennese bookshop. That word *complete* must be used cautiously. Landon's copy is the only one possessing a chorus; both sources listed in Hoboken have only the aria. Since there is no autograph or other record of the chorus, its authenticity will be questioned. That aside, it is a fine piece, its fifty-one measures of *alleluia* (see Ex. 3.12) making at least as joyful and varied a noise as the finale of *Applausus*, and a longer one than that of *Dictamina mea*. The aria shows a number of Haydn's early-1760s fingerprints, especially his dotted "Esterházy" figures and Lombard snaps.

There are two contrafacta with chorus drawn from the Esterházy cantatas: *Plausus honores date* (from *Da qual gioja*) and the so-called "Eibiswald" contrafactum. In *Plausus*, Haydn uses as instrumental prelude a shortened version of the grandiose opening ri-

---

[46] Robbins Landon provided both sets of text throughout his edition of this work. See his summary of Becker-Glauch's research, to which he added new data from other sources, in *HCW* 2, 495-503.

[47] Becker-Glauch "Neue Forschungen," 182. Does this mean that the other Esterházy cantatas should also be prefaced with an Allegro? Not necessarily: common sense says that they are much shorter works than *Applausus* and would be overbalanced by such an addition, but then we may be laying an anachronistic sense of proportion into that.

tornello. The chorus follows immediately. We have already examined the chorus to the "Eibiswald" work (named for the Parish Church of Eibiswald [Graz]): it is the *Sit laus plena* of Haydn's very early years. For an aria, the contrafactum uses the lovely *allegretto* duet from *Destatevi, o miei fidi*, here rescored for soprano and tenor.

Conductors planning programs with this literature may also want to examine some contrafacta for solo voice and small orchestra from the same period: the *Magna coeli Domina* (XXIIIa:C7) for bass and *Ego virtus* (*deest*) for soprano.[48] Both are C-major works in the heroic Esterházy manner.

HAYDN'S FIRST *TE DEUM*

In the fall of 1765, Gregor Joseph Werner, now old, bedridden, and no longer able to supervise the chapel music at Eisenstadt Castle, wrote to Prince Nicolaus concerning his deputy's failures:

> I am forced to draw attention to the gross negligence in the local castle chapel, the unnecessarily large princely expenses, and the lazy idleness of the whole band, the principal responsibility for which must be laid at the door of the present director, who lets them all get away with everything, so as to receive the name of a good Heyden [*sic*]; for as God is my witness, things are much more disorderly than if the 7 children were about; it seems that there are only libertines among the chorus people, who according to their fancy take their recreation for 5 or even 6 weeks at a time: the poor chapel thus has only 5 or six at a pinch, also not one of them pays attention to what his neighbor is playing. Over half the choir's instruments are lost, and they were collected only seven years ago, after many requests, from the late lamented Prince. Apart from all that, now most of the church music itself goes out to all the world. . . .
>
> The church choir will be . . . depleted completely unless Heyden is seriously ordered to prepare a catalogue of at least of what pieces remain.
>
> Incidentally, it is humbly requested: Your Princely Highness should give him a severe order that he must issue the strictest command to the princely musicians that they appear in the future, all of them without exception, at their duties. And because it is likely that he, Heyden, will try to lie his way out of it, the order must come from on high, that the extant choir instruments be examined, among which there must be 12 old and new violins.[49]

---

[48] Both available in practical editions from Verlag Doblinger, ed. H. C. Robbins Landon. The bass aria is scored for strings and organ continuo (Landon's edition includes two *clarini* and timpani, clearly a local addition to the scoring), the soprano aria for two oboes, two *clarini* and timpani in addition to strings and organ continuo (of which at least the timpani part, and possibly the *clarini*, are a local addition).

[49] Werner to Prince Nicolaus Esterházy, trans. in Landon *HCW* 1, 418.

It would seem that Werner's charges were at least partly true. Much of the church music from his time and before has disappeared from the Eisenstadt chapel archives; the easygoing Haydn may have been to blame for some of that. When the Prince directed him to take better charge of matters, he did so. Although the thematic catalog that Haydn was asked to make of the chapel's music has not survived, the start of his own *Entwurf-Katalog* also dates from this time. He may have presented a copy of it to Prince Nicolaus as a further sign of devotion.

It is not only the letter above that lets us know Haydn had begun taking over many of Werner's duties. Records show that on December 24, 1765, Haydn collected for the first time the musicians' money for the annual *Rorate* service; that means he was in charge of this Chormusik affair, a traditional Advent observance in Austria for which the musicians were paid with a meal (*Rorate-Suppe*, literally "Rorate-soup"). Haydn also felt well enough established by this time to ask that his brother Johann be brought in as an unpaid tenor in the choir.

That Haydn, rather than the venerable Capellmeister, was asked at some point early in the 1760s to provide a *Te Deum* for a princely occasion speaks volumes about the increasing esteem he enjoyed. Werner had continued to compose prolifically in his later years, so he must have found this favoritism a bitter pill to swallow; perhaps it was his jealousy that made him refer to Haydn as a *Modehansl* ("fashion-monger") and *G'sanglmacher* ("cheap tunester").[50] Haydn, for his part, respected Werner's music and eventually acquired a large number of his autograph scores.

Haydn's early *Te Deum* in C (XXIIIc:1) remained almost unknown until the 1960s. The *Te Deum* was one of the most popular forms in *settecento* Austria, being as often employed for civic celebrations as for church services. Haydn wrote another *Te Deum* around 1800 that stands as a summation of his life's art; within his choral music it is not easy to find another ten minutes of such shining invention. This first setting knows how to make a merry noise, too. If it sometimes bears its combination of Baroque and progressive elements rather awkwardly, perhaps it can be forgiven that on account of youth.

Like the second *Te Deum*, the first is in C and is organized in three parts. That was typical of these festive pieces. Even a conservative example like Gregor Werner's *Te Deum* shows a basic tripartite division, although its seven movements recall the length and grandeur of Fuxian works.[51] For the young Haydn, grandeur must still have meant Reutter—his scurrying violins and variously churning rhythms fill every measure of the first section

---

[50] According to Pohl (*Haydn* 1, 366), Werner wrote sixteen Masses, a Requiem, five *Salve Regina*, four *Regina Coeli*, and four *Alma Redemptoris* between 1759 and 1765. There is no record of whether they were all performed, but it is likely Haydn had to rehearse and conduct any that were. It was also Pohl, drawing upon the memories of Eisenstadt musicians, who reported the disparaging terms Werner used for his younger, better-appreciated colleague (*Haydn* 1, 211f.)

[51] MS in the Domarchiv collection, Cathedral Church of St. Martin, Eisenstadt. See Dack "Origins," 253-254.

and return at the very end. By comparison the choral writing seems simple and sturdy (see Ex. 3.13).

In the middle Adagio, violins *à la* Reutter briefly give way to a gentle pulsation that gives the text, declaimed in loosened homophony, more prominence. Only the church trio accompanies.

The final section shows both Haydn's skill at handling the contrast of solo and tutti vocal ensembles and his burgeoning contrapuntal talents. He brings in a solo trio (the tenor already having delivered a solo in the first section) at "Per singulos dies" and continues to alternate SA with B phrases effectively until the climactic choral "Fiat misericordia." A fugue ensues, also traditional at this point. Haydn enlivened it by setting a buoyant "non confundar in aeternum" countersubject almost immediately against his "In te Domine speravi" subject (Ex. 3.14). With details like these, and in his overall economy of form, Haydn looks forward to his great sacred choral works of the 1790s. Small wonder that his Prince saw fit to ask works like this of Haydn even when he had an older, more practiced church composer in his stable.

We cannot be sure of the occasion for which this *Te Deum* was written. It may have been part of the welcoming ceremonies for Prince Nicolaus in May of 1762. There is also a description of the wedding of Nicolaus's eldest son Count Anton with Countess Erdödy in January 1763, which contains specific mention of a *Te Deum* being sung:

> In the middle of the square in front of the castle, a portal of honor had been erected, whereupon trumpets and kettledrums were heard. The Princely Guard, consisting of a Grenadiers' Company of selected men, stood to attention. After the happy arrival of the noble Count and Countess, with their company, the Te Deum was celebrated in the Castle Chapel. . . .
>
> The next day, after solemn Mass, His Serene Princely Grace had arranged for a [great common feast]. . . . On the third day an *opera buffa* was given with exceptional applause [Haydn's *Acide* had been given the day before], and afterwards a ball began, during which the entire castle garden was magnificently illuminated and the number of masks even greater than [at the first evening's ball].[52]

---

[52] *Wienerisches Diarum*, trans. in Landon *HCW* 1, 382.

Example 3.1a: Haydn, Cello Concerto (VIIb:1), I, mm. 1-6

Example 3.1b: Haydn, Cello Concerto (VIIb:1), I, mm.18-21

Example 3.2: Haydn, *Acide*, "La beltà che m'innamora," mm. 1-10

Example 3.3a: Haydn *Destatevi*, Duetto, mm. 1-7

Example 3.3b: Haydn *Destatevi*, Duetto, mm. 43-50

Example 3.4: Haydn, *Destatevi*, "Quanti il mar," mm. 1-14

Example 3.5: Haydn *Da qual gioja improviso*, II, mm. 26-39

(cf. V.)

Example 3.6a: Haydn *Qual dubbio omai*, I, mm. 1-10

Example 3.6b: Haydn, *Qual dubbio omai*, I, mm. 21-34

Example 3.7: Haydn *Qual dubbio omai*, IV, mm. 33-50

Example 3.8: Haydn *O Jesu, te invocamus*, mm. 1-17, strings and voices

Example 3.9: Haydn *Alleluia*, mm. 1-13

Example 3.10: Haydn *Quis stellae radius,* I, mm. 29-40

Example 3.11: Haydn *Quis stellae radius*, II, mm. 1-7

Example 3.12: Haydn *O coelitum beati*, II, mm. 1-13

Example 3.13: Haydn *Te Deum* 1, mm. 1-16

Example 3.14: Haydn *Te Deum* (XXIIIc:1), mm. 97-105, vocal lines (begins above)

4

MASSES 1766-1782

MISSA CELLENSIS IN HON. B.V.M.

On March 3, 1766, Werner died.[1] Haydn became Capellmeister-in-full to Prince Nicolaus without any outward ceremony marking the occasion. But an inward event of some magnitude must have taken place, because Haydn shortly began work on his most ambitious sacred work (perhaps his most ambitious work in any genre) to that point, the *Missa Cellensis in honorem Beatissimae Virginis Mariae* (XXII:5). This work had been known as the *Cäcilienmesse* or *Missa Sanctae Caeciliae* because of the title given on an early nineteenth-century manuscript in the Austrian State Library.[2] In the mid-1970s, newly-discovered fragments of the autograph[3] established once and for all the work's actual name and also cast new light on its dating. Whereas scholars had previously placed the music somewhere between 1769 and 1774, it is now thought that Haydn began it in 1766, perhaps to fulfill a private vow he had made involving Our Lady, the church at Mariazell (*Cellensis:* "Celle" = "Zell"), and his accession to the post of Capellmeister.[4]

Earlier in these pages, the story of Haydn's own youthful ties to Mariazell was told. The Esterházy family also enjoyed a long association with this Styrian pilgrimage church. In 1692, Prince Paul had led a procession of 11,200 believers. He managed to visit Mariazell himself fifty-eight times and eventually dedicated a side-chapel there which still stands. We can assume that Prince Nicolaus, following the Esterházy tradition, encouraged

---

[1] Gregor Joseph Werner, Capellmeister to the Esterházys from 1728 on, is discussed in Chapter 3.

[2] Haydn had termed this work *Missa Cellensis* in both *EK* and *HV*, but that was laid to confusion on the composer's part with the later work of the same name.

[3] Signed and dated title page plus two sections of the Kyrie.

[4] See Landon "Autograph."

his chapel-master's vow. Haydn would have been anxious in any case to demonstrate his skills in church music for Nicolaus. No doubt he keenly anticipated creating the major works he could only dream of while Werner was Capellmeister.

The story of the first *Missa Cellensis* (hereafter called the *Cäcilienmesse*, in deference to tradition) should go on something like this: Haydn labors successfully at a great "number" Mass; his prince praises his efforts; the work in all its admirable excess is finally given at Mariazell, glorifying the Virgin and adding to the fame of both composer and patron. But it does *not* go on like that. First of all, we cannot know whether Haydn finished the Mass in 1766 (see below). Secondly, there is no record of its ever having been performed at Mariazell. Such an omission in the chronicles is not uncommon and not by itself conclusive but, if we consider that no other work of the time in the Mariazell repertoire approaches the *Cäcilienmesse* in length, scoring, or character, the likelihood of its performance there does seem remote. Biba has suggested that Haydn composed the Mass for Vienna, where numerous opportunities to perform a Mass in honor of the "Muttergottes von Mariazell" would have presented themselves.[5] There also Haydn would have had no problem gathering the needed singers and players, especially the high trumpets called for in his score.[6]

But even if Vienna answers the question of a 1766 performance, the end of the story is not yet in sight. Further problems loom: unlike the Kyrie sections, the other autograph fragment (part of the Benedictus and all of the Dona[7]) must be dated somewhat later than 1766—perhaps as late as 1773, to judge from its watermarks, layout, and sloppy "hand." And performers who study this Benedictus and Dona will immediately notice a change in styles between these movements and the earlier sections, a change even greater than what we would expect given the stylistic range of a late-eighteenth-century number Mass (again, see below). How can this obviously later manuscript fragment, and its music's markedly different style, be reconciled with the authentic title-page date of 1766?

It need not be. The best hypothesis, given the evidence we now have, is that Haydn revised or completed the Mass after 1766. This second version would be what we know today.[8] To reach its present form, it can have taken any number of paths.

The reader should first bear in mind that Haydn may not have written a complete setting of the Mass Ordinary in 1766. No composer of that time regarded the Mass Ordinary as an inviolable cycle or necessarily as a cycle at all. Practical needs often dictated sub-

---

[5] For example, the yearly commemoration of the Feast of Mary's Birth, marked by a Pontifical Mass at the Augustinerkirche honoring both the patron of Styria's *Landesgenossenschaft* and "the most blessed Mother of God in her holy dwelling, Maria Zell." Biba "Werke," 142-143.

[6] Although archival records show that two *clarinistae* were also a regular part of the musical forces at Mariazell, and that in 1766, "hoc anno interu[m] Tympana introducta sunt." See Dack "Dating," 108.

[7] Not, as Robbins Landon states, "the whole Agnus." Cf. *HCW* 2, 228.

[8] Most of the details and reasoning for this explanation—but not necessarily the specific conclusions reached here—are drawn from Dack "Dating," an excellent guide to the complexities of the whole issue.

stitutions (akin to insertion arias in opera) and reworkings in the Ordinary; the insertion numbers best-known to modern church musicians are probably Mozart's isolated Mass movements.[9] It frequently happened, especially at elaborate Pontifical Masses, that not all parts of an Ordinary would be by the same composer. Nor was this considered undesirable, since within the service various liturgical acts and other music separated nearly every part of the Ordinary anyway. The more splendid and richly divided a work, the more likely it is to have been created as a single Ordinary setting: thus Vivaldi's *Gloria*, or the originally isolated compositions of Kyrie-Gloria (*Missa*), Credo (*Symbolum Nicenum*), and so on in Bach's B-minor Mass.[10]

Let us assume that Haydn wrote only a Kyrie-Gloria-Credo cycle for that commemoration at Mariazell or Vienna. Let us further assume that he copied out only one set of parts from his autograph score and, after the performance, took the parts back with him to Eisenstadt. There they remained in his private possession, since the Castle chapel could not then support a performance of this ambitious work. But—and this is no assumption—in 1768 a disastrous fire burned Haydn's house and destroyed many of his compositions. Perhaps the parts and most of the score of this 1766 Mariazell Mass were lost in the fire.[11] Thus a scant year and a half or so would have existed in which the 1766 Mass could have been copied and used elsewhere. Because of its special nature, its distribution was apparently limited, for no manuscript copies of it exist today.

As we have seen with the cantatas and their contrafacta, Haydn was not one to let good music lie. Sometime around 1770 he may have revived the Mass, reconstructing any lost parts and adding the missing sections, probably for an occasion that warranted the opulence of the existing music and at a time when the press of other matters prevented him from undertaking composition of a wholly new Mass.[12] A number of such occasions can be found in the early 1770s, revolving around noble marriages, name-days, or the visits of considerable personages to Esterháza.[13] Nor can we rule out the possibility of a commission from Vienna or elsewhere, one that has so far escaped discovery by scholars. It may be that a link will yet be found between Haydn and that Viennese Brotherhood whose members yearly celebrated the Feast of St. Cecilia (they gave a Litany on November 21st evening and a High Mass at the Stephansdom on the 22nd). Only one such performance for them, lingering in the minds of the congregation, would have been needed to beget a mi-

---

[9] For example the Kyrie in D Minor, K. 341, from 1780-81.

[10] See Mac Intyre "Mass," 109-110.

[11] As well as the newly copied parts to the *Missa Sunt bona mixta malis* of 1768; for this latter work, not a single manuscript copy exists, only the Kyrie-Gloria autograph fragment recovered in 1984 (see text following).

[12] A number of similar instances in Haydn's creative life can be cited: in 1774 he wrote and conducted a new version of *Acide* (1763); around that time he also added trumpet and timpani parts to the *Grosse Orgelmesse*; in 1785 he revived *La vera costanza* (1778), which the Esterháza fire of 1779 had largely destroyed. See Dack "Dating," 109-110; Landon *HCW* 2, 210-211.

[13] See Dack "Dating," 110 for a list of six occasions culled from Landon *HCW* 2.

nor legend, perpetuated in later manuscript copies of this *Missa Cellensis*. In 1774, the Brothers would have celebrated the silver anniversary of their society's founding.[14] Could this *Missa Cellensis* have been their jubilee piece and thus truly a *Cäcilienmesse*?

Certainly the music seems fit. It ranges far and wide stylistically, including within its nearly two hours' length both past and future: fugues in *stile antico* and *moderno*, several full-blown arias, even a *recitativo accompagnato*. The last pages display that *Sturm und Drang* manner which haunts so many of Haydn's works composed in the ten years after 1766. Any group of music lovers would have discovered in it much to savor.

Hearing it, some of the true connoisseurs might also have sensed Haydn engaged in rediscovery, a musician gradually reawakening to the text and traditions of the Mass (remember that he had not composed a setting of the Ordinary since 1749). The present work begins very much in the vein of that earlier setting, its Reutteresque fiddling and foursquare choral phrases showing, in 1766, the stiffness of another age. In spite of all its activity, this is not very lively music. The "Christe," a tenor solo which might be expected to add some intimacy to the proceedings, also seems rather cold; it is followed by a Kyrie II fugue so dependent on sequential episodes that it too fails to sustain interest, let alone build to any climax. Throughout his career, Haydn would seek various technical solutions to the problem of setting the Kyrie. Its three-part, simple text called for a formal scheme, not the expressively varied rhetorical landscape of the Gloria and Credo. Haydn would eventually find a stronger design but, in the Kyrie of the *Cäcilienmesse*, we are still a long way from the symphonic sweep of the late Masses.

The seven-movement Gloria is another story. Beginning with a unison choral statement that strides, Colossus-like, on tonic and dominant from c' to g" in about five seconds (Ex. 4.1), Haydn called forth music of a diversity, drama, and richness equalled in only one other number Mass of the time, Mozart's mighty C-minor torso of 1782 (K. 427).[15] As would Mozart, Haydn here used the most intense contrasts of style to create a feeling of magnificent breadth and life. Yet nothing seems out of place. After the driving choral tutti of the "Gloria in excelsis," with its signature trumpet calls and dynamic contrasts, the mincing operatic charm of the "Laudamus," a soprano aria, refreshes us.

Haydn's "Gratias" is a fugue in almost-proper *stile antico*: at least no independent instrumental parts intrude until measure 243. This chorus, too, features effective dynamic contrasts, and it builds solidly into its homophonic portions so that a fine sense of unity is maintained. Example 4.2 shows the beginning and conclusion of the movement.

Again a solo movement follows, here the well-constructed "Domine Deus." It is actually a succession of three long solos, alto-tenor-bass (the last with quite difficult leaps);

---

[14] For details, see Landon *HCW* 2, 229-230; Feder "Manuscript Sources," 108.

[15] But cf. also Caldara's *Missa dolorosa* (1735; practical edition Carus CV 40.080) and *Missa in honorem Sanctificationi Joannis Nepomucensis* (1726), Reutter's *Missa Sancti Caroli* (1734; see Chapter 1) and esp. Florian Leopold Gassmann's *Missa Sanctae Caeciliae* (ca. 1765).

the soloists share a great deal of motivic material, but through a process of thematic transformation and continuous tonal progression, the music continually unfolds in beautiful new ways. At the end the singers join in a trio.

In Mozart's C-Minor Mass, the "Qui tollis" is one of the most powerful choruses, drawing upon Handelian antiphony and lightning dynamic strokes. Haydn's *Cäcilienmesse* uses another kind of opposition: juxtaposed question-and-answer phrases. The massive homophonic *forte* of "Qui tollis" is followed by a quiet, imitative "peccata mundi" limned with Baroque pathos. These joined figures reappear, ritornello-like, in relative major, then in the subdominant. A separate orchestral ritornello introduces each of these appearances and ends the movement.

The next movement could hardly provide greater contrast. It is another soprano solo, brighter and even more effervescent than the first (Ex. 1.11a). These polished arias, effortlessly balancing vitality and taste, indicate how well-versed Haydn had become at opera-seria forms through his experience with the Italian comedies and cantatas.

A brief Largo ("Cum sancto spiritu" in choral declamation) introduces the final movement of the Gloria, a fugue on "In gloria Dei Patris." Although a fugue was customary here, we could scarcely have expected one this magnificent, considering the precedent set by Kyrie II. At times it exudes a rhythmic crackle reminiscent of Bach (Ex. 4.3a), and the two well-placed stretti, the second over a dominant pedal (Ex. 4.3b), really drive the piece to a fine climax.

After all that, Haydn may be forgiven if the beginning of his three-part Credo recalls the everyday quality of the Kyrie. That was probably intended as a means of rounding out the Kyrie-Gloria-Credo structure. The soprano soloist, alternating with the choir in a kind of ritornello, provides some interest. And the composer gives us something entirely different in the "Et incarnatus est": it commences as a *recitativo accompagnato* for tenor, straight out of the opera house, before settling into a long and beautiful aria in florid, somewhat improvisatory style. Alto and bass join the tenor for the "Crucifixus." Here again the bass voice is shown to particular advantage, with dramatic intervals throughout and ending on a low F ("sepultus est"). The *allegro* third section takes advantage of its text ("Et resurrexit . . . judicare . . . vivos et mortuos") to deliver many of the rhetorical gestures associated with the Viennese Classic Mass and especially with Haydn's later Masses. The fugue with which it ends ("Et vitam venturi," Ex. 4.4) is likewise linked in style to later works; we might rightly consider it their proud parent. The forthright theme, given out by the trumpets too, finds an echo in the *Heiligmesse*, as does its moment of rising syncopated figures (Ex. 4.4b; in the later work, they are expanded after being suggested by the countersubject). Besides the propulsion created by these figures, Haydn employs far-reaching but smoothly consistent harmonic excursions to reach the goal. "At the end, the first trumpet, rising to the highest *clarino* register, flashes like a shining sword across the horizon. It is one of the greatest movements in all Haydn."[16]

This brings us to the second half of the Mass, that part which may have been composed as late as 1773/4. A span of five years may not seem too great a passage of time. But for Haydn's music, the years immediately after 1766 saw an unparalleled process of experiment and expansion. Authorities sometimes speak of this period as Haydn's "romantic crisis" (*vide* Wyzewa and Geiringer) or else borrow the term *Sturm und Drang* ("Storm and Stress") from Germany literary history. When they do so, they are thinking above all of the minor-key symphonies, and perhaps of certain string quartets.[17] Yet the period makes itself equally felt in Haydn's choral music; it deserves a brief overall description before moving ahead in this Mass.

The roots of eighteenth-century musical *Sturm und Drang* can be found in the eccentric but forceful music of C. P. E. Bach—sometimes described as in the *empfindsamer Stil* ("expressive" style)—and in works of the 1760s such as Gluck's ballet *Don Juan*. That piece concluded with a fiery D-minor descent into hell, a "Dance of the Furies" which Gluck later adapted for the Paris version of *Orphée*. The *Sturm und Drang* era did more than simply encourage renewed use of the minor keys, however. Works like *Don Juan* encouraged the wholesale testing of new materials and methods, and among them lay what composers of the emerging Classic style needed in order to create more serious and complex music. Counterpoint became fashionable again—witness the double and triple fugues of Haydn's Op. 20—and a number of other old techniques too: slow opening movements from the *sonata da chiesa*, Gregorian chant as a cantus firmus. The temporary license to commit extremes was extended beyond sudden and frequent dynamic contrasts, insistent syncopations, wide melodic leaps, unison *forte* themes and the like, into reconsiderations of form and harmonic rhythm.[18]

For Haydn, *Sturm und Drang* definitely meant more than fiery contrasts: when all his works of the time are surveyed, we can see him reaching for a truly Shakespearian breadth of expression. Within his range now were also a newly sharpened wit, a still more frivolous pastoral manner. As much as anything, the essential quality of Haydn's music ca. 1767-72 is that one can never be sure which of his masks will be in place, what gesture will occur in the next movement or even the next measure.

And so it is in the present Sanctus, Benedictus, and Agnus. The Benedictus is long— 123 mm. of moderate four, not counting the reprise of the 12-bar "Osanna"; it is in a mi-

---

[16] Landon *Symphonies*, 311.

[17] See esp. the Symphonies No. 39 (upon which Mozart based his first G-minor symphony, K. 183 of 1773), 49 "La Passione," 45 "Farewell," 26 "Lamentatione," and the quartets Op. 17/6 and all of Op. 20. Or the Piano Sonata in C Minor, No. 33 of 1771.

[18] Robbins Landon noted a "new sense of long harmonic line, particularly noticeable in the construction of [symphonic] slow movements, where one sometimes has the impression that time seems to stand still." *HCW* 2, 273-274.

nor key; its wind writing shows new independence and color (see mm. 34, 119; also solo bassoon doubling violin I, mm. 1-9, 95-99); its harmonic rhythms are generally slower and simpler; and—most telling of all—it seems to have been conceived as an instrumental movement upon which the vocal lines were laid. All these factors point to Haydn's style of the 1770s and beyond.[19] What the listener will hear immediately, however, is the uneasiness in this music. It careens between minor and major, encountering diminished-chord outbursts and martial rhythms en route to its ultimately tragic ending. Blessed, but cruel also, is he that cometh in the name of the Lord: here is a feeling akin to those in the great minor-key Benedictus movements of the late Masses, especially the *Nelsonmesse*.[20] When the little "Osanna" from the Sanctus is tacked onto the end of this brooding monument, the effect is almost of black comedy. Example 4.5 quotes only the movement's main ideas; also striking is the choir's initial entrance—*forte,* in octaves, mid-phrase—at measure 13 (see Ex. 10.71).

A brief bass solo (Agnus Dei) with some peculiar features[21] raises the curtain on the final fugue of the Mass ("Dona nobis pacem"). As in the Benedictus, moody feelings lurk not far beneath the surface. This Dona may be a C-major Presto, but its subject, a broken, chromatically descending line ending in a new key, sways the harmony of the whole movement, resulting in modulations far more remote than those of the earlier fugues. With episodes like measures 127-136 (diminished chords, sudden *piano,* and—significantly—the Agnus Dei text again), one's first impression of the music is confirmed: this is a troubled yet exciting Dona, musically much more advanced than anything Haydn had written before or would write again at this spot in a Mass.[22] He once reproached himself, while writing a symphony, with the scribbled words "This was for far too learned ears."[23] One cannot doubt that these final pages likewise appealed most to the connoisseurs in Haydn's congregation.

---

[19] Dack "Dating," 103-104.

[20] To compare only the tonal outlines of Benedictus movements in the *Mariazellermesse* (*Missa Cellensis 2*), *Paukenmesse,* and *Nelsonmesse* with this one: *1)* all begin with extended orchestral introductions, i - III - i; *2)* whereas the present movement ends in i, the *Mariazellermesse* and *Paukenmesse* movements end in the parallel major (after vacillating similarly between i and III), and the *Nelsonmesse* Benedictus moves to a climactic episode in VI (all the more chilling for its emotional ambiguity).

[21] Dack has speculated about the authorship of this section, wondering whether it is from the master or only his *atelier.* "Dating," 104n.

[22] Cf. the much milder effects of similar passages in the *Heiligmesse*: mm. 79-92, 95-101.

[23] Autograph of Symphony No. 42 in D, 1771, second movement after bar 45.

"GREAT" ORGAN MASS

Prior to 1975 it was thought that Haydn's first great effort in sacred music as Esterházy Capellmeister had been the *Missa in honorem Beatissimae Virginis Mariae* (XXII:4), the so-called *Grosse Orgelmesse* or *"Great" Organ Mass*. Now that the first part of the autograph for the *Cäcilienmesse* has been discovered, we know it to be the work Haydn began shortly after assuming command in Eisenstadt (see above). And the *Grosse Orgelmesse*, which is after all entered in *EK* alongside pieces from 1768, can assume its rightful place as a later work.[24]

It is not surprising that the chronology of the two Masses should have been confused. Both are said to show the somewhat undigested mélange of styles that would become reconciled in Haydn's later works. Both are ambitious longer pieces, although the *"Great" Organ Mass* is about half the length of the other. In the end, it is the differences between these two pieces that matter. The *Cäcilienmesse* breathes the air of some extraordinary occasion, a festival in the heavens; that makes it a rarity in Haydn's *oeuvre* at any time. But with the *"Great" Organ Mass*, we can see our worthy Capellmeister fashioning something more to the measure of his Prince's taste and the performers at hand. Although it has met with critical abuse for two hundred years, this Mass is a great work. It presents a more mature and artistically unified whole than the *Cäcilienmesse*, all the while working from lesser materials. In the end, it plucks triumph from *galant* fripperies that could have overwhelmed it and makes a virtue of the intimacy and simplicity at its core.

The *"Great" Organ Mass* is cast in ten movements, two of them linked. Thus it falls somewhere between a *Missa brevis* and a number Mass in terms of its divisions; its forty-minute duration puts it in a class with the later Masses. The basic church-trio instrumentation is filled out with two *cor anglais* and two horns, to which, around 1775, Haydn added two trumpets and timpani (in 1768 his Esterházy band did not yet have those players).[25] There is also a prominent organ concertante part, which we may assume the composer himself played.

The opening measures of the Kyrie signal Haydn's artistic stance immediately. Although it is marked *Allegro*, the syncopated and filigreed organ/violin line demands delicate treatment: this landscape should be a Watteau, not a Breughel (it bears also just a trace of the old Esterházy manner). The choir follows with a contrapuntal treatment that lends dignity and an expansive quality to the subject, making us realize, after all, just how apt a melody this is (Ex. 4.6). A twittering organ interlude, the first of many, emerges from

---

[24] See Landon "Autograph" for details surrounding the original misdating, by Pohl and others, of the two Masses. Feder had considered it possible the "Great" Organ Mass was composed as late as 1768 or 69, based on the watermarks of the autograph fragments.

[25] The added parts should be considered optional at best; as is the case in other Haydn sacred works, the earlier instrumentation represents the composer's first, and perhaps finest, intentions. Certainly it was seldom possible for Haydn to rethink his entire timbral concept when he was called upon, or found it expeditious, to add extra winds.

the last eight bars of the first "Kyrie" and brings the music round to the dominant, where the solo quartet is introduced two by two for a brief "Christe." As we might expect by now, the first subject is recapitulated at movement's end for the final "Kyrie."[26] Haydn also recalled the general character of this movement in his Sanctus setting, so that in effect the same musical curtain is raised on both halves of the Mass liturgy, Synaxis and Eucharist.

It is in the six movements of the Gloria and Credo that more similarities to the *Cäcilienmesse* surface. Haydn seems to have reprised the 3/8 *andante* manner of his earlier "Domine Deus" in the "Gratias agimus tibi" here, and his present fugue on "In gloria Dei," with its sequences and Italianate thirds, is very like the final Kyrie fugue in the earlier Mass. Fortunately, the *"Great" Organ Mass*'s homelier context allows this counterpoint to emerge as pleasant rather than dim; a later fugue on "Et vitam venturi" is topnotch but also maintains simple outlines. One other paraphrase: like its counterpart in the 1766 Mass, the "Et incarnatus est" is an ornate tenor aria in C minor and *largo* tempo.

Yet the main impression left by both Gloria and Credo is not that of patches on older works but of a fresh use of old and new expressions (i.e., Fuxian and *galant* idioms) that somehow reconciles them to each other. The traditional features of the Viennese Mass are certainly present: witness the sudden drop to *piano* at "et mortuous" or the strongly sung unisons at "et unam sanctam catholicam [etc.]" in the Credo. But just as often, such clichés are transformed with a Haydnesque twist. The beginning of the Gloria is one such place. Underneath the hushed choral declamation of "Et in terra pax" throbs enough rhythmic activity in the strings to make the outburst of Esterházy-style dotted sixteenths at "Laudamus te"more a fulfillment than an aberration (Ex. 4.7). Likewise the Credo's "Et resurrexit" provides the standard rising line and lively tempo but surprises us with its alto solo and minimal, quiet accompaniment.

All the soloists have their moment in this Mass, and the writing for solo quartet is likewise well-distributed and confident. Quartet and choir alternate skillfully in several movements; Haydn's assurance in handling this essential texture is now as profound as his command of the choir. The major case in point is the Benedictus, an extended movement in the pastoral manner featuring quartet and organ soloist.

The most striking choral movement may be the often-maligned Agnus/Dona. Following an "Agnus Dei" that moves chromatically from the subdominant (A♭) through a number of keys to a dominant in home key E♭, the "Dona nobis pacem" takes off at a rapid clip, a fugue with subject and countersubjects suitably trimmed for flight. What happens not once but four times in the course of this little scherzo is shown in Example 4.8.

That last part, the *jongleur*'s final tumble before the Virgin, has been an object of scorn since Haydn's time; critics considered it not only silly but a poor bit of composition as

---

[26] James Dack has pointed out that Haydn is here actually combining the sonata idea with the ritornello principle of the Baroque concerto. But the solo organ ends up providing the ritornello, while the choir sings through the modulatory linking passages that are usually given over to the soloist. "Origins," 132-133.

well.[27] That judgment seems overly harsh. Taken as a whole, the Dona in this Mass, as in other Viennese Masses, will not garner any prizes for depth of expression. But it is not poorly constructed, especially in regard to the organ interpolations. The movement's every measure has been buffed up to accommodate as much homophony as possible within a fugal context, and the character of the organ interpolations is consistent with that style. When so little counterpoint is occurring, the organ part can scarcely be accused of interrupting it. The Dona should be taken as it was meant, an unfeigned dance of joy at the end of the Mass. Movements like this can help us see the whole of the *"Great" Organ Mass* for what it is—endearingly human. It succeeds, not because of its frailties, but because it embraces so many sides of our nature and does so with such equanimity.

MISSA SUNT BONA MIXTA MALIS

Nowadays we have another Mass from 1768 to consider. As of this writing, the *Missa Sunt bona mixta malis* (XXII:2) is the most recently recovered of Haydn's lost choral works; more than one mystery still clings to it. The *Missa*'s existence had long been known through an entry Haydn made in the *EK* (between Symphony No. 41 and the "Great" Organ Mass). He appears to have sent the autograph to Artaria, the Viennese publishing house, in 1805.[28] They in turn sold it to Vincent Novello, English organist, composer, and publisher, in 1829.[29] Neither Artaria nor Novello saw fit to publish the work. The autograph disappeared without a trace and had remained missing until its discovery a few years ago in a farmhouse in Northern Ireland. After that, it was auctioned with great fanfare at Christie's (March 28, 1984), transcribed, and performed at the Vienna *Haydn-Tage 1985*. It has recently been published.

Only the Kyrie and the first movement of the Gloria have survived. They are both written in the *stile antico* described earlier in these pages: there are no violin parts, and the choral writing recalls as much of Palestrina as the eighteenth century could bear.[30] In this case, the SATB choir is supported by a figured bass marked "Organo." Like the later *Libera me* and *Non nobis, Domine* (see Chapters Six and Seven), the work is in D minor. David Wyn Jones offered this brief description of its content:

---

[27] "It is not only because the solo organ part in the 'Dona' is frivolous or unchurchly that it disturbs: rather the great fugal line is broken off by a stylistic element that is, to say the least, musically incongruous." Landon *HCW* 2, 244. Cf. Carpani *Haydine*, 159.

[28] See his letter of August 17, 1805: "I hope that for these twelve pieces of music [including the *Missa*] the old Haydn shall have merited a small reward." In Landon *HCW* 5, 336.

[29] Details of the sale recorded in Novello *Mozart Pilgrimage*, 203.

[30] See Chapter 1.

In the *alla breve* first movement the phrases "Kyrie eleison," "Christe eleison," "Kyrie eleison" are announced in turn in a similar way, in the form of a four-part fugal exposition that continues in a contrapuntal fashion before culminating in stretto. Two brief interludes for organ separate the three main paragraphs, making conventional use of sequential patterns. The opening subject and the subsequent subsidiary motif to the word "eleison" (bar 30 etc., anticipated in bars 13-14) seem unnerving anticipations of passages from the opening movement of Mozart's Requiem, but as in Haydn's use of the so-called "Jupiter" motif, these contrapuntal subjects and others in the mass are part of a shared musical heritage; the opening motif occurs, for instance, in Mozart's Misericordias (K. 222).

Formal counterpoint plays a less pervasive part in the Gloria. It contains two expositions on the phrases "Laudamus te" and "Gratias agimus tibi," each subsequently leading to skilful overlapping of entries. Elsewhere the texture is either freely contrapuntal in a reduced number of parts, as in the carefully judged climax to the Gratias, or predominantly homophonic, as in "Et in terra pax" which, often in Haydn's masses, is sung in a low, as it were, "terrestrial" register. Two continuo links precede the two fugal expositions and, like those in the Kyrie, make perfunctory use of sequence.[31]

The *Missa Sunt bona mixta malis* is one of the few pieces Haydn wrote in *stile antico* despite a lifetime of involvement with church music. For him to have turned in that direction implies that special circumstances lay behind the composition of the work. It has been suggested that this Mass was some kind of votive offering, its contrapuntal rigors further encouraged by the period of experimentation in which it was written.[32] That seems reasonable on both counts. The "hand" of the autograph is especially neat and precise, with no corrections. After the first movement of the Gloria, there are five blank pages of manuscript paper. One may assume that the work was being scrupulously recopied from sketches when something interrupted the process. That could have been the 1768 fire at Eisenstadt, or it could simply have been the new opera (*Lo speziale*) in need of rehearsal. Jones has suggested that it may also have been Haydn's reluctance, having written five separate fugal expositions plus their succeeding developments, to proceed further with this particular experiment.[33] In any case the work may never have been sung in Haydn's life-

---

[31] Landon/Jones *Haydn*, 142-143; p. 142 also contains a musical example showing the first 17 measures of the Kyrie.

[32] See Landon "Lost," 7-8. Landon mentions the minor-key Symphonies No. 49 ("La Passione") and 26 ("Lamentatione") as having been composed in the same year. A comparison with No. 26 is of particular interest, as it appears to have been based musically on an ancient Holy Week drama known throughout Austria in Haydn's time. See Landon *HCW* 2, 291-295.

[33] That might also explain the title, *Sunt bona mixta malis*. In speaking of his works, Haydn had once quoted half of the old Latin proverb *sunt bona mixta malis, sunt mala mixta bonis* to Griesinger, adding, "there are good and bad children, and here and there a changeling has crept in"; Griesinger *Notizen* (3), 55-56. Perhaps the nomenclature of this Mass is thus a wry comment on the work's style. Cf. Landon/Jones *Haydn*, 143.

time: no performance materials have been located anywhere in Europe. As we said, more than one mystery remains.

MISSA SANCTI NICOLAI

One of the delicious ironies that the student of Haydn's Masses encounters is the historical juxtaposition of the *Missa Sancti Nicolai* (XXII:6) with the "Farewell" Symphony (I:45). No two works could be less alike—further evidence of Haydn's frequent change of masks in the early 1770s.[34] The events surrounding the Symphony have become well-known:

> Among Prince Esterházy's *Capelle* there were several vigorous young married men who in summer, when the Prince stayed at Esterháza castle, had to leave their wives behind in Eisenstadt. Contrary to his custom, the Prince [in 1772] wished to extend his stay in Esterháza by several weeks. The fond husbands, especially dismayed at this news, turned to Haydn and pleaded with him to do something.
>
> Haydn had the notion of writing a symphony (known as the Farewell Symphony) in which one instrument after the other is silent. This symphony was performed at the first opportunity in the presence of the Prince, and each of the musicians was directed, as soon as his part was finished, to put out his candle, pack up his music and, with his instrument under his arm, to go away. The Prince and the audience understood the meaning of this pantomime at once, and the next day came the order to depart from Esterháza.[35]

The "Farewell" Symphony begins violently, by hurtling *allegro assai* down an F♯-minor triad against a restless syncopated accompaniment. No relief theme appears until the development section; throughout the first movement Haydn forges a riveting sense of strength and unity from quite unorthodox formal procedures. Whatever the ultimate message of this music, it is shocking enough to give us new respect for Prince Nicolaus's tolerance as a patron.

Perhaps as little as a week or so after that first performance of Symphony No. 45, the Prince was treated to a new Mass on the occasion of his name-day, December 6. We have seen that Haydn had offered his patron cantatas and possibly other works on name-days or homecomings, but never before a Mass. That this particular Mass is so thoroughly ingratiating, so much in Nicolaus's favored Italianate style, tempts one to believe it was a thank-offering for the Prince's considerate departure from Esterháza. The manuscript shows signs

---

[34] Anyone seeking a Haydn symphony of this time more like the "Nicolaus" Mass in style need not look too far, however: the sunny Symphonies No. 35 (1767) and (especially) No. 43 (c. 1772) both show the kind of alternating lyricism and *buffa* touches that delighted the Prince. Both are scored for the *Missa*'s two oboes, two horns, and strings.

[35] Griesinger *Notizen* (3), 19.

of hasty composition, as if the work had been conceived and copied in record time follow-ing the Capelle's bundling-off to Eisenstadt. Later Haydn evidently used it for another occasion: the name "Nicolai" in its *EK* entry has been crossed out and "Josephi" substi-tuted.[36]

The most characteristic movement of the "Nicolaus" Mass is its Kyrie, the music of which is repeated for the Dona at the end.[37] Its pastoral character, echoed in many of the remaining sections, is immediately established by an easily flowing melody harmonized in thirds and sixths. Example 4.9 shows the first vocal entrance; only fifteen of the move-ment's fifty-seven bars are choral. Haydn shows his preference for the solo quartet else-where by writing an especially fine "Et incarnatus est/Crucifixus"—chromatic and con-trapuntal but never tortuous—and a warmly expressive Benedictus.

The Gloria (Ex. 4.10) is cast in a more extrovert mold (note Haydn's signature martial rhythm in m. 1) and features the choir, with the solo soprano intruding only for the "Gratias." An agile, brief "Amen" fugue ends the movement. Perhaps the other outstand-ing choral movement is the Sanctus. Here, as in the Kyrie, Haydn has suggested a pastoral setting without allowing monotony to set in.

It is remarkable that so few clichés are present in the *Missa Sancti Nicolai*, considering how quickly it was made. True, the first sixteen bars of the Credo overlap text in the old *Missa brevis* tradition. This passes quickly and in any case presents a more unified and com-prehensible surface than many other polytextual Credos. Here the passagework in the string parts helps bind things together, showing us moreover just how far Haydn had come from his days of slavishly imitating Reutter: his ascending runs, alternating between unison violins and *basso*, are both more simple and more interesting than what the older composer might have done. And he makes very good use of the modest instrumentation; later additions to the scoring (flute, two bassoons, two D trumpets, and timpani in one Eisenstadt source) add nothing of musical value.[38]

"LITTLE" ORGAN MASS

After the *Nicolaimesse* of 1772, Haydn evidently felt little motivation to compose an-other large-scale sacred work for his master. Prince Nicolaus had become increasingly in-terested in opera production at Esterháza, causing him by 1775 or so to neglect other musical activites. He seems to have left no more than a skeleton crew behind at Eisenstadt

---

[36] Likewise on the title page of the Eisenstadt parts. See Landon *HCW* 2, 251.

[37] That is not uncommon in Austrian Masses of the time. Considering the time constraints under which Haydn and his musicians were working, it must have been particularly helpful in this instance. Haydn did not even bother to write out the Dona in his autograph, relying instead on the singers to insert the second text as best they could during the performance. Landon *HCW* 2, 251.

[38] See descriptions of manuscript sources in Landon *HCW* 2, 251 and esp. Landon "Preface" 1, vi-vii.

for the musical needs of the chapel there; as for Esterháza, not a single contemporary reference to figural music at its services has been found.

Both of the Haydn Masses written between 1772 and 1796—two, over a span of nearly a quarter-century!—were prompted by external commissions. The *Kleine Orgelmesse* of ca. 1775[39] was shaped to suit the needs of the Order of the Barmherzige Brüder in Eisenstadt. The *Mariazellermesse* of 1782 was commissioned by Haydn's friend Anton Liebe as a thank-offering upon his elevation to the nobility.

These works, taken together with other choral music of that period, represent something of a mixed grill stylistically. The Janus-faced *Mariazellermesse* evokes, in alternating pages, shades of Haydn's earlier Masses and prophecies of his late ones. The *Kleine Orgelmesse* is a singular piece shaped very much by the individual circumstance for which it was created.

We have seen that, in his young years, Haydn was Sunday organist at the Vienna house of the Order of the Brothers of Mercy.[40] In 1768 at that same house he had performed his *Stabat Mater* in the presence of Johann Adolf Hasse.[41] After coming to Eisenstadt he established a relationship with the chapter there.[42] The Brothers of Mercy owed their foundation to the Portuguese monk Juan Ciudad (1495-1550), who, after leading a rootless and dissolute early life, devoted himself to caring for the poor and sick. He became known as "John of God" and was made a saint in 1690 (thus Haydn's formal title for his Mass: *Missa Sancti Joannis de Deo*).

Several factors influenced the creation of the *Kleine Orgelmesse*. First of all, Haydn wrote it at a time when he was once again a practicing organist. Franz Novotni, princely organist at Eisenstadt, had died in 1773. Rather than incur the expense of hiring another musician, Haydn and the Prince agreed that Sunday organ responsibilities at the castle would be divided between Joseph Dietzl, castle schoolmaster and sometime tenor in the choir, and Haydn himself. Dietzl was to play while Haydn was at Esterháza, and Haydn would play during the winter months; each would receive extra compensation. The most likely date for the first performance of this new Mass would have been March 8, the Feast of St. John of God. Thus Haydn knew he could count on one skilled soloist—himself—for the first performances in the Brothers' chapel and later at the castle. He wrote a beautiful organ solo in the Benedictus, traditionally the one place in an Austrian *Missa brevis* where an extended musical treatment was allowed.

A second factor Haydn had to consider was the worship situation peculiar to the Brothers' Eisenstadt house. The Barmherzige Brüder are a nursing order, and when cele-

---

[39] Robbins Landon has most recently proposed 1777-78 as the winter in which the Mass was composed, based upon watermark evidence and the distribution of the earliest MS copies; *HCW* 2, 407.

[40] See Chapter 2.

[41] See Chapter 5.

[42] See Schmid "Brüder."

brating Mass they felt an obligation to leave their patients unattended for no more than half an hour. Therefore any musical setting of the Ordinary had to be the briefest of *Missae breve*. Haydn's Mass, with a performing time of fifteen minutes, provided a maximum of musical interest without delaying the service. Its Gloria is only thirty-one measures long, its Credo only eighty-two (of which almost half is devoted to the "Et incarnatus est . . . sepultus est").

A third factor was the performance space itself. Although the chapel adjoining the Brothers' hospital is small, its organ loft is comparatively roomy.[43] But Haydn was surely also considering the situation in the Esterházy Castle Chapel, where he would also have performed the Mass. Its tiny size and limited personnel[44] would certainly have restricted the composer to traditional church-trio scoring.

All these things explain Haydn's return to the *Missa brevis* genre after a lapse of at least twenty-five years (the *Nicolaimesse* can't really be considered a full member of the *brevis* club). The *Kleine Orgelmesse* was to become one of the most popular of all Haydn's Masses, celebrated as much for its musical richness as for its convenient scale. Briefly: *1)* the Kyrie is *adagio* throughout, providing a contemplative yet magisterial tone that would not be captured again until the *Harmoniemesse* of 1802; *2)* the Gloria so radically condenses its text via overlapping that brother Michael felt it needed revision;[45] *3)* the best part of the Credo is a lovely "Et incarnatus est," especially its "Crucifixus" with chromatically descending choral bass line; *4)* The Sanctus is a 6/8 Allegro unique to Haydn's Masses—perhaps its inevitable suggestion of the hunt or peasant dance is a reference to St. John's past as shepherd and soldier; *5)* the Benedictus (Ex. 4.11), for soprano solo with organ obbligato, is usually considered the high point of the Mass; *6)* the Agnus/Dona, all *adagio* (and thus another inventive departure from Viennese tradition), ends with the merest whisper, a fitting final bow to the caregivers for whom the Mass was written.[46]

---

[43] It is definitely *not*, as per Landon *HCW* 2, 407, "very restricted." On the contrary, I was told by officials of the Order that as many as sixty musicians have crowded into it for festival Masses.

[44] See Chapter 6.

[45] His version of the Gloria, "un poco più prolungato," is included in *JHW* XXIII/2, 247-252. For a slightly differing view, see the Preface (p. 4) by Willi Schulze to his edition of this Mass (Carus-Verlag CV 40.079; Stuttgart, 1980), in which he notes that the Gloria's *Agnus Dei* line "clearly provides melodic and rhythmic contrast [to] the more animated motion of the *Gratias*." Whether this can actually be heard is questionable. Other lengthened versions of the Mass are also available; see the listing for this Mass in Chapter 11.

[46] See Ex. 2.4. At the end of the autograph Haydn wrote: "laus Deo: et B.V.M. et S. Joanni de Deo." Hoboken *Verzeichnis* 2, 84.

MARIAZELLERMESSE

By the late 1770s, Prince Nicolaus was dividing his time between Esterháza, where he could spend lengthy "summers" enjoying opera and other diversions, and Vienna, which was after all the social and political center of the empire; Eisenstadt became little more than a stopping-off place for his entourage. The gravitation to Vienna in the winters allowed Haydn to develop social ties with various Viennese whose homes were now becoming centers of the empire's renewed intellectual life. The death of Maria Theresa in 1780 meant the end of her conservative stranglehold on literature and philosophy within Austria. Censorship was lifted, ideas from abroad were allowed to enter and circulate, and Viennese intellectuals took advantage of the new freedom by building libraries and establishing literary salons. Haydn was no intellectual, but he enjoyed the mix of well-to-do bourgeoisie, poets, musicians, and bright young women he encountered at such gatherings. Besides the important salon of Franz Sales, Hofrat von Greiner, he was a frequent guest at the homes of Anton Liebe and the Hofrat von Keeß, who gave orchestral concerts.[47] Haydn's ties with the Liebe household are especially important to us. He dedicated his first volume of *Lieder* to Francisca, Anton's daughter (she received a copy bound in red taffeta), and it was probably she who suggested that her father commission a Mass from Haydn. The recently ennobled Herr Liebe "von Kreutzner" wished to undertake a pilgrimage to Mariazell, where this new Mass would be performed as a thank-offering. Haydn was probably approached at the beginning of 1782; he would have written the music between March and June of that year, and it presumably received its first performance at Mariazell the same summer.[48] At least one of its movements contains an explicit reference to Herr Liebe's pilgrimage experience.

The *Missa Cellensis, Fatta per il Signor Liebe de Kreutzner* (XXII:8) shows some of the characteristics of Haydn's earlier "solemn" Masses, but it also contains many of the elements of the symphonic Mass style he would develop in the 1790s. The newer ingredients are the more striking, as in the slow introduction and first theme of the Kyrie (Ex. 4.12). Here is an opening Adagio worthy of any of the late Masses; in fact it reaches somewhat ahead of the symphonies composed at about the same time (Nos. 76-78). The following Vivace's tune is a fine example of the "popular" style, or *Volkstümlichkeit*, that Haydn now sought to make an integral part of all his music. It may not be as elegant as the soprano solo in the *Paukenmesse*, but then Haydn was not writing for his Princess here. The layout of the first movement, with solo giving way to choir (supported by trumpets and timpani) and the whole effort moving through a kind of sonata-form-plus-coda, is in fact very similar to that of the later Mass. But an incomparable verve emanates from this piece's clean,

---

[47] Landon *HCW* 2, 501-503, provides an overview of this development in Haydn's life, from which we have drawn the present summary.

[48] Details taken from Pohl *Haydn* 2, 196f., and Brand *Messen*, 150f.

simple choral declamation, driven by an even simpler "drum" bass line and complementary violin motive. To lend a cyclic quality to the work, Haydn brought back the rhythms and textures of this movement in the Credo.

Another movement containing an unabashed popular reference is the Sanctus. Within its first section's choral parts is embedded an ancient Marian pilgrimage song; the sound of it must have warmed the hearts of "Signor Liebe de Kreutzner" and his fellow pilgrims when they heard it at Mariazell. (In 1796, Haydn repeated this trick with the Sanctus of another Mass, in which he hid the tune of the old German hymn "Heilig, heilig, heilig.") Note (in Ex. 4.13) that after their first, *forte*, entrance, the trumpets and timpani remain to add *piano* punctuation to the chorus's hushed phrases. The movement ends with a fugato on "Osanna in excelsis" (Ex. 4.14). Once again the energized texture from the Kyrie and Credo has surfaced, to clothe a rather plain subject in as much brilliance as Haydn's new style will allow. By this point in the work it is obvious that unity and simplicity have become the composer's paramount concerns.

The more old-fashioned side of the second Mass for Mariazell can be seen in its solo sections. When he returned to Mass composition in the 1790s, Haydn would dispense with arias, relying more on the flexible deployment of the solo quartet. But here we have an "Et incarnatus est" for tenor (Ex. 4.15a) that echoes the Baroque rhetoric of its predecessors in the first *Missa Cellensis* (*Cäcilienmesse*) (Ex. 4.15b) and the *Grosse Orgelmesse* (Ex. 4.15c). Note the similar handling of the transition from florid solo to starkly hewn choral fugue in *Mariazellermesse* and *Grosse Orgelmesse*. Likewise the earlier "Gratias agimus tibi" is an Allegro in 3/8 reminiscent of the "Gratias" in the *Grosse Orgelmesse*.[49]

Elsewhere this book briefly discusses Haydn's operatic music; here we encounter it again, in the Benedictus of this Mass. It is adapted from an aria, "Qualche volte non fa male," in Act II of *Il mondo della luna*; this is the only such self-borrowing in any of the Haydn Masses. The text of the opera aria is concerned with strife and reconciliation; Haydn made several changes to accommodate the differing message and length of the Benedictus text. At times the melody was altered to emphasize a key word (e.g., "Domini," m. 19); also some of the original aria's modulations were removed.[50] The movement begins in G minor, its tone at first martial and then forgiving (cf. the *Nelsonmesse* Benedictus). The beautiful relief tune anticipates Haydn's "Gott erhalte Franz den Kaiser."

---

[49] See also the Gratias of the *Harmoniemesse* of 1802, Haydn's last Mass (but one containing a number of retrospective elements); Chapter 8.

[50] A sudden shift from D major (V of g) to B♭ major, and from choral to quartet textures, in m. 27 calls to mind the technique, if not the effect, of the D-minor to B♭-major shift of the *Nelsonmesse* Benedictus. See the excellent Introduction by Andreas Ballstaedt and Volker Kalisch to their edition of this Mass for Carus-Verlag (CV 40.606; Stuttgart, 1986), 5 (Ger.)/6 (Eng.), which first drew our attention to this.

JOSEPH II AND JOSEPHINISM

Broader historical reasons also exist for Haydn's neglect of the Mass between 1772 and 1796. As early as 1749 the Church had taken steps to remove secular or operatic elements, including the use of orchestral instruments, from church music.[51] This trend was further encouraged in Austria by the rising spirit of the Enlightenment. The aim of Baroque church music had been to awaken in the beholder an emotional reaction to, and a sense of mystery and awe about, the central rituals of Christian belief. This it accomplished with forms and textures akin to the exaggerated visual art and architecture of the time. But the coming idea was that worship should serve a mainly educational function, helping to inculcate morality and virtue in the people. Religious practice was to be made simpler and more "natural," superstition and pointless ritual discouraged. To that end, congregational singing in German was increasingly preferred over extravagant orchestral settings of the Ordinary. The reforms of Archbishop Colloredo of Salzburg, Mozart's legendary nemesis, were part of this general trend.

As we have seen, the reign of Charles VI, with its full-blown *Reichsstil*, stands at the end of the Baroque era in the life of the Austrian Church. Maria Theresa, who generally shared her father's ideals in this area, lacked the economic means to continue their development and therefore became a transitional figure. Her son Joseph II (1741-1790) made radical changes in the character of Austrian church music and can be said to have launched, somewhat prematurely and arbitrarily, a new age in religious practice.

When Maria Theresa died in 1780, Joseph II assumed full control of the Austrian dominions. Many of his sweeping reforms, now referred to *en masse* as Josephinism, were concerned with church practices and had a direct influence on the development of sacred music. His decree of February 25, 1783, established among other things these restrictions on parish churches: *1)* instrumental (i.e., concerted) music would be permitted at High Mass only on Sundays and holidays; *2)* Vespers could not feature instrumental music, although organ accompaniment would be permitted on high feast days; and *3)* all other music (e.g., symphonies, trio sonatas, organ concerti) was forbidden.[52]

Other Josephine decrees resulted in the closing of many monasteries, the elimination of the musicians' guild, and the restriction of scholarships for choirboys to cathedrals, courts, and cloisters, thus forbidding such support in ordinary churches. Altogether these moves had a chilling effect on the creation of new sacred choral music. It may be significant that, like Haydn, Mozart broke off Mass composition in the early 1780s (with the incomplete C-Minor Mass, K. 427); he did not continue until 1791, well after Joseph's death. By

---

[51] Benedict XIV's encyclical of 1749 restricted orchestral accompaniment of the voices to strings; an Imperial decree of 1754 forbade the use of trumpets and drums in churches or processions within the Holy Roman Empire; Fellerer "Liturgical Basis," 164-165.

[52] Pass "Josephinism," 170.

then, Leopold II had to some degree lifted the ban against concerted music in the parish churches.[53]

Josephinism was in effect for less than ten years. But much of the damage done to the Church's musical infrastructure could not be easily repaired: money had been reallocated and was not restored, players and singers had found other jobs, monasteries remained closed, and the evolution of a new church style had been interrupted or perhaps permanently forestalled.[54]

---

[53] According to Pass "Josephinism," 171; cf. Fellerer ("Liturgical Basis," 166), who points to Frances II's response to repeated entries from Cardinal Migazzi for the resumption of instrumental Masses following his assumption of the throne in 1792.

[54] Robbins Landon notes that manuscript copies of the *Mariazellermesse* do not seem to have circulated with their usual speed. No one seems to have gotten the Mass during the 1780s, which is understandable; even after 1791 the monasteries, publishers, etc., were somewhat slow in acquiring it. *HCW* 2, 555.

Example 4.1: Haydn *Cäcilienmesse*, Gloria, mm. 1-14

Reprinted from Henle HN 5562 (*JHW* 23/1a). © 1992 G. Henle, Munich; used by permission.

Example 4.2a: Haydn *Cäcilienmesse*, Gloria, mm. 189-211, vocal lines

Reprinted from Henle HN 5562 (*JHW* 23/1a). © 1992 G. Henle, Munich; used by permission.

Example 4.2b: Haydn *Cäcilienmesse*, Gloria, mm. 300-334

Reprinted from Henle HN 5562 (*JHW* 23/1a). © 1992 G. Henle, Munich; used by permission.

Example 4.3a: Haydn *Cäcilienmesse*, Gloria, mm. 768-780, vocal parts with bass

Example 4.3b: Haydn *Cäcilienmesse*, Gloria, mm. 808-821

Example 4.4a: Haydn *Cäcilienmesse*, Gloria, mm. 275-290

Reprinted from Henle HN 5562 (*JHW* 23/1a). © 1992 G. Henle, Munich; used by permission.

Example 4.4b: Haydn *Cäcilienmesse*, Gloria, mm. 326-330

Reprinted from Henle HN 5562 (*JHW* 23/1a). © 1992 G. Henle, Munich; used by permission.

Example 4.5: Haydn *Cäcilienmesse*, Benedictus, mm. 39-57

Reprinted from Henle HN 5562 (*JHW* 23/1a). © 1992 G. Henle, Munich; used by permission.

Example 4.6: Haydn *Grosse Orgelmesse*, Kyrie, mm. 1-24

Example 4.7: Haydn *Grosse Orgelmesse*, Gloria, mm. 1-15

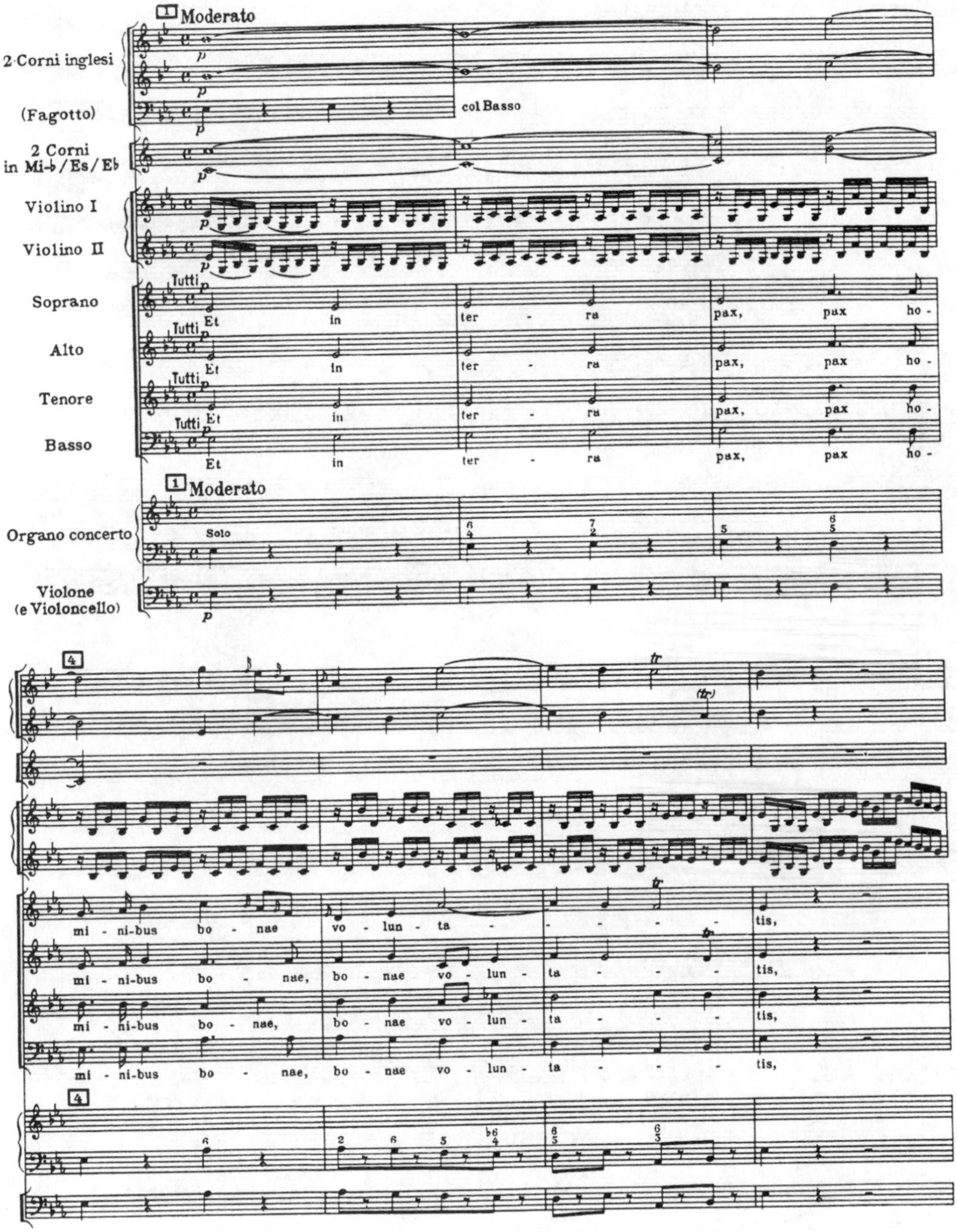

Example 4.8: Haydn *Grosse Orgelmesse*, Dona, mm. 33-38

Example 4.9 begins on next page.

Example 4.15c: Haydn *Grosse Orgelmesse*, Credo, mm. 1-6

Example 4.9: Haydn *Nicolaimesse*, Kyrie, mm. 9-19

Example 4.10: Haydn *Nicolaimesse*, Gloria, mm. 1-9

Example 4.11: Haydn *Kleine Orgelmesse*, Benedictus, mm. 11-21

Example 4.12: Haydn *Mariazellermesse*, Kyrie, mm. 1-23

Example 4.13: Haydn *Mariazellermesse,* Sanctus, mm. 1-14

Example 4.14: Haydn *Mariazellermesse*, Sanctus, mm. 28-36

Example 4.15a: Haydn *Mariazellermesse*, Credo, mm. 84-91

Example 4.15b: Haydn *Cäcilienmesse*, Credo, mm. 102-107

Example 4.15c follows Example 4.8.

5

ORATORIOS 1767-1784;
OPERA CHORUSES

Asked in 1776 to provide an autobiographical sketch for an Austrian dictionary of celebrities, Haydn included this statement:

> Among my works, the following have been most approved of—: the operas *Le pescatrici*, *L'incontro improvviso*, and *L'infedeltà delusa*, performed in the presence of Her Imperial and Royal Majesty; the oratorio *Il ritorno di Tobia*, given in Vienna; also a *Stabat Mater*, for which I received, through a kind friend, a testimonial from our great composer Hasse, containing many undeserved eulogiums.[1]

Note that the composer, today popularly considered the father of the string quartet, master of the symphony, and so on, mentioned only vocal works, none of them still well-known. For an eighteenth-century composer, the road to fame and a good position customarily lay not in string quartets but in opera and—to a lesser degree—church music. Clearly Haydn expected to be remembered for his large vocal works. He composed operas not only at Esterháza but also for London audiences. Whenever he had an opportunity, he applied himself to extended sacred music as well, from the childish twelve-voice *Salve* that drew Reutter's scorn all the way to the great Masses and oratorios of his later life.

History has not been kind to Haydn's middle-period oratorios or to his operas. The operas observe the conventions of the day without rising above them, and the oratorios, although more skillful, are similarly cramped by forms and texts that no longer hold our interest. Yet not all these works deserve oblivion; within each, there are pages that show Haydn at his best and that will still command attention from discerning listeners.

---

[1] Trans. by Robbins Landon; quoted in Haydn *CCLN* 18-20, Geiringer *Haydn* 69, *HCW* 2 398. Complete text of Haydn's "autobiography" in Geiringer *Haydn*, 67-70; also in Landon *HCW* 2, 397-399.

STABAT MATER

The outburst of big church works Haydn delivered after Gregor Werner's death gives special testimony to his interest in that genre. Among those pieces, the *Stabat Mater* (XX*bis*) was considered for many years his finest achievement.

Between *La canterina* of 1766 and *Lo speziale* of 1768, Haydn composed no operas; this gave him the necessary time to prepare a work on the scale of the *Stabat Mater*. It consists of thirteen separate numbers, nearly half of which feature the choir (*viz.*, two numbers for choir alone and four with the soloists). The orchestration of oboes, strings, and organ continuo with bassoon would have permitted performance at Eisenstadt in 1767, although no record of that exists. A letter of March 20, 1768, from Haydn to the Prince's secretary is the first we hear of this great work:

> Nobly born, Highly respected Sir!
> You will recall that last year I set to music with all my power the highly es-
> teemed hymn, called Stabat Mater, and that I sent it to the great and world-cele-
> brated Hasse with no other intention than that in case, here and there, I had not
> expressed adequately words of such great importance, this lack could be rectified
> by a master so successful in all forms of music. But contrary to my merits, this
> unique artist honored the work by inexpressible praise, and wished nothing more
> than to hear it performed with the good players it requires. Since, however, there
> is a great want of singers of both sexes in Vienna, I would therefore humbly and
> obediently ask His Serene and Gracious Highness through you, Sir, to allow me,
> Weigl and his wife, and Friberth to go to Vienna next Thursday, there on Friday
> afternoon at the Brothers of Mercy to further the honor of our gracious prince by
> the performance of his servant; we would return to Eisenstadt on Saturday even-
> ing.
> If His Highness so wishes, someone other than Friberth could easily be sent
> up. Dearest Mons. Scheffstoss, please expedite my request; I remain, with the
> most profound veneration,
>
> > Your most devoted servant
> > HAYDN[2]

This letter is informative on a number of counts. First, we can predict that Haydn's setting will have fallen safely within the Neapolitan tradition, since it met with the unquali-fied approval of Hasse, one of Naples' foremost adopted sons. Second, we see here another evidence of Haydn's desire for meticulously coached performances of his own works. Re-gardless of what is said in the letter, talent was not lacking in Vienna. But by taking him-self, the cellist Weigl, Weigl's wife the soprano Anna Maria Scheffstoss, and tenor Carl Friberth there, Haydn could exercise much more control over his work than otherwise. Third, Haydn the courtier here demonstrates his skills, by asking leave in such a way that

---

[2] Quoted in Landon *HCW* 2, 144; also in Geiringer *Haydn*, 66.

his Prince will be flattered (imagine having not only a celebrated composer in your Capelle, but irreplaceable singers too!). The performance in Vienna evidently took place on the Friday before Palm Sunday (this letter having been written two weeks before Easter), which accords with one of the prescribed usages of the *Stabat Mater* hymn in the Catholic liturgy.[3]

We can see why the Haydn of 1767 chose this text. Aside from exhibiting another facet of the Marian adoration so appealing to his culture, it gave him the opportunity to set a great number of passionately expressive movements in minor keys. With the *Stabat Mater* he was able to expand his large-scale language without leaving behind the traditional rhetoric of church music—indeed, he increased its usage at many points. What he did manage to avoid was the superficial operatic idiom of Pergolesi, whose own *Stabat Mater* was immensely popular throughout Europe. Many better musicians disdained its excesses.[4]

The first movement (Ex. 5.1) provides a good example of this *Stabat Mater*'s overall style. Its florid, rhythmically mercurial vocal lines show a Rococo aesthetic that would vanish in Haydn's later works. Nevertheless it sets the text well.

Less dust has settled on the tenth movement, "Virgo virginum praeclara." Its simpler *galant* contours, assured solo quartet writing, and masterful choral interjections look forward to mature Classic style. Example 5.2 quotes about one-sixth of the movement, showing the play of light and shade Haydn creates by varying dynamics and phrase lengths.

The *Stabat Mater* was instrumental (perhaps we should say *vocal*) in establishing Haydn as a composer of large choral/vocal works. It was performed to great success in Vienna, Paris, and London and became his first "oratorio" to appear in print. As late as 1831, the Oxford Professor William Crotch would opine that

> Of [Haydn's] vocal sacred productions his Stabat Mater is the best. The first chorus is learned, ingenious, and dignified; the songs for a bass voice are extremely fine, and the accompaniments throughout the piece delicate and fanciful, particularly that to the chorus "Quis est homo." The extraneous modulations and passages in counterpoint are, in all his works, admirable: his fugues are, on simple subjects, not treated with much skill, the interest often declining instead of increasing, and the terminations being abrupt, or in a modern style.[5]

---

[3] L. E. Cuyler, "Stabat Mater," *New Catholic* 13, 626.

[4] Padre Martini, the mentor of Mozart's youth, declared that on the whole, that work was indistinguishable from Pergolesi's famous comic opera *La serva padrona*. Robbins Landon noted that at one point, Haydn even dropped the words ("Inflammatus et accensus") that Pergolesi had set as an "unchurchly and gay" duet, going on instead with a bass aria "Flammis orci." The implication is that Haydn "was at considerable pains to circumvent the pitfalls which Pergolesi had failed to avoid" or at least, we might add, to prevent Pergolesi's more famous work from being called to mind at that point. Landon *HCW* 2, 234-235.

[5] Crotch *Substance*, 140-141.

If interest in the *Stabat Mater* has waned since then, it is probably due to the frequent successive slow tempos in the piece and to some of the stylistic eccentricities hinted at by Crotch: one blatant example is the interruption of the final fugue for a coloratura soprano solo.[6]

On Good Friday of 1771 Haydn conducted another importance performance of the work in the Piaristenkirche, Vienna.[7] The chronicles show that a very large congregation was present and sixty musicians were employed, a large number for any such performance at that time. The intimate quality of the *Stabat Mater*'s music may mislead us as to Haydn's desires for performance; evidently he favored sizable forces whenever they could be assembled.[8]

IL RITORNO DI TOBIA

By 1775 Joseph Haydn was developing a symphonic language far more varied, yet more balanced than his earlier Rococo or *Sturm und Drang* manners. But the pace of operatic activity at Esterháza was now continually accelerating, and a lack of time for study and experiment prevented Haydn's works of this period from achieving the polish we find in the more mature "popular" symphonies of the '80s and '90s. It was at this point he received his first major commission from Vienna since beginning service with the Esterházys: an oratorio, *Il ritorno di Tobia* (XXI:1). Rather than attempt the integration of new elements in this work, Haydn looked to the past for its form and spirit.

The commission came from the Tonkünstler-Societät, a charitable organization founded in 1771 by Imperial Court Capellmeister Florian Leopold Gassmann to provide funds for the widows and children of its members. Twice a year, at Advent and Lent, they performed an oratorio in the old Italian tradition to benefit the fund. Close to two hundred musicians would form the orchestra for these events; usually a concerto or some other special instrumental selection would be played between the first and second part of the oratorio itself. When Haydn conducted *Tobia* on April 2, 1775, Esterházy concertmaster Luigi Tomasini played his own violin concerto during this intermission. On April 4, when the oratorio received its customary second performance, Haydn's cellist Marteau played a concerto.

Tomasini and Marteau were not the only musicians Capellmeister Haydn brought with him to Vienna. As he had done for his *Stabat Mater* performance in 1768, he took key vocal soloists from his own group as well. Magdalena Friberth, her husband Carl, and bass Christian Specht sang the parts of Sara, Tobia, and Tobit respectively. Margarethe Span-

---

[6] Criticized in Pohl *Haydn* 2, 65f.

[7] Also the site of the first Vienna performance of the *Paukenmesse*. See Chapter 8.

[8] Landon *HCW* 2, 170.

gler, Magdalena's sister, and one Barbara Teyber filled the remaining roles of Anna and Azaria. Although we may wonder just how cordially these interlopers were received, their presence apparently only aided the performances: Haydn's music was praised everywhere, and the coffers of the Societät were enriched by 1,712 gulden. Landon noted dryly, "the Oratorio was such a success . . . that it was three years before the members could bring themselves to invite the composer to join their ranks."[9]

This was not the only humiliation Haydn would suffer at the hands of the Societät. Following his acceptance of their invitation of membership in December 1778, he was sent a letter implying that he could remain a member only if he composed "oratorios, cantatas, choruses, symphonies, etc., as they require," a condition he had already discussed with the officers and rejected. He was moved to an angry reply:

> This clause, with the so-called DISCREET demands, depends in my opinion wholly on the fancy, or the envy, of some of the members; in time it might depend largely on those who have the least possible insight into the art of composition, for they could judge as DISCREET that which is INDISCREET (for instance, a whole oratorio instead of a few symphonies). I should be forced to compose the most DISCREET oratorios *in plurali* as a result of the INDISCRETION which they consider their right; and if not, the majority of the *vota*—purely out of DISCRETION, of course—would demand my suspension *sine jure* (just as is now threatened). . . .
>
> Now, my good friend! I am a man of too much sensitivity to permit me to live constantly in the fear of being quashed: the fine arts, and such a wonderful science as that of composition allow no fetters on their handicraft: the heart and soul must be free if they are to serve the widows and collect profits.[10]

Haydn demanded the return of his 368-florin deposit, yet promised "despite such a crude and threatening treatment" to compose "various new pieces for the widows" if time permitted. In fact, he made important revisions to *Il ritorno di Tobia* in 1784 when it was revived by the Societät. But only in 1797, after his second trip to London, was he finally voted an honorary membership.

The piece was given a third time in 1808. It is instructive to compare the reviews that followed the first performances with critical opinion as it stood after the last. In 1775: "Expression, nature and art were so finely woven in [Haydn's] work that the listener must perforce love the one and admire the other. Especially his choruses glowed with a fire that was otherwise only in Handel."[11] Yet in 1810 Griesinger could only manage this: "The choruses in it are full of strength and vigor, and they received the greatest applause; but the plan of the oratorio as a whole is unsuccessful and much too monotonous. From be-

---

[9] Landon *HCW* 2, 215.

[10] Entire letter in Landon *HCW* 2, 418-420.

[11] *k. k. priviligierte Realzeitung*, Vienna, 14. *Stück* of April 6, 1775, 219, quoted in Landon *HCW* 2, 215.

ginning to end the not-very-interesting dialogue is followed always by an aria, without any alteration with duos and trios."[12] Another nineteenth-century observer noted, "it was not well received" and dubbed it "an antiquated pot-boiler [*veraltetes Machwerk*]."[13]

Il ritorno di Tobia's few commanding moments stem from the talent of its creator; its weaknesses lie in all those things inextricably binding it to the eighteenth-century traditions of the Italian oratorio. That was a genre very different from what the term *oratorio* calls to mind today. In Roman Catholic countries during the 1700s oratorio meant unstaged opera on a religious text. In all other respects, both libretto and music mimicked the preeminent operatic species of the day, opera seria.[14]

The classic libretti of Pietro Metastasio[15] established the tone for much of Italian oratorio, just as they had for opera; his oratorio books were set numberless times. We can count Reutter, Wolfgang Mozart, Gassmann, and Ignaz Holzbauer among those who composed a work on *La Betulia liberata*, for instance. Metastasio's clear, simple structures and polished verse were also imitated by any number of other poets including the librettist of *Tobia*, Giovanni Gastone Boccherini (1742-ca. 1800).[16]

A Metastasian oratorio libretto was expected to base its dramatic conflicts on moral issues derived from religious history and doctrine. Respect for the three unities of time, place, and action was also prescribed. That is, the drama had to take place within a twenty-four-hour time span and within the same place; only one dramatic action was to occur. In the case of *Il ritorno di Tobia*, as in many other such oratorios, adherence to the unities meant that much action was narrated in the past tense rather than conveyed through dialogue or stage business in the present. Thus although Tobias is, in the course of the biblical account (from Tobias 5-12, part of the Apocrypha), attacked by a monstrous fish, married, and saved from a devil, Boccherini's libretto allows the audience to witness none of this. Rather the action takes place at the home of Tobit and Anna, Tobias's parents, who are anxiously awaiting the return of their son. Much of Part One is consumed by a philosphical dialogue between the two, Tobit exhibiting his steady and forgiving faith, Anna her weakness and doubt. The Angel Raphael, who has disguised himself as the guide Azarias and accompanied Tobias on his journey, arrives first and retells their various adventures. He predicts that Tobias will cure Tobit's blindness. In Part Two Tobias makes several unsuccessful attempts to do that, using the gall of the monstrous fish he killed. This gives

---

[12] Griesinger *Notizen* (3), 18.

[13] Diary of Joseph Carl Rosenbaum; see Radant "Rosenbaum," 146.

[14] The following discussion of style in Italian oratorio and Il ritorno di Tobia owes much to Smither *History* 3, esp. 3-5, 35-54, and 160-181. For more specific and extended discussions of the relationship of this work to the Italian tradition, see also Smither "Haydns ritorno" and Michel "Tobias-Dramen."

[15] See Chapter 2 for details of Metastasio's role in the young Haydn's career.

[16] Giovanni was an older brother of the more famous Luigi and also wrote opera libretti for Gassmann and Salieri. Sometime after 1781 he went to Madrid. See Mutini, "Giovanni Antonio Gastone Bocherini," *Dizionario biografico degli italiani* 2, 59-60 (Rome, 1960-).

Tobit and Anna another opportunity to examine their faith (not unexpectedly, it is found wanting). Finally comes the expected *lieto fine* or happy ending: in a long accompanied recitative for the entire cast, Sara (Tobias's bride) reveals that Tobit's sight has been restored and that she, acting on Raphael's instructions, was able to gradually accustom his eyes to the light; Tobit enters and rejoices at seeing his family; Azarias enters, reveals himself as Raphael, and explains that he has done everything in answer to the prayers of Tobit and Anna; he then makes various prophecies and ascends to heaven on a cloud. In a final chorus, the remaining four characters and their servants praise God for his mercy.

The oratorio in its 1775 version contains eight numbers in Part One and seven in Part Two, typical of the genre. It begins with an overture and a chorus; each part also ends with a chorus. Otherwise the music consists of alternating recitatives and arias, with one duet. The large orchestra at Haydn's disposal for the Tonkünstler-Societät concerts offered him a greater-than-usual chance to play with instrumental sonorities, and he used it skillfully. Sara's aria in Part Two, for example, employs the solo colors of flute, oboe, bassoon, and horn at various points against muted strings, as she compares being with Tobias's family to being with angels rather than men. Another pleasant feature is Haydn's avoidance of the full da-capo form (there are "half" da capos for two of the arias in Part One). That helps the pacing of the work somewhat. Yet the overall impression it gives is that of a series of lengthy, lovely *Koloraturarien*, not a drama.

That Haydn was not unaware of his oratorio's shortcomings (one might rather say *longcomings*) is shown in the revisions he made for its 1784 revival.[17] Two new choruses, "Ah, gran Dio" and "Svanisce in un momento," were added; these were inserted about midway through Part One and Part Two, respectively, so that some relief was obtained from the stream of arias and "not-very-interesting dialogue." In addition, extensive cuts were made in the arias. Haydn shortened all but two (Anna's F-minor "Come in sogno" and the duet "Dunque, oh Dio"), cutting repetitive measures in the instrumental introductions and ritornellos and likewise in the vocal parts. The reprises of two- and three-part arias were shortened, while the arias "Quando mi dona un cenno" and "Del caro sposo" lost both middle section and reprise; all superfluous coloratura was removed too.[18] Oddly

---

[17] A repeat performance planned for 1781 came to naught, because Haydn had asked for compensation for revisions (primarily shortening; see text following) the Societät had asked him to make. The Tonkünstler-Societät declined to provide any such favors and instead gave a cantata by Hasse. Haydn was told that "because of the departure of an alto singer your oratorio cannot be produced," which may in fact have been so. See Edelmann "Haydns Il ritorno," 189-190.

[18] This may have been part of the process of adapting the music to a new cast of singers, one less well-versed in the rapidly disappearing Baroque art of florid song. See text following plus the commentary in Chapter 10 on the change in vocal skills in the eighteenth century.

enough Haydn let the lengthy recitatives stand. Perhaps he felt that revising the libretto would simply have taken too much time.[19]

In any event, the 1784 performances can hardly have been received as well as the premiere. The Societät encountered multiple problems casting the oratorio: Christian Specht had to bow out, and his initial replacement, one Francesco Bussani of the Vienna Court Theater, was dismissed after several Societät members objected. Eventually Steffano Mandini sang the part. The Tobia, Valentin Adamberger, became indisposed immediately before the performance; Carl Friberth had to step in. For the part of Anna, Nancy Storace was engaged, and Haydn may have had to rewrite this alto role for her soprano voice. Altogether these were not the kind of events likely to produce a sparkling performance.[20]

After 1784 *Tobia*'s star dimmed further. One sign of changing tastes in Vienna was the occasional performance by the Tonkünstler-Societät of German oratorios, perhaps at the urging of Baron Gottfried van Swieten (1733-1803). As Imperial Court Librarian from 1778 on, he was an ardent advocate of both "serious" (read *old*) music and all things German. One of the first works given in the vernacular at a Societät concert was his translation of Handel's *Judas Maccabeus*. Although German oratorio never become a sweeping trend, such Haydn works as *The Seven Last Words, The Creation*, and *The Seasons* may be considered part of a general assertion of German culture at century's end.[21] Swieten served as librettist for the latter two works.[22]

In Vienna a relatively new dramatic form, opera buffa, had also made strong inroads in public taste by the mid-1780s. Its emphasis on characters drawn from everyday life opened to it a wealth of musical possibilities—patter songs, ensembles, choruses—that opera seria could not match. And its rapidfire comic plots, which invariably depicted good sense triumphing over wealth and status, fit perfectly with the temper of more Enlightened times.

---

[19] All these cuts are clearly indicated in E. F. Schmid's edition of the oratorio (*JHW* 28/1, 2 vols.). Haydn eventually did improve the accompanied recitatives in the autograph, erasing some of the long held chords in the strings and leaving only a *secco* recitative. By providing greater contrast, this enhanced the force of the remaining *accompagnato* sections; the *secco* portions also allowed the singer greater declamatory freedom. Schmid marked these variants in the recitatives as "Zweitfassung." But Edelmann asserted that surviving performance parts from the Societät show no evidence these variants were ever used, not even by Neukomm in 1808; thus exactly when they were made cannot be ascertained. Edelmann "Haydns Il ritorno," 199-200.

[20] See Schmid "Haydns Oratorium," 296-298; also Edelmann "Haydns Il ritorno," 189-190. Yet Landon called this a "great" cast, pointing out that two years earlier Theresia Teyber (Sara) had been Mozart's Blondchen in *Die Entführung aus dem Serail*, Catharina Cavalieri (Raffaelle) his Constanze, Adamberger the Belmonte, and that two years later Mandini would be his Count Almaviva in *Figaro*. A score with Anna's part (re?)written for a soprano and highly ornamented, discovered before World War II by Dr. Schmid, has since disappeared. Landon *HCW* 2, 489.

[21] See Smither *History* 3, 361-376, for a discussion of related works from Protestant North Germany. Although Temperley found German oratorio in Austria a significant development (*Creation*, 2), Olleson (*NOH* 7, 327) did not. The splendid isolation of Haydn's great late oratorios may be the most telling means of measuring German oratorio's progress as a genre.

[22] See Chapter 9.

Audiences would soon begin to demand the variety and quickened pace of buffa style in other musical genres as well.

By the 1780s, the Tonkünstler-Societät had come to rely upon revived, revised, and shortened versions of works in the older Italian tradition. In 1786 it decided to deal with the oratorio problem more directly. Lorenzo Da Ponte, a rising young theater poet, was commissioned to rework eight libretti on biblical themes, tailoring them for more modish musical settings. He would provide in each work, he told the Societät, only short *secco* recitatives, none longer than five or six verses (three of Haydn's *Tobia* recitatives have over *fifty*), five or six choruses, and eight other pieces divided among arias, duets, trios, or quartets. Four main vocal soloists would be the standard. If this seems to us more like a "real" oratorio, it was also to the Viennese more like opera buffa, a genre in which the Abbate Da Ponte would soon distinguish himself mightily: that same year he fashioned *Le nozze di Figaro* for Mozart.

In the end, Da Ponte's experiments with oratorio produced little. Because he continually put the project off in favor of more interesting work, the Societät was forced to ask Esterházy court poet Nunziato Porta to finish it. Porta produced a total of thirteen libretti, only two of which were ever set to music. The shift away from Italian oratorio was coming more quickly than anyone had anticipated. By the 1790s, the Societät itself had turned its benefit concerts into "academies" offering more varied musical fare.[23] And in 1797, when Empress Marie Therese was looking for a copy of *Il ritorno di Tobia*, she approached the Tonkünstler-Societät only to be told they had discarded their parts, had presumably swept them away with other old rubbish.

Reaction to *Tobia*'s 1808 revival, also mounted by the Tonkünstler-Societät, was noted earlier in this chapter. From a musical standpoint, the revisions done by Haydn's pupil Sigismund Neukomm for this performance are of little interest. Neukomm actually made fewer and shorter cuts in the original material than had Haydn himself for the earlier revival. His added wind parts reflect a late-Classic aesthetic, not the Baroque style that had governed the original composition; thus, like Mozart's wind writing for *Messiah*, they cover the sharp detail and vivid colors of a great artwork with an incongruous plaster-and-fresco veneer. *Il ritorno di Tobia* is best approached in its original form (for sheer vocal glory) or its 1784 version (for the added choruses).

One of those choruses, "Svanisce in un momento," has become well-known as a separate work. Its style sums up an entire subgenre of the time, the "storm" chorus, and that makes it even more worth examining. The words of the text ("Svanisce in un momento dei malfattor la speme, come il furor del vento, come tempesta in mar. . . . De' giusti la speranza con cangia mai sembianza, costante ognor si fa . . . ed è lo stesso Iddio la lor tranquillità") call forth contrasting musical imagery: D minor and lightning-like string pas-

---

[23] Smither gives 1788 as the last year the Societät gave a complete Italian oratorio at its concerts; Edelmann cites the 1790 revival of Kozeluch's *Moisè in Egitto* (written one of Porta's libretti) as the "last great success of an Italian oratorio" for the Societät. *History* 3, 49; "Haydns Il ritorno," 198.

sagework for the stormy sea (Ex. 5.3), the relative or parallel major and a *dolce* relief subject for "tranquillità" (Ex. 5.4).

Although the orchestra provides most of the fireworks, the choral texture occasionally breaks free of its blocks of homophony. Each section is heard twice for an ABAB, d-F-d-D form; the emphasis is on immediate effect rather than any sort of musical progression. That is what we would expect from a Baroque work, and it stands as one more sign of *Tobia*'s basically backward-looking aesthetic stance.

Especially in England, "Svanisce in un momento" became popular as the sacred contrafactum "Insanae et vanae curae." Perhaps it reminded the English of the chorus Haydn composed for them in 1792, *The Storm*.[24] And well it should have—its text, form, and orchestral usage are strikingly similar.

THE CHORUS IN HAYDN'S OPERAS

Opera occupied a significant part of Haydn's life, both as composer and performer. He wrote operas of all kinds: Singspiel, opera seria, opera buffa (or more often the mixed heroic-comic genre his Prince preferred). Unfortunately, a number of these works have been lost, and other remain neglected in spite of some modern revivals. There are a number of reasons why Haydn's operas have not held the stage. They were not written for "the public," but for the intimate, peculiar environment at Esterháza. Also, many of them suffer from inferior libretti. And it must be said that Haydn did not bring to opera the supramusical talent of a Mozart or a Rossini—the ability to unify a story, galvanize a drama, from beginning to end. The music in Haydn's operas is usually no more than a series of interesting or delightful set pieces. That may actually work to the modern conductor's advantage, since it allows excerpts to be presented from these works with little damage to the material.

In Haydn's operas, the chorus plays a relatively minor role. The Italian operas composed for Esterháza have no choruses at all, due to the small size of the company and the intimacy of its performance situation. Only two surviving Haydn operas contain choral material of any substance. One of these is the charming *Philemon und Baucis* (XXIXb:2), the first marionette opera Haydn is known to have written. The surviving version of *Philemon* is, however, not the puppet opera that Haydn gave at Esterháza for Maria Theresa's visit in 1773, but a Singspiel devised around 1776 from that piece's music.[25]

Besides a fine D-minor overture and some pleasant arias, *Philemon* contains two extended choral scenes that could stand alone in concert or be performed as part of a selection from the opera. The opening chorus is a "thunderstorm" number painted with broad brushstrokes, well suited to the fairy-tale action about to unfold. Haydn's choral style is

---

[24] See Chapter 7.

[25] Cf. Geiringer *Haydn*, 271-272; Landon *HCW* 2, 197, 257-258; and esp. Landon "Marionette."

homophonic and declamatory throughout, although he effectively employs alternating unison men's and women's voices after the first tutti. "Suddenly," the stage directions tell us, "the storm vanishes; the heavens brighten again; and a beautiful sunset appears." As the chorus breaks into a joyful little D-major *contredanse* (Ex. 5.5), we half expect to see the Three Ladies or Papageno appear on the scene: here Haydn has captured a mood perhaps more naive than Scene One of *Die Zauberflöte* but no less infectious.

The final chorus is a da-capo construction in which the beginning and ending statements (Ex. 5.6) frame a quartet number of exceptional beauty. It begins with each character (two sopranos, two tenors) in turn stating a portion of the tune, then goes on to a brief duet followed by chorus or quartet statements. The 3/4 tune itself is one of those warmhearted hymns that would be labeled "Masonic" in another context. Like Mozart, Haydn could occasionally achieve something quite wonderful by mingling the sublime with the faintly ridiculous.

A number of fine choruses can also be found in *L'anima del filosofo* (XXVIII:13), a serious opera on the Orpheus legend that Haydn composed for his first London visit in 1791.[26] Political problems prevented the opera from being given, but an incomplete autograph and other authentic sources have survived. The English scholar Rosemary Hughes was particularly fond of the choral writing in this "hopelessly undramatic" work, arguing that Haydn's future achievements in Mass and oratorio could be glimpsed in its "ominous C-minor opening chorus, the deceptive gaiety of the women's chorus at the wedding, the warm and tender funeral dirge, and in the choruses of the spirits of the underworld."[27] Typical of the more sophisticated language of these pieces is No. 2b, "Ferma il pede, o principessa" (Ex. 5.7), in which the chorus warns Euridice not to enter the forest.

In addition to SATB or SSBB numbers, the opera includes both men's and women's choruses. One of the choruses for women, "Finché circola il vigore" (Ex. 5.8), was arranged by Haydn for STB chorus and performed in London as "Su cantiamo, su beviamo."

THE SEVEN LAST WORDS

Given the advent of Josephinism in Austria, it is significant that Haydn's last major sacred work of this period was produced for a church in Spain and, furthermore, that it was entirely instrumental in its first conception.[28] When Breitkopf & Härtel published the score in 1801, Haydn contributed the following explanation in his preface:

---

[26] See Chapter 7.

[27] Hughes *Haydn*, 200-201.

[28] Regarding Josephinism, see Chapter 4.

About fifteen years ago I was requested by a canon of Cádiz to compose instrumental music on *The Seven Last Words of Our Saviour on the Cross*. It was customary at the cathedral of Cádiz to produce an oratorio every year during Lent, the effect of the performance being not a little enhanced by the following circumstances. The walls, windows, and pillars of the church were hung with black cloth, and only one large lamp hanging from the center of the roof broke the solemn obscurity. At midday the doors were closed and the ceremony began. After a short service the bishop ascended the pulpit, pronounced the first of the seven words (or sentences) and delivered a discourse thereon. This ended, he left the pulpit and prostrated himself before the altar. The pause was filled by music. The bishop then in like manner pronounced the second word, then the third, and so on, the orchestra following on the conclusion of each discourse. My composition was subject to these conditions, and it was no easy matter to compose seven Adagios to last ten minutes each, and succeed one another without fatiguing the listeners.[29]

Haydn's music had been well received in Spain since at least 1779; the future King Carlos IV had sent the composer a gold snuffbox set with diamonds, and two other members of the Spanish aristocracy had arranged for him to send yearly a number of symphonies, quartets, and other chamber music scores. This particular commission apparently was the brainchild of a well-known priest, Marqués de Valde-Inigo, who had decorated the church in which the above-mentioned exercises took place (not the cathedral, but the grotto Santa Cueva, built underground in 1756). The Marqués asked Father Don Francisco Micón, who knew Haydn, to approach him with the idea of the work. Father Don Francisco wrote to Haydn and explained the ceremonial in detail, including the role of the music.[30] According to a later story, Haydn found it quite difficult to remain within the ten-minute limit set for each movement and asked the Bishop of Cádiz to grant him an occasional indulgence. The Bishop readily agreed, saying he would instead limit the length of his sermons.[31]

This was the year 1786, one of the busiest in Haydn's life. He conducted 125 opera performances at Esterháza, wrote three of the "Paris" Symphonies, some concertos and insertion arias, and began *The Seven Words*, probably finishing them in 1787. In his *Kritische Bericht* to the Köln Haydn-Institut edition, Hubert Unverricht commented on the evidence of extreme haste with which the sketches for this work were done. Haydn seems to have written as long as the pen contained any ink, only stopping to dip it after it went dry. This of course resulted in manuscript of continuously varied dark and light passages (the correct way to use a quill is to dip it at regular intervals so that a uniform ap-

---

[29] Quoted and trans. in Geiringer *Haydn*, 83.

[30] This account from Hoboken *Verzeichnis* I, 845.

[31] *The Morning Chronicle* (London), 1791 (day unspecified), summarized in Landon *HCW* 2, 617.

pearance results). Said Unverricht, "The outward picture of these sketches makes an almost Beethoven-like impression."[32]

Haydn was at least momentarily perplexed by his basic task. The Abbé Maximilian Stadler, a friend of both Haydn and Mozart, recalled in his autobiography that Haydn had asked his advice about how to get on with writing such an unusual piece. This was confirmed years later by Vincent and Mary Novello, who visited Vienna in 1829:

> Stadler was with Haydn when he received the commission to write the seven Adagios—and as he seemed comparatively at a loss to proceed in introducing sufficient variety in writing seven Adagios directly following each other, it was the Abbé Stadler who advised him to take the first words of the text and write a melody to each which should be the leading feature of each movement; he followed the Abbé's advice and with a success that requires no eulogy from me.
>
> A [priest] afterwards adapted words, but not in a satisfactory manner, and Baron Swieten engaged Joseph Haydn to adapt some words to the music himself which he accordingly did. Stadler said he preferred these beautiful compositions without the words just as they originally were conceived by their Author. . . .
>
> In Novello's edition (vocal score) of *The Seven Words*, some of the above conversation was incorporated, with the addition that "L'Abbé Stadler also corroborated the truth of the tradition that Haydn himself considered this 'the very finest of all his works.'"[33]

Basic facts concerning the composition of the vocal versions by Joseph Friebert (the priest cited by Novello) and Haydn are given in chronological context in Chapter 9. The following musical discussion of *The Seven Words* focuses on Haydn's vocal version of 1796, as that will be the work with which our readers are most concerned.[34] But words—the Latin words of the Vulgate—were central to the original conception of the work as well, so that Haydn's eventual adaptation of it to a vocal text, and our present overriding concern with that adaptation, makes both historical and practical sense.

The work in its original scheme consisted of seven "sonatas" (one on each Word), a D-minor introduction, and a depiction of the earthquake after Christ's death on the cross. It was scored for flutes, oboes, bassoons, and trumpets in pairs, four horns, timpani, and strings. Upon Haydn's instrumental framework Friebert had imposed a four-part chorus, using a pietistic German text partly based on Carl Wilhelm Ramler's oratorio libretto *Der*

---

[32] Unverricht *Bericht/Sieben*, 41a.

[33] Novello *Mozart Pilgrimage*, 172.

[34] In 1787, the year that Artaria published parts for the orchestral version, arrangements for string quartet (by Haydn) and piano (edited by Haydn) also appeared. These should be considered versions for home and amateur use (rather like a recording), not performance alternatives to the original scores of 1786-87 and 1796.

Tod Jesu.[35] By repeating certain parts of the instrumental music, Friebert devised ritornellos, and he had also added accompanied recitatives between the sonatas.[36]

In adapting Friebert's choral version, Haydn mainly kept his 1786 orchestration, but he added pairs of clarinets and trombones, reduced the four horns to two, and amplified the original flute and bassoon parts. He accepted most of Friebert's choral parts while rejecting his extra ritornellos and accompanied recitatives. Swieten (see above) aided him in revising Friebert's text. To the existing introduction, sonatas, and finale Haydn added an "Introduzione" to Sonata V for wind band only. In place of the recitatives he composed short unaccompanied choral intonations, setting forth each Word before the sonata that would (now literally) comment upon it (Ex. 5.9).

Like an aria from a Baroque Passion setting—after all, this text has roots in *Tod Jesu*—the sonata provided a personalized explication of the Word. Haydn used all his timbral prowess here to provide a warmhearted vision of Paradise. At the beginning, a muted solo cello doubles the melody, while horns and bassoon enrich the texture (Ex. 5.10a).

By measure 21 the modality has become major, and the solo quartet enters to a lighter string accompaniment (note the pizzicato violas and bassi in Ex. 5.10b). The solo cello continues to double the tune, which shifts between soprano and alto. (This play of colors and textures should be a warning, incidentally, to the conductor to avoid gargantuan performing forces in this music; there is no surer way to blunt its subtle effects.) The tonal scheme of the movement reveals itself to be c-E♭-f-g-C, with the f-g section contributing fine moments of chromatic/dynamic *chiaroscuro* (Ex. 5.11).

Elsewhere the influence of the old Baroque picture-painting is strong, as when, several times in Sonata IV (". . . why has thou forsaken me?"), all instruments and voices but the first violin drop away to depict Christ's feeling of abandonment. At the end of the "earthquake," Haydn wrote *fff*, an unusually explicit and extreme marking for his day.

In its orchestral version, *The Seven Last Words* helped spread Haydn's fame throughout Europe in the 1780s. This first version became popular once again in the 1950s, after Bärenreiter printed performance material based on the new Haydn-Institut edition. One can only hope that the choral version will not now be forgotten. It is extremely well written but of a somewhat old-fashioned cast, with a mawkish text difficult to render convincingly in our vernacular. Perhaps German-language performance, which would encourage an American audience to find meaning mainly within the music itself, is the answer.

---

[35] Ramler (1725-98) was a well-known German poet whose contributions included not only *Der Tod Jesu*, in its musical setting (1755) by Karl Heinrich Graun the most popular German oratorio before Haydn's *The Creation*, but also *Die Auferstehung und Himmelfahrt Jesu*, set by C. P. E. Bach in 1778. His oratorio libretti have been criticized for their shallow and sentimental approach, but this hardly prevented their widespread adoption by contemporary composers. Ramler also contributed to the reform of poetry for song composition; his *Lieder der Deutschen* (Berlin, 1767), a song collection compiled with Christoph Gottfried Krause, was an early harbinger of the trend toward simpler, more "natural" song settings in Germany.

[36] See Bartha "'Sieben Worte'" and Saam "'sieben Worte'".

Example 5.1: Haydn *Stabat Mater*, I, mm. 20-39

Example 5.2: Haydn *Stabat Mater*, X, mm. 37-59

Example 5.3: Haydn *Il ritorno di Tobia*, 13c, mm. 16-21

Reprinted from Henle HN 5815 (*JHW* 28/2). © 1963 G. Henle, Munich; used by permission.

Example 5.4: Haydn *Il ritorno di Tobia*, 13c, mm. 157-161

Reprinted from Henle HN 5815 (*JHW* 28/2). © 1963 G. Henle, Munich; used by permission.

Example 5.5: Haydn *Philemon und Baucis*, 2, mm. 127-136

Reprinted from Henle HN 5612 (*JHW* 24/1). © 1971 G. Henle, Munich; used by permission.

Example 5.6: Haydn *Philemon und Baucis*, 8, mm. 1-6

Reprinted from Henle HN 5612 (*JHW* 24/1). © 1971 G. Henle, Munich; used by permission.

Example 5.7: Haydn *L'Anima del filosofo*, 2b, mm. 32-55

Reprinted from Henle HN 5752 (*JHW* 25/13). © 1974 G. Henle, Munich; used by permission.

Example 5.8: Haydn *L'Anima del filosofo*, 12, mm. 1-13

Example 5.9: Haydn *Seven Last Words*, 2

Example 5.10a: Haydn *Seven Last Words,* 2, mm. 1-6

Example 5.10b: Haydn *Seven Last Words*, 2, mm. 21-24

Reprinted from Henle HN 5822 (*JHW* 28/2). © 1961 G. Henle, Munich; used by permission.

Example 5.11: Haydn *Seven Last Words*, 2, mm. 67-80

6

SMALLER SACRED WORKS
AFTER 1766

The writing of shorter works for church use occupied Haydn throughout his lifetime. Some of these efforts rank among the eighteenth century's acknowledged masterpieces, while others will be seen as *Gebrauchsmusik*. None of them is unworthy of its creator. Whether he was delivering an "old order" for the Empress or merely coming up with the right piece for an Esterházy funeral, Haydn took his customary care. The result was a body of music that completes the profile of Haydn we find in his Masses and oratorios.

For the reader's convenience, this chapter groups together nearly all the short sacred works, making reference to the discrete chronology and circumstances of each. Only some early works and the first *Te Deum* have been relegated to other parts of the book.[1] This approach should more easily reveal both the distinctive features of each piece and the common stylistic threads that many possess.

THE CASTLE CHAPEL FROM 1771 TO 1785

We have seen that, once Haydn was established as the primary musical leader at the Esterházy court, Prince Nicolaus began to focus ever greater resources on the performance of symphonies, opera, and chamber music. His parallel neglect of the Chormusiker eventually caused it to dwindle to a handful of musicians. In the summer of 1771, Estates Director P. L. Rahier summarized for his Prince the sorry state to which the chapel music establishment had fallen since the death of Capellmeister Werner:

---

[1] Regarding the *Ave Regina*, *Salve Regina* in E, and first *Lauda Sion*, see Chapter 2; the first *Te Deum* is discussed in Chapter 3.

SERENE HIGHNESS AND NOBLE PRINCE OF THE HOLY ROMAN EMPIRE,
GRACIOUS AND DREAD LORD[:]

Since our Choir here only consists of
an Organist
a Discantist [soprano]
a Bassist and
a violinist
in the absence of the rest of the court musicians, it
would be necessary to add
an Altist
a Tenorist
and a violinist,
in my opinion one could engage the daughter of the bass singer Grießler, who for some time has been singing alto without pay, and give her yearly 50 f., Johann Haiden, who has been singing tenor hitherto without pay . . . and the Rent Master Frantz Nigst, who despite the fact that his previous pay of 50 f. and the musician's uniform have been taken away from him, continued to play first violin without neglecting his other duties, and ought in grace to have 50 f. annually given to him; . . . there were, apart from the above musicians, also a violonist [double-bass player], and a bassoon player, but since all the other musicians are mostly here the whole winter period, perhaps these two could be omitted.[2]

Eleonora Jäger, a contralto who had been singing in the chapel choir for almost twenty years, also thought things were now bad enough to warrant writing her own letter to Prince Nicolaus:

Your highness knows that the choir, as it is normally constituted, has to have at least 4 vocal parts, 2 violins and the organ in order to perform the usual kind of music; and this is also a Parish Church with its unavoidable ceremonies, and we are just 4 persons here, and the other 2 have helped out just the last 2 summers because we asked them, and all this is something that a great Prince and Lord doesn't have to put up with, so if Your Highness would turn his attention to the glory of God, it would be to get Grissler's girl who (because I'm singing discant) sings alto, the young Haÿden [Joseph's brother] (because the Schoolmaster plays second fiddle) who has to sing tenor, Nigst who plays first fiddle because Sturm is dead and that Nigst always helped us out, anyway Your Highness could distribute the jobs to these 3 persons from your highest grace, so that our music could be supported a little, and Your Highness has much too much respect for the glory of God to be ungracious with us, and I ask Your Highness this in the greatest submission and in the absence of Haÿden I throw myself at your feet and may it please Your Highness,

I am, Your Highness's
most obedient
Eleonora Jäger, Singer.[3]

---

[2] Quoted and trans. in Landon *HCW* 2, 83.

[3] Quoted and trans. in Landon *HCW* 2, 84.

Rent Master Nigst and the others were hired, and for a time the chapel choir again had four singers, two violinists, and an organist. To augment the basic group, they could probably call upon other persons like Nigst who would play even though their official salaries had been cancelled; there was also the nearby Parish Church of St. Martin, which had its own choir and orchestra. After 1774, records show that one Anton Höld, the Eisenstadt Thurnermeister, was also reimbursed for "services rendered to the Castle Choir in the period in summer when the *Kammer Music* is absent."[4] Höld was listed as a violinist, but his main duty probably was to contract for musicians as needed, especially the trumpeters and drummers that the village Thurnermeister traditionally supervised.

LAUDA SION (RESPONSORIA DE VENERABILI)

Given the vicissitudes of the Castle Chapel music, Haydn might understandably have tried to avoid any compositional duties connected with that group. But in fact he contributed steadily to the Chapel repertory throughout the 1760s and '70s. About the time of the *Stabat Mater* (1767), Haydn also composed the modest four-movement *Lauda Sion* or *Hymnus de venerabili* (XXIIIc:4; hereafter *Lauda* 2) and two "offertories" (i.e., works with nonliturgical texts), *Ens aeternum* (XXIIIa:3) and *Animae Deo gratae* (XXIIIa:2).

With *Lauda* 2 again we have music for Corpus Christi.[5] As the set of parts found in the Kuks Collection at Prague puts it, these are "Quatuor Station / pro Festo Corporis Christi /à / 4tuor Voci Concertandi / Due Violini / Due Corni / Violone/ con / Organo." The composer's autograph having disappeared, the only source for the work is the Kuks manuscript.[6]

This time Haydn chose verses 1-5, 7, 9, and 10 of Thomas Aquinas's sequence for the four stations. Whether he originally intended performance by four solo voices cannot be determined, although it seems likely; by 1768 the opera house at Esterháza had opened, and Haydn along with most of his musicians would have been there for the summer (Corpus Christi fell during June in 1767 and 1768). If *Lauda* 2 was written for the Eisenstadt chapel, probably no more than four singers were available, and not the best. The need to make the most of meager forces seems to be reflected in the writing. There are no solo passages, and the vocal quartet is set throughout in a simple, mostly homophonic texture. A small choir could also easily perform the work.

---

[4] Details in Landon *HCW* 2, 85.

[5] See Chapter 1 for a discussion of the Feast of Corpus Christi; Haydn's first setting of *Lauda Sion* excerpts for this great Feast is described in Chapter 2.

[6] Discovered in 1964 by Irmgard Becker-Glauch. See "Neue Forschungen," 204-206.

Considering its modest resources (even the horn parts[7] should be considered optional), *Lauda* 2 succeeds in offering celebration, strength, and some mystery. The conventionally celebratory movements are I and III; both are in the popular 3/4 style of *Lauda* 1 and other earlier works. Movements II and IV depart from this to bring a wider range of feelings into the piece. In IV, an initial *forte* proclamation (Ex. 6.1) leads ultimately to a quiet plagal cadence. Movement II is the most enigmatic, as shown by its opening measures (Ex. 6.2).

After a good deal of parry and thrust—supplied, respectively, by chromatic harmonies and the dynamic scheme—the movement ends in a plagal cadence, leaving an overall tonal plan of d-F-D. Unlike the other movements, which use repeated musical material to provide a sense of unity (approaching sonata form in I and III), II seems open-ended and incomplete. Perhaps the liturgical situation somehow made it possible to perform III directly after II, with very little intervening ritual.

Becker-Glauch has theorized that the disparate keys (B♭-D-A-E♭) of the four movements, especially the uncommon succession of A major and E♭ major, imply performance at four different churches in Eisenstadt: the Bergkirche, the two cloister churches of the Brothers of Mercy and the Franciscans, and the Parish Church of St. Martin—although the Castle Chapel may have been used as a station instead of one of the others.[8]

ENS AETERNUM; ANIMAE DEO GRATAE

Because of its sophisticated part-writing, *Ens aeternum* was once considered a work of Haydn's from the 1780s. But its violin writing, its rather soloistic vocal style, and its slightly pompous manner are now seen as evidence of an earlier origin. Haydn may have written it for the Order of the Brothers of Mercy (for whom he later composed the *Kleine Orgelmesse*); their chapter in Graz possessed a copy dating from 1772.[9] It was originally scored for chorus, strings, and organ. Later various wind parts were added, but it is unlikely these came from Haydn's hand. The piece begins with a twenty-six-measure instrumental ritornello, the music of which is repeated under the choral entrance (Ex. 6.3).

---

[7] See Becker-Glauch "Remarks," 207.

[8] Becker-Glauch "Neue Forschungen," 205. Berkenstock has suggested a more specific scheme—Franciscans to Brothers of Mercy/Bergkirche to St. Martin's—that would account for both the weakness of the cadence in II and the A-to-E♭ jump between III and IV. The proximity of the Brothers of Mercy and Bergkirche would have meant virtually linked performances of II and III (perhaps, in fact, both were performed at one church); the long walk back to St. Martin's would then have justified the awkward key succession from III to IV. "Smaller Sacred Compositions," 85-89.

[9] See Becker-Glauch "Neue Forschungen," 210-211, for details of the work's sources and dating; also Landon *HCW* 2, 245.

Animae Deo gratae, with its C-major key and slightly fuller scoring, strikes an unabashedly festive note. It is somewhat surprising that this pleasant little work, which in Haydn's time found its way to Mariazell, Göttweig, and the Pitti Palace of Florence, has not yet been printed in a modern edition.[10] Example 6.4 shows the first choral entrance.

SALVE REGINA IN G MINOR

As the 1770s began, Haydn found himself in an enviable position. He had been able to engage a number of fine singers, either Italian or trained in the Italian manner, and had built the strength of his orchestra to about sixteen players, not counting the Castle chapel's small band. Construction of Esterháza, Prince Nicolaus's lavish summer castle, had proceeded far enough that in 1766 the first musical performances could be held there. Although eventually the operatic activities at Esterháza would consume most of Haydn's time, in the early 1770s he was still able to devote himself to a wide range of compositional and performing activities. At least twenty-two symphonies, eighteen string quartets, and a great many piano sonatas, duets, baryton[11] trios, and other works were written between 1768 and 1774; they are among Haydn's most interesting works. During these years his operas *Lo speziale*, *Le pescatrici*, and *L'infedeltà delusa* also received their first performances (*Lo speziale* was even taken to Vienna).

Haydn apparently fell ill later that year. His sickness was serious enough that in 1771 brother Michael was granted leave from Salzburg to visit him. By that time, however, he had recovered and may even have begun to sketch the second *Salve Regina* (XXIIIb:2, hereafter *Salve* 2). At any rate Michael did not make the trip. Haydn himself, in a conversation years later with the Moravian musician Christian Latrobe, spoke of this illness:

> "I was," said [Haydn], "not prepared to die, and prayed to God to have mercy upon me & grant me recovery. I also vowed, that if I were restored to health, I would compose a Stabat Mater in honor of the Blessed Virgin, as a token of thankfulness. My prayer was heard & I recovered. With a grateful sense of my duty, I cheerfully set about the performance of my Vow, & endeavoured to do it in my best manner. . . "The tears glistened in his eyes, while he gave me this account, of which I have remembered the very words.[12]

---

[10] One has been prepared by this author.

[11] The Prince played the baryton, a bass string instrument that is simultaneously bowed from above and plucked from behind. By the end of the eighteenth century it had faded into obscurity.

[12] Quoted in Landon *HCW* 3, 58.

Yet it was not the *Stabat Mater* that Haydn composed at this time, but the deeply devotional G-minor *Salve* 2. In it he indeed displays his "best manner" of the early 1770s, and the result is a small masterwork in the *empfindsamer Stil.*

A comparison of this work's opening measures (Ex. 6.5) with those of the 1756 *Salve* indicates just how much ground the composer had covered in the intervening years. Haydn's new attitude is immediately apparent in the orchestral introduction. Gone are the monumental polar phrases that launched—with drama but also with a sense of grand proportion—his first *Salve.* Instead we are met by a series of off-center utterances that would seem to have sprung from one of Emanuel Bach's Württemberg Sonatas. Indeed, the instrumental parts maintain the intimate quality of keyboard improvisation throughout the movement—aided mainly, of course, by the organ soloist. Note the upward leap of a tenth in measure 1 with which the piece pitches forward, and the ornamentally prolonged semicadence in measure 5, forcing that phrase to linger beyond its expected conclusion. It is shortly followed by four long measures of a syncopated figure. The whole introduction is then capped by the first entrance of the singers, on a German-sixth chord. To this point all has been *piano;* a sudden *forte* now underlines the surprise of the vocalists' arrival. Taken together, these contrivances provide an effective and unsettling way to begin.

One of the paradoxes of this work is that, even though it takes several minutes longer to perform, its scale seems much smaller than that of the 1756 *Salve.* Haydn has matched his singular expressions here to the more subjective sounds of solo quartet[13] and organist, supported by a modest string group. That is a Romantic way of looking at it, of course. The far greater probability is that the composer, faced with the customary meager resources for church music at Eisenstadt Castle, turned those constraints to advantage in the process of casting the piece in the "expressive style."[14] A further indication of the scant number of musicians available (and their quality?) can be seen in the avoidance of a full-blown aria anywhere in the work. The closest Haydn comes is in the tenor's ten-measure "Et Jesum," which serves as slow introduction to the third and final movement. Its tempo, arioso quality, and broken string accompaniment are highly reminiscent of the tenor arias in the *Cäcilienmesse* and the "Great" Organ Mass. Soprano and alto are allotted brief expository solos in the second movement ("Eja ergo"), a C-minor Allegro in 3/8. Other-

---

[13] The autograph specifies "Quattro voci ma Soli," but we have elected to discuss it as a choral work, since it is more likely to be performed today by some kind of larger vocal ensemble. The parts can be easily divided into soli and tutti passages; see this work's listing in Chapter 11.

[14] In a concise and persuasive presentation at the 1975 International Haydn Conference, Walter Pass compared melodic style in the two *Salve Regina* settings. The relative absence of Neapolitan melodic patterns and coloratura passages in the G-minor *Salve* contributes greatly to its quality of intimacy and individuality, of course. Pass outlined this change and also provocatively suggested that Haydn responded to the loss of Neapolitan decoration as a primary (expressive) element by altering word order; see Pass "Melodic Construction," esp. 373. The reader may notice that we have forborne referring to this style of Haydn's as *personal.* Although it radiated "individualism" as a matter of course, the *Sturm und Drang* manner was no more self-expressive for Haydn than any of his other masks.

wise, Haydn relies heavily on the collective strength of the quartet, using occasional voice pairing or loosened homophony to provide a variety of textures.

Example 6.6 shows two of the devices used to unify *Salve* 2. At the end of the tenor arioso, the solo organ again comes forth with a descending four-note motive first heard in the first movement (Ex. 6.5, mm. 1-16); in fact it is the same phrase as that of Example 6.5, measure 11, and it is followed by a vocal entrance identical with Example 6.5, measure 12. By this time the motive is recognizable as a prime organizing factor in the solo organ part, having been used throughout the first two movements. Its transformation into the propulsive figure of Example 6.6a, measures 16-18, 20-22, etc. seems only natural. Likewise the quartet's German-sixth sonority is replaced by a prominent diminished seventh (that is, $V°/6/5$ of V becomes $V°/9\flat$ of I) as the third-movement Allegretto gets underway. That seventh is echoed poignantly in the concluding measures of the work (Ex. 6.6b). As with his first *Salve* setting, Haydn has triumphed over circumstance to create something of considerable beauty.

LIBERA ME, DOMINE

The Prince's chapel choir subsisted on minimal resources throughout the 1780s, and Haydn seems to have had little time or inclination to compose for it. Aside from the *Kleine Orgelmesse*, which could readily be done by small forces, only one other work written in this period reflects musical realities at Eisenstadt Castle.

That is the *Libera me, Domine* (XXIIb:1) for tenor solo, mixed choir, string trio, and organ. A set of parts, mostly in Haydn's own hand, was discovered in 1966 at the Cathedral Church of St. Martin in Eisenstadt.[15] No autograph score has been found, and no reference is made to the work in any of Haydn's or Elssler's catalogs. For these reasons, and also on stylistic grounds, the piece's authenticity has been doubted.[16] It is quite possible that Haydn copied and/or adapted the work from another source. Evidence indicates that he was asked to provide a bit of service music for an important Esterházy burial and found himself pressed for time. That occasion may have been the death of Princess Marie Elisabeth, wife of Prince Nicolaus I, on February 25, 1790. At that point Haydn would have been at Esterháza, absorbed in opera productions. Robbins Landon theorized that a memorial service for the Princess was held soon afterward at St. Martin's and that Haydn's *Libera* was written for that occasion, hurriedly copied, and dispatched there by courier. He also speculated that it might have been intended to round out a D-minor setting of the Requiem by Gregor Werner, which music St. Martin's church already had.[17]

---

[15] See Landon "'Responsorium.'"

[16] Cf. Georg Feder's Worklist in Larsen *New Grove Haydn*, 125.

[17] Landon "'Responsorium,'" 143-144.

This *Libera me* is an *alternatim* setting of the Responsory of Absolution, that part of the Catholic burial service sung immediately after the Requiem Mass. The tenor soloist sings phrases from the service's Gregorian chant (a unison ensemble could be substituted). These phrases are interspersed with homophonic choral settings in severest *stile antico* that continue the ritual text; the strings double the choral lines throughout.

Readers may find it hard to believe that the composer of the "Surprise" Symphony could also resort to such antique language. If so, they should look back at the *Cäcilienmesse* "Gratias," or ahead to the offertory *Non nobis Domine*, composed probably between 1790 and 1795 (see below).

NON NOBIS DOMINE

Two short sacred choral works can be traced to Haydn's years in England. One is the *stile antico* offertory *Non nobis Domine* (XXIIIa:1), whose text (Psalm 115:1), "Not unto us O Lord, but unto thy name give glory," received its widest circulation in William Byrd's famous canon. Musically speaking, these words had gone virtually unused in Austria before 1800. That, along with a preponderance of other evidence, makes it fairly safe to assume that the work was inspired by the English visit and composed between 1790 and 1795 (revised ca. 1802).[18]

Non nobis Domine is thus Haydn's last contribution to the old a cappella tradition he had cultivated throughout his life. Its closest relative within the composer's own body of works is the recently rediscovered *Missa Sunt bona mixta malis*. Both pieces are in D minor and have similar thematic material.[19] The present work ends with a powerful section of pedal point (Ex. 6.7), showing the wonders that can be wrung from an obsolete style by the hand of a master.

SIX ENGLISH PSALMS

In December of 1794, the Reverend William Dechair Tattersall published the first volume of an *Improved Psalmody*, settings of the psalms for three voices using Merrick's metrical poetry. Tattersall's aim was to "silence the many ludicrous reflections, that are perpetually cast upon our psalmody" by making more attractive melodies in easy harmonizations available for congregational singing. To this end, the Reverend Tattersall and his

---

[18] Haydn owned two copies of Byrd's canon, one in his copy of Mattheson's *Der vollkommene Kapellmeister* and the other a printed arrangement by his London friend Joseph Diettenhofer, *The Celebrated Canon. Non nobis Domine, adapted as a Fugue for the Organ*. For a history of the work's varied dating, probable revision, etc., see Landon *HCW* 4, 77-78, and esp. Becker-Glauch "Neue Forschungen," 224-228.

[19] For a discussion of this work and the curious details of its recent recovery, see Chapter 4.

contributors were "all perfectly agreed that plainness and simplicity are the grand criterion, that ought to guide us."[20] In his Preface, Tattersall waxed eloquent about the current state of congregational psalm-singing in England:

> The performance of the psalmody in London is open to many objections. Whatever be the subject of the psalm, the tunes that are chosen, are very solemn, and, in most of the parish churches they are rendered still more solemn, by the slow manner, in which they are usually played. The clerk and the charity children are almost the only performers, and although a person is employed to instruct the young people, nevertheless there seems to be no management in the regulation of their voices. Each child seems to think it necessary to be heard, in consequence of which, instead of that easy and pleasing manner . . . [customary] at the Magdalen, the Asylum, and other places . . . the children most commonly rise beyond the natural pitch of their voices, and it becomes rather a general unisonous scream. . . .
>
> In country parishes, the psalms are chosen, that consist of four parts, and it is thought by the people, who form themselves into a choir, that their performance will be very defective, if they do not contrive to fill them all. . . . The harmony is generally very indifferent; but if it were faultless, the counter tenors [i.e., high male voices] are for the most part poorly managed. On this account I have been very anxious to restrain the tunes to two trebles and a bass, that singers of this class may not be induced to attempt things beyond their ability.
>
> . . . The congregation and children, led and supported by good voices, should join in the upper part. In the choir the treble should be divided, half to the first, half to the second: men's voices may join each part according to their compass, and there should be a sufficient number of basses to support them all, which parts can be performed by men only. In singing different stanzas to the same tune, a long note may occasionally meet a short syllable, or the contrary; but this may be tempered with a little care.[21]

Haydn was in England when Volume One was being compiled (see Chapter 7) and contributed six psalm settings to the effort. They deserve to become much better known. The melodies to these *Six English Psalms* (XXIII:Nachtrag) seem already familiar the first time we hear them, but they are not borrowed from other works. Instead they form one more example of Haydn's success at composing "popular" music, as direct and accessible as any British or Austrian folk song. Most of the settings are homophonic and strophic in the manner of hymns. But the imitative, through-composed Psalm 41 runs to 93 measures. Its opening strophe (verse 12) is given here as Example 6.8.

Verse 15, which ends on the words "To him through endless ages raise / One song of oft repeated praise," inspires Haydn to a buildup of phrases reminiscent of the climactic

---

[20] Tattersall *Psalmody*, preliminary "Advertisement."

[21] The final paragraph seems to imply that some men may join in singing the upper two parts, but (considering the author's dislike of "counter tenors") possibly an octave lower. That would parallel the practice of the "singing schools" led in early North American by Billings and others; Tattersall *Improved Psalmody*, 14-16.

passages in "The heavens are telling": polyphony alternates with declamation, masterful *piano* sections appear, tessituras stretch ever higher, note values longer, and the whole effort is capped with a powerful unison restatement of the opening melody.

Like Psalm 41, Psalm 50 has a heroic character; its twenty-six measures anticipate the Credos of the late Masses and whole choruses in *The Creation*. The other psalms receive more *gemütlich* settings marked by triple meter, slow to moderate tempos, and impeccably constructed melodies like the one for Psalm 61 (Ex. 6.9).

TE DEUM FOR EMPRESS MARIE THERESE

The first reference made by Haydn or any of his contemporaries to the remarkable second *Te Deum* occurs in a letter written in the spring of 1799 to Breitkopf & Härtel by Georg August Griesinger. Griesinger, who would later become Haydn's first biographer, was acting as an agent for the publisher and had just succeeded in making his first contact with the composer. But the only news Griesinger could report was that Haydn appeared to be "swamped with business," including "old orders for the Empress . . . and many other wealthy Viennese" and would have little to offer for publication in the near future.[22] His "old order" was the *Te Deum*; it received its first performance on September 8, 1800, at Eisenstadt in lieu of the new Mass Haydn customarily provided during this period for his Princess Marie Hermenegild. We know of no specific performance for the Empress.[23]

After this work was resurrected in the late 1950s by H. C. Robbins Landon, it became one of the most popular of all Haydn's choral pieces. Brief and full of life, it is completely dominated by the chorus, which appears in all but 17 of its 194 measures; there are no soloists. The choral writing is good enough to make even a competent performance without orchestra enjoyable.

In many ways the second *Te Deum* is a compendium of the devices by which Haydn renewed sacred music in his time without loosening its ties to a magnificent past. Thus the first theme heard is a recasting of the Eighth Psalm Tone—and by no means is it a hidden reference:[24]

VIII Ctávus Tónus sic incípi-tur, sic fléctitur, † et sic medi- átur.*   Te, te De - um lau-da - mus;

---

[22] Quoted in Landon *HCW* 4, 466; from Olleson "Griesinger," 9.

[23] See Chapter 8 for further historical details.

[24] The idea put forth earlier by Robbins Landon (*Symphonies*, 262) and Geiringer ("Small Sacred Works," 468) that the *Te Deum* chant melody is found in the inner voices is now considered fallacious.

The concluding section begins as a double fugue, yet veers into less confining counter-point to build a powerful climax. Its exposition opens at a high level of energy and with every appearance of strictness, but the treatment soon assumes a textural freedom allowing it first to reach a crisis worthy of any of the late symphonies (Ex. 6.10) and then to resolve with Wagnerian expansiveness.

Between psalm tone and fugue lie three major sections, as in the first *Te Deum*.[25] And, as in the earlier work, C major is the overall key. But there are important differences between the two. The concluding fugue is treated more strictly in the first *Te Deum*. The orchestration is imcomparably richer and more skillful in the second. Form also seems tighter in the second: its first section is a clearly delineated sonata structure, its middle section a more elegantly unified Adagio. Note the simple power of this Adagio's first two measures (Ex. 6.11). Besides being an effective contrast to the bustle of the preceding section, they are mimetic of the congregation, which must kneel at this point. This second *Te Deum* is another example of music by Haydn that lay virtually forgotten for a century and a half, yet is today widely performed and appreciated.

Example 6.1a: Haydn *Lauda* 2, IV, mm. 1-10

Reprinted from Henle HN 184. © 1965 G. Henle, Munich; used by permission.

---

[25] Robbins Landon pointed to an emphasis on "three-ness" in the work that fits its Trinitarian text well. In the first section, cast in modified sonata or ABA form, Haydn takes care to iterate portions of the text ("Sanctus," mm. 28-30) or musical figures ("aperuisti eredentibus regna caelorum") three times; *HCW* 4, 607.

Example 6.2: Haydn *Lauda* 2, II, mm. 1-15

Reprinted from Henle HN 184. © 1965 G. Henle, Munich; used by permission.

Example 6.3: Haydn *Ens aeternum*, mm. 25-30

Example 6.4: Haydn *Animae Deo gratae*, mm. 15-19

Example 6.5: Haydn *Salve Regina* in G Minor, I, mm. 1-16

Example 6.6a: Haydn *Salve Regina* in G Minor, III, mm. 8-29

Example 6.6b: Haydn *Salve Regina* in G Minor, III, mm. 183-202

Example 6.7: Haydn *Non nobis Domine*, mm. 101-130

Example 6.8: Haydn "Maker of All" (Ps. 41), mm. 1-20

Example 6.9: Haydn "Long life shall Israel's king behold" (Ps. 61), mm. 1-8

Example 6.10: Haydn *Te Deum* 2, mm. 174-186, strings and vocal lines

Example 6.11: Haydn *Te Deum* 2, mm. 83-86, strings and vocal lines

7

LATE SECULAR MUSIC

HAYDN IN LONDON

In 1790 Princess Maria Elizabeth Esterházy and then Prince Nicolaus died, whereupon the *Burgherrschaft* passed into the hands of Anton Esterházy. Not a music lover like his father, he quickly dismissed all the chamber musicians except Haydn and his concertmaster Tomasini. The Feldmusik and the meager chapel choir remained, while Haydn was allowed to continue as titular Capellmeister with no real responsibilities. He moved to Vienna, intending to enjoy at last a more relaxed existence than he had known in his years at Esterháza.

This long-sought peace was not to be. Johann Peter Salomon, German violinist and London concert impresario, was on the Continent when he heard of Prince Nicolaus's death. Sensing that Haydn might now be free to consider other offers, Salomon quickly traveled to Vienna. There he introduced himself to the composer and won him over ("I am Salomon from London and have come to fetch you. Tomorrow we shall conclude an agreement."). Joseph Haydn, fifty-eight years old and now a man of some leisure, agreed to compose a new opera, six new symphonies, and twenty other works to be performed in London under his own direction, for which he would be paid a great deal more than he had received for such tasks during his years with Prince Nicolaus.

Haydn ended up making not one but two trips to England, from January 1791 to June 1792 and from February 1794 to August 1795. The twelve "London" symphonies are the best-known products of the period 1791-95, but they reflect only a part of his rich experiences abroad. He was deeply impressed by the Handel Commemoration of 1791 and by other choral concerts, making them touchstones of his memory during the years when he fashioned his own greatest choral works. And besides encountering London's great public concerts, its professional orchestras and able choirs, Haydn was constantly involved in informal and amateur music-making among the English that stimulated him in other directions.

London's musical vitality must have astonished the composer. Of course he had had some idea of the excellent orchestras that London could boast. At the time of his first visit a group of forty players was the norm; during his second visit he used a group of about sixty. A contemporary account, published just before Haydn's arrival, offers a few more details about the professional concert life of the great city:

> The musical arrangements now making promise a most *harmonious* winter.
>
> Besides two rival *Opera* houses, a Concert is planned under the auspices of *Haydn*, whose name is a tower of strength, and to whom the *amateurs* of instrumental music look up as a *god* of science. Of this concert *Salomon* is to be the leader, and *Madame Mara* the principal singer.
>
> The professional concert under the able conduct of *Cramer*, is to be reinforced by Mrs. Billington, assisted occasionally by Mr. and Mrs. Harrison.
>
> The *Antient* concert under the patronage of their Majesties will continue soon after the Queen's Birth-day, with Cramer as their leader and Storace as the principal singer. The *Ladies subscription concert* is to be continued as usual on the Sunday evenings by permission (we hope) of his Grace the Archbishop of Canterbury.
>
> There will be Oratorios twice a week, at the Theatres of Drury-Lane and Covent-garden during Lent.
>
> These with the *Academy of Antient Music* will constitute the principal public musical entertainments of the winter.[1]

Besides Mara, Cramer, and Nancy Storace (Mozart's first Susanna), many other well-known musicians were in London when Haydn arrived. The composer Gyrowetz, an old friend, helped him get around in English society. The pianists Muzio Clementi and Jan Ladislav Dussek were also cordial; even Ignatz Pleyel, a former pupil now dubbed Haydn's "rival" by the journalists, took time to dine and walk with his old master.

In fact Londoners from every walk of life showered Haydn with kindnesses, showing him a nearly oppressive hospitality. Early in his stay he wrote to Maria Anna von Genzinger in Vienna, "Everyone wants to know me. I had to dine out 6 times up to now, and if I wanted, I could dine out every day."[2] In this regard, it is important to remember the significant role that amateur music-making occupied in London society. As he made his way from one fashionable town house or country estate to another, the composer invariably found himself at the keyboard, surrounded by household Apollos and Cecilias. Throughout his English stay, Haydn the social musician—whether as keyboardist or as string player in so-called "quartet parties"—was a prize keenly sought.

---

[1] The *Morning Chronicle*, December 30, 1790; quoted in Landon *HCW* 3, 31.

[2] Quoted in Landon *HCW* 3, 36.

Haydn's diverse London experiences provided him an opportunity to compose a number of short secular choral works, to which we have added for discussion here those pieces written later but strongly influenced by the same experiences. This chapter accordingly treats three categories of his late secular music: music in informal style or for social occasions, i.e., canons, catches, and glees; partsongs; and single-movement orchestrally accompanied works.

CANONS, CATCHES, AND GLEES

Chief among Haydn's "informal" pieces from his time in London are the set of canons known as *The Ten Commandments* (XXVIIa:1-10). Between 1791 and 1799 he also wrote many other canons (XXVIIb:1-47) as delightful as the *Heiligen Zehn Gebote*, an "Italian catch" (Haydn called it a *Maccone*) now lost but extremely popular during the first London visit, and keyboard accompaniments for twelve catches and glees by an English nobleman.

It is not surprising that the English had long since invented various handy forms to accommodate their appetite for music at social gatherings. Two such forms were the catch and the glee. A catch is an unaccompanied round or canon at the unison for three or more male voices, often featuring a suggestive text. Such works had been popular in England since the sixteenth century. By Haydn's time, a number of well-organized clubs were meeting "at taverns of convenient distance from each other" in order to sing catches under a competent musical director.[3] These groups also sang glees, which are distinguished from catches by their simple homophony and less vulgar words. A glee might even be suitable for singing in mixed company; as the clubs began to hold ladies' nights, the production of more such refined catches and glees became a priority. Haydn himself took part in this form of convivial concertizing, although he did so not with amateurs, but with Oxford alumni:

> This eminent man became a member of the *Society of Musical Graduates*, to whom he would often express the great pleasure which he felt in hearing glees, adding, with a smile, "Ah! if I were to stay long enough in England, I would study and write glees myself!" and he evinced his respect for the society, by presenting it with a canon on the first commandment, composed both in three and four parts, which is read forwards and backwards, then inverted, and sung in the same manner.[4]

---

[3] Henry Playford, 1702, quoted in Jack Westrup, "Catch," *New Grove* 3, 7.

[4] Crosse *Account*, 273n.

That canon (Ex. 7.1) was the same work (with the text "Thy voice, O Harmony, is divine") Haydn presented to the faculty at Oxford University when, in 1791, he was honored with a Doctor of Music degree. By the end of his second London visit, Haydn had completed all of *The Ten Commandments* and dedicated them to Count Hans Moritz von Brühl, the Saxon Minister to England. He continued to write canons for the remainder of his life, often framing fair copies of them to adorn the walls of his house in Vienna. In 1810 his total accumulation was published by Breitkopf & Härtel in two editions, *The Ten Commandments* and *Forty-Two Canons*.[5] A reviewer for the *Allgemeine Musikalische Zeitung* wrote:

> The character of these pieces is, as the text requires, almost throughout a solemn one, and the composition is simple and easy. . . . The Canons are, by the way, all without accompaniment, and in two-, three-, up to eight-parts. . . . The great artist, who more, perhaps, than anyone else of the modern age, understood not only with simple means but also in a restricted genre to express himself completely and easily, has made only very moderate demands in the vocal parts: any feminine, and any masculine, voice, who is not just a high tenor or a low bass voice, can perform these Canons.[6]

We would only qualify this by adding that these works are not so "simple and easy" that they can be performed successfully without the same attention to correctness of pitch and rhythm, and refinement of musical expression, that any other good music should receive—they do not make much of an effect at first reading. Performers should also be aware of that very important *almost* in the reviewer's phrase "almost throughout a solemn [character]." For in a number of the canons, Haydn's impish sense of humor is freely at play. The Sixth Commandment is quoted here as Example 7.2; note the effect of the meter and the occasional chromaticism. The Ninth Commandment, "Thou shalt not covet thy neighbor's wife," is like unto it, combining a mock-pompous tempo and *parlando* text setting to give a pronounced tongue-in-cheek effect.

Nevertheless Haydn seems to have largely avoided the kind of scatalogical humor that made Mozart's canons notorious—and led to their frequent expurgation. Some of Haydn's canon texts have also been altered over the years for one or another reason (even Breitkopf & Härtel indulged in this practice). That is particularly unfortunate in the case of the more "solemn" pieces. Taken with their original texts, they are often among Haydn's best music—as Example 7.3, a dignified and simple setting of an epigram by Horace, makes clear.

The story of Haydn's "faithful dog" canon provides a good example of the spirit and circumstances in which most of these works were created. In 1794, Haydn sojourned in the English countryside, including a stop at Bath. There he visited the composer Henry

---

[5] The actual German titles were *Die Heiligen Zehn Gebote als Canons* and *40 [sic] Sinngedichte als Canons*, fifty-six canons in all have come down to us.

[6] *Allgemeine Musikalische Zeitung*, December 12, 1810, 1006ff. Quoted in Landon *HCW* 3, 358-359.

Harington (see below) and was a houseguest of the famous castrato Venanzio Rauzzini, who had retired to the area in 1787. Rauzzini was the soprano for whom Mozart had written the motet *Exsultate, jubilate* (K. 165) some twenty years earlier; he in turn became Storace's teacher. In one of his London notebooks, Haydn described his visit in interesting detail.[7] But it was Dies who provided an account of Haydn's gift to the old singer:

> Rauzzini had placed in his garden a monument to the honor of his best friend, whom death had snatched away from him. He lamented, in an inscription, the loss of a friend so true, etc., and concluded his lament with the words: "He was not a man—he was a dog."
>
> Haydn copied the inscription in secret, and made a four-part canon to which he set the words. Rauzzini was surprised. The canon pleased him so much that he had it carved on the monument to the honor of Haydn and of the dog.[8]

The actual words on the monument were "Turk was a faithful dog—and not a man." It is said that in his well-known canon (XXVIIb:45), Haydn preserved not only Rauzzini's inscription but also a famous old bell-chime he may have heard in Bath.[9]

We began this section by briefly discussing catches and glees, and we cannot go on without filling in what is known about Haydn's most celebrated catch, the *Maccone* he wrote for the Gallini concerts of 1791 (see below). It was in seven parts, at least to judge from the newspaper announcements ("a CATCH . . . / Sung by . . . / Signoras MAFFEI, SESTINI, CAPPELLETTI; Signors CAPPELLETTI, TAJANA, ALBERTARELLI, / And Signor DAVID.").[10] And it was a large-scale piece (filling "6 sheets," or twenty-four pages, of manuscript paper), to judge from Haydn's description of it in his *Catalogue of Works Composed in England*.[11] Its first performance took place on June 2. It was then repeated at the Gallini concerts of June 4, 6, 7, 10, 18, and 21 that year, so it must have been quite popular. No copy of the work has yet turned up, however, so we must await its recovery before further descriptions—or any performances—can be given.

Although the *Maccone* was included at orchestral concerts, it was doubtless performed in the customary manner, without accompaniment. Later Haydn would break with this tradition. Around 1794 his friend Willoughby Bertie, Earl of Abingdon, induced him to write "Harp or Piano-Forte" accompaniments to *Twelve Sentimental Catches and Glees* (XXXIc:16) for which the Earl himself had written the melodies. Haydn probably became

---

[7] See Landon *HCW* 3, 266-267, or Geiringer *Haydn*, 145.

[8] Dies *Nachrichten* (3), 153.

[9] Among his notes on Bath (Landon *HCW* 3, 266), Haydn had written, "Every Monday and Friday evening all the bells are rung." The chime is expressed in the pattern of descending thirds, mm. 3ff. of the canon. See Mansfield *Bath*, 201ff.

[10] The *Morning Chronicle*, June 1, 1791; quoted in Landon *HCW* 3, 79.

[11] Described in Landon *HCW* 3, 72ff., from which we have gratefully drawn the other details furnished here (the catalogue itself is given in 316-317).

acquainted with Lord Abingdon while visiting his country estate. He was an amateur musician and, one gathers, something of an eccentric. In one of his London notebooks, Haydn jotted this amusing story:

> Lord Avington [*sic*] had an organ built in the church on his estate. When the Archbishop of the diocese heard about it, he wrote a letter reproving him for having done this without his knowledge, inasmuch as one cannot do such a thing without previously informing the authorities. He got an answer: The Lord gave it, and the Lord can take it away again. This is most ambiguous, but very good.[12]

Later Abingdon was convicted and sent to prison after a notorious libel trial in London; he had written and published accusations "of the most scandalous and malignant nature" against one Thomas Sermon, an attorney of Gray's Inn and could find no attorney willing to defend him at court.[13]

Lord Abingdon's *Catches and Glees* turn out to be trifling but pleasant pieces. The vocal settings are all for three voices in treble clef (i.e., equal voices) and of an undemanding technical nature. Similarly, Haydn's accompaniments can be read at sight by a moderately well-trained amateur. One of the catches is reproduced in its entirety here as Example 7.4. Bear in mind that it is to be sung as a round, with singer A singing the first line alone, then proceeding to the second line while singer B commences with the first line, and so forth. The little ritornello at the end is to be played only at the conclusion of the piece, after each voice has entered in turn and sung at least one line.

PARTSONGS

Haydn began his foray into the partsong genre with a ditty he christened *Dr. Harington's Compliment* (XXVIb:3). We owe the survival of this little-known piece to the composer himself, who took a copy back with him to Vienna and eventually sold it to Breitkopf & Härtel. It was written in 1794 while Haydn was visiting Henry Harington. Dr. Harington, founder of the Harmonic Society of Bath, had written Haydn a welcoming poem, "What Art expresses." To return the compliment, Haydn set it to music that must have been particularly suited to Dr. Harington's circle.

The piece begins as if it were a song for soprano in A major. But after one verse with eight-measure keyboard introduction and interlude, it becomes a vocal quartet with keyboard accompaniment, repeating the words of Harington's poem. That gives way, after a scant thirteen measures, to a section more than twice as long: *variazione*—including a very

---

[12] Haydn *CCLN*, 300f.; quoted in Landon *HCW* 3, 271.

[13] Quotation and details from the *Sporting Magazine* (London) for February 1795; see Landon *HCW* 3, 289-290.

empfindsamer A-minor interlude—for the keyboard alone. Then the soprano solo and the major tonality return, while the keyboard continues in its *variazione* texture. The quartet is not heard from again. All of this makes for a rather curiously shaped work; it is not so curious, however, that it could not make a nice effect within a group of other partsongs or *Lieder* by Haydn, Mozart, Schubert, or Brahms. A good pianist is required.

Haydn's finest efforts inspired by English social music came after he had left England for the second time. In 1796 he began composing a series of partsongs for three or four voices with keyboard accompaniment.[14] Old age and other responsibilities prevented him from completing more than thirteen, although he seems to have planned a set of twenty-four or -five.[15] The thirteen were completed by 1799 and published by Breitkopf & Härtel in 1803; these *Mehrstimmige Gesänge* (*Aus des Ramlers Lyrischer Blumenlese*) (XXVb:1-4; XXVc:1-8) have since become favorites with singers and choral directors alike. Stylistically they cast a fond glance backward, both at Rococo German poetry and the convivial social music of London. A German critic of Haydn's time gave as good a summary of their virtues as we are ever likely to have:

> The collection itself consists of comic, serious, and religious songs, which are not only beautifully and intelligently composed but are also especially satisfactory exercises for smaller singing groups. They are all in the fugal style and this requires each singer to pay attention. The use of the fugal style for the comic pieces, the simplicity of the accompaniment, the lovely and unfettered expression which abounds in each part: all this is as new as it is instructive for young composers in our times, when everything is calculated to the vast effect of instrumental accompaniment. One sees here how easy, natural and flowing is a good leadership of several simultaneous parts for one who was trained in the best school and is master of the tones. If only the noble Haydn would deign to present the world with more examples of this kind, in particular on religious, Latin or German Bible texts! The comic is certainly not to be spurned; yet we have a great deal of the comic nowadays and not nearly enough of the serious and religious.[16]

As a prelude to remarks about the chronology and character of these pieces, here is a list of the partsongs' titles and voicings in the order of their first publication:

1. *Der Augenblick.* ("The Moment") SATB

---

[14] One trio and three quartets have simple accompaniments; the others are actually furnished only with a continuo line, implying accompaniment by keyboard and (if desired) a bass instrument such as cello.

[15] In reference to these plans, the Swedish diplomat F. S. Silverstolpe noted that "[Haydn] sang some arias for me which he intends to issue by subscription when their number reaches 24" (letter of June 14, 1797, quoted in Landon *HCW* 4, 255). And G. A. Griesinger, acting in his capacity as an agent for Breitkopf, told the publisher that "Haydn is holding off until there are a full twenty-five, for 'nowadays if I am going to print something, it has to be a bit big.'" (letter of ca. December 16, 1801, from Pohl *Haydn* 3, 336; quoted in Olleson "Griesinger," 29.).

[16] Anonymous review in Leipzig's *Allgemeine Musikalische Zeitung* 5 (1803), 799ff.; trans. in Landon *HCW* 4, 193.

2. *Die Harmonie in der Ehe* ("Harmony in Marriage") SATB
3. *Alles hat seine Zeit* ("Everything has its Day") SATB
4. *Die Beredsamkeit* ("Eloquence") SATB
5. *Der Greis* ("The Old Man") SATB
6. *An den Vetter* ("Cousin") TTB
7. *Daphnens einziger Fehler* ("Daphne's One Flaw") TTB
8. *Die Warnung* ("An Admonition") SATB
9. *Betrachtung des Todes* ("Reflection on Death") STB
10. *Wider den Übermut* ("Invocation") SATB
11. *An die Frauen* ("On Women") TTB
12. *Aus dem Danklied zu Gott* ("Thanksgiving Song") SATB
13. *Abendlied zu Gott* ("Evening Song to God") SATB

This numbering reflects the approximate order in which the partsongs were composed, as can be deduced from the texts used and the accompaniment. Nos. 1-9 were all composed in 1796; instead of an actual keyboard accompaniment, Haydn provided only a figured bass (which Breitkopf realized in their edition). The texts of the first seven pieces (also of the eleventh) are taken from a collection of poems entitled *Lyrischer Blumenlese*, assembled by the poet and critic C. W. Ramler (1725-98). Haydn probably had intended to draw words for the whole set from Ramler's collection, but in the end he turned to other sources: no. 8 is a translation by Hagedorn of an anonymous Greek poem; nos. 9, 10, 12, and 13 are from C. F. Gellert's *Geistliche Oden und Lieder* (1757) and cast a decided religious tone on the latter part of the set. The last four pieces were composed between 1796 and 1799 and feature complete (i.e., right hand/left hand) keyboard accompaniments.[17]

One would not expect the old Haydn, whose literary tastes were in any case formed haphazardly, to look to the rising generation of poets for pieces written "*con amore* in happy hours, not to order."[18] Instead Haydn sought familiar voices from his youth. Ramler was a well-known literary figure slightly older than the composer; his *Tod Jesu* had served as the basis for the text of Haydn's *Seven Last Words* in its choral version.[19] Friedrich von Hagedorn (1708-1754) had brought a new grace and lightness of touch to German verse in his time; today his work is often simply lumped together with the frivolous pastel art of the German Anacreontics. Christian Fürchtegott Gellert (1715-1769) wrote religious poems and hymns that combined piety with the rationalism of the Enlightenment. Singers may associate his name with Beethoven, who set Gellert's famous "Die Ehre Gottes aus der Natur." No doubt it was Gellert's directness and simplicity, not his moralizing, that appealed to Haydn.

---

[17] Landon *HCW* 4, 189-190, provides details of the evidence from watermarks, etc., which further support this chronology.

[18] As he told Griesinger in 1801; see Pohl *Haydn* 3, 336, or Olleson "Griesinger," 29.

[19] See Chapter 5.

From a musical standpoint, even the simplest of these songs shows its composer's experienced hand. One of the best demonstrations of Haydn's "fugal" style in the service of comedy is No. 8, *Die Warnung*. Its opening measures (Ex. 7.5) provide a sensation similar to that of watching a horror film: one can enjoy being a bit frightened and be further amused by one's fright, a *very* Classical balance of dread and delight. The composer's ability to quickly change texture and tonality provides an added pleasure.

No. 5, *Der Greis*, evokes considerable pathos, not least because Haydn used its first two lines ("Gone is all my strength, / Old and weak am I") for his calling card during his declining years. The infirmities of age are deftly called to mind by the music's short, limping phrases. But the most moving part of the song comes when the composer first acknowledges Death (Ex. 7.6, m. 17) and then fearlessly welcomes it as his fate (m. 21). This is part of a series of strong dramatic contrasts on an intimate scale, calling to mind some of Schubert's best songs,[20] yet here it is handled with the abiding calm of one fortunate enough to have lived much longer and in a different age. A work like *Der Greis* is actually more Romantic than—to name something often linked with Romanticism—the "Chaos" prelude to *The Creation*: the former is a personal utterance and structurally episodic, whereas the latter is impersonal and highly unified in its structure (see the discussion in Chapter 9).

The range of these partsongs cannot really be encompassed by quoting short excerpts from a couple, of course. There is a clever bit of theatre at the end of No. 4, *Die Beredsamkeit*, that the reader will need to discover for him- or herself. And no musician should be denied the full experience of No. 13, *Abendlied zu Gott*. It is one of those works of great feeling and utter simplicity that imparts a transcendant awareness of the human condition.

Haydn first performed seven of these songs on October 16, 1799, at an "academy" in Eisenstadt held in the home of Provost Andreas Seitz. Like many other things we know about Haydn's activities in his old age, we know this because one Joseph Carl Rosenbaum, a young official in the Esterházy administration, kept a careful diary of events that concerned him at Eisenstadt. He was very fond of music—and of the lovely soprano Therese Gassmann, who sang many solo parts in Haydn's late works.

> In the evening Therese came to me gaily, and we went to the Provost's to hear the academy. There were several pieces from [Peter von Winter's] *Das unterbrochene Opfer Fest*, Pölt played a piano sonata by Haydn, [the young] Tomasini played variations by his father on the violin, and Haydn, at popular request, did 7 new

---

[20] For example, *Der Tod und das Mädchen* or the version of *Gesang der Geister über den Wassern* for male octet and strings, Op. 167.

German Songs, which are unusually lovely. — The young Prince and Princess were there with several of the Court and a few of the clergy.[21]

That performance was doubtless with a solo quartet. But the German critic quoted above felt the songs would work well with "smaller singing groups," and we know of at least one large-scale performance of Nos. 12 and 13. In 1804 Haydn wrote to Karl Friedrich Zelter, urging him to "go to the trouble of taking Gellert's Abend Lied . . . from my score, and arrange it for his whole choir, alternating 4 soloists with the semi-chorus and full chorus."[22] Zelter replied that he had in fact already arranged the last two numbers and performed them with his 200-voice Singakademie:

> I do wish I could give you the pleasure of hearing your choruses sung here. . . . The best and finest youths of Berlin assemble here with their fathers and mothers, like a heaven filled with angels, praising in joy and honor the glory of Almighty God, and practising the works of the greatest master the world has yet seen.[23]

ORCHESTRALLY ACCOMPANIED WORKS

Only a handful of choral-orchestral efforts were actually composed for London: *1)* a "madrigal," *The Storm* (XXIVa:8), *2) Mare Clausum* (XXIVa:9), a fragment from a projected oratorio (to be discussed in the next chapter), and *3,4)* two pieces adapted from earlier music, "Su cantiamo, su beviamo" (ii, 433) and an "Italian oratorio chorus" with new words by Charles Burney which cannot be traced further.[24] Given the potency of England's choral tradition at the time, we can well ask why so little "big music" came forth from Haydn's pen. There are two reasons. The chief one was that choristers, specifically the boys who sang soprano and alto in the great churches, were hard to come by. These performers had already been booked well ahead of Salomon's hastily assembled concert schedules and were not available in 1791-92.[25] Nor were Haydn and his colleagues more

---

[21] Radant "Rosenbaum," 69; trans. in Landon *HCW* 4, 490.

[22] Letter of February 25, 1804, to Zelter, trans. and quoted in Landon *HCW* 5, 284.

[23] Letter of March 16, 1804, trans. and quoted in Landon *HCW* 5, 285.

[24] Burney probably "Englished" one of the choruses from the revised version of *Il ritorno di Tobia*, perhaps "Ah gran Dio" or "Svanisce un momento."

[25] Cf. Haydn's letter of April 24, 1792 to Maria Anna von Genzinger. In reference to *The Storm*, he wrote, "I must admit that this little choral piece, my first attempt at the English language, has earned me considerable credit as a composer of vocal music with the English. It is only a pity that I could not compose more such pieces during my present stay here, but we couldn't have any boy choristers on the days our concerts were held, because they had already been engaged for a year past to sing at other concerts, of which there are a great number." Quoted and trans. in Landon *HCW* 3, 158.

successful in obtaining them during his second visit. By that time, Haydn was also doubt-lessly aware of the potential difficulties involved in presenting any grand choral works in the land of Handel. Years later he suffered criticism when *The Creation* was given its first London performances—the English could not help comparing it unfavorably with *Messiah*, *Judas Maccabeus*, and the other works of oratorio's first, truest genius. In the face of such prejudice, Haydn might understandably have decided to retreat from the field even had he commanded battalions of troops. He would certainly have seen that an old-fashioned Italian oratorio like *Il ritorno di Tobia* was unsuited to English taste.

Haydn's choral triumphs in London were to prove modest but very important for the future. First there was the "Italian catch." Though this *Maccone* had proven the hit of the 1791 Salomon concert series (see above), one could still hear mutterings in London that the visiting Austrian had not properly distinguished himself as a vocal composer. A com-ment in the *Oracle* for January 27, 1792 was typical:

> HAYDN, though in instrumental composition so *various* and *original*, has yet but slender merit as a Writer for the *Voice*. He once wrote, however, an *Opera* at Vienna, and the late EMPEROR would not hear of its being performed.[26]

The latter comment was a twist on the truth which Haydn later took pains to correct.[27] But the operatic venture he had planned for London with Sir John Gallini had also gone awry; officials intervened at the last moment to prevent Haydn's performance and to pro-tect the monopoly enjoyed by the Italian opera at the Pantheon.[28]

So the desire to firmly establish himself with the English public as a vocal composer may have played a strong part in Haydn's composition of *The Storm*. It received its first performance on February 24, 1792. This was the second concert of that year's Salomon series, at which the Symphony No. 93 ("new Grand Overture") was also repeated. The newspaper notices for the event read as follows:

> Mr. SALOMON's CONCERT
> HANOVER-SQUARE
>
> Mr. SALOMON most respectfully acquaints the Nobility and Gentry, that the Second Performance will be on FRIDAY next, the 24th instant,
>
> PART I.
> Overture, CLEMENTI.—Song, Miss POOL.
> New Quartetto M.S. for Two Violins,
> Tenor and Bass, Messrs, SALOMON, DAMER, HINDMARSH
> and MENEL.—Gyrowetz.
> Song, Mr. NIELD.
> (with an Accompaniment of a Bassoon Obligato, by Mr. HOLMES.)
> Concerto, German Flute, Mr. ASH.

---

[26] Quoted in Landon *HCW* 3, 125.

[27] See Griesinger *Notizen* (3), 36, and Dies *Nachrichten* (3), 107-108.

[28] This opera, *L'anima del filosofo*, contains a number of excellent choruses and is discussed briefly in Chapter 6.

(Being his first appearance in London.)

PART II.
The new Grand Overture M.S. HAYDN.
(as performed last Friday.)
Song, Miss CORRI.
New Concerto Pedal Harp, Madame KRUMPHOLTZ—
Dusseck.
Song, Signor CALIAGNI.
THE STORM.
A new Quartetto, composed by HAYDN, for four voices, and
a Full Band.
Sung, by Miss CORRI, Miss POOL, Messrs NIELD, and
BELLAMY.
(The words by an eminent English Author.)
FINALE.

This advertisement, which appeared in all the major London newspapers, reveals the customary format and length of the Salomon concerts, and indeed of most eighteenth-century public musical events. They were mélanges of vocal and instrumental works, new and familiar pieces. Although no mention of a chorus was made in Salomon's notice, some critical reports of the evening imply that the vocal responsibilities were shared: "The new Chorus and Quartetto of HAYDN is the first attempt of that great Master on English words, and he has succeeded admirably in representative harmony—his *storm* and *calm* being wonderfully expressed."[29]

The text was by "Peter Pindar," a pseudonym for the well-known British author Dr. John Wolcot. His words provided Haydn with all he needed to bring forth a dramatic but tightly controlled bit of program music:

> Hark! the wild uproar of the winds, and hark,
> Hell's Genius roams the regions of the dark;
> And thund'ring swells the horrors of the main.
> From cloud to cloud the moon affrighted flies,
> Now darken'd and now flashing through the skies—
> Alas! bless'd calm, return, return, again.

Now it so happens that Haydn had recorded many of his first impressions of London in a letter to his friend Maria Anna von Genzinger. Particularly interesting, in light of *The Storm* to come, are his reactions to bad weather at sea:

> During the first four hours there was scarcely any wind and the vessel made so lit-
> tle way that in that time we went only one English mile. Fortunately toward
> eleven-thirty such a favorable breeze began to blow that by four o'clock we had
> come twenty-two miles. I remained on deck during the whole passage, in order to
> gaze my fill at that huge monster, the ocean. So long as there was a calm I had no

---

[29] Salomon's advertisement and the excerpt from a critical report are taken from the *Morning Herald* for 22, 24 February and 25 February, respectively; quoted in Landon *HCW* 3, 136-137.

fears, but when at length a violent wind began to blow, rising every minute, and I saw the boisterous waves rushing on, I was seized with slight alarm, and a little indisposition likewise.[30]

Thus it appears that Haydn had drawn a little unbidden inspiration from his own recent experiences.

The work takes twelve to fourteen minutes to perform and is roughly in AA'BAB form, with A and A' representing the tempestuous lines 1-2 and 3-5, respectively, and B the hoped-for calm in the final line. D minor and D major alternate, bringing to mind not only Gluck's *Don Juan* ballet music but also—and much closer to home—Haydn's great chorus "Svanisce in un momento" from *Il ritorno di Tobia*. As we might expect, a lot depends on variously diminished chords, judicious dynamic pacing, and orchestral colors, especially—in the first or London version—the string writing. Characteristic choral textures from the work are shown in Examples 7.7 and 7.8.

The Storm was performed again at the fifth Salomon concert of 1792 (March 16) and was acclaimed even more heartily than at its first hearing. *The Diary, or, Woodfall's Register* for March 17 remarked that, of all Haydn's works heard the previous evening,

> a Concertante [I:105], and the fine representation of harmony, entitled, THE STORM, were the most striking; but particularly the latter, which was alternately tremendous and delightful, according to the perdominance [*sic*] of the imitation hurricane, or the approaching calm.[31]

Clearly the critical reaction had not yet begun against "representations of harmony" (i.e., program music in the Baroque tradition); by the time of *The Seasons,* it would plague Haydn. *The Storm* was scored for pairs of flutes, oboes, bassoons, trumpets, horns, and strings plus timpani.

Back in Vienna in 1793, Haydn enlarged the wind parts (adding clarinets and trombones) and mounted successful German-language performances, possibly for Baron van Swieten's Gesellschaft der Associirten and certainly for the Christmas concerts of the Tonkünstler-Societät. It is also most likely that Swieten supplied the German text. As we shall see, this little chorus helped convince first the English and then the Baron that Haydn was capable of writing great choral music in the spirit and manner of Handel. *The Storm* would steer its composer toward *The Creation* and *The Seasons.*

We mentioned above that the opera Haydn composed for London was never performed, due to the intervention of government officials bent on protecting London's established Italian opera. Gallini, the impresario with whom Haydn had been working, managed to pull together a short season of miscellaneous programs in the spring of 1791 and

---

[30] As quoted in Geiringer *Haydn*, 100; cf. complete version in Landon *HCW* 3, 36-37.

[31] Quoted in Landon *HCW* 3, 147.

thus utilize many of the performers contracted for the opera. Although surviving records of Gallini's concerts make it difficult to prove, we can assume that much of Haydn's music for *L'anima del filosofo* (XXVIII:13) was also salvaged for these concerts. That would best explain the existence of *Su cantiamo, su beviamo*, an adaptation of the opera's Act II opening number.[32] For the chorus's independent performance, Haydn enlarged the instrumentation, adding flute, two trumpets, and timpani to the original strings and pairs of oboes, bassoons, and horns. The two-part female chorus became an STB setting with indications for soli and tutti. Not only is this one of Haydn's few three-part choruses (some *divisi* numbers in *The Seasons* really fall into another category), it is one of his simplest and most charming.

Example 7.1: Haydn "Thy Voice O Harmony"

Reprinted from Henle HN 5882 (*JHW* 31). © 1959 G. Henle, Munich; used by permission.

---

[32] See Example 6.8. For the Act II opening of the London opera, Haydn had actually borrowed music from one of his earlier operas, *Orlando Paladino* (XXVIII:11; 1782), so this little chorus has quite a history. For details on the autograph and its dating, see Landon *HCW* 3, 356-357.

Example 7.2: Haydn *Die heiligen zehn Geboten*, VI

Example 7.3: Haydn "Vixit"

Example 7.4: Haydn/Abingdon "Some kind angel"

Example 7.5: Haydn *Die Warnung*, mm. 1-9, 17-23

Example 7.6: Haydn *Der Greis,* mm. 12-23

Example 7.7: Haydn *The Storm,* mm. 62-82

Example 7.8: Haydn *The Storm*, mm. 193-204

8

LATE MASSES

After Haydn returned from his second London trip, he was able to settle permanently in Vienna. He quickly became a fixture in that city's musical life, absenting himself only in the summers when Prince Nicolaus II took up residence at the Esterházy Castle in Eisenstadt. This Nicolaus had succeeded his father Anton in 1794, only four years after the death of the elder Nicolaus. Nicolaus II did not seem to have inherited any of his grandfather's musical talent, although oddly enough he had a keen interest in music for the church.[1] Haydn remained Capellmeister to the Prince, with his only real duty being to compose a Mass once a year in celebration of Princess Marie Hermenegild's name-day. This he did every year but one between 1796 and 1802; these six late Masses are among the chief glories of Haydn's lifework. Chapter 8 is devoted to a chronology of their composition and first performances, followed by a discussion of their musical content.

COMPOSITION AND FIRST PERFORMANCES

Work on the Masses was spread around the composition of *The Creation* and *The Seasons* and of an 1800 *Te Deum* for Marie Therese (discussed in Chapter 7); altogether these nine masterpieces occupied most of Haydn's creative time between 1796 and 1802. Aside from them, we have from Haydn's last years only some partsongs and canons (also dis-

---

[1] The Prince balanced this penchant with far more profane activities. Contemporary accounts spoke of Nicolaus's owning "ten or twelve houses, inhabited by different ladies, who share his favors and diminish his faculties." And: "The Prince used to go to church [in the Bergkirch] surrounded by his guard. He rode on horseback through the church, to the door of his tribune, where he sat in solitary grandeur." Not, we hope, for any of Haydn's Masses. Landon (quoting the diary of Frances, Lady Shelley) *HCW* 4, 41-48 *passim*.

cussed in Chapter 7), the nine string quartets Opp. 76, 77, and 103, and the famous hymn *Gott erhalte Franz den Kaiser*, for many years Austria's national anthem.

Haydn wrote the first of his Masses for Princess Marie between Easter and September of 1796; according to Robbins Landon, that was the *Missa Sancti Bernardi von Offida* (*Heiligmesse*).[2] Evidently Haydn had become aware of Bernard of Offida, the dedicatee of this Mass, because the composer's apartment was in the same square as Vienna's great Capuchin monastery, of which order Bernard had been a member. In 1795 Pius VI had beatified this good and simple monk (d. 1694), and there would have been much talk around the monastery about the general celebration of Bernard's sainthood scheduled to take place in 1797.

Haydn traveled from Vienna to Eisenstadt at the beginning of September, taking score and parts with him for the Mass's first performance on the eleventh or perhaps later. A theatrical troupe led by one Johann Karl Stadler was also in residence at the Castle, presenting a series of plays and operas including *Die Zauberflöte*. Robbins Landon's summary estimate of the forces available to Haydn for the premiere of the Mass is worth quoting in full:

> He obviously had a much larger group available than the meagre forces of his own *Capelle*, but he cannot have known, when he began the Mass, how many voices and instruments (if any) the Stadler group had at their disposal; so Haydn wisely scored the new Mass for the wind players he knew he had at his disposal: by making the two horn players of the *Harmonie* play trumpets, he had, as wind players, two clarinets, two bassoons, two trumpets, and otherwise a timpani player who was also a bassoonist. . . . The strings will have been augmented by the theatrical orchestra, and everyone who could sing will have helped in the choir: the theatrical group boasted many trained singers who will have been proud to contribute their bit. . . . Later authentic sources indicate horns doubling the trumpets; Haydn may have done so, using the theatrical brass players, even at this first performance.[3]

To this we need only add that the Stadler troupe comprised approximately eight men and six women; Haydn may also have called upon choristers from St. Martin's Church. In any case the authentic performance materials include only two copies each of the soprano and alto choral (ripieno) parts, along with one each of tenor and bass.[4] Evidently more sopranos and altos were used than tenors and basses. That was no doubt done to lay greater emphasis on the upper lines and to compensate for the soft, piping quality of con-

---

[2] The traditional chronology of Haydn's works also places the *Heiligmesse* first among the late Masses. Schnerich and Brand felt that the *Paukenmesse* was probably the first composed, owing (among other things) to its textual omissions and mistakes in the Credo which would have resulted from Haydn's being out of practice at Mass composition. Landon has reasons of his own for respecting the traditional chronology; see Landon *HCW* 4, 102-105.

[3] Landon *HCW* 4, 107.

[4] Becker-Glauch "Remarks," 206.

temporary treble voices, whether boys or women. We may further assume that at least two choristers shared a ripieno part, that (since their parts also contained the ripieno passages) the soloists sang at least some choral sections, and that additional choristers could have shared those parts as well. Even so, it must be concluded from the historical evidence that Haydn's choir numbered no more than thirty, and probably closer to fourteen. This seems a paltry crew by modern standards, but in fact the *lower* figure agrees best with what we know of contemporary choral-orchestral balances, including the estimated size of Haydn's band that day (about twenty-six players). The relative choral-orchestral balance for the Eisenstadt performances of Haydn's other late Masses cannot have been much different, although the sum total of performers for the *Harmoniemesse* in 1802 was greater.[5]

On September 9 Stadler's troupe performed an historical drama, *Alfred, oder der patriotische König*, for which Haydn wrote and conducted the incidental music, including a chorus discussed in Chapter 5 together with the other theatrical works. It uses approximately the same orchestra as the *Heiligmesse*.

Haydn must have remained in Eisenstadt long enough to begin work on the *Paukenmesse*; the autograph is dated "Eisenstadt 796 Haydn [mpria]." At the end of the (autograph) Credo is written the prayer "Laus Deo," usually placed at the end of a Mass but here indicating that the composer stopped work at this point before returning to Vienna. In the meantime the Viennese population was becoming increasingly upset by news of Napoleon's victories to the south; in 1797 his army would advance into Austria as far as Graz. This turmoil is doubtless reflected in the title and sometimes-martial content of the new Mass: *in tempore belli*.

At the end of the year Haydn conducted the first performance of the *Missa in tempore belli* at the Piaristenkirche, a lovely Baroque church in one of the Vienna suburbs. Joseph von Hofmann, son of the Imperial-Royal Minister of War Finance, had been admitted to the priesthood. His parents spared no expense in observing their son's first celebration of Mass (*Primitae*). Not only were Haydn and the other necessary musicians brought in for the figural music, but a priest "formerly . . . in the Hungarian province" was imported for the sermon.[6] Two contemporary accounts, the first official, the second a bit of dialect humor by a Viennese wit, provide some of the flavor of the event:

> On 26 December, that is the Feast of Saint Stephen, our *Professkleriker* Joseph
> Hofmann, who was ordained on the 18th of this month, celebrated his *Primitae*

---

[5] According to Becker-Glauch "Remarks," the original performance material for the *Harmoniemesse* includes eighteen parts for the ripieno voices, an increase of eight parts. Robbins Landon noted: "There are remains of some kind of fanfare on the trumpet parts of the original performance material. . . . The fanfare is marked 'furioso.' Can it be the remains of the *intrade* which were used in church performances? . . . No doubt the entrance of the Prince and Princess into the Bergkirche at Eisenstadt was greeted with fanfares of this 'furioso' kind." *HCW* 4, 109; cf. Burney *State*, 115f., quoted in n. 49 below.

[6] Among other expenses incurred by *Kriegszahlmeister* Hofmann on this occasion were "7 *Plutzer* [Austrian measure] of beer for the musicians, 42 xr."

in our Parish Church in the Josephstadt, to which a colossal crowd of people came from all over, also many of the nobility, the more so since the most respected and world-famous *Herr* von Heydn [*sic*], whom the parents of the new priest had invited and asked, performed his new and certainly solemn Mass (*The War Mass*), which he conducted.

The famous Haidn [*sic*] wrote the music for it, and by a special favor I received an entrance ticket up in the choir balcony; otherwise I'd have been squeezed to death down in the church itself. Dear Cousin, there hasn't ever been a sermon to pack 'em in like that, but it was well worth while, Dear Cousin, 'cause I never heard such beautiful music even in the theatre.[7]

The year 1797 began auspiciously for Haydn. Either he approached or he was asked by Count Saurau, President of the Lower Austrian Government, to set to music a patriotic text by the poet Lorenz Leopold Haschka. Thus the Austrian national anthem, "Gott erhalte Franz den Kaiser" was born. Haydn had come to know the British anthem "God Save the King" and was said to envy that nation for having "a song through which it could, at festive occasions, show in full measure its respect, love and devotion to its ruler."[8] The French, against whom the Austrians were engaged in an increasingly serious war, had recently made the stirring *Marseillaise* their national anthem; this also must have contributed to the desire among German-speaking peoples for their own *Volkslied*. Haydn's hymn was distributed to all the theatres in the provinces and sung there variously by the assembled crowds, actors, etc. on the Emperor's birthday (February 12). It was reported to be an immediate success, a spur to national unity at a time when that was sorely needed. The anthem has of course survived as the Protestant hymn "Glorious things of Thee are spoken," also in Haydn's popular string quartet "The Emperor," (Op. 76 No. 3). We mention it in this narrative because, considered broadly, it is the most popular and effective choral work Haydn ever wrote.[9]

As the year 1797 wore on, there was growing public unrest over the approach of the French army. A projected performance of *The Seven Words* at the Schwarzenberg Palace on April 7 was cancelled because of the situation. At some point that summer Haydn went, as always, to Eisenstadt, in order to make ready for the celebration of Princess Marie Hermenegild's name-day (September 10). But the Mass that day was not by Haydn, as this entry from the diary of the Esterházy official Rosenbaum makes clear:

For the Feast of St. Mary we had a new Mass, the music by Fuchs, also a new chorus by Joseph Haydn; Baroness Walterskirchen sang an aria. At mid-day a banquet,

---

[7] Quotations and records from Landon *HCW* 4, 120-21, who drew from the Piaristenkirche Archives, Brand *Messen*, Pohl *Haydn* 3, et al. See also, and esp., Biba "Pflege."

[8] Quoted in Landon *HCW* 4, 242; from Anton Schmid, *Joseph Haydn und Niccolò Zingarelli* (Vienna, 1847).

[9] Haydn prepared his own orchestral accompaniment for the anthem; the unison chorus is preceded by a G chord "so that the people may find the right pitch." Full score reprinted in Landon *HCW* 4, 279-283.

vespers later in the afternoon, then Turkish music on the square. In the evening, fireworks . . . then illumination of the castle, garden, and town; finally a ball in the grand hall, lasting until 4 a.m. The company numbered 800.[10]

Finally, on September 29, Haydn's "new Mass in C," the *Missa in tempore belli*, was given. As in 1796, a theatrical troupe was resident along with a number of noble guests. "On the 28th two choral singers [i.e., soloists] arrived from Pressburg [another princely Esterházy establishment]: Anna Rhumfeld, a soprano, and Frl. Hammer, an alto . . . both women sang [on Friday] and both were very successful."[11] About the same performance conditions existed, then, as for the *Heiligmesse* the year before.

Having written two Masses in 1796, Haydn could devote himself during the summer and autumn of 1797 to finishing *The Creation*. By early 1798 he and his copyist Joseph Elssler were copying out performance materials for the first performances (audience limited to the nobility), which took place on April 29 and 30. It was to be a tumultuous, exciting, and exhausting spring.[12] The doctor seems to have ordered rest. Pohl wrote that Haydn, now sixty-five years old, had suffered from fatigue after the first performances of *The Creation* and had to be confined to his rooms; Griesinger had gotten that story from the composer's own mouth, reporting that "[Haydn] required—naturally beside other occupations—one month [to write a Symphony], for a Mass three months; but he remembered having written one in a month, because he was ill and thus could not go out."[13]

This was undoubtedly the *Nelsonmesse*, the autograph of which is signed "di me giuseppe Haydn mp[ria] 798 10ten Juli Eisenstadt" at the beginning and "Fine. Laus Deo 31 August" at the end. That such a complex and intensely dramatic work could have been written in six weeks, and moreover when Haydn was suffering from exhaustion, is incredible. Perhaps the composer's enforced isolation actually aided his concentration on this incomparable piece. We shall see also that contemporary events played no small part.

As part of a general belt-tightening period at the palace, Nicolaus had dismissed the musicians of the Feldmusik, thus depriving Haydn of wind players for the new Mass. That explains its scoring for solo organ, strings, choir, soloists, and three trumpets with timpani (Haydn had to bring in the three trumpet players). This *Missa in angustiis* or "Mass in the

---

[10] Radant "Rosenbaum," 25. Joseph Carl Rosenbaum eventually married Therese Gassmann, a well-known soprano who sang in several Masses at Eisenstadt; his accounts of musical events there and in Vienna are unusually accurate and helpful. "Fuchs" is Johann Nepomuk Fuchs, Haydn's successor with the Esterházy family, who later arranged wind parts to the *Nelsonmesse* and *Theresienmesse*. The "chorus" by Haydn may have been *Non nobis Domine* or the more elaborate *Insanae et vanae curae*.

[11] Radant "Rosenbaum," 26. But Robbins Landon felt that Therese Gassmann was probably the principal soprano soloist; she could have done the first performance, at the Piaristenkirche, and was due to perform *The Seven Words* later that year in Eisenstadt; *HCW* 4, 162-163.

[12] Described more fully in Chapter 9.

[13] Pohl *Haydn* 3, 132; Griesinger *Nachrichten* (3), 62.

narrow (i.e., affliction)" had its first performance on Sunday, September 23, at the Parish Church of St. Martin in Eisenstadt.

Exactly how the nickname *Nelsonmesse* became attached to the D-minor Mass is not known. It may have happened when Lord Nelson paid a visit to Eisenstadt in September of 1800 (see below). It is also possible that the congregation at its first performance immediately associated this fiery music with recent events in the Mediterranean. Napoleon had continued to menace Austria and her neighbors with aggressive military actions; in retaliation the still-powerful British navy placed a sea blockade around Europe from Denmark to Egypt in the hope of containing the French and eventually defeating them. But in May of 1798, Napoleon and his fleet slipped through this blockade and headed for Egypt. There he defeated the main Egyptian army; by late July, he had entered Cairo. Nelson's line gave chase, but for some time they were unable to locate the enemy. It looked as if once again the French conqueror had escaped.

After a series of abortive maneuvers up and down the Mediterranean, on August 1 Nelson sighted the French fleet at anchor in the harbor of Aboukir. Although nightfall was near and they lacked a chart of the harbor's dangerous shoals, the British sailed in and literally blasted the French out of the water. Midshipman John Theophilus Lee, whose *Swiftsure* had engaged the French flagship *L'Orient*, remembered that

> the incessant flashes of the numerous guns, discharged at nearly the same instant, were so vivid at times as to enable each party to distinguish clearly not only the colours of the respective contestants, but the disastrous results of battle upon them. . . . The brave [French admiral] Brueys, having lost both his legs, was seated with torniquets on the stumps in an armchair facing his enemies; and giving directions for extinguishing the fire [which had started near the mizzen chains], when a cannon ball from the SWIFTSURE put a period to his gallant life by nearly cutting him in two.[14]

News of this stunning victory, one of the few bright moments in the allies' long struggle, reached Vienna about September 15.[15] Thus it is not possible that Haydn had received news of the Battle of the Nile while he was still composing the *Nelsonmesse*.[16] All the same, his music furnishes us with a striking portrait of Europe's emotional state during the summer of 1798. The name "Nelson Mass" is well deserved.

---

[14] Quoted in Michael Glover, *The Napoleonic Wars: An Illustrated History 1792-1815* (New York, 1979), 57. Glover's book (esp. Chapter II, pp. 50-59) provides a compelling account of the entire battle and the events leading up to it.

[15] Olleson cites the diary entry of Count von Zinzendorf for September 15, 1798, which mentions Nelson's victory "dans le port d'Alexandrie" (corrected in the following day's entry to "Abukir"); "Diaries," 54.

[16] Cf. for example Geiringer *Haydn*, 347: "The striking use of the trumpets in the Benedictus is usually thought to be associated with the report of Nelson's decisive victory over Napoleon, which made a tremendous impression all over Europe."

On March 2 and 4 of 1799 came the first two public performances of *The Creation* in Vienna, at the Schwarzenberg Palace. Within a week Prince Lobkowitz hosted a grand concert that included Haydn's *Der Sturm*, perhaps also choruses from *Il ritorno di Tobia*. The Tonkünstler Society gave *The Seven Words* on the 17th and 18th of the month. And on the 19th, in the Burgtheater, there was yet another public performance of *The Creation*. It was an incredibly busy month for the old composer. Moreover he was beginning to be involved in a series of business deals and increased inquiries from various publishers, not to mention his own project of printing *The Creation* for subscription sale. Georg August Griesinger entered Haydn's life about this time as an agent for Breitkopf & Härtel of Leipzig. He succeeded in making contact toward the late spring and wrote to Gottfried Christoph Härtel that "[Haydn] is swamped with business, and has to take care of old orders for the Empress, for Prince Esterhasy [*sic*] and many other wealthy Viennese."[17]

That "old order" for the Empress was undoubtedly the *Te Deum* (XXIIIc:2). Prince Nicolaus would have been expecting another Mass for the autumn. Haydn left Vienna for Eisenstadt on the 10th or 11th of July, where he finished the Mass in Bb (XXII:12) now called the *Theresienmesse* (it was once believed to have been composed for Empress Marie Therese).

Haydn was in and out of Eisenstadt during the summer, leading us to assume his musical duties there were limited. The meagerness of the resources at Schloss Esterházy continued. Haydn's three trumpet players had evidently been kept on: the Prince wrote, asking his advice about establishing some kind of yearly contract for them.[18] The *Theresienmesse* orchestration calls only for two clarinets, two trumpets, and drums in addition to the strings. A bassoon or two doubled the basso continuo (there are authentic parts for them) as well, and Haydn may have been able to scare up those players in Eisenstadt; it is more likely that he had to bring in the clarinetists from Vienna.

About all we know of the *Theresienmesse* premiere is that the weather, which had been miserable all summer, continued to plague Eisenstadt, its Prince, and his subjects. Rosenbaum wrote:

> [Saturday, September 7:] Cold and dull. . . . At about six in the evening there was Turkish music on the square, then a French play. At the end there was a decoration with the Princess's portrait.

He did not mention Mass, which would have been celebrated the following morning in the Bergkirche with Haydn's new music. But for that afternoon, he noted

> the banquet in the grand hall, 54 persons strong. There were many healths drunk, each announced by trumpets and drums in the gallery and by the thunder of can-

---

[17] Quoted in Landon *HCW* 4, 466; from Olleson "Griesinger," 9.

[18] Landon *HCW* 4, 476-77; Haydn *CCLN* 158-59.

non in front of the castle. The Prince also drank Haydn's health, to general con-
currence. . . . They were at table until 5 o'clock, but real merriment was lacking
despite 80 items to eat and all sorts of wines.[19]

In 1800 there would be no new Mass for the name-day of the Princess. Instead, Haydn
saw to the first performance of his new *Te Deum* in Eisenstadt on Monday, September 8.
It is thought that the Mass performed on Sunday the 7th was the *Missa in angustiis*, since
Lord Nelson, Lady Hamilton, and their entourage were resident at Schloss Esterházy from
September 6 to 10. The appearance of this great hero of the Napoleonic wars was a thoroughly exciting event to the Austrians and was marked by a number of other musical observances, especially at Eisenstadt. Lady Hamilton was an accomplished singer who had in
her repertory Haydn's cantata *Arianna* (1790) and other songs; he now set verses for her
to "Lines from the Battle of the Nile," written by a Miss Cornelia Knight of the Nelson
party. Nelson and Haydn exchanged mementoes, Nelson's watch for Haydn's quill. There
may also have been a "small" performance of *The Creation*.[20]

The reason there was no new Mass in 1800, of course, is that Haydn was engulfed in
the composition of *The Seasons*, upon which he and Swieten had begun work soon after
the enormous success of *The Creation*. The new work was given its first private performances in Vienna on April 24, 27, and May 1 of 1801, followed by the first public performances a month later. Haydn, who had experienced considerable strain in composing another monumental oratorio, had been forced to interrupt his work repeatedly due to illness. Therefore it hardly seems possible that he would have had the strength to compose
another Mass that summer. Nevertheless he went to Eisenstadt about the middle of June;
his autograph score for the *Schöpfungsmesse* begins with the notation "di me giuseppe
Haydn mpria 1801 ai 28^{tro} di/Iuglio." The Mass was performed in the Bergkirche on
Sunday, September 13, the Princess's name-day. These two dates encompass a period of
about six weeks within which the Mass must have been composed, a truly Herculean accomplishment given its length and the composer's health. Haydn's brother Michael may
have been present at the first performance; we know he had made a grand journey to
Vienna and had an audience with the Empress on September 9. She had invited him to
compose a new Mass.[21]

---

[19] Radant "Rosenbaum," 68.

[20] See Deutsch *Nelson und Haydn*. The *Creation* mounted for Nelson would have been one of the most intimate,
in terms of performing forces, that Haydn oversaw during his lifetime; see Part Two and esp. Brown *Performing*,
3. We also read about numerous arrangements of the two late oratorios for string quartet, quintet (with flute), etc.
These arrangements allowed for performance of the music in private gatherings or for those with limited
resources. The question of whether Haydn approved of such versions is almost beside the point; he obviously
preferred large-scale performances when they could be mounted. But the "quartet version" was as ubiquitous in
Haydn's time as the cassette or compact disc is in ours, and served much the same purpose.

[21] This *Missa sotto il titulo di S. Theresia* was completed by August 3 and performed in Empress Marie Therese's
presence on October 4 at Laxenburg Castle, the summer residence of the court. Robbins Landon believed it was

The period of musical austerity at Eisenstadt was nearing its end. Nicolaus II had re-engaged a number of the former wind players (some of whom had evidently gone on serving without pay) and otherwise strengthened the Capelle, so that for the *Schöpfungs-messe* Haydn had two oboes, one clarinet, two bassoons, two horns, two trumpets, kettle-drums (probably handled by the third trumpet player), six violins and violas, one cello and one double bass. The second clarinet required by the music had to be brought in. The choir contained (in terms of the professionals) two each of sopranos, altos, tenors, and basses. Robbins Landon estimated the total violins and violas at about 4-4-2 or 5-4-2, which means Haydn must have prevailed on the *Regens chori* at St. Martin's for some ad-ditional players. And as we have seen before, there were doubtlessly additional choristers.[22]

Haydn began work on the *Harmoniemesse*, the last Mass for his Princess, rather early. It was evidently a more attractive task to him in that autumn of 1801 than correcting the proofs sent from Breitkopf for *The Seasons* or arranging more folk songs for Mr. George Thomson of Edinburgh, which would otherwise have occupied his time. In his correspon-dence with Breitkopf & Härtel, Griesinger refers to the Mass on October 24 and again on January 20 of 1802: "Hn. is again working on a new Mass for Esterházy and is arranging some Scottish songs for Thompson [*sic*] in Edinburg [*sic*]."[23]

The *Harmoniemesse* of 1802 was to be Haydn's last Mass and is in fact one of his very last finished works. That he was forced by age and poor health to proceed slowly with it is evident from the length of time he spent, from October 1801 through the summer of 1802. He wrote to his Prince on June 14, "I am laboring WEARILY on the new Mass, though I am ANXIOUS whether I shall receive any applause because of it."[24] On September 8, the Mass was performed in Eisenstadt with somewhat larger forces than usual (Becker-Glauch counted eighteen vocal parts among the original performance materials).[25] The trumpets were evidently doubled for this first performance as well.[26] Afterwards, Haydn sat at table with the Prince and his guests while the musicians, directed perhaps by their new Assistant (after 1804, Full) Capellmeister Johann Nepomuk Fuchs, played *Tafelmusik* for them.

---

the success of this Mass (described as "masterly" by one Abbot Domenikus of St. Peter's Abbey, Salzburg) that prompted Prince Nicolaus II to offer Michael a "handsome" job. So once again we hear of Michael's acclaimed skill in church compositions. Landon *HCW* 5, 76-77.

[22] Landon *HCW* 5, 63-67.

[23] Landon *HCW* 5, 215.

[24] Quoted in Landon *HCW* 5, 227.

[25] Becker-Glauch "Remarks," 206.

[26] Brand *Messen*, 461.

STYLE

In Chapter 7, we mentioned the general effect of London's musical life on Haydn. Working for a large but cultivated audience stimulated him to produce a body of music more consistently excellent than any in his career. And the psychological freedom Haydn enjoyed in London allowed him to begin experimenting again, after he had settled into a somewhat slick manner in the 1780s. But what more specific stylistic developments can be seen to come from the London years?

Just as the *Mehrstimmige Gesänge* from later years show Haydn using a more personal and expressive musical language, so do the chamber and keyboard works of the London period show him developing it. Of the three piano sonatas (XVI:50-52) written for English pianist Theresa Jansen in 1794-95, Karl Geiringer (ever the historical determinist) compared No. 51/1 to the music of Schubert and other movements to that of Chopin and Beethoven. In the Op. 74 string quartets (III:72-74), with their use of mediant key relationships, expansive second subjects, and developments resurfacing in the recapitulations, Geiringer found further evidence of the "dawn of romanticism."[27]

Nevertheless it is the twelve symphonies associated with Haydn's London years (the so-called "London" or "Salomon" Symphonies Nos. 93-104) that are most closely linked in style to the late Masses. In them can also be found elements of Haydn's new proto-Romanticism, although these elements have been transformed into gestures more suitable to a large ensemble. The last twelve symphonies are more to be distinguished by their other innovations: more varied and skillful instrumentation, a direct result of the virtuoso bands with which Haydn worked in England; unorthodox treatment of forms, including in sonata-allegro the use of more flexible approaches (segues) to the recapitulation, imaginative variations within the recapitulation, and a new emphasis on the coda; increased and freshened use of counterpoint, especially in development sections and finales; a unified sense of motivic construction, in which the "germ" or basic cell could as easily be derived from the filling and accompanying voices as from the *Hauptstimme*; and inclusion of audience material—popular elements such as familiar tunes, surprises, and other witty musical usages.

All of these innovations turn up in the six late Masses. First, each features a different wind complement. For Haydn this was a matter of necessity, since the orchestra available to him varied from year to year (see above). But he turned obstacle into advantage, melding the character of the music he wrote to the sound of each group he had. Thus three trumpets, timpani, and organ, in addition to the obligatory strings, have come to seem for many of us the ideal means of delivering the *Nelsonmesse*'s dramatic, acid-tinged rhetoric. And the phrases of the *Harmoniemesse*, by turns powerful and elegiac, need the weight of the largest wind body among these Masses for full impact. Furthermore the instruments are now used with a greater independence than before. The beautiful cello solo in the

---

[27] Geiringer *Haydn*, 315, 320-321.

"Qui tollis" of the *Paukenmesse*[28] is a good example of this; in earlier sacred music by Haydn that instrument never broke free of its continuo function.

As we examine individual movements, we will have an opportunity to see Haydn's creative treatment of structure. One innovation in the Masses that widened the composer's range of structural choices was his elimination of the unalloyed vocal solo. There are no real arias in the late Masses. Instead Haydn made the solo quartet much more important, using it not only as "soloist" but also as one more agent of color and texture within a symphonic framework. Thus solo, quartet, choral, and instrumental utterances alternate and combine freely and can be readily shaped to sonata, rondo/ritornello, and other forms. We shall also see that the enriched textures of the vocal symphony are well suited to Haydn's technique of unified motivic construction, in which one motive can be tossed from voice to voice and transformed to build up an entire movement's worth of music.

It may seem naïve to make much over the counterpoint in these Masses, since learned style was a staple of sacred music in the eighteenth century. But surely the contrapuntal play of the "London" symphonies also spurred Haydn to the bright uses he made of imitative writing in his later music. Any number of fine fugues could be cited—Geiringer singled out the *Paukenmesse* Credo and the "In gloria Dei" of the *Heiligmesse*, but he could just as easily have mentioned half-a-dozen others—and some ingenious canons too. The Credo of the *Nelsonmesse* is a canon at the fourth between high and low voices; for the "Et incarnatus est" of the *Heiligmesse* the composer adapted one of his earlier three-part canons.[29]

That brings up the matter of popular and humorous elements in these Masses, and they are plentiful. That a sacred work could contain such things, even a sacred work admittedly written in theatrical or "elegant" style, has been a continuing source of complaint from certain parties over the years. As we have seen, this perceived gap between style and function was not new to eighteenth-century sacred music. Perhaps Haydn was singled out for special criticism because of his proven mastery in so many other genres, also because of his position at the end of an era. By the 1790s another, more superficially serious age was approaching, one which could not understand the Viennese Classic school's drive to include (and then balance) disparate elements. Haydn himself was unquestionably devout. However, Griesinger reminds us that he "left every man to his own conviction, and he recognized them all as his brothers. Altogether his devotion was not of a sort which is gloomy

---

[28] It bears more than a passing resemblance to "Mit Staunen sieht dies Wunderwerk" from *The Creation*, and is shaped to a ritornello-like form.

[29] It is based on music Haydn had (presumably) set earlier to the German text, "Gott im Herzen, ein gut Weibchen im Arm, / jenes macht selig, dieses g'wiss warm." ("God in the heart, a good woman on your arm, /that gives a blessing, this makes you warm.") Haydn evidently withheld this German canon from Breitkopf & Härtel, because it was not published with the *40* [sic] *Sinngedichte als Canons* in 1802. Landon *HCW* 4, 148-149.

and forever in penance but rather cheerful, reconciled, trusting—and in this mold his church music, too, is composed."[30]

There are various levels on which the popular and humorous are employed in the late Masses. It is pointless in this context to question the use of "elegant" musical style itself—what Charles Rosen, for example, found so distasteful about the first Allegro of the *Paukenmesse*.[31] Haydn did not use that style referentially (i.e., to provoke recognition and then affection, or shock, or laughter from his congregation/audience) but as part of his everyday language, the language of Italian opera and Viennese serenade. To provide what would be called a musical *topic*, he had to reach a bit further afield. One example is his quotation of an old German Sanctus melody, "Heilig, heilig, heilig," in the inner parts of that movement of the *Heiligmesse*. This was undoubtedly recognized and appreciated by many hearing it. Haydn's quotation of himself in the "Qui tollis" of the *Schöpfungsmesse* was intended to be similarly recognized, perhaps with amusement. But for at least one listener that was not the result:

> In the Mass that Haydn wrote in 1801 it occurred to him in the "Qui tollis" that frail mortals sinned mostly against moderation and chastity only. So he set the words *qui tollis peccata, peccata mundi* to the trifling melody of the words in *The Creation*, "Der tauende Morgen, o wie ermuntert er!" ["The dew-dropping morn, oh, how she quickens all!"] But in order that this profane thought should not be too conspicuous, he let the *Miserere* sound in full chorus immediately thereafter. In the copy of this Mass that he made for the Empress, he had to alter the passage at her request.[32]

Haydn was more often successful with witty and surprising uses of musical syntax itself, the kind of rhetorical spark that animates the "Surprise" or "Clock" Symphonies (and the *Heiligmesse* Kyrie—see the discussion below).

It should be clear from everything said so far that in many ways the Masses are constructed as if they *were* symphonies for choir and orchestra. Robbins Landon was the first to acknowledge this in his great book on the Haydn symphonies;[33] later Martin Chusid

---

[30] Griesinger *Nachrichten* (3), 54.

[31] Saying, among other things, that it "can only have sounded as trivial to Haydn's contemporaries as [it does] to us today"; *Style*, 369.

[32] Griesinger *Nachrichten* (3), 63. Brand (*Messen*, 426-428) felt that Haydn had changed the accompaniment, dynamics, and, by augmentation, the theme, so that the passage was, "if not profound, still full of churchly gravity and thus quite transformed."

[33] Landon *Symphonies*, 596.

Vocal Symphony No. 1				
MVT	TEXT	TEMPO AND NO. OF BARS	METRE	KEY
I	Kyrie	*Largo* (10 bars) —	4/4	C major-minor→V
		Allegro moderato (83 bars)	4/4	C major
II	Gloria	*Vivace* (124 bars)	3/4	C major
III	Qui tollis	*Adagio* (71 bars)	alla breve	A major-minor
IV	Quoniam	*Allegro-più stretto* (102 bars)	3/4	C major

Vocal Symphony No. 2				
MVT	TEXT	TEMPO AND NO. OF BARS	METRE	KEY
I	Credo	*Allegro* (33 bars)	4/4	C major
II	Et incarnatus	*Adagio* (60 bars)	3/4	C minor
III	Et resurrexit	*Allegro* (91 bars)	3/4	C major→
				A minor→V
IV	Et vitam	*Vivace* (128 bars)	alla breve	C major

Vocal Symphony No. 3				
MVT	TEXT	TEMPO AND NO. OF BARS	METRE	KEY
I	Sanctus	*Adagio* (13 bars) —	4/4	C major→V
	Pleni	*Allegro con spirito* (25 bars)	4/4	C minor→C major
II	Benedictus	*Andante* (111 bars)	6/8	C minor→C major
III	Agnus	*Adagio* (39 bars) —	3/4	F major→C major→V
IV	Dona	*Allegro con spirito-più presto* (125 bars)	3/4	C major

Table 8.1: *Paukenmesse* as **Vocal Symphony**

showed that each Mass could be considered a cycle of three "vocal symphonies."[34] Because of the way the Mass Ordinary is broken up during the service by parts of the Proper, the Kyrie-Gloria, Credo, and Sanctus-Benedictus-Agnus are heard as discrete musical systems. Haydn took advantage of this circumstance in the last six Masses by casting each system as a three- or four-movement unit, often adopting symphonic structures (sonata, rondo) in the process. Chusid added:

> The first movement may have a slow introduction, and the last movement is usu-
> ally in a quicker tempo than the first. Each of the vocal symphonies has at least
> one slow or moderate movement, and it is always in a contrasting key or mode. As
> is to be expected in sacred compositions, there is no counterpart to the minuets or
> scherzos of the instrumental symphony. However, one of their principal functions,
> that of providing a contrast with an earlier, more solemn movement, is assumed by
> the more consistently cheerful sections such as the openings of the Gloria or the
> Et Resurrexit.

Table 8.1 gives Chusid's analysis of the *Paukenmesse* as vocal symphony. In the following brief discussion of the individual Masses, we will have an opportunity to see how symphonic form and style were adapted to the various texts of the Mass Ordinary.

---

[34] Chusid "Liturgy." Block quotation, 127; chart of vocal symphony, 128.

MISSA SANCTI BERNARDI VON OFFIDA

The *Heiligmesse* may have been the first Mass Haydn wrote after his return from England, making it the first he had composed in fourteen years. Yet it is a sure-handed bit of work, incorporating features associated with his earlier liturgical music as well as his recent symphonies. The use of an old Sanctus melody has already been mentioned. This kind of usage is hardly an innovation for Haydn; plainsong can be found variously worked into the Symphonies No. 26 ("Lamentatione") and 45 (in the Trio of the third movement), also the early Corpus Christi music (*Lauda* 1). More of a new development is Haydn's choice of key, on which Robbins Landon expounded convincingly and at some length:

> In using B♭ with a large orchestra, Haydn had several things in mind: first, the use of trumpets and timpani in B♭. They did exist in Austria, and Michael Haydn wrote for them at Salzburg . . . but they were rare, and it was not till he went to England that [Joseph] Haydn wrote for them. In that key, the trumpets have a curiously sonorous, almost silvery tone, quite different from the aggressive brilliance of their sound in D or the martial "open" quality they have in C; similarly, the kettledrums are less prominent, for one thing because low F (the dominant) is one of the lowest effective notes for the instrument. On the other hand, the wind instruments sound particularly full and attractive in B♭, which was always a favorite key for late eighteenth-century wind-band *Parthien* and serenades. The strings sound less brilliant than in sharp keys such as D major (where more open strings can be brought into play). The voices lie particularly well in B♭: the top B♭" for the sopranos is at the one end of the gamut, while low F in the basses . . . is at the other. The subdued brilliance—a typically Haydnesque tautology—of a Mass in B♭ was obviously so attractive to its composer that he wrote no less than four of his last six Masses in that key . . . and some of the most exalted choral movements of the last two oratorios are also in B♭, including the final chorus of *The Creation*.[35]

Much the same sort of considerations of color and mood can be seen to lie behind Haydn's choices of keys, and modulations, in the other late Masses.

The Kyrie of the *Heiligmesse* provides an excellent example of Haydn's adaptation of the symphonic sonata form to these Masses. Table 8.2 provides an outline of its thematic and tonal structure.[36]

---

[35] Landon *HCW* 4, 139.

[36] Here and elsewhere, PTSK are used to indicate the major thematic components of sonata form, usually found intact in the exposition and repeated variously elsewhere: P = primary, T = transition, S = secondary, K = cadential. See Jan LaRue, *Guidelines for Style Analysis* (New York, 1970), 154ff.

Th:	Exposition				Development		Recapitulation	
	Introd.	P	T	S	T + P		P	T¹ (as coda)
Key:	I (V)	I (V)	I →	V →	X	→	I	I
Mm:	12	22	44	9	24		23	25

Table 8.2: Sonata Form in the Heiligmesse Kyrie

Following a slow introduction that harbors thematic elements of both P and T, the P tune ("Kyrie"), a graceful popular melody in triple time, gets underway:

Example 8.1: Haydn Heiligmesse, mm. 13-20

It is quickly swept up by the orchestra ("drum" bass, scurrying sixteenths in the violins) and propelled through a brief period to a half cadence. The T section is a strong fugato (Ex. 8.2a) extended by bringing back motives from P—it becomes the biggest development section in the piece. Finally the dominant is achieved, and with it a new motive (S, which moves upward slowly) and the "Christe" text (Ex. 8.2b). But this harmonically unstable relief section is quickly dispatched by a return of the T motive: the development proper has gotten underway. T is again met with motives from P (more quickly this time) and swings around to the recapitulation. Here the composer plays with the folk-like tune (and with the listener) in the manner of one of the "London" symphonies (Ex. 8.3).

In spite of a thrilling coda, it is all over much too soon. The most compelling features of this movement formally are its seamless rush from initial statements to developments and, of course, its two "developments," since the first T virtually displaces the customary development area as a harmonic and thematic proving ground. The insertion of a fugue for an exposition and/or development section is not unknown in the other late Mass movements (see the Kyrie of the *Theresienmesse*), but that can be expected in church music. What we had not expected was the way in which the piece continually plays with our expectations and defeats them: first with the two developments, next with the instant dismissal of the "Christe" relief tune, and finally with the insouciantly varied recapitulation of the P tune. Was church music meant to be this joyfully witty?

The *Heiligmesse* has other outstanding parts: its Benedictus in particular has been dubbed "remarkable" (Brand), "ideal" (Schnerich), and "most excellent" (Rochlitz).[37] It employs the whole wind section, including trumpets and drums, in one of those *gemütlich* marches so characteristic of this movement in Viennese Masses. Somewhat uncharacteris-

---

[37] Brand *Messen*, 300; Schnerich *Messe*, 37; Rochlitz in *AMZ* IV (1802), 715f., trans. in Landon *HCW* 4, 153, 158-161.

tically, no vocal soloists are present, only the choir and orchestra. In fact soloists are less often employed in this Mass than in any of the other six, being confined to relatively simple passages in the "Gratias" and "Et incarnatus est." This is a further clue that the *Heiligmesse* was the first of the late Masses to be composed; Haydn may not have known who his soloists would be, so he took care to minimize his writing for them.

MISSA IN TEMPORE BELLI

In the *Paukenmesse*, next of the six to be written, vocal solo writing occurs more often and is more difficult, especially for the soprano and bass. The soprano will be forever identified with the Kyrie's ebullient solo, of course, while the bass delivers the "Qui tollis" in tandem with the cello. This is one of a pair of noble "Qui tollis" settings for the bass (the other is in the *Nelsonmesse*) written perhaps for Christian Specht, a singer whom Haydn remembered fondly for creating many of the *basso* roles in his Esterháza operas. Elsewhere the solo writing is given over to the quartet, although both alto and tenor are given brief and untaxing moments in which to shine.

The *Paukenmesse*, or, as Haydn titled it, *Missa in tempore belli* (*Mass in Time of War*), has always been popular. Its orchestration is one of Haydn's best efforts, combining the festive quality of many earlier C-major settings[38] with Romantic drama in the Agnus Dei. As with the *Heiligmesse*, Haydn later expanded his original scoring, this time ending up with (for winds) a single flute plus pairs of oboes, clarinets, bassoons, trumpets, and horns. The enlarged version adds extra weight and color and includes some wonderful fillips of melody (e.g., the clarinet run at the beginning of the Gloria).[39]

The *Paukenmesse* Credo typifies Haydn's approach to this long, central text in all the late Masses. The first section of the creed, full of dogma and short on imagery, gets a hearty if somewhat old-fashioned sendoff that emphasizes the steadfast nature of faith. This particular setting is a fugue (Ex. 8.4). The same kind of Baroque starch can be seen in any of the other Credo settings, as these excerpts demonstrate. Compare the stereotyped continuo rhythms of Ex. 8.4, 8.5b, and 8.5c (Ex. 8.5a, a canon, manages more originality).

It was in the "Et incarnatus est" that tradition allowed Haydn to display personal eloquence. The first twelve measures are given in Chapter 10 as Example 10.44; but what happens next is the phenomenal part. Although the passage is too long to quote here, it merits careful consideration from the reader. Functioning in C minor, the key of "Chaos" in *The Creation*—and with somewhat the same eerily fragmented orchestration—the initial

---

[38] The *Cäcilienmesse* and *Mariazellermesse*, not to mention a whole string of symphonies ending with No. 97.

[39] Robbins Landon felt that the special qualities of the *Paukenmesse*'s orchestration, and its kinship with the two earlier C-major Masses, might be related to the relatively livelier acoustics of the pilgrimage church at Mariazell and the Piaristenkirche, as opposed to the drier acoustic of the Bergkirche in Eisenstadt, where the other late Masses were first performed. *HCW* 4, 163.

melody is gradually reduced to motives and the motives then reduced to mere rhythms and murmurs, as the text proceeds from Christ's life to his crucifixion and death. It is a *Creation* in reverse. This anti-development is another stunning example of Haydn's power to unify music with little more than a few notes played or withheld at the right moments.[40]

The trumpets and drums now burst in with C major and all the stock devices of the time—ascending lines for "Et resurrexit" and "et ascendit in coelum," a sturdier I-V motive for "judicare," strict choral homophony for "Et unam sanctam catholicam . . ." and so forth, taking us to the final glory of this movement, the *vivace* finale of "Et vitam venturi." For although it begins in the traditional manner (i.e., as a fugue), that procedure soon breaks off with some Handelian *amens* and proceeds to the first of two interludes for the solo quartet. We are in the middle of an operatic ensemble finale. Or, since that may be too grandiose a way to describe this 128-measure Vivace, one might better say that Haydn has here used the form and language of *Le nozze di Figaro* to provide a happy ending for this vocal symphony.

The Sanctus and Benedictus of the *Paukenmesse* are lightweight enough to shift considerable emphasis to the Agnus Dei, which is no doubt what Haydn had in mind. It is this movement that gave the work its German nickname ("Kettledrum-Mass"). As Griesinger related, "the words 'Agnus Dei, qui tollis peccata mundi' are performed in singular fashion with timpani accompaniment, 'as though one heard the enemy coming in the distance.' At the following words, 'dona nobis pacem' he has all the instruments enter in a very striking way."[41] Prompted by the threat of Napoleon's approach toward Vienna from Italy, Haydn decided to dramatize the plea "give us peace" for his own time. He used not only timpani but also insistent trumpet calls to shock his listeners—and to bend the course of church music toward ever more contemporary references. Beethoven was one of the first to apply this lesson: he too used timpani in the Agnus Dei of his *Missa solemnis.*[42]

MISSA IN ANGUSTIIS

As shocking as the final movement of the *Paukenmesse* must have been, it could not have prepared Haydn's patrons for the nearly unrelenting fury of the *Nelsonmesse*. Haydn called this work *Missa in angustiis*, which may be translated as "Mass in time of affliction

---

[40] Note also the reappearance at measures 65-66 of the ornamental figure first associated with the *largo* introduction to the Kyrie, then with the "Qui tollis."

[41] Griesinger *Nachrichten* (3), 62.

[42] It must also be noted that Haydn was hardly the first to include such military episodes in a Mass. Kirkendale "New Roads," a goldmine of information on rhetorical tradition in the Mass before Beethoven, traces this practice back to the oldest collection of prayers for the Mass, the Leonine Sacramentary. Its *Missae tempore hostili* was motivated by the barbarian sieges of Rome in the fifth and sixth centuries. Many later examples, from Clement Jannequin to the Austrian Christoph Straus, are cited as well; 693-694.

[or danger]". It is the most dramatic Mass setting he ever wrote. No *adagio* introduction graces the first movement; instead, strings, trumpets, timpani, and organ[43] break immediately into the silence with stark, unyielding calls (Ex. 8.6). Using a tightly constructed network of motives, the Kyrie builds to a strong climax.

Not every movement in the *Nelsonmesse* is full of such terror. The Gloria and Credo, centered in D major, are no less exciting because they share the sunny qualities of many other such Haydn settings. But if one were to choose a section that epitomizes the character of this Mass, it would be the Benedictus. Its opening measures are given as Example 8.7. Like its sisters in the *Mariazellermesse* and *Heiligmesse*, this movement is styled as a march. But we are again in D minor: "he who comes in the name of the Lord" approaches with menacing tread and unknown motives. The explosive entrance of the trumpets and drums makes one rather doubt that a blessing will result. The piece alternates skillfully between choral statements and solo sections (in formal terms, an exposition and a development occur), building to an unforgettable climax. Musically this is accomplished with a sudden break-off of the recapitulation and a move to B flat. Then, as Robbins Landon wrote, "The trumpets hammer out a fanfare on unison d' and the chorus also sings its text on the note d, its message interrupted by the 'clash of arms and the horrid sublimity' that is war."[44]

THERESIENMESSE

In this country the *Theresienmesse* and *Schöpfungsmesse* have been unfairly neglected. Both contain a wealth of beautiful and interesting music. Like the *Nelsonmesse*, the *Theresienmesse* calls for fewer wind instruments than the norm: pairs of clarinets, trumpets, and bassoons (not independent parts, but implied as part of the continuo). As in the *Nelsonmesse*, the organ is occasionally used as a solo instrument too. But once again these reduced forces have in no way caused a reduction in the size or variety of Haydn's musical conceptions.

From its very beginning the *Theresienmesse* teems with novel ideas. The Kyrie is an ABA in the Adagio-Allegro-Adagio cast of the old French overture.[45] That the Allegro is the first of many good fugues adds no little interest to this opening movement.

The Gloria is even more intriguing. Its opening section is a good example of the basic texture of so many quick movements in these Masses: against a background of rapid pas-

---

[43] The orchestration was later expanded to include woodwinds, but not by Haydn. One set of currently available woodwind parts is by the previously mentioned Johann Nepomuk Fuchs; another was commissioned by Breitkopf & Härtel ca. 1802 and includes certain other alterations. See the Chapter 11 entry for this work; Schenbeck "Missa" provides a concise description of all changes to the vocal and instrumental parts.

[44] Landon *HCW* 4, 442.

[45] Cf. the early Symphony No. 15 in D.

sagework or repeated short notes in the strings, with the winds filling in the harmonies, the choir declaims the text in the basic tempo (see Ex. 8.8). The winds add fanfares after "Benedicimus te" and "Adoramus te"; from "Glorificamus te" to the movement's end, these fanfares are worked into the general fabric, providing (along with the sopranos' high B♭) a thrilling culmination for this part.

The "Gratias" which follows (Ex. 8.9) is a suave Moderato for the solo quartet (at "Qui tollis" and "Qui sedes" the choir re-enters). It features the sort of irregular phrase-structure seen in Haydn's early Marian antiphons: the opening ritornello is nine measures long, its basic structure, which is taken over by the soloist, 3 + 2 + 2, etc. Perhaps the composer used this wilfullness of form as a metaphor for the feminine.[46] The Gloria ends with a stirring Vivace, knit even more tightly together by Haydn's now-familiar motivic development. Thus the ritornello subject of the opening (Ex. 8.10a) is taken over by the solo quartet and eventually appears as subject and countersubject of the "Amen" fugue (Ex. 8.10b).

The *Theresienmesse* has encountered a mixed reception from critics over the years, but from the vantage point of the late twentieth century it is difficult to see why. Gross contrasts of style exist within its pages, but that is equally true of the other Masses. Considering its musical strengths (particularly its many excellent fugal passages), it deserves to receive many more performances.

SCHÖPFUNGSMESSE

Johann Adam Hiller (1728-1804), the great Leipzig composer and choral director, revered the *Schöpfungsmesse* above all Haydn's other compositions. On a score he had made for himself by copying the published parts (full scores themselves were seldom published), he printed in large capitals: *Opus summum viri summi I. Haydn* [Greatest work of a very great man].[47] The work's greatness is primarily a matter of two factors: it is constructed on a somewhat larger scale than any of the other late Masses to 1801;[48] and its musical power owes less to dramatic or extramusical associations than other works (e.g., the *Nelsonmesse*) and more to an absolute mastery of the symphonic idiom.

By 1801, Prince Nicolaus II had restored much of the Esterházy orchestra, so that Haydn had pairs of all winds except flutes for his Mass. From the first notes of this Kyrie we can sense its composer's happiness at being able to unleash his creative powers on a full

---

[46] Here one is reminded that all these Masses were composed for a woman, the Princess Marie Hermenegild Esterházy (see text above). This Mass also bears a nickname linking it to Empress Marie Therese; Robbins Landon looked beyond those Maries, writing that the *Theresienmesse* "is obviously Haydn's thank-offering [to the Virgin] for the gigantic success of the first public performance of *The Creation*, in April 1799"; *HCW* 4, 526.

[47] Dies (3), 136n.

[48] Although the *Heiligmesse* takes longer to perform because of its preponderance of moderate tempos.

band, and with no "Frenchified trash" to set (*The Seasons* had occupied him for the past year). Here he uses the Kyrie—the text of which was generally treated abstractly anyway—to create a joyful and formally unique opening movement. After a slow introduction with the by-now customary fanfare motives, the piece takes wing in a 6/8 Allegro that could almost pass as a symphonic finale. It is in sonata form, but the basic simplicity of the themes (Ex. 8.11a; derived from a motive in the slow introduction) and their episodic usage give it a rondo-like quality (see esp. Ex. 8.11b, which moves to B♭ minor). Yet the combination of Haydn's hammer-stroke insistence on the "Ky-ri-e!" rhythm and the quicksilver changes to minor mode, Neapolitan harmonies, et al., gives the movement a more serious cast. It affords pleasure to the listener as absolute music without seeming the least bit frivolous for that.

Inevitably some of the movements in this penultimate sacred work by Haydn will seem to have a retrospective quality, something even more notable in the *Harmoniemesse*. Here, it is the Credo that seems deliberately old-fashioned, not just in its opening section but in its continuing use of old Baroque text painting. One of these "old" devices is actually new to Haydn and thus bears mentioning. In the "Et incarnatus est," the *Flauto* (flute) stop of the organ is used to represent the presence of the Holy Spirit. The dove had long been a symbol of this part of the Trinity, especially in connection with Mary, Mother of God. The twittering, bird-like motives given out by the organist here correspond gracefully with that usage and again remind us of Beethoven, who used a flute trill to similar effect in the "Et incarnatus est" of the *Missa solemnis*.[49]

Aside from the remarkable Agnus of the *Paukenmesse*, we have not yet paid much attention to an Agnus Dei/Dona from any of these late Masses. The Agnus of the *Schöpfungsmesse* is more typical of the group. It begins in *adagio* tempo, with the solo quartet and strings, and in the submediant key of G. Example 8.12 includes that beginning and then the breathtaking first entrance of the brass and timpani on a single B♭, a harmonic shock that returns in a slightly altered form later in the section. This is the kind of bold stroke by which Haydn so often transformed his material.

After a thorough working out of these ideas (and a last twist to half-cadence in G minor), the Dona commences in B♭ major with a tutti figure that probably called to mind for Haydn's congregation the traditional brass *intradas* still used in many Austrian churches.[50] This Dona builds to an enormous climax, alternating homophonic sections with free fugato and using extreme dynamic contrasts to generate additional energy. At the very end, the B♭-minor tutti dies down to a piano, only to roar up again, *fortissimo*, with the chorus making great octave strides down the dominant and tonic chords (Ex. 8.13).

---

[49] Cf. Kirkendale "New Roads," 679-680, which also cites various eighteenth-century Masses using the flute in this way.

[50] Cf. Burney *State*, 115f.: "[in Augsburg] there was a rude and barbarous flourish of drums and trumpets at the elevation of the Host, which was what I had never heard before, except at Antwerp."

HARMONIEMESSE

As we have seen, the *Harmoniemesse* was Haydn's valedictory to Mass composition. It is distinguished from the first five Masses in this series chiefly by its performing time—at fifty-five minutes, it is the longest—and by its scoring, the richest and most fully exploited among the late Masses. To the instrumentation of the *Schöpfungsmesse* was added one flute; Haydn also doubled the trumpets at the first performance.[51] That enhanced the typically festive passages like the "Gloria in excelsis" or the Dona. But Haydn found places in which the winds could bear more special fruit: the "Et incarnatus est," for example, in which the soprano soloist's words are first introduced by the woodwinds ("ex Maria Virgine") and then by soft brass and timpani ("Et homo factus est").

Two of the Ordinary texts also received unusual settings. The Kyrie (Ex. 8.14a) is a long Poco Adagio standing in vivid contrast to the merry or dramatic treatments that had flowed from Haydn's pen for so many years. It is as if the composer of *Der Greis* and "Chaos" had finally met up with the composer of the *Paukenmesse* and showed him what a Kyrie should be: humble, contemplative, but never lacking in strength of feeling. This elegiac treatment was, for its composer, a fresh vision of the Kyrie message, proof of his continuing struggle to expand his language. As stated before in this chapter, much of the power of Haydn's expressive late style derives from timing and harmonic surprise. The first entrance of the choir in this Kyrie (Ex. 8.14b) demonstrates both. It is followed by a reprise of the opening measures, into which solo quartet lines are now laid with considerable sensitivity.

The other movement that breaks stylistic ground is the Benedictus. Robbins Landon felt that the "bizarre" originality of this piece, which is marked *Allegro molto* and *pianissimo*, was "as Rococo as Vierzehnheiligen or Wilhering Monastery."[52] William Herrmann, who edited the work for G. Schirmer, was understandably puzzled by Haydn's tempo indication and suggested that "something closer to Allegro moderato was intended."[53] This Benedictus is in sonata form, and the relief subject is particularly lovely.

Elsewhere the *Harmoniemesse* somewhat resembles a catalog of Haydn's earlier works. The "Gratias" is in a moderately quick 3/8 that recalls the *Cäcilienmesse* or *Grosse Orgelmesse*. There is a magnificent double fugue at "In gloria Dei patris," and another Baroque-sounding Credo. Undoubtedly Prince Nicolaus II, who later experienced Beethoven's Mass in C Major with confusion and dismay, was able to regard this final Mass by his servant Haydn as a nearly perfect example of the proper churchly manner.

---

[51] Brand *Messen*, 461.

[52] Landon *HCW* 5, 250.

[53] In the G. Schirmer vocal score (New York, 1966), 99.

Example 8.2a: Haydn *Heiligmesse*, Kyrie, mm. 13-28, vocal lines and bass

Reprinted from Henle HN 5572 (*JHW* 23/2). © 1958 G. Henle, Munich; used by permission.

Example 8.2b: Haydn *Heiligmesse*, Kyrie, mm. 73-82

Reprinted from Henle HN 5572 (*JHW* 23/2). © 1958 G. Henle, Munich; used by permission.

Example 8.3: Haydn *Heiligmesse*, Kyrie, mm. 109-117

Reprinted from Henle HN 5572 (*JHW* 23/2). © 1958 G. Henle, Munich; used by permission.

Example 8.4: Haydn *Paukenmesse*, Credo, mm. 1-8, choral lines and continuo

Example 8.5a: Haydn *Nelsonmesse*, Credo, mm. 7-13, choral lines and continuo

Example 8.5b: Haydn *Theresienmesse*, Credo, mm. 1-7, choral lines and continuo

Example 8.5c: Haydn *Harmoniemesse*, Credo, mm. 1-3, choral lines and continuo

Ex. 8.5b reprinted from Henle HN 5582 (*JHW* 23/3). © 1965 G. Henle, Munich. Ex. 8.5c reprinted from Henle HN 5602 (*JHW* 23/5). © 1966 G. Henle, Munich. Used by permission.

Example 8.6: Haydn *Nelsonmesse*, Kyrie, mm. 1-6

Reprinted from Carus-Verlag 40.609. This Carus Verlag reproduction is made with the express consent of Carus Verlag of Stuttgart and Mark Foster Music Company, Inc., of Champaign, Illinois, Sole U. S. Selling Agent, in accordance with the provisions of the United States Copyright Law.

Example 8.7: Haydn *Nelsonmesse*, Benedictus, mm. 1-11

Exx. 8.7 and 8.8 reprinted from Henle HN 5582 (*JHW* 23/3). © 1965 G. Henle, Munich; used by permission.

Example 8.8: Haydn *Theresienmesse*, Gloria, mm. 1-9

Example 8.9 follows Example 8.11b.

Example 8.10a: Haydn *Theresienmesse*, Gloria, mm. 249-253

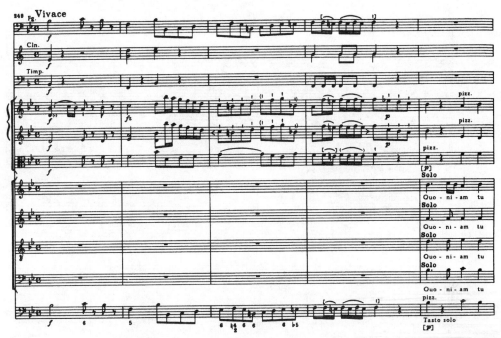

Example 8.10b: Haydn *Theresienmesse*, Gloria, mm. 281-285

Example 8.11a: Haydn *Schöpfungsmesse*, Kyrie, mm. 29-33

Exx. 8.11a and 8.11b reprinted from Carus-Verlag 40.611. These Carus Verlag reproductions are made with the express consent of Carus Verlag of Stuttgart and Mark Foster Music Company, Inc., of Champaign, Illinois, Sole U. S. Selling Agent, in accordance with the provisions of the United States Copyright Law.

Example 8.11b: Haydn *Schöpfungsmesse*, Kyrie, mm. 63-73

Example 8.9: Haydn *Theresienmesse*, Gloria, mm. 112-126

Reprinted from Henle HN 5582 (*JHW* 23/3). © 1965 G. Henle, Munich; used by permission.

Example 8.12: Haydn *Schöpfungsmesse*, Agnus Dei, mm. 1-18, strings and voices only

Example 8.13: Haydn *Schöpfungsmesse*, Agnus Dei, mm. 149-159

Example 8.14a: Haydn *Harmoniemesse*, Kyrie, mm. 1-6

Exx. 8.14a and 8.14b reprinted from Henle HN 5602 (*JHW* 23/5). © 1966 G. Henle, Munich; used by permission.

Example 8.14b: Haydn *Harmoniemesse*, Kyrie, mm. 18-24

9

THE CREATION AND
THE SEASONS

THE ROAD TO THE CREATION

In the years following his return from England, Haydn became as much an institution as a composer. He now took time to pursue only the musical paths that interested him, and what interested him most was the prospect of carving a niche among the immortals. This he did not only with his Austrian hymn[1] but also, and in all nations, with *The Creation*.

Haydn appears to have conceived the idea of writing an oratorio in the Handelian manner while still in England. As mentioned in the previous chapter, he had attended the gigantic Handel Commemoration at Westminster Abbey in 1791:

> [Haydn] confessed . . . that when he heard the music of Hendl [sic] in London, he was struck as if he had been put back to the beginning of his studies and had known nothing up to that moment. He meditated on every note and drew from those most learned scores the essence of true musical grandeur.[2]

He must also have meditated on another thing: the English public's almost-religious veneration of Handel and his music. From his box near the royal family at the Commemoration, Haydn would have wonderingly beheld the King, the Queen, and the entire congregation rising as the "Hallelujah" chorus began.

---

[1] *Gott erhalte Franz den Kaiser;* see Chapter 8.

[2] Carpani *Haydine,* 162.

We can also mark Haydn's early interest in an English-style oratorio from the so-called *Mare Clausum* (XXIVa:9), two movements he set of a rather strained six-stanza allegorical poem by Marchamont Nedham on British naval power (see below).[3] Haydn had undertaken this work at the behest of his English friend and patron the Earl of Abingdon, whose estate he visited in September 1794. We have seen that Lord Abingdon induced Haydn to write keyboard accompaniments for some catches and glees he had "melodized"; those were published in 1795. The projected oratorio (really more of a cantata, considering its presumed six-movement length) never got beyond the two movements mentioned above. The first is a very singable aria for bass soloist and full orchestra that strikes a hearty "nautical" pose rather in the manner of Sir Arthur Sullivan. The strings accompany with pizzicati at first; then flute and oboe enter with sprightly passagework leading into some typical martial tuttis on Haydn's favorite rhythms. The second movement is an SSATTB chorus with full orchestra accompaniment, in D. We will recall that Handel also favored this key for festive and triumphant choruses. The choral ranges are moderate, the parts themselves easy; the piece lacks any real counterpoint but makes a fine effect by alternating blocks of declamation with loosened homophony.

Yet neither chorus nor aria is likely to gain wider acceptance until some inventive person fits them with new texts. The verses Haydn had to use are spectacularly bad. They may in fact have been the reason he broke off work on the project (it also didn't help that Lord Abingdon was imprisoned in 1795).[4] Even with his limited command of English, Haydn must have known that lines like these—

> Thy great endeavors to encreas[e]
> The Marine power, do confess
>   thou act'st som[e] great design.
> Which had Seventh *Henrie* don[e], before
> *Columbus* la[u]nch'd from Spanish shore,
>   the *Indies* had been thine.
> Yet do thy Seas those Indian Mines excell
> In riches far: the *Belgians* know it well.

—scarcely afforded a path to musical immortality. After reading Nedham's poetry, one is more inclined to view Swieten's merely third-rate verse for *The Seasons*, and Haydn's willingness to cope with it, in a charitable light.

---

[3] This oratorio fragment is referred to in Feder's *New Grove* Worklist as "Nor can I think/Thy great endeavors." Feder pointedly notes that the text is not drawn from John Selden's Latin treatise on maritime law *Mare Clausum* (London, 1635). It is comprised of the second and third stanzas of Nedham's "Neptune to the Commonwealth of England," which Nedham included as a pendant to his English translation of the Selden work (*Of the dominion, or, ownership of the sea, two books,* London, 1652; repr. New York, 1972. The book is irregularly paginated, but any interested reader can find Nedham's complete poem on its last page.). Thus the title used by Robbins Landon for his edition (cf. Landon *HCW* 3, 271, 356) has some relevance.

[4] Pohl said Haydn lost interest in the work after he discovered that three other composers, including Pleyel, had worked on the same subject before him (*Haydn* 3, 84; cf. Geiringer *Haydn*, 350-351).

A happier choral circumstance for Haydn in England, later in Vienna, was the popularity of his "madrigal," *The Storm* (XXIVa:8). Evidently this work (discussed in Chapter 7) impressed various persons in London so much that they presented its composer with the original libretto of *The Creation*:

> Since Handel's death there had been resting a vocal libretto in England put together from Milton's *Paradise Lost* and called *The Creation*, because it was thought that only the singer of *Messiah* could have been expected to provide this text with an harmonic garb worthy of it. Meanwhile Haydn appeared in London, and recalled, with his great and powerful works, the giant strength of Handel. One's hopes were once again raised, and they hoped to see this poem worthily set to music also by Haydn; they looked for it, and gave it to Haydn to compose.[5]

> The first idea for the oratorio *The Creation* belongs to an Englishman, Lidley by name, and Haydn was to have composed Lidley's text for Salomon. He soon saw, however, that his understanding of the English language was insufficient for this undertaking; also the text was so long that the oratorio would have lasted close to four hours. Haydn meanwhile took the text with him to Germany. He showed it to Baron van Swieten, the royal librarian in Vienna, who arranged it as it now stands. Salomon was going to sue Haydn for this, but Haydn protested to him that he had used only Lidley's idea and not his words; Lidley moreover was already dead, and so the matter was dropped.[6]

By the end of 1793 Baron van Swieten would become familiar with *The Storm*, now reorchestrated for performances in Vienna: in fact he probably prepared its German translation and thus had a real share in its triumphant reception that year.[7] This experience further convinced him that Haydn was capable of writing "in the spirit and manner of Handel." Swieten had already offered Haydn a libretto, *Die Vergötterung des Herkules* by one Johann Baptist von Alxinger, in which places for arias, duets and choruses were fully prescribed, probably by the Baron himself. Haydn did not set this work, but after his second London trip he did bring Swieten the "Lidley" text.

Besides being Imperial and Royal Librarian, Gottfried van Swieten was himself a composer (his symphonies said to be "as stiff as he was"[8]) and a great promoter of early music—which for his time will have meant Bach and Handel. As life secretary of a group of noble patrons who arranged occasional performances of this music, he had been Mozart's

---

[5] Gerber *Lexikon* (2), 2, 543.

[6] Griesinger *Notizen* (3), 37-38.

[7] It is thought the madrigal was performed as an insertion chorus in Handel's *Alexander-Fest* in (Swieten's ?) performances of March and/or December 1793, also at the Tonkünstler-Societät's Christmas concerts that year. Landon *HCW* 3, 216-228 *passim*.

[8] Haydn to Griesinger; Griesinger *Notizen* (3), 38. Cf. Haydn's remarks to Silverstolpe about Swieten's talent, quoted in the text following.

generous supporter. It was for concerts of this Gesellschaft der Associirten that Mozart arranged and reorchestrated Handel's *Acis and Galatea, Messiah,* and other works. Now it was to Haydn that Swieten turned to create a newly classic work; we are fortunate that the Baron was a relatively gifted and discriminating connoisseur, both in his choice of musicians and in his ability to shape a text.

And *shaping* is the best way to describe Swieten's part in delivering a German text to Haydn and helping him make good use of it. The libretto, and the collaboration of wordsmith and composer, will be discussed more fully below. Herewith, a few more details about Haydn's activities from 1795-98: It would seem that in the months of 1795 remaining after his return from England, Haydn did little but reacquaint himself with his Prince and Princess, enjoy the stimulations of Viennese life, and organize a concert of "three grand Symphonies" for December 18 in the Redoutensaal.[9] At this marathon affair, Beethoven, who had lately been Haydn's pupil in counterpoint, also performed his own Piano Concerto No. 2 in its newly revised version.

Haydn had of course purchased the house in Gumpendorf that his wife requested for her widowhood, but he found it more convenient to lodge at various apartments in the city. There he could more easily make his way to rehearsals and concerts and also work closely with Swieten on their oratorio project. But that was not to occupy him greatly for another few months. The spring of 1796 found Haydn working instead on his own vocal version of *The Seven Words.* On his journey back from London he had heard at Passau a vocal arrangement done by the Cathedral *Capellmeister* Joseph Friebert. Having decided he could improve on Friebert's efforts, in Vienna Haydn asked Swieten to adapt Friebert's text to the music. He then added choral parts and additional wind instruments to the existing score. The new version was heard at the Schwarzenberg Palace on March 26 and 27, probably under the sponsorship of Swieten's Gesellschaft.[10]

During the summer and fall of 1796 Haydn completed the *Heiligmesse* and much of the *Paukenmesse.* His work on *The Creation* had also been proceeding apace. Some of the sketches for it appear to date from the same time as his sketches for the *Heiligmesse* Gloria and Credo; thus we know it occupied Haydn's thoughts from at least the spring or summer on. Presumably his work with Swieten on the libretto began even earlier. By December he was playing parts of it to Albrechtsberger, who wrote to Beethoven that "[Haydn] is carrying round in his head the idea of a big oratorio. . . . I think it will be very good."[11]

A letter from the Swedish diplomat Frederik Samuel Silverstolpe to his father in the spring of 1797 confirms Haydn's progress on *The Creation.* Silverstolpe had chanced to

---

[9] Landon *HCW* 4, 55-60. Becker-Glauch ("Neue Forschungen," 224-228) also assigned Haydn's offertory *Non nobis, Domine* (XXIIIa:1) to a period roughly between 1790 and 1802 (cf. Landon's "c. 1795, revised c. 1802"), noting its use of a Psalm text associated mainly with the English. We discuss this work in Chapter 6.

[10] An Italian text was also prepared by Carpani; Landon *HCW* 4, 95-97, quoting Neukomm et al. We discuss this work in connection with its original composition as a string quartet during Haydn's "Opera Years" (Chapter 5).

[11] Quoted in Landon *HCW* 4, 115.

meet Haydn after a performance of Handel's *Acis and Galatea* at the Schwarzenberg Palace and gave this account of their conversation:

> [Haydn] then lived in the Krüger-Strasse No. 1075; the house was called *der blaue Säbel*. He only rented this lodging for a short period to be near Baron van Swieten, the librettist of that great musical work on which Haydn had been engaged for some weeks. It was *The Creation*. Baron van Swieten, at the head of 12 or 13 other music lovers, had ordered the piece so that it could be performed the next year at Prince Schwarzenberg's, who likewise belonged to the Society. "I find it necessary," said Haydn, "to confer often with the Baron, to make changes in the text and moreover it is a pleasure for me to show him various numbers in it, for he is a profound connoisseur, who has himself written good music. . . ."—Soon Haydn let me hear the introduction of his oratorio, describing Chaos. He asked me to come and sit beside him, so as to follow the score. When the piece was ended, he said: "You have certainly noticed how I avoided the resolutions that you would most readily expect. The reason is, that there is no form in anything [in the universe] yet."[12]

A fascinating addendum to the story of Haydn's work at this time has come down to us from the poet Franz Grillparzer, who would have picked it up in 1820 or 1830 from some survivor of Swieten's circle:

> [The Baron] had each piece, as soon as it was ready, copied and pre-rehearsed with a small orchestra. Much he discarded as too trivial for the grand subject. Haydn gladly submitted, and thus that astonishing work came into being which would be admired by coming generations. I have all this from the lips of a well-informed contemporary who himself took part in these pre-rehearsals.[13]

Although such a procedure would have been unusual, it does not seem improbable. Swieten had the means, Haydn the time and desire to make sure his new venture would crown his other triumphs. Grillparzer's story may also help explain the large number of extant sketches and discarded versions of single numbers from *The Creation*. And it fits with what we know of Haydn's continuing experimentation with the score after its first performances (see below).

Silverstolpe's memoirs take us further into 1797:

> When Summer began Haydn moved back to his own house in the suburb of Gumpendorf, Kleine Stein-Gasse No. 73. . . . When I entered the room I heard a parrot calling "Papa Haydn!" . . . *There* it was that he showed me the D major Aria from *The Creation* ["Rolling in foaming billows"] which describes the sea

---

[12] Trans. and quoted in Landon *HCW* 4, 251–252; full German text of Silverstolpe's reports on musical life in Vienna in Mörner "Haydniana," 24ff.

[13] Quoted in Walter "Textbücher," 242.

moving and the waves breaking on the shores. "You see," he said in a joking tone, "you see how the notes run up and down like the waves: see there, too, the mountains that come from the depths of the sea? One has to have some amusement after one has been serious for so long." —But when we arrived at the pure stream, which creeps down the valley in a small trickle, ah! I was quite enthusiastic to see how even the quiet surface flowed.[14]

Later that autumn Haydn gave a performance of *The Seven Words* in its new choral version, for which the soprano Theresa Gassmann was brought in. He also received a visit from Silverstolpe:

In September 1797 I gave myself the pleasure of seeing Haydn in peace and quiet in the country. I visited him in Eisenstadt in Hungary, almost a day's trip from Vienna. It is a so-called *Landstadt*, free of all noise, with a castle which is used at certain times by the owners, the Princes Esterházy. The view of the Neusiedlersee was most pleasant. In this place of refuge, Haydn completed his Oratorio, *The Creation*.[15]

By January Silverstolpe and other insiders knew that the first performances of the new work would take place during the Lenten season of 1798. The Tonkünstler Society's Lenten concerts would also feature Haydn with the vocal arrangement of *The Seven Words*; a chorus of 150 was assembled for that series.[16]

Among their many other chores of early 1798, Haydn and his assistant Johann Elssler were mightily occupied with copying out performance materials for the upcoming *Creation* performances. Adjustments continued to be made up to the day of the premiere, and indeed afterward (see below). At Prince Schwarzenberg's a public rehearsal (presumably following one or more private rehearsals) was held on April 29, the official first performance there the next day. Silverstolpe wrote:

I was among the audience, and a few days beforehand I had attended the first rehearsal. . . .—No one, not even Baron van Swieten, had seen the page of the score wherein the birth of light is described. That was the only passage of the work which Haydn had kept hidden. I think I see his face even now, as this part sounded in the orchestra. Haydn had the expression of someone who is thinking of biting his lips, either to hide his embarrassment or to conceal a secret. And in that moment when light broke out for the first time, one would have said that rays

---

[14] Mörner "Haydniana," 26; trans. in Landon *HCW* 4, 256.

[15] Mörner "Haydniana," 27; trans. in Landon *HCW* 4, 264.

[16] Landon *HCW* 4, 312-317 *passim*. At the second of these concerts, Beethoven played his own new Quintet, Op. 16, for piano and winds, between halves of the oratorio. This kind of intermission concerto was a customary practice that we have noted earlier in connection with *Il ritorno di Tobia;* see Chapter 5.

darted from the composer's burning eyes. The enchantment of the electrified Viennese was so general that the orchestra could not proceed for some minutes.[17]

The principal performers were Christine Gerardi, soprano; Matthias Rathmayer, tenor; and Ignaz Saal, bass. Antonio Salieri sat at the fortepiano and Haydn conducted. Robbins Landon described Gerardi and Rathmayer as well-known amateurs (in the eighteenth-century sense); Saal was a versatile professional with a great deal of theatrical experience. His daughter Therese "would soon become the toast of musical Vienna" and in fact succeeded Gerardi as soprano soloist in the 1799 performances of *The Creation*.

Other witnesses also testified to the tremendous excitement felt by musicians and audiences alike at the first performances. Here is Griesinger:

> I had the fortune to be a witness of the deep emotion and the most lively enthusiasm which were felt by all the audience at several performances. . . . Haydn admitted to me, moreover, that he could not describe the feelings with which he was filled when the performance went just the way he wished, and the audience listened to every note in total silence. "Sometimes my whole body was ice-cold, sometimes a burning heat overcame me, and more than once I was afraid that I would suddenly have a stroke."[18]

And Carpani:

> La megliore orchestra possibile; *Haydn* stesso alla testa; il più perfetto silenzio e l'attenzione più scrupolosa; una sala favorevole; un'esattezza somma negli esecutori; un sentimento quasi di divozione e di rispetto in tutta l'assemblea: ecco le disposizioni con che partì il primo colpo d'orchestra, che dischiuse le porte alle non più intese armoniche bellezze.[19]

After April 29 and 30, Haydn conducted several more performances with approximately the same forces and the same overwhelming response. These concerts were held on May 7 and 10, 1798, at the Schwarzenberg Palace; March 2 and 4, 1799, also at the Schwarzenberg Palace (the first performances open to the general public); March 19, 1799, at the Burgtheater; and December 22 and 23, 1799, also at the Burgtheater (the Tonkünstler Society Christmas benefit). From the very beginning, *The Creation* was acknowledged as a masterpiece in the oratorio literature.

---

[17] Mörner "Haydniana," 28; trans. in Landon *HCW* 4, 318.

[18] Griesinger *Notizen* (3), 38.

[19] Carpani *Haydine*, 165.

THE CREATION: LIBRETTO AND GENERAL PLAN

The textual roots of *The Creation* lay in rational Georgian England, yet its first and greatest success came in the conservative Catholic Austria of Francis II.[20] That the work could travel so widely and so well is due in no small part to the libretto's spirit of inclusion; it points to the wonders of the earth as proof of a loving Creator. That would have been in tune with all but the most skeptical of English thinkers in Handel's day. Science and reason were not yet seen as contradicting Christian teachings, but more often as affirming them: Newton's studies of the physical world thus reinforced the image of God as the architect of an orderly universe. Only the Deists, who believed in a divine creator but drew the line at biblical miracles, might have quibbled with those few portions of the libretto in which God intervenes arbitrarily in human affairs. Most of the text espouses a comfortable optimism: Nature is celebrated and the Fall of Man is pushed nearly out of the picture, producing a version of Genesis that Anglicans, skeptics, and Freemasons alike could enjoy.

As for German-speaking believers, it must be admitted that the influence of liberal theology was felt far more strongly in the Protestant North than in the Catholic South. The Austrian Church had undergone its own sort of reformation during the reign of Joseph II (see Chapter 4), so its adherents were by the early nineteenth century presumably more capable of appreciating *The Creation*'s worldview. But Enlightenment philosophy had less to do with making the Viennese ready for *The Creation* than had earlier performances of German oratorios and—especially—Handel's oratorios in German translation. Those works radiated a sense of religious freedom without challenging the letter of Catholic dogma. The Church reacted quickly to the popular success of *The Creation* by banning performances of the work within its own buildings,[21] yet it could hardly prevent music or message from entering the souls of the faithful. A place was already waiting there, prepared by Handel.

Like most of Handel's oratorios but few such German or Italian works, *The Creation* is in three Parts. Undoubtedly the original English libretto was too, because Swieten wrote

> I followed the plan of the original faithfully as a whole, but I diverged from it in details as often as musical progress and expression, of which I already had an ideal conception in my mind, seemed to demand. Guided by these sentiments, I often judged it necessary that much should be shortened or even omitted, on the one hand, and on the other that much should be made more prominent or brought into greater relief, and much placed more in the shade.[22]

---

[20] For a concise yet thorough examination of the theological bases of *The Creation*, see Temperley *Creation*, 9-16, from which we have drawn, with thanks, for the present discussion. Stern "'Schöpfung'" presents a detailed analysis of the libretto's Enlightenment roots, with emphasis on German sources.

[21] Landon *HCW* 4, 346.

[22] Letter in *Allgemeine Musikalische Zeitung* 1 (1798-99), 254-255; trans. by Olleson in "Origin," 150.

In general the libretto also took Handel's path in ordering the smaller structures within each Part. Parts I and II are comprised of a series of recitative-aria-chorus or recitative-aria-recitative-chorus units, each built around a single theme or idea.[23] First a recitative states one of the acts of creation in the words of the English Bible (Genesis); then an aria follows which paraphrases and comments on that act (Milton); then there may follow another recitative in the style (but not the words) of the Bible, introducing a Psalm-like chorus from the heavenly host. Thus, scripture-commentary-praise: the text is narrative-reflective after the general manner of *Messiah* or the *Matthew Passion*. Wherever the plan departs from this, we may presume that Swieten cut material from the original libretto to tighten the work (see Table 9.1). In this connection, note that Haydn set in recitative all of the biblical and pseudo-biblical passages but one: the famous "And there was light" sequence, sung by the chorus. This type of change is probably what Swieten meant by bringing some things "into greater relief" and putting others "more in the shade." It also compensates formally for a (presumably omitted) chorus of angels at the end of the First Day.[24] In any case Haydn would have wanted to avoid overemphasizing the chorus's role; that was Handel's miscalculation in *Israel in Egypt*. *The Creation*, with its succession of recitatives, arias, and choruses (and a shrewd variation of texture within that succesion, e.g., duet, solo with chorus, etc.) provides a nearly ideal balance of genres.

Part I treats the first four Days of creation according to the story in Genesis. Part II describes (also following Genesis) the more complicated Fifth and Sixth Days, culminating in the creation of man. Part III focuses on the Garden of Eden before the Fall. There are no more events to describe, and the resulting idyllic text dictates a less dramatic musical setting; thus text and music present a considerable contrast here to Parts I and II. In Part III the solo characters also change: the three angels who earlier narrated and commented on events—Gabriel (soprano), Uriel (tenor), and Raphael (bass)—are mainly absent now, and in their stead mere mortals—Adam (bass) and Eve (soprano)—hold forth with a hymn of praise and a love duet. Throughout the oratorio, the chorus (always SATB) generally represents the Heavenly Host.

Most of our readers will be concerned about the effectiveness and authenticity of the oratorio in its English-text version. For a long time critics assumed that Swieten must have significantly altered the original, English libretto in preparing his German text—so much so that the German version became virtually his own invention and thus the "original"; that assumption made it easier to believe that the English text used in the first British performances (and printed in Haydn's authorized edition) was derived from Swieten's German version, hence was what Donald Francis Tovey condescendingly called "a re-

---

[23] Cf. Jens Peter Larsen's description of the recit.-aria-chorus structure in *Messiah; Larsen Messiah*, 97-103.

[24] The angels join Uriel at the end of her aria (No. 2); the "Lidley" text probably provided words for an independent chorus.

translation by a German from the German."[25] As such, its stilted language became a safe target for ridicule throughout the nineteenth and twentieth centuries. The idea that no proper English poet could have forged such banal, archaic verse was aided by scholars' inability to find another copy of the original "Lidley" libretto. Neither Lidley nor his heirs nor his friends could be turned up (Tovey thought Griesinger's reference must surely have been to the Linley family, who *could* be turned up).[26]

Two recent studies have proven that an original English libretto did exist and that Swieten and Haydn relied heavily upon it. In 1968 Edward Olleson compared *The Creation*'s English "translation" to its probable sources in Milton and the English Bible, found similarities too striking to be coincidental, and concluded that

> The English text to the *Creation*, as we know it from the printed score, was to a considerable extent simply compiled by van Swieten from his model. It seems safe to assume that those parts of the "Lidley" libretto which were used in Haydn's oratorio have by and large survived—not dimly visible through a translation and a re-translation, but *in their original form*. Van Swieten's general method of working was to *leave the English of his model as it stood*, and to write his German text around it. His own metaphor describes the process exactly: he "resolved to clothe the English poem in German garb". . . . The German libretto was written in such a way that Haydn's music would fit the original English too.[27]

In 1983 Nicholas Temperley made a similar comparative study, this time of *a)* the sources (i.e., *Paradise Lost* and the Authorized Version of the Bible), *b)* the English texts as found in Haydn's published score plus an important authentic manuscript, and *c)* the texts of the word-books distributed at the first English performances. Like Olleson, Temperley found evidence of an existing English libretto, one from which Haydn may even have derived some early musical inspiration.[28] It is profitable to compare our much-maligned English version with its supposed German source, then with the poetic ancestors cited by Swieten and confirmed by Olleson and Temperley.[29] When we do so, we can easily see Swieten's debt to Milton. The famous recitative describing the animals (see Ex. 9.1) begins in the German with:

> Gleich öffnet sich der Erde Schoß,
> Und sie gebiert auf Gottes Wort
> Geschöpfe jeder Art,
> In vollem Wuchs' und ohne Zahl.

---

[25] Tovey *Essays* 5, 120; (2) 355.

[26] Tovey *Essays* 5, 120. (2), 354. Cf. Landon *HCW* 4, 118-119, which ties together later scholarship.

[27] Olleson "Origin," 160. Italics added.

[28] Temperley "New light," esp. 204-208.

[29] Temperley *Creation*, 10-11, also cited Joseph Addison's paraphrase of Ps. 19:1-6 (*The Spectator*, 23 August 1712) as a remarkable precursor of "The heavens are telling."

In the English version this is:

> Strait opening her fertile womb,
> The earth obey'd the word, and teem'd
> Creatures numberless,
> In perfect forms and fully grown.

Which is easily traced to Milton's:

> The Earth obeyd, and strait
> Op'ning her fertil Woomb teemd at a Birth
> Innumerous living Creatures, perfet formes,
> Limbd and full grown . . .
> *(Paradise Lost*, vii. 453-6)

Sometimes Milton's poetry can *only* be traced from the English version, as with the passage "In serpent error rivers flow" (No. 6). That language is quite similar to "with Serpent errour wandring" (*Paradise Lost*, vii. 302), but one could never infer the same connection from Swieten's prosaic German: "in mancher Krümme." Clearly the Baron was working (as he said) from an English libretto based on Milton, and just as clearly he left most of that libretto intact in the English version: it is no "re-translation."[30]

In like fashion the English version's wordings of Genesis and paraphrases of the Psalms can be seen to reflect the Authorized Version, the Psalter, and the Book of Common Prayer, not the Vulgate or Luther Bibles to which Swieten would naturally have turned for an "original" German text.[31] A final proof of the English version's legitimacy is this: ridiculous as its language may sometimes seem (and Handel's texts could be ridiculous too), it stands head and shoulders above Swieten's English efforts for *The Seasons*, in which he is known to have fashioned first a German text and then translated it.

For performers, one especially pleasant result of Temperley's study has been the discovery of some historical but clearer English that could well be used in place of Swieten's least gainly utterances. This discovery came from careful examination of the word-books printed for the first London performances; they turned out to be *de facto* copies of "Lidley." When the texts of these word-books were compared with Swieten's English version, his alterations of "Lidley" (whether the result of miscopying or done for other reasons) became obvious. Thus we now have two possible authentic texts. Table 9.1 shows some examples of the variants.

---

[30] This assumption did not die with Tovey but as recently as 1966 was prevalent in German scholarship; cf. Stern "'Schöpfung'".

[31] "It is unlikely, for example, that the similarity between the words from Haydn's sunrise, 'A giant proud and glad / To run his measured course,' and the verse from the Book of Common Prayer, '...and rejoiceth as a giant to run his course' is purely coincidental." Olleson "Origin," 158.

One or two words can make a difference, and the cumulative effect of such changes is very strong. Temperley's discoveries have been incorporated into the Peters Edition (London) score; since they are so often happier English, it is fortunate that the music will accommodate most of the "Lidley" variants.[32]

In any case, we now have a much better insight into the provenance of the English version, and we should no longer have any qualms about presenting *The Creation* in Milton's native language. The English version is not bastardized *Hochdeutsch* but has in fact remained faithful to its roots. We can no longer doubt that Haydn intended the work to be equally effective, equally authentic, in either tongue.

THE CREATION: MUSIC

Much has been written about the music of *The Creation*. Certainly any conductor planning a performance of this great work will want to begin with Nicholas Temperley's *Haydn: The Creation*, which manages to be both comprehensive and relatively concise. Then one can turn to the more than eighty pages on the subject in Robbins Landon's *Haydn: The Years of "The Creation"* (*HCW* 4) and from that to the excellent studies by Tovey, Brown, and others mentioned in this chapter.[33] Here we have just enough space to introduce the wonders of this work with an example or two. Perhaps our unavoidable neglect of many other aspects will give the reader more impetus to make an individual investigation.

General structure and symbolism

Howard Smither has compiled an excellent short summary of *The Creation*'s tonal organization, gratefully quoted below. When it is read while holding Table 9.2 within glancing range, it should provide a good foundation for more detailed study (note also the tempo architecture given in Table 9.2 and its relationship to the tonal plan).

> The main tonal center of the work is C, a key that is introduced at several significant points: Number 1 begins in C minor and closes in C major; C major returns at the end of the second Day (No. 4) and at the end of the fourth Day (No. 13, which closes Part I); in Part II, C major is heard after God creates man (No. 24); and in Part III, when Adam and Eve first sing, in paradise (No. 30). Yet Part III ends in B-flat, rather than C, for symbolic reasons: Adam and Eve, central to Part III, are lower beings than the angels, and as Uriel suggests in a recitative (No.

---

[32] Complete table of variants, with annotations, in Temperley "New light," 200-204.

[33] A new study of *The Creation* by Bruce Mac Intyre, due in 1996, also promises to be a major contribution to the literature.

33), they will fall from Grace. Their position and their fall are symbolized by the B-flat ending of Part III. Long before, however, Haydn had prepared for the final deflection to B-flat: the first stable key in Part II is F, and Part II closes in B-flat. . . . [Furthermore, Adam and Eve's] first duet (with chorus, No. 30) begins and ends in C major (for they are still associated with the Heavenly Host), but in the center section of that number the tonality moves remarkably far afield on the flat side, passing through F, B-flat, A-flat, G-flat, E-flat minor, F minor, G minor, G major, and again to C major (for the last time in the oratorio); and their love duet (No. 32) is in the key of E-flat. The tonal symbolism with respect to Adam and Eve is matched by stylistic symbolism, for in comparison with the magnificent C-major duet with chorus (No. 30), the love duet and the final chorus of the oratorio are notably simpler and of a "lower" style.[34]

Haydn carefully marshalled other aspects of the work to offset this asymmetrical shift to another tonal center and "lower" style. One of his most successful unifying efforts was the grand triumvirate of choruses that end Parts I, II, and III. All use the same forces: full orchestra, chorus, and concertante vocal soloists. Yet without disturbing the intended overall affinities between these structural pillars, Haydn also introduced subtle but effective contrasts within each number to mark the advancement of the creation story. Thus the first finale, "The heavens are telling the glory of God," features Gabriel, Uriel, and Raphael providing, as a trio, the relief material in a kind of giant choral rondo; form and content are relatively simple, after the manner of a symphonic fourth movement, and the alternating praise statements of the Heavenly Host and the three angels no more different than two sides of a coin.

By the end of Part II, however, all of the creation has been completed, including humanity. Haydn here separated the soloists from their counterparts in the choir and gave them their own number (27, "To Thee each living soul"). It is framed by two choruses in B♭ with much the same text and musical material ("Achieved is the glorious work"). These choruses of the Heavenly Host are (*vide* Smither) tonally affected by the new presence of mortals. So is No. 27, and to a far greater degree. Although the solo trio is still nominally angelic, this supplicative Adagio in E♭ (the "Masonic" key—see below—and also tonic to B♭), is more priestly than divine and provides an endearingly human center to the finale. It is surely no coincidence that Eve and Adam sing a love duet soon afterward in the same key, the same tempo, and with similar brushes of woodwind color.

Having introduced incarnate beings in Part III, Haydn chose nevertheless not to include them specifically in its choral finale. Instead, the last chorus of *The Creation* conspicuously omits giving names to the soprano, alto (!), tenor, and bass soloists who figure so heroically at the climax of this movement, repeatedly entering on an "amen" in florid counterpoint. Perhaps at the very end, the composer wished to recall the great German

---

[34] Smither *History* 3, 497-498, based on Levarie "Closing," esp. 319-320, and Landon *HCW* 4, 397 and 399-403.

Passion tradition by having his singers represent not merely angels or men but all of creation.

If that was Haydn's intent, it was unfortunately lost on many of his nineteenth- and early-twentieth-century critics. A significant amount of negative comment has occurred over the years regarding the perceived anticlimax of Part III. Why not just end the piece after No. 30's gigantic C-major cadences, it has been asked, after Adam, Eve, and the Heavenly Host have sung "one of the most inspired and powerful numbers of the entire work"?[35] Nothing could top that, and in fact Haydn made no effort to do so. Tovey advocated cutting the rest of Part III in performance.[36]

But there are two major reasons why "solving" the "problem" of Part III in that way would be wrong. First of all, Tovey and his colleagues suffered from what might be called the climax syndrome; the eighteenth century did not. For Haydn and his contemporaries, a Classical work of music demanded, like a classical drama, that the high point come somewhere *before* the very end and that it be followed by something more decorous, an interval of comparative repose. Thus the last movement of a symphony will never be as intense or complex as the first. The development section, not the recapitulation, of a sonata movement will contain its climax; within that development, the moment of greatest drama will occur well before the end. In opera the ideal is the same: after Don Giovanni is dragged into the flames of hell, the other characters sing us the moral in a merry sextet. After Tamino and Pamina undergo the trials of fire and water, Papageno and Papagena get to play. And in Handelian oratorio: after the "Hallelujah" chorus, we are granted an intermission and then a long, placid soprano solo—if *Messiah* is done as Handel wished, that is. Siegmund Levarie convincingly argued that the closing numbers of *The Creation* follow in this honorable tradition, that they are "the *Singspiel* counterpart to the grander preceding scene."

Levarie also spoke to the second major reason for letting Part III stand as written:

> To Haydn, man was the crown of all creation. Man, therefore, has to be shown in both his aspects as partaking of divinity and succumbing to worldly pleasures. God has touched him, but the snake will get him.[37]

As Levarie's words imply, we would be remiss in accepting the final numbers of *The Creation* only in terms of their function as "comparative repose" or their style as "Singspiel." Most listeners will sense something nobler behind Haydn's turn from angels to mortals in Part III. The fondest hope of the Enlightenment was that humans would somehow prove worthy of the universe they had come to inhabit. That makes Haydn's final scene, a vision of Adam and Eve at play in the fields of the Lord, infinitely more

---

[35] Geiringer *Haydn*, 358.

[36] Tovey *Essays* 5, 124-125, 145-146; (2), 359-360, 380-381.

[37] Levarie "Closing," 317 (quote in body of text), 316.

touching than any angelic chorus might have been. Whether or not we can still share the Enlightenment's hope, if we recognize it as the guiding myth of this oratorio, we can find Part III moving and necessary after all.

An issue somewhat related to tonal organization and symbolism is the use of Masonic symbols in the music. It is clear by now that Haydn's membership in a Viennese lodge of Freemasons meant more to him than his early biographers realized.[38] Baron van Swieten was also a Mason, and the whole of *The Creation* is deeply imbued with reverence for the "Great Architect of the Universe," as the order conceived of God. We draw attention again to No. 27, "To Thee each living soul." Besides the obvious devotional quality of the text, it is worth noting the many "threes" that it embodies (this number had mystical significance in Freemasonry): it is the central movement of three linked numbers (26-28); it is sung by a solo trio; it is in E-flat, the so-called Masonic key (three flats); it is in 3/4 time with prominent anacruses of three eighth-notes throughout. The use of woodwinds, specifically the clarinets associated with Mozart's Masonic music, further suffuses every measure with the gentle spirit of Freemasonry.

Tone painting; accompanied recitatives

The Creation is full of what eighteenth-century Viennese called *Thonmahlerey*, "tone painting" or musical pictorialism. That ancient Baroque tradition could bring drama (raging seas, thundering heavens) and humor (Vivaldi's barking dog) by turns to any work. Its appeal was immediate and obvious, and Haydn's audiences surely enjoyed it. But already—by the time of *The Seasons* if not sooner—a younger, more humorless generation had begun to quarrel with such devices, which they saw as frivolous and naive. Beethoven was very careful to say that his "Pastoral" Symphony depicted nothing more specific about nature than his *feelings* for it. But, as we can infer from his remark to Silverstolpe ("One has to have some amusement"), Haydn felt perfectly free to indulge in a little frivolity. And he could scarcely be accused of naiveté. In producing these settings Haydn had calculated, with a wisdom born of many years' craftsmanship and political maneuvering, their precise effect upon his audiences.

To this end he had almost overbearing assistance from Swieten. The Baron's manuscript libretto for Haydn is littered with suggestions for musical setting, many of which the composer adopted:

> [No. 1 "And the Spirit of God"] In the Chorus, the darkness could gradually disappear; but enough of the darkness should remain to make the momentary transition to light very effective. "And there was light &c." must only be said once. . . .

---

[38] See Chailley "Création" and esp. Hurwitz "Freemasons."

[No. 16 "Be fruitful all"] Here it seems that the bare accompaniment of the bass moving solemnly in a straight rhythm would create a good effect. [This was Haydn's first idea of the final, finished version and it would seem that it was performed that way on the first evening; then he added two violoncelli and still later the divided violas.] . . .

[No. 18 Terzetto] For these strophes, a quite simple and syllabic melody would probably be the best thing to have, so that the words can be understood clearly; but the accompaniment could paint the course of the brook, the flight of the bird and the quick movement of the fishes. [Haydn in the middle and sometimes also upper strings gives a convincing feeling of flowing water, and he also imitates the birds, the bottom of the ocean and, delightfully, "th'immense Leviathan."].[39]

We reproduce at this chapter's end, as Example 9.1, the conclusion of No. 21, "Strait opening her fertile womb," the most famous piece of tone painting in *The Creation* and a fine example also of Haydn's skill with accompanied recitative. An immense variety of tempos, textures, colors, and rhythms is presented in very little space. Note that the orchestra depicts each animal (in Ex. 9.1 the horse, cattle, sheep, insects, and lowly worm) *before* Raphael introduces it vocally. This is a pattern that can be traced in other passages as well: compare for example in No. 1 the choral phrases "Let there be light!" and "And there was light." (Ex. 9.2). Each is preceded by an orchestral statement that harmonically anticipates it. Symbolically, the first orchestral statement represents God speaking; the second—a masterfully simple pizzicato on a dominant seventh—represents the moment at which God wills the light into being.[40]

Arias

Only five numbers in *The Creation* are arias without chorus; even in these, a more modern style is apparent. One can easily point out archaisms: Gabriel's "With verdure clad," for example, is a true *siciliano*, in lilting compound meter like "He shall feed his flock," and furthermore containing a certain amount of florid passagework. But those elements are wedded to an altogether Classical sense of form. The introduction takes just four measures; it becomes part of a sonata procedure with astonishingly neat, incremental periods:

Tonal structure	I	→	V	‖	X	→	I	K
No. of measures	16		17		18		24	14

---

[39] "Gottfried van Swieten's Suggestions to Haydn: English Translation" in Landon *Creation*, 84-86. Bracketed comments by Landon.

[40] We owe this interpretation partly to Smither *History* 3, 506, which also cites Handel's setting of "Let there be light" in *Samson* as a possible inspiration for Haydn's use of ascending fourths in the soprano here.

The melodic style of the number is genuinely folk-like too, holding the coloratura factor in check. Not a whiff of the Rococo mock-pastorale intrudes here—Haydn's angel apparently knows that loamy soil is needed to nourish the scented herb and healing plant.

Gabriel's aria in Part Two, "On mighty pens" (No. 15), is more of a soprano show-piece, with proportions and *passaggi* that recall the Baroque concerto or opera seria. Yet its pretensions are masterfully undercut too, and with one of the principal devices of Haydn's "popular" manner, namely tone-painting. This aspect has retained its interest for succeed-ing generations largely because of the composer's uncanny musical eye. We can ascribe his pictorial talent to his love of the countryside (he was fond of hunting) and his artisan's at-tention to detail. Before the aria runs its course, it thus provides the highly distinguishable antics and songs of the eagle, lark, dove, and nightingale. A similar use of tone-painting is threaded through the rest of the arias, revealing at times Haydn's childlike side as well: in No. 22 a quiet passage occurs where Raphael sings of the "heavy beasts"; there Haydn gleefully inserted two loud, low grunts from the bassoons and contrabassoon.

Three numbers are solo ensembles; the two trios, being "angel" music, are written in an elevated style with occasional patches of counterpoint. The duet for Adam and Eve is, as noted above, less elevated. In fact, its second section is built on the rhythms of the *écos-saise*, a type of contredanse that was all the rage in turn-of-the-century Viennese ball-rooms.[41] We will have more to say below about the style and interpretation of the arias.

Choruses

The chorus appears in ten of *The Creation*'s thirty-four numbers; that is a nice bal-ance.[42] It is a further tribute to Haydn's imaginative integration of elements in this work that only three of these numbers are for chorus alone: "Awake the harp" (No. 10), "Achieved is the glorious work" (No. 26/28, which is nevertheless part of a chorus-trio-chorus form), and "Sing the Lord, ye voices all!" (No. 34, which includes a *concertante* solo quartet). The others are all linked to solos (three numbers, if we count the opening recitative), a duet (No. 30), or trios (Nos. 13 and 19).

A number of the choruses bear the unmistakable imprint of time spent in England. In these, Haydn's own well-developed orchestral craft and Fuxian counterpoint are fortified by a truly Handelian sense of drama—that is, of timing and structure. Thus the D-major vitality of "Awake the harp" (No. 10; see Ex. 9.3) is buoyed up by spurting call-and-re-sponse motives that frame a longer (mm. 3-6) choral declamation. And that is mere intro-duction; it goes on just long enough to set up the fugue, also handled in a brilliant but economical manner. Tovey praised this "admirably terse" movement and went on to re-

---

[41] Levarie "Closing," 318.

[42] Cf. *Messiah*, with twenty-one choruses out of fifty-seven numbers, or *Israel in Egypt*, with its twenty-seven out of forty.

mark on Haydn's device of "prolonging the first note backward," using a touch of the-matic augmentation here and there to produce a sense of breadth in a very small space (m. 23ff).[43] Robbins Landon has shown how the clever disposition of the trombone parts in this section, sometimes doubling the voices and sometimes not, provides another illu-sion—obbligato lines—without cluttering the texture.[44]

Two other choruses demonstrate the wide variety of manners or types present in these movements. Number 13, "The heavens are telling," was always immensely popular with the British. Its text is a paraphrase of Psalm 19:1-2; in the previous chapter, we noted the-matic similarities between one of Haydn's English Psalm settings and this movement. Haydn has complemented its sturdy Anglicized melodies with his own deft orchestration: a flute that joins the solo trio at measure 55, the reservation of trumpets and drums until the very end of the fugue, and *then* a thrilling headlong descent into chromaticism for the coda, with violins hammering away in the highest leger-lines.

Number 2, Uriel's aria with chorus, is more charmingly Viennese. It has a symmetrical three-part form (aria "Now vanish . . .," chorus "Despairing, cursing . . .," aria + chorus "A new-created world") and key structure (A-c-A) which comforts and moves us still to-day, even if our hopes have dimmed considerably of seeing a time when "disorder yields to order fair the place."[45] As in many earlier works, Haydn's impeccable sense of thematic unity guides us through the well-trimmed *chiaroscuro* of the movement.[46] The leading motive of the "Chaos" prelude has gradually made its way into No. 2. It is first recalled in Raphael's accompanied recitative at the end of the prelude, in both its original form (Ex. 9.4b) and in a sort of inversion (Ex. 9.4a):

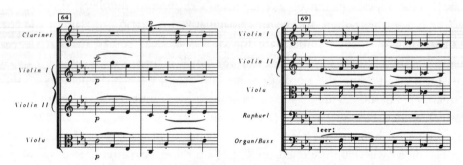

Example 9.4a: Haydn *The Creation*, 2, mm. 64-65; 9.4b: Haydn *The Creation*, 2, mm. 69-70

Then its inverted form is turned to radiant major and becomes the tune of Uriel's "Now vanish . . .":

---

[43] Tovey *Essays* 5, 130; (2), 365.

[44] Landon *HCW* 4, 419.

[45] Consider also its Masonic implications (architecture, keys).

[46] Much of the following analysis is derived from Landon *HCW* 4, 414-415.

Example 9.5: Haydn *The Creation*, 2, mm. 16-19

But when the chorus arrives, describing in C minor the rage of "hell's spirits," this motive undergoes another transformation:

Example 9.6: Haydn *The Creation*, 2, mm. 76-77]

Finally, the arrival of "A new-created world" brings not only the comforting return of A major, but something new-created indeed—a virgin motive (see Ex. 9.7, end of chapter). The introduction of this folkish but delicate tune was a master-stroke on Haydn's part, exactly what was needed to evoke wonder at the freshly minted universe. He saved the "Verzweiflung" motive for one last transformation in the final bars (Ex. 9.8, e.o.c.).

THE CREATION: FIRST PERFORMANCES; EDITIONS

Modern musicians will find extremely helpful a recent comprehensive study by A. Peter Brown of the earliest *Creation* performances.[47] In spite of an unbroken tradition of performance in Vienna and elsewhere and in spite of the presence of an authorized printed score, much remained unknown about Haydn's own renditions of his most popular oratorio. We have drawn heavily on Brown for the comments which follow; his little study should be required reading for every Haydn conductor.

---

[47] Brown *Performing.*

Between April 29, 1798, and 1810, Vienna heard *The Creation* more than forty times. Haydn himself presided at nearly half these performances and attended several others.[48] The sizes of the chorus and orchestra at these events cannot always be determined, but they appear to have varied widely. Typical of the small-scale performances was one given at the Esterházy Palace in Eisenstadt for the visit of Lord Horatio Nelson in September of 1800. Haydn conducted, employing about twenty-four instrumentalists and eight singers—eight paid singers, that is; there may have been a few servants commandeered without compensation. On the other end of the size spectrum, we have firm reports of 180 executants (perhaps 120 instruments and 60-80 singers) taking part in the first "public" performances of March 1799.[49] Probably the forces at the Schwarzenberg Palace in 1798 also approached this number. We know that Haydn preferred the bigger performances, although he must have considered more intimate versions—like the one for Nelson—tolerable. His biographer Carpani did not: for him, the minimum requirement for a respectable *Creation* performance was sixty instruments and twenty-four voices.[50]

We do not know whether the soprano and alto parts at the first performances were sung by boys or women. The evidence leans toward boy singers, however, since boys were used by the Tonkünstler Society, which had established the big-oratorio tradition in Vienna. In 1781, for example, Albrechtsberger recruited a total of twenty-eight boys from three Viennese churches for a performance of his own oratorio.[51] Brown: "The first documentation of women participating in the chorus begins after the founding of the Gesellschaft der Musikfreunde [1812]."[52] As we mentioned in connection with the Masses, the soloists' parts contained the choral sections also, so the male choral sound may well have been colored by doubling from the female soloists. We have also seen that Haydn used three soloists, not five, for his performances.

For the instrumental forces there is a bit more evidence, both of their balance/disposition and of the seating arrangement. The approximately 120 instrumentalists

---

[48] A table in Brown *Performing*, 2-7, shows the date, place, sponsor, principal performers, number of performers, and scholarly references to each of these performances.

[49] Cf. "Das Orchester wird aus 180 Personen bestehen" (*Allgemeine Musikalische Zeitung* February 1799); "181 Instrumenten" (Constanze Mozart); "Der Sänger- und Orchesterchor bestand aus mehr als 180 Personen" (*Allegemeine Musikalische Zeitung* April 1799); "The orchestra which together with the chorus consisted of some 400 persons" (Johan Fredrik Berwald [*not* his father Georg Johan Berwald as stated in Brown *Performing*]). Quoted in Brown *Performing*, 20, also in Landon *HCW* 4, 448-458 *passim*. The term "orchestra," not incidentally, often included soloists, chorus, and instrumentalists. Berwald was eleven years old when he attended the performance, so his memory may be faulted; his story is certainly contradicted by several other points of evidence, not the least of which is the surviving performance materials: they were used for many years afterwards in Tonkünstler Society performances for groups of about 180 and could not reasonably have accommodated an assembly of 400. Ibid., 20-21.

[50] *Haydine*, 186.

[51] Biba "Beispiele," 100.

[52] Brown *Performing*, 23.

will have included about 72 string players, distributed approximately 18/18/12/12/12; in addition one cello and one double bass player stood by the keyboardist to form a continuo ensemble (especially useful in the recitatives). Winds (*Harmonie*) were more or less tripled and divided into three groups plus a brass-and-timpani complement. Solo and tutti divisions were carefully marked in these parts; Brown proposed (referring also to general contemporary practice) that *Harmonie 1* (see Fig. 10.8) was the solo group, *2* and *3* the tutti. But *Harmonie 3*'s role may have been even further limited, e.g., to playing only in the choruses and at other climactic points. At any rate an extremely wide range of dynamic and color contrasts would have been possible: Brown noted that "solo and tutti distinctions are to be found in the most delicate of the arias, and a tutti may occur in the briefest of interludes."[53] Remarkable also is the relative strength of the wind and string choirs and their seating arrangement, given in Figure 10.8.[54]

This diagram is a reconstruction based on an account by Johan Fredrik Berwald, a Swedish violin prodigy whose father took him to the March 1799 performance in the Burgtheater. He was particularly struck by the multilevel "amphitheater" aspect of the stage arrangement:

> Down below at the fortepiano [!] sat *Capellmeister* Weigl, surrounded by the vocal soloists, the chorus, a violoncello and a double bass. At one level higher stood Haydn himself with his conductor's baton. Still a level higher on one side were the first violins, led by Paul Wranitzky, and on the other the second violins, led by his brother Anton Wranitzky. In the center: violas and double basses [*sic*; cellos?]. In the wings, more double basses; on higher levels the wind instruments, and at the very top: trumpets, kettledrums and trombones.[55]

This story is comparable to Charlotte Papendiek's diary entry describing the orchestra setup at Haydn's London concerts (see Fig. 10.7). Evidently it proved succesful then, so Haydn continued to employ it. The reference to a baton in Berwald's memoir can be regarded cautiously; he was recollecting the event years later, when such things would have been more common. Compare this excerpt from a letter of Princess Eleonora Liechtenstein, written the day after the second performance of 1798: "La musique a été parfaitement executée, dirigée par Hayden [*sic*] qui donait la mesure des 2 mains."[56]

The autograph score of *The Creation* has been lost. Haydn prepared another score for an edition that he himself had printed and sold by subscription in 1800; it was reprinted by Breitkopf & Härtel in 1803. Eusebius Mandyczewski used that score for the first critical

---

[53] *Performing*, 24.

[54] Brown *Performing*, 24-30.

[55] As given in Brown *Performing*, 29. Trans. in Landon *HCW* 4, 455; Mörner "Haydniana," 5.

[56] Quoted in Pohl *Haydn* 3, 130.

edition in 1924. The 1925 Eulenberg score, used for most performances today, is in turn based on Mandyczewski.

Because of their lineage, one would expect all these editions to be scrupulously faithful records of the composer's final wishes, but that expectation must be qualified. Brown came to a rather extreme conclusion:

> Haydn's primary objective [in his first edition] was to secure for himself a substantial financial return. The edition had all the trappings of a souvenir of already legendary music from the hands of the most revered musical personality of his day, with its prestigious subscription list, special paper, and title page signed and sealed by Haydn himself; for the royalty, the nobility, and the gentry, it was a significant addition for their collections.[57]

According to Brown, at least three sets of manuscripts from Haydn's time provide a more accurate picture of his own performances:

1) Haydn's own conducting score and parts for the "big" performances, now housed in the Wiener Stadtbibliothek. Prepared by Haydn's personal copyist Johann Elssler and others working under his direction, the score contains cues and other emendations by Haydn. Because of their association with the Tonkünstler Society's concerts, Brown dubbed them the *Tonkünstler Score and Parts.*

2) Another set prepared by Elssler et al. with numerous corrections by Haydn. They were found in his library at his death and thus called the *Estate Score and Parts.* The score contains the most extensive figures for realizing the basso continuo.

3) The *Elssler Parts*, an incomplete set by Elssler now in the Gesellschaft der Musikfreunde. These probably date from the 1808 performance at the University Hall honoring Haydn.

All these scores and parts contain a number of fascinating details omitted from the authorized edition of 1800 but undoubtedly used in Haydn's performances:

1) Eight additional passages are scored for the bass trombone and/or contrabassoon.[58] Moreover, in No. 21, mm. 8-13, the lion roars rather more loudly, since Haydn added bass trombone and *all* bassoons to the trombone I and II parts and contrabassoon specified in the authorized edition. These changes may have been made specifically to provide the extra bass sound needed by a large group playing in a large room.[59]

---

[57] *Performing*, 74.

[58] The music for each of these is provided in Brown's Appendix 5; *Performing*, 92-110.

[59] See William Gardiner's comments on similar problems at the Westminster Abbey Handel concerts, quoted in Brown *Performing*, 28.

2) The opening measures of the Elssler Parts contain some mysterious "dynamic-staccato" markings. Whether these represent a sort of *Luftpause*, or the exact mid-point of the "hairpin," or something else, is unclear.[60]

3) At the beginning of No. 1, not only the strings but also the trumpets, horns, and timpani are instructed to play *con sordini*, thus enhancing the movement's initial sombre colors and quiet dynamic; the mutes are removed just before the burst of light.

4) In No. 12, the lines for the trumpets and horns at the "sunset" passage (m. 17ff.) are reversed in the parts. In performance Haydn must therefore have heard the horns, not the trumpets, sustain through m. 18.

5) There are other small changes in the orchestration, principally in Nos. 1 and 14.[61]

Should then Haydn's 1800 edition and its descendants be dismissed as inauthentic and irrelevant? Hardly. The subscription edition bears the composer's imprimatur; it must remain a primary point of reference. Although he may not have proofread it well, Haydn undoubtedly viewed his printed score not merely as a collectors' item, but also as a reliable guide to performance. Any eighteenth-century musician would have been expected to create a "realization" of that score according to his own performing circumstances; the Tonkünstler, Estate, and Elssler parts should be seen as products of that flexible attitude toward music-making, not as second and third thoughts on the road to a more definitive version of the work. No such version will ever be found.[62]

AT WORK ON *THE SEASONS*

Back in Vienna after the Princess's name-day, Haydn wrote to the German musical lexicographer Ernst Ludwig Gerber about two new projects:

> Since this subject [an oratorio, *The Seasons*] cannot be as sublime as that of *The Creation*, comparison between the two will show a distinct difference. Despite this, and with the help of Providence, I shall press on, and when this new work is completed I shall retire, because of the weakened state of my nerves, in order to be able to complete my last work. This will consist of vocal quartets, with accompaniment only of the pianoforte, based on German texts of our greatest poets; I have already composed thirteen such pieces, but have not yet performed any of them.[63]

---

[60] Cf. Landon *HCW* 4, 395, with Brown *Performing*, 32.

[61] See Brown *Performing*, 37-39, 39-41.

[62] Some scholars have also quibbled over discrepancies between Mandyczewski's edition and the authorized edition of 1800. See Lucas "Analysis," esp. 112-116, which gives a list of over 200 additions, deletions, and substitutions of various markings (mainly dynamics and solo/tutti indications) made by Mandyczewski but not listed as part of his editorial revisions.

[63] Landon *HCW* 4, 487-488; Haydn *CCLN* 166-167.

The "quartets" were the partsongs "Aus des Ramlers lyrischer Blumenlese" (XXVb:1-4; XXVc:1-9), of which Haydn completed no more than the thirteen mentioned in his letter. In October at Eisenstadt he performed seven of them for an "academy" held at a private house; these *Mehrstimmige Gesänge* are discussed in Chapter 7.

Haydn had been at work on *The Seasons* for some time. Back in March, a German correspondent reported that "he has already completed the first part, 'Spring.' The curiosity of all music lovers is already stretched to the breaking point."[64] Once again, Haydn's collaborator was the indefatigable Baron van Swieten. In fact, it was no doubt Swieten who instigated the project and persisted with the composer until it was completed. This time, moreover, the Baron had set himself the double task of abridging the poetry and translating it freshly into English. Although *The Seasons* had its roots in English verse—James Thomson's poem of 1726-30, later much revised—Swieten appears to have worked from the German side of a dual English-German edition brought out in 1745 by B. H. Brockes.[65] German or English, the final libretto is universally acknowledged to be far inferior to that of *The Creation*, and Haydn found setting it a difficult task. His advancing age also exacted a price. Griesinger noted:

> The best in [Swieten's] poems was not that which he expressed but rather that which he imagined, and it was amazing to find in his works none of the beauties by which, according to his intention and his emotion, they ought to have been distinguished.
>
> Haydn often complained bitterly over the unpoetic text of *The Seasons*, and how hard it was for him to find inspiration to compose "Heysasa! Hopsasa! Long live wine! Long live the cask in which it's kept! Long live the pitcher from which it pours!" and so on. When he came to the place "Industry, noble industry, from thee comes all prosperity!", he remarked that he had been an industrious man all his life, but that it had never occurred to him to set industry to music. Haydn attributed to the strain that the composition of *The Seasons* cost him the weakness that grew ever greater from this time. He was seized with a brain fever shortly after completing the work, and at that time he described how his mind's incessant activity with notes and music was the cause of his greatest suffering.[66]

Haydn's "brain fever" caused him to cancel his conducting of two *Creation* performances on April 12 and 13, 1800. Maria Anna Haydn had died on March 20, but it is questionable whether that caused further stress to the composer that spring. Perhaps, as Silverstolpe rather maliciously suggested in a report to Stockholm, "Haydn is now writing with new zeal, since he has recently had the fortune to lose his evil wife."[67] In any case, his

---

[64] Quoted in Landon *HCW* 4, 454.

[65] The same Brockes (1680-1747) who compiled the text of the German Passion set by Handel and others.

[66] Griesinger *Notizen* (3), 39-40.

[67] Trans. in Landon *HCW* 4, 547; Mörner "Haydniana," 351.

convalescence took quite some time, and work on the "Summer" dragged well into the winter.

In October Haydn traveled to Esterháza, the castle at which he had spent so much time in the service of Nicolaus I, for what was probably the last concert he and his musicians would ever give there. After this point Haydn began to withdraw from many of his public obligations; he ceased attending meetings and "academies" of the Tonkünstler Society after November, complaining of a cold draft in the hall at performances. In December Haydn asked Paul Wranitzky, his concertmaster on previous occasions, to conduct the Society's *Creation* performances that month.

The new year brought, at least for a while, an end to the hostilities with France. Shortly before the Treaty of Lunéville was signed, Haydn had conducted a benefit performance of *The Creation* (January 16) for wounded soldiers. He was again ill in bed with a *Kopffieber* in February. On March 28, Silverstolpe wrote

> Haydn's *Seasons* is finished, however, but a sickness which Haydn suffered postponed everything for so long that I think the performance will be put on next year. Too bad, for who can guarantee that the master will then be able to perform his work. He is old. His works can only lose if they later fall into strange hands.[68]

But *The Seasons* did receive its first performances that spring, on April 24, 27, and May 1 at the Schwarzenberg Palace. Haydn used the same large forces as for *The Creation*, with chorus drawn from several church choirs and orchestra made up mainly of players from the German and Italian opera establishments in Vienna. The soloists, Therese Saal, Matthias Rathmayer, and Ignaz Saal, were the same three singers who appeared in most of the later *Creation* performances. Once again the Gesellschaft der Associirten was the sponsor, and Pohl informs us that Prince Schwarzenberg paid for a police guard to keep the traffic under control before performances; he also saw that the kiosks on the Neuer Markt were cleared away each evening well before crowds began arriving, and that the market place was illuminated.[69]

The Seasons was received enthusiastically by its first audiences. But in the reviews, correspondence, etc., which followed those initial concerts, an air of balanced judgement, a somewhat more ambiguous response, can be detected. Typical is this comment from the *Zeitung für die elegante Welt*:

> The performance was worthy of Viennese artists, the applause undivided and noisy.
>
> It would be more than daring to wish to judge such a masterpiece on the basis of a single hearing; thus only a few general remarks here. Even during the composition, *Herr* Haydn stated that he would rather have composed another subject

---

[68] Trans. in Landon *HCW* 5, 33; Mörner "Haydniana," 367-368.

[69] Pohl *Haydn* 3, 177.

than the four seasons, for example the last judgement or something similar, because some ideas from *The Creation* involuntarily insinuated themselves into "Spring"; also one noticed in the new work that some arias and choruses displayed a relationship, albeit a small one, with some [numbers] of *The Creation*. Who would want to blame the great master for that? *The Four Seasons*, instead, contained many passages which must move the coldest heart to the most gentle emotions, and many which are great, sublime, that sweep us along like a great river and excite one to the greatest enthusiasm. But the imitation of the cock's crowing at dawn, the gun's explosion during the hunt, seem to me to be a mistaken concept of tone-painting in music, perhaps even a degradation of this divine art.[70]

Among the general praise, these two objections—to the unfortunate similarities of some parts of the work to moments in *The Creation* and to one aspect or another of the *Thonmahlerey*—would appear again and again. The Romantic tide, sweeping out the *Mechanismus* of the old century for a renewed emphasis on pure feeling, was making itself felt. Another critic wrote:

Music ought to describe only passions, emotions and objects that can be heard. . . . Joys and sorrows, which [poetry] often deems inexpressible, can be portrayed by the composer completely and with all their delights and disasters. . . . A composer may describe natural objects; but how? He should describe them, not as they are—their absolute appearance as physical nature—but only through the impressions they make upon us. He must describe them in the reaction that they produce in our souls, but made more beautiful as in a mirror. . . . Haydn is to be excused on account of the badly selected material because the choice was not of his doing; for it is obvious how little suited for music the material really is. It offers neither passions nor emotions, even too few objects for the ear; the dominating objects of nature are not, in this case, seen by the poet in their reactions on our emotions but simply in their physical appearance as part of nature.[71]

It is significant that when the first public performance of *The Seasons* was held, at the Redoutensaal on May 29, it was not well attended. A triumphant string of encore performances was not in store for *The Seasons* in Vienna. Nor did it fare well elsewhere: the French barely noticed it, and the English pointedly avoided performing it during Haydn's lifetime. For the former circumstance, the execrable French translation (perhaps also by Swieten) in the authorized first edition may be partly to blame.[72] For the latter, the situation was more complicated. The English resented what they saw as Haydn's effort to compete with the

---

[70] 1. Jahrgang (1801), 427-428; trans. in Landon *HCW* 5, 45.

[71] *Journal des Luxus and der Moden*, 16 (Weimar 1801), 414; quoted in Pohl *Haydn* 3, 371-372; trans. in Landon *HCW* 5, 46.

[72] Published by Breitkopf & Härtel in 1802, the edition came out in two versions: one with German-French texts, the other with German-English. Carpani referred to this first edition as "tradotto barbaramente in varie lingue" (*Haydine*, 212).

immortal Handel by bringing forth not one but now two oratorios; even *The Creation* had suffered from this prejudice. Furthermore, the text translation provided for *The Seasons* was truly (*vide* Carpani) "barbarous" and cannot have improved its reception. To top it all off, the name of Haydn was at this time involved in a bizarre controversy. When elected a member of the Institut National de France, he had unknowingly beaten out Richard Brinsley Sheridan for that honor. Sheridan and his friends in the British press mounted a campaign of calumny against Haydn that quickly degenerated into flag-waving; in the process it drove Haydn's art further downward in the estimation of the public.

In none of these matters did the music for *The Seasons* play an important part. In fact, large portions of it are equal or superior to that of *The Creation* and well deserve further attention.

THE SEASONS: LIBRETTO AND GENERAL PLAN

The libretto is in four parts: "Spring," "Summer," "Autumn," and "Winter." No plot drives these four segments toward a climax, no overarching literary theme connects them; the effect is much more that of four related cantatas. Besides the German translation of Thomson's poem mentioned above, Swieten incorporated into "Winter" the *Spinning Song* by Gottfried August Bürger and the *Romance* by Madame Favart in its German translation by Christian Felix Weisse. He also added several sections of his own invention. In general Swieten may be said to have excised the philosophical and political overtones in Thomson's poetry while preserving its lyrical evocations of nature. Both Thomson and Swieten saw nature, however, through the eyes of Watteau and Fragonard. As Geiringer said, "The exaggerated praises of the 'merry shepherd,' the 'gay herd,' and the wonderful 'daughters of nature' all breathe the shallow playfulness of rococo art."[73] Their visions of swains and farm girls were not made to arouse deep feelings, only to present pleasant scenes. Modern audiences will find *The Seasons*'s nature scenes quaint by comparison with any of the well-known Romantic depictions. Somehow those later works, through their emphasis on the natural world's beauty *and* infinite power *and* utter indifference to human life, cut deeply into us, whereas Swieten's charming portraits of the hunt and the harvest do not.

Swieten made one other important thematic change from his sources. Thomson's poem contains a strong element of Deism, that eighteenth-century movement which advocated a "natural" religion based on reason and emphasizing morality. To this element Swieten added his own German pietism, as we can see in the oratorio's concluding number. It is a divided chorus that attempts, perhaps, the middle-class mysticism of *Die Zauberflöte* but

---

[73] *Haydn*, 359.

passes from that into a conventional Christian panegyric, echoing the Psalmist in its structure:

> Who may enter these gates?
> He who avoided evil and did good.
> Who may climb this mount?
> He from whose lips came truth.
> Who may dwell in this tent?
> He who helped the poor and needy.
> Who will enjoy peace there?
> He who gave protection and law to the innocent.
> See, the great morning approaches! ...
> Lead our hand, O God!
> Give us strength and courage!
> Then we shall sing,
> > then we shall enter
> in the glory of this kingdom. Amen.

There are three *dramatis personae*, who narrate in the manner of *The Creation*'s angels: Simon (bass), a farmer; Hanne (soprano) (Jane in the English version), his daughter; and Lucas (tenor), a country boy. Although the chorus at times is given a role to play ("Chorus of Peasant-People," "Girls and Lads," etc.), it appears more often as itself. Swieten's autograph libretto shows that he made specific musical suggestions, many of which Haydn followed.

Each of the cantatas begins with an instrumental introduction depicting something appropriate to the overall program; the overture to "Spring" expresses the passage from winter to spring. That is followed by a recitative and a chorus of peasants, "Come gentle spring." The succeeding scenes show a plowman happily tilling his field (bass aria), the peasants praying for God to bless the crops (trio and chorus), and a Song of Joy over the fields in bloom (soprano solo and then "alternating chorus of girls and lads"). That finally gives way to a great hymn to the Creator ("Endless God, mighty God. . . . From thine abundant meals hast thou repasted us.") ending in a choral fugue.

For "Summer," a short introduction "representing the idea of morning twilight" leads directly into a recitative describing the retreat of the night and its fearsome inhabitants ("To gloomy cells repairs of fun'ral birds the lurid tribe. Their moaning hollow cries no more affect the tim'rous heart."). Simon and Jane describe the shepherds going forth with their flocks as sunrise approaches. Then, in No. 12, solo trio and chorus describe the arrival of the sun (Haydn set this in no less a magnificent manner than the parallel number in *The Creation*; see Ex. 10.53). A hymn of praise follows. Farmers work the fields, the sun's heat grows ever more oppressive, and finally (No. 15, Cavatina) "Distressful nature fainting sinks. Drooping flowers, singed meadows, drained fountains, show the rage of tyrant heat." Jane welcomes the "shady groves" in the ensuing recitative and aria, providing an effective contrast to the thunderstorm chorus which follows. "Summer" ends with trio and chorus describing the peace after the storm.

The introduction to "Autumn" indicates "the husbandman's satisfaction at the abundant harvest." It is followed by a trio with chorus in praise of Industry (see Haydn's remarks above). Next there is a slightly less ambitious duet between Jane and Lucas, in which each praises the other's wholesomeness and pledges undying love. Perhaps that scene was inserted in order to bring the last two tableaux into sharper relief, for they offer more vivid opportunities to the composer. Nos. 27-29 depict a hunt, with dogs, birds, hares, horns, and the noble stag. The final chorus depicts merry-making after a grape harvest, and, with Geiringer, "one is reminded of old Dutch paintings, showing lusty peasants dancing, drinking, and shouting."[74]

It speaks volumes that most of "Winter" is arranged so as to take place indoors. In the eighteenth century, no rational person would have taken joy in the approach of the fourth season, so it is hardly surprising that its introduction is in the same key, and just as bleak, as the "Representation of Chaos" in *The Creation*. The succeeding recitative, the Cavatina No. 34 (Ex. 10.54), and the next recitative-aria pair all describe the countryside's icy desolation; eventually the poet's eye falls on someone who has unexplicably ventured out. When at last this wanderer sees a farmhouse, he gratefully he joins its warm inhabitants (the wanderer of Thomson's poem perished in the snow). Here is the point at which Swieten inserted Bürger's *Spinning Song*, sung by Jane and the chorus. It is followed immediately by the Favart *Romance*, in which Jane tells the story of an "honest country lass" who thwarts an attempt at seduction by her lord. The chorus listens and, at precise intervals, laughs uproariously. Then the mood becomes serious again: No. 42 compares the progress of the seasons with the stages of a man's life ("and winter bleak is drawing near, to show at last the yawning tomb"). Thus chastened, the poet meditates on virtue and, in No. 44, for solo trio and double chorus, awaits God's mercy. The concluding words of that chorus are given above.

THE SEASONS: MUSIC

The Seasons begins in G minor and ends in C major. Each of the individual cantatas exhibits a similar flexibility in terms of key: "Spring" moves from G minor to B flat, "Summer" from C minor to E flat, "Autumn" from G major to C major, and "Winter" from C minor to C major. There may be some tonal symbolism scattered throughout the work: G major, the key of Singspiel, is used for Jane's folksy little "Romance" (No. 40), also for the chorus "Come gentle spring" and the genial introduction to "Autumn." As noted above, C minor, the "Chaos" key, has returned as the sound of bleakest winter,

---

74 *Haydn*, 364.

while C major is again the key of heaven (in the finale). But C major is also used for the chorus No. 23 in praise of Industry, which makes it sound rather more like "The heavens are telling" than it should; and the happy plowman of No. 4 also whistles his tune in C, probably because it originally appeared that way in the slow movement of the "Surprise" Symphony. Robbins Landon had a few things to say about D major:

> D major, of course, is Haydn's old hunting key. He wrote three symphonies (Nos. 31, 72, 73) on "chasse" motifs and one *Cassatio* in D with four horns. There is a special twist to the hunting chorus in *The Seasons*, however, because the music shifts from D to E flat. D major, the key of sunrise in *The Creation*, is also the key for the rising sun in *The Seasons*, but otherwise it is never used, except in passing. The surprising shift from D major to E flat illustrates the stag deceiving the hounds.[75]

It hardly seems necessary to say much about tone-painting in *The Seasons*, that is after all one of its most famous ingredients. Haydn had complained about some of the settings in a letter to Müller, the Capellmeister at Leipzig: "NB! This whole passage [No. 20, mm. 53-58], with its imitation of the frogs, was not my idea; I was forced to write this Frenchified trash."[76] But what delightful trash! And how much more gracefully it fits into Haydn's scenes of rustic life than some of his fugues or grand-scale arias (e.g., the duet No. 25 for Jane and Lucas). Some of Haydn's simplest ideas in this genre, for example the "crested harbinger of day" (No. 10, mm. 29ff), are his most effective. Messiaen would never make a better bird-call than this:

Example 9.9: Haydn *The Seasons*, 10, m. 29 oboe

The orchestra for *The Seasons* is substantially the same as for *The Creation*: piccolo; pairs of flutes, oboes, clarinets, and bassoons; contrabassoon; four horns; three each of trumpets and trombones; timpani and other percussion; strings. Although there is no single movement as innovative as the "Representation of Chaos," Haydn continues to show his com-

---

[75] The whole of our discussion of the tonal plan is drawn gratefully from Landon *HCW* 5, 128-129. Nevertheless Landon, in speaking of the key shifts in each cantata, went rather too far in calling them instances of "progressive tonality." One might as easily, and wrongheadedly, assign significance to *Messiah's* beginning in E minor and finishing in D major. The nineteenth-century sense of harmonic macrostructure implicit in such terms is anachronistic when applied to Haydn and his contemporaries.

[76] Quoted in Landon *HCW* 5, 89; Haydn *CCLN*, 197. This part of the letter found its way into print, which predictably enraged Swieten. Griesinger reported that the Baron "intends to rub into Haydn's skin, with salt and pepper, the assertion that he was *forced* into composing the croaking frogs." Griesinger's letter in H. von Hase, *Joseph Haydn und Breitkopf und Härtel* (Leipzig, 1909), 33-34.

mand of orchestration throughout the work. The striking realism of the "Storm" chorus (No. 19) is accomplished through a combination of "chaotic" scoring in the strings (different figures and articulations) and brutal hammering from woodwinds, brass, and especially timpani (e.g., *ff assai*, mm. 2-4). The preceding recitative, describing the approach of the storm, is no less evocative for having been scored with great economy and delicacy. In a similar fashion, the introduction to No. 44, the double-choir finale, manages to conjure up the Last Judgment with truly Viennese felicity (Ex. 9.10). Only winds are used, and these are scored *piano* except for the first trumpet and the contrabassoon. Haydn once said he would have preferred to set this subject—judgement day and universal resurrection—rather than the farmers' antics that Swieten presented him. Here his use of only a few woodwinds and brass to suggest both peace and triumph is a master stroke; it even lends an exalted air to the pseudo-Sarastro of the text.

Haydn's colorful use of the brass, especially the horns, also deserves mention. In No. 11 not only does the horn solo provide a vivid splash of sound against its lightly scored accompaniment, it is also authentic: a contemporary critic noted that "the horn sounds with a call which is the signal in every village for the herds to go out."[77] Likewise the horn calls in No. 29 of the Hunting Scene are drawn from real signals that would have been recognizable to every hunter in eighteenth-century Austria—and there were many, Haydn among them.[78]

Considering what has been said about libretto and orchestration, we could rightly assume that the choruses in *The Seasons* are among Haydn's most varied and appealing. He took more care than in *The Creation*, in fact, to introduce fresh vocal shadings: the loveliness of "Come gentle spring" (No. 2) is further refined by its alternating groups of men and women (both four-part *divisi*); this device is echoed in Nos. 19, 29, and 31 (2- or 3-part men, 2-part women); in No. 8 the "Girls and Lads" are mainly SATT; the magnificent antiphonal scoring of No. 44 adds yet another choral dimension. Haydn expected more of his chorus technically too: in No. 8 the sopranos must hold a high B♭ for nearly two measures; numerous other spots demand more agility of all the parts (e.g., No. 12 m. 82ff.). All this variety and drama are compounded by the practice Haydn followed in *The Creation*, of interlacing solo, duet, and trio pieces with choral passages, and vice versa. Of the twelve numbers containing chorus, only four are for chorus alone.

Four of the choruses (Nos. 6, 9, 23, 44) contain fugues. Yet it is not necessarily Haydn's most characteristic choral writing that wins us over in *The Seasons*. The industrious No. 23 is certainly well crafted: it moves inexorably from one soloist and light accompaniment, through three modulations, more soloists and the whole orchestra, to pedal point, fugue and *più allegro*—in short, the composer's entire battery of tricks. But the effort al-

---

[77] G. A. Griesinger in the *Allgemeine Musikalische Zeitung* 3 (1801), 575-579; trans. in Landon *HCW* 5, 43-45.

[78] Facsimiles of the original hunting calls reproduced in Landon *HCW* 5, pls. 13-18; see also Ringer "Chasse" and Heartz "Hunting."

most backfires, and just because of the almighty arsenal deployed. We cannot quite forget that this massive hymn is not an "in gloria Dei, Amen" but a *Lauda* for something less divine. The famous "drunken" fugue of No. 31 is more successful; Tovey described it with dry humor and great relish:

> We are told that "the bulky tuns are filled." From the music it would rather appear that they were being emptied. . . . The first section, in quick common time, modulates widely and wildly. . . . Then the dance begins. Skirling pipes, rolling drums, scraping fiddles, and snarling drones are duly catalogued and illustrated. The chorus is ejaculatory and spasmodic, but the music is gloriously continuous in a way which possibly inspired Mahler in one of his best movements, the Scherzo of his Second Symphony. At last the orchestra becomes learned and works out a quite solid fugue on the following subject:

> It is some time before this theme penetrates the intellect of the chorus; but at last the whole chorus, having been helped into the home tonic, joins *en masse* to an extempore accompaniment of triangle and tambourine. Thus ends the *Autumn*, with a display of Haydn's highest symphonic powers.[79]

THE SEASONS: FIRST PERFORMANCES; EDITIONS

Haydn had no further interest in self-publishing after his experience with issuing *The Creation* by subscription. Instead he prepared an edition for immediate publication by Breitkopf & Härtel; it appeared in 1802. The autograph was lost, so (as with the *Creation*) the practical editions of Peters and Eulenberg and the Philharmonia pocket score are all based on this source, as is Mandyczewski's critical edition of 1922. But apparently the Breitkopf score is no more reliable a document of Haydn's own performances than was his authorized *Creation* score. What we may, after Brown's nomenclature for the *Creation* materials, call the *Tonkünstler Score and Parts*[80] differ in a number of significant ways from the Breitkopf edition:

[79] Tovey *Essays* 5, 158; *Concertos*, 393. Cf. Haydn's remarks as quoted in Dies *Nachrichten* (3), 187: "Haydn said . . . that in order to lift [*The Seasons*] out of the eternal monotony of imitating, he hit on the notion of representing drunkenness in the final fugue [of "Autumn"]. 'My head,' he said, 'was so full of the crazy nonsense *Es lebe der Wein, es lebe das Fass!* that I let everything fly hither and yon; so I call the final fugue the tipsy fugue.'"

[80] Because they were used by Haydn and in succeeding years by the Tonkünstler Society for their large-scale performances; now in the Stadtbibliothek, Vienna; copied from the lost autograph by Johann Elssler and his assistants with many additions in Haydn's hand.

1) The authentic contrabassoon parts to Nos. 1-17 were never printed at all. From No. 17 to the end, discrepancies occur between the part as found in Elssler's copy and as printed by Breitkopf: Elssler's (which is to say Haydn's) is more idiomatic and usually at a lower tessitura.[81]

2) The orchestral introductions to "Autumn" and "Winter" are substantially longer than in the Breitkopf printing. Haydn probably felt, after the experience of the first performances, that these numbers would benefit from shortening. Both Geiringer and Robbins Landon second that decision: "The composer always avoided drawing out a composition unnecessarily if he could achieve the same effect with fewer notes"; "there is no doubt that *The Seasons* is a very long work and that the cuts were well advised."[82]

3) The introduction to "Summer" was originally scored without violins, so that "in a grey veil [of violas, cellos, and double basses] the gentle morning light increases." But perhaps Haydn wanted to avoid comparisons with the "Be fruitful" section in *The Creation*, or perhaps the violas found the long passage too exposed for their capabilities. It was evidently rescored as it appears in Breitkopf.[83] A careful study of the Tonkünstler materials by some diligent future editor will doubtlessly reveal other discrepancies; we need a new critical score of *The Seasons* almost as badly as we did one of *The Creation*.

In this country more negative attention has focused on the English text of *The Seasons*. From the examples we have quoted in passing, it would seem that Swieten's English version is beyond hope. Its absurdities, which range from archaic usage to awkward word order to outright mispronunciation (e.g., "globe" set as a two-syllable word) have unjustly placed the music in a shadow. Several attempts have been made at new English librettos, among them *1)* a version for the Novello edition (taken over in the G. Schirmer score) which sought to remove Swieten's most egregious gaffes while preserving the flavor of Thomson's language; *2)* a version by Alice Parker and Thomas Pyle, published by Lawson-Gould; *3)* a new translation done for the (English) Decca Record Company;[84] and *4)* a version by the American choral director Leonard Van Camp. Table 9.3 compares a portion of No. 35 as given in the original and each of these versions.

The question of performance cuts is also appropriate. For a number of reasons, the desire to cut parts of *The Seasons* is less questionable than it might be in *The Creation*. First of all, the work has only the loosest connections among its four parts. Secondly, each part is composed of contrasting, often unrelated episodes. Thirdly, the entire work is long: it runs

---

[81] The authentic contrabassoon parts to Nos. 1-17 have been printed in Landon *HCW* 5, 132-137. Landon noted "Conversely, the double-bassoon part for No. 20 is not found in all the authentic parts; . . . we see no particular reason to doubt its authenticity."

[82] Respectively in *Haydn*, 364; *HCW* 5, 149. The uncut introductions are published in Mandyczewski *Jahreszeiten*, "Revisionsbericht"; along with the overture (introduction to "Spring") they also form part of an edition by Robbins Landon intended for concert performance (G. Schirmer, 1973).

[83] Original version in Mandyczewski *Jahreszeiten*, "Revisionsbericht"; also in Landon *HCW* 5, 150-152.

[84] Included in Robbins Landon's edition of the authentic word-books, etc; see Landon *Creation*, 125-135.

over two hours in performance, not counting intermissions. And finally, it must be admitted that the subject matter, for all its charm, is more bound to Haydn's time and place than our own. Modern audiences will not gladly suffer as much of it as Haydn's did.

There are two main ways of cutting *The Seasons*. One or two individual parts can be presented whole; the most successful candidates for this approach are "Spring"-plus-"Summer" or else "Summer"-plus-"Autumn." The latter has the advantage of ending with a choral extravaganza. One can also wander throughout the oratorio, excising those numbers that least appeal to modern audiences; Tovey hinted at ways of accomplishing this. A third way to present *The Seasons* would be to give it uncut, but in two or four evenings consecutively or spread over a concert season. That way listeners would at least have the advantage of fresh ears and minds when they reach the final chorus. Haydn was once asked which of his late oratorios he preferred. The first one, he replied, because "in *The Creation*, angels speak and tell of God, but in *The Seasons* only Simon talks."[85] It would be a shame to dull the listeners' senses with too much Simon before the angels get to speak, as they surely do, in No. 44.

HAYDN'S LAST YEARS

In 1803 Haydn made his last appearance as a conductor, performing *The Seven Words* as a benefit for the Hospital of St. Marx, a charitable institution in which he had long taken an interest. In honor of his services, the City of Vienna conferred on him a "twelve-fold golden citizens' medal," of which Haydn became more proud than any of his many other honors.[86] More and more his age and poor health caused him to retire from public life. A signal occasion for the old composer was the Vienna performance of *The Creation* held on March 27, 1808. He rode to the University Hall in Prince Nicolaus II's carriage and occupied a seat of honor beside the Princess, who wrapped him in her own shawl when he began to shiver. Salieri conducted; among those attending were Beethoven, Hummel, and Gyrowetz. The performance obviously moved Haydn deeply. After the famous "... and there was LIGHT," the audience erupted in thunderous applause, and Haydn, "the tears streaming down his pallid cheeks and as if overcome by the most violent emotions, raised his trembling arms to Heaven, as if in prayer to the Father of Harmony."[87] He was unable to stay for the entire performance and was borne out to the carriage in his armchair as the crowd continued its acclamations.

---

[85] Dies *Nachrichten* (3), 188.

[86] Cf. letter quoted and trans. in Landon *HCW* 5, 260. Of this so-called "Salvator Medal," Haydn told Griesinger, "I thought to myself, *vox populi, vox Dei.*"; Griesinger *Notizen* (3), 44-45.

[87] Journalist's report in the *Allgemeine Musikalische Zeitung*, quoted and trans. in Landon *HCW* 5, 361-362.

Haydn died on May 31, 1809, and was buried at the Hundsturm Cemetery the next day, Corpus Christi day. On June 2, a Requiem Mass with music by Michael Haydn was celebrated at the church in Gumpendorf. Two weeks later, a great memorial service was held at the Schottenkirche in the Inner City. There the Tonkünstler-Societät performed the Mozart Requiem with a "double orchestra"; Rosenbaum noted that "the whole [ceremony] was most solemn and worthy of Haydn."[88]

We close this narrative not on that grand note, but with one last, telling glimpse of Haydn the choral musician. About a year earlier the choir of the Esterházy Capelle had made a visit to Haydn's home. The princely Esterházy forces gave a Mass by Hummel and a Vesper by Fuchs at a church in the Johannesgasse on the 22nd and 29th of May, 1808. At some point between these engagements, Capellmeister Hummel took the choirboys and male choristers to the little house in Gumpendorf. After congratulating Hummel on his new Mass, Haydn made a few remarks to the younger visitors. His brief utterance serves as valediction for a whole life and body of work:

> I was once a choirboy. Reutter took me from Hainburg to St. Stephen's in Vienna. I was diligent. When my comrades went to play, I took my little *Clavierl* under my arm and went up to the attic, where I could practice on it undisturbed. When I sang solo, the baker next to St. Stephen's always gave me a bun as a present. Go on being good and diligent, and never forget about God.[89]

HAYDN'S CHORAL LEGACY

Nourished by the Baroque era in music, Joseph Haydn helped create Viennese Classicism and introduced elements of the coming Romantic period in his late works as well. Few other composers have been so providentially placed in history. That Haydn was able to make use of all these styles to create a body of music with its own strong identity is due to his unique genius, of course, and not merely to an accident of birth.

Haydn's early- and middle-period choral works can be seen to alternate between or combine the two aspects of Italo-Austrian Baroque church practice described in Chapter 1, namely the aristocratic-ceremonial and the "popular," the latter meant in the sense of emphasizing simplicity, faith, and folk-like musical elements. But even as Joseph Haydn was absorbing the Italian Baroque manner from Porpora and others, its days of musical currency were numbered. The omens for church music after the disintegration of Baroque style were not heartening. To many musicians, the emerging *galant* manner lacked the splendor, complexity and utter seriousness needed to celebrate either earthly lords or heav-

---

[88] For details of the various funeral ceremonies (including Rosenbaum's critique of the performances—"Campi has no more middle-voice," etc.), see Radant "Rosenbaum," 149-151; trans. in Landon *HCW* 5, 388-389.

[89] Pohl *Haydn* 1, 68; quoted and trans. in Landon *HCW* 1, 60.

enly ones. When Haydn stopped writing church music during the early 1780s,[90] it may have been as much because he felt stymied by this aesthetic dilemma as because of any outward obstacles (e.g., the Josephinian reforms or his operatic activities at Esterháza). It should be noted that Mozart's efforts in church music also ceased at this time.

Neither composer could have returned to the genre without having had his resources renewed through contact with earlier styles capable of supporting the sacred message. For Mozart, the study of Bach and Handel encouraged him to struggle with a number of experimental works, including the unfinished Mass in C Minor, K. 427. His Requiem benefitted from the same deepened understanding of Baroque art, but it too was destined to remain incomplete.[91]

Haydn was more fortunate. His experiences in the London of the 1790s provided him with not one but several avenues by which he could see his way to a rebirth of sacred style—one that would match his highly developed skills as a symphonist and the new social conditions as well. First he encountered Handel, whose command of dramatic counterpoint and choral writing was far removed from the stiff exercises Haydn had remembered in the music of Fux. And in evolving a symphonic style for middle-class concert audiences, Haydn found other musical processes whose flexibility and depth could be adapted to serve the needs of church music. But it was in the overall experience of creating art for an intelligent, non-patrician audience that Haydn's heart must have found its most fundamental renewal. By witnessing the English canonization of Handel and his oratorical works, and by having both his own person and his music accepted by a wide spectrum of society, a society far freer and more open than any he had known before, Haydn would draw fresh breath and set his sights on making his own contributions to a more universal art form. From then on, his audience would be an entire nation, if not a world. And by tailoring his output to suit that wider audience, he could someday hope to be called *genius* and *immortal* like Handel.

Haydn realized those dreams most unequivocally in his two late oratorios, with their various Masonic and popular elements ("universal" libretti, glorification of nature and the simple life, etc.). But they also shine through in the wit, accessibility, and warmth of the late Masses. In addition a host of other sacred and secular works reveal the composer's breadth of achievement within this new style and new world.

That Haydn's accomplishment would be discounted, even forgotten, by the generations that followed him was to be expected. First there came a rush to do things more grandly, more sententiously, more personally than Haydn or his time had found proper: Beethoven and Berlioz encouraged that line of development, whereas Mendelssohn and Brahms may be said to have maintained a certain restraint and sense of proportion in cho-

---

[90] See Chapter 4.

[91] See Schenbeck "Baroque Influences."

ral music, at the same time using more "serious" materials than they had perceived coming from the Viennese Classical school.

Mendelssohn's great hero in sacred music was Bach, of course: he modeled his own oratorios after the cantatas and Passions he so admired. But he had been raised to respect the achievements of Haydn as well, as this excerpt of a letter from his father, the philosopher Moses Mendelssohn, makes clear:

> How, then, is the wealth of the [modern symphony] orchestra to be applied? What guidance can the poet give for this and in what regions? . . . An object must be found for music—just as for painting—which by its fervor, its universal sufficiency and perspicuity may take the place of the pious emotions of former days. It seems to me that also from this point of view both the Oratorios of Haydn are very remarkable phenomena. The poems of both, as poems, are weak, but they have happily substituted the old positive and almost metaphysical religious impulses with those which nature, as a visible emanation of the Godhead, in her universality and her thousandfold individualities, instils in every susceptible heart. Hence the profound depth, but also the cheerful efficiency, and certainly genuine religious influence of these two works, which hitherto stand by themselves. Hence the combined effect of the playful and detached passages with the most noble and sincere feelings of gratitude produced by the whole; hence it is, also, that I, individually, would like as little to be deprived—in *The Creation;* and in *The Seasons*—of the crowing of the cock, the singing of the lark, the lowing of the cattle, and the rustic glee of the peasants, as in nature herself.[92]

Yet Moses's views were the product of another era; Felix's own understanding of the Viennese Classical language, like that of his peers, was sharply limited. What Haydn had once meant was no longer what people heard. Mendelssohn's sister Fanny unwittingly described that in a letter to Ignaz Moscheles:

> One evening during the autumn that he spent with us Felix played the wonderful Adagio in F-sharp major from a Haydn Quartet[.] Father loved Haydn especially, every piece was new for him and moved him strangely. He wept when he heard it and said afterwards that he found it so profoundly sad. This description astonished Felix greatly, because *Mesto* [i.e., "sadly"] was in the tempo [marking], and all the rest of us in fact found that it made a rather jolly impression on us.[93]

It is not surprising, considering the "jolly impression" made on Romantic musicians by even the most profound of Haydn's works, that Haydn's Masses were decried as frivolous, degenerate, and the like. Performance of his music was banned in many churches, although it never lost its hold on the Austrians for whom it was first written. The harshest criticism of Haydn came from the conservative "Cecilian" faction that arose in reaction to perceived

---

[92] Mendelssohn *Letters,* ed. G. Selden-Goth (New York, 1945), 241-242.

[93] Pohl *Haydn* 3, 313.

excesses in church music style. Here is a typical comment on the *Nelsonmesse* from an Austrian critic writing in 1844:

> [It is] formidable, excellent and a work of genius in *musical* aspects, but from the *churchly* standpoint hardly to be tolerated. . . . Jos. Haydn took the worldy (operatic) music of his period, put it in the church and made almost a concert hall out of the house of God.[94]

This attitude was echoed well into our own century by the most celebrated of modern composers:

> Why, then, did I compose a Roman Catholic Mass? . . . My Mass was partly provoked by some Masses of Mozart that I found in a secondhand music store in Los Angeles in 1942 or 1943. As I played through these rococo-operatic sweets-of-sin, I knew I had to write a Mass of my own, but a real one.[95]

The widespread acceptance of such sentiments accounted for such uncharacteristic Haydn products as *The Seven Words* (in its oratorio version) becoming popular with the Victorians. Robbins Landon cited Queen Victoria herself as a great admirer of *The Seven Words*, although she had to allow that all oratorios, including that "very beautiful" work, tended to "affect my nerves if they last above three quarters of an hour and make me sleepy (I think from the slow time and the attention one naturally pays)."[96]

The early twentieth century saw two great centenary celebrations, that in 1909 marking the anniversary of Haydn's death and that in 1932 his birth. Between them, they could have done much to rehabilitate Haydn's music, including his sacred choral works. But the spirit of the 1909 musicological conference at Vienna seems to have remained strongly conservative in that regard: for example Alfred Schnerich, to whom we are indebted for so many fine early editions of Bach and Handel, confined himself to a paper on "The Textual Omissions in Haydn's Masses and Their Correction."[97]

The 1932 celebrations bore more interesting fruit. Soon after this bicentennial, Karl Geiringer's new biography appeared, then Jens Peter Larsen's *Die Haydn-Überlieferung* and also Tovey's essays, including his engaging analyses of the two late oratorios. Robbins Landon has also cited from this period the recording projects that got underway, principally of the quartets and symphonies. After World War II, attempts were made to launch a new Haydn *Gesamtausgabe*, first in Boston with the Haydn Society in the early '50s, and then—more successfully—in Cologne with the Joseph Haydn-Institut a few years later.

---

[94] Höslinger "Standpunkt," 130.

[95] Igor Stravinsky (with Robert Craft), *Expositions and Developments* (New York, 1962), 65.

[96] *Dearest Child, Letters between Queen Victoria and the Princess Royal 1858-1861*, ed. Roger Fulford (New York, 1965), 246; cited in *HCW* 5, 422.

[97] Schnerich "Versehen."

A new attitude toward Haydn emerged in the years following, and his choral music has benefitted from it as much as any genre in his output. Having reliable editions of the Haydn Masses, and lately editions of the less-well-known works also, has been a great help to conductors in this country. For both performers and audiences, the role of recordings has been possibly even more significant. Many of us first became acquainted with the Haydn Masses through some of the good recorded performances available in the '50s and '60s, especially those directed by Wöldike, Willcocks, and Guest. Willcock's and Guest's LPs, which usually featured all-male choirs, resonant chapel acoustics, and the Academy of St.-Martin-in-the-Field, were a ubiquitous presence on record-stores shelves until the late '70s. Their vitality, precision, and somewhat other-worldly quality (Cambridge University certainly qualifying as another world to most Americans) combined to provide compelling sound-portraits of music that did not invariably suggest such potential when read at the keyboard.

The renaissance of Haydn scholarship begun by Geiringer and Larsen has multiplied geometrically with fine contributions from Feder, Becker-Glauch, Brown, Dack, Temperley, and many others. During the thirty years following Word War II, H. C. Robbins Landon became a virtual one-man Haydn *Verlag*, churning out editions, scholarship, and popular treatments alike at a rate that astonished (and probably alarmed) many of his colleagues. During the same period, the early-instrument movement grew up and eventually annexed Haydn, Mozart, and Beethoven; to that development we owe a spate of interesting new Haydn recordings from Hogwood, Pinnock, Preston, Gardiner, and others.

Has all this settled Haydn's place in history? To raise the thorniest problem for choral musicians, does it imply that his sacred music should by now be a more widely accepted part of the church repertory? To the first question, it is possible to answer an unequivocal yes. As to the second, many honest differences of opinion remain, including a strong sensation that the question itself may no longer be relevant. The issue of proper sacred style has played an ironic trick on Haydn and posterity. Haydn's own faith was unquestionable; his Masses and other sacred works were created as an integrated response to his own culture and its belief system. But cultures change, beliefs as well. Haydn's sacred settings fell into disrepute at least partly because their style came to imply a shallow cosmology, a lightweight view of Christian principles. From that perspective, it must be admitted that part of Haydn's rehabilitation has come about for suspect reasons: our appreciation of his artistic discourse has deepened at the very time that we are more willing to ignore or accept whatever spiritual weaknesses may be implicit within it. In other words, we have come to revere Haydn's language and to care little about what he may have been saying. That attitude trivializes anew the basic integrity of his work. For whether or not we care one whit about Haydn's brand of Catholicism, it is a critical element in the style of his sacred choral music. Understanding it can only add to our appreciation of a Haydn Mass. Beyond appreciation, however, the question of acceptance will remain to vex the believer.

Is it necessary, or even possible, that music for worship be pious and interesting in equal degrees? And how can music of another culture, whether that culture is eighteenth-century Austria or twentieth-century Zaïre, effectively serve in modern worship? Such fundamental questions about sacred art can scarcely be addressed in so meager a space as this. But we can acknowledge a few simple truths: first, that piety ultimately resides more in the listener, less in what is being listened to; second, that music of another culture is only effective to the degree that it causes our own sensibilities to resonate in sympathy. On the first count Haydn's music is at least acquittable, and on the second it probably deserves an award. Few composers have held a comparably continuous position in their own land and also been so successfully reborn and exported over the years. Beyond whatever numinous expression it may have aspired to or that we may now aspire to on its behalf, Haydn's choral music continues to make a profound *human* impression, and that may be the best indication of its continuing value. If we are successful, coming generations will love and understand it as well.

Table 9.1: Comparison of Texts in *The Creation*

Swieten	"Lidley"
No. 6:	
Softly purling glides on	In silent vales soft gliding brooks
Tho' silent vales the limpid brook.	By gentle noise mark out their way.
No. 21:	
In whirl arose the host of insects.	In whirls arose the host of insects.
No. 22:	
Now heav'n in fullest glory shone:	Now heav'n in all her glory shone;
Earth smiles in all her rich attire.	Earth smiles in her rich attire.
No. 23:	
Male and female created he him.	Male and female created he them.
No. 24:	
The Lord and King of nature all.	The Lord of earth, and nature's king.
No. 33:	
O happy pair, and always happy yet,	O happy pair, and ever happy still,
If not, misled by false conceit,	If not, by false conceit misled,
Ye strive at more, as granted is,	Ye strive at more than granted is,
And more to know, as know ye should.	And more to know, than know ye should.

Table 9.2 follows overleaf.

Table 9.3: Haydn *The Seasons*, 35, Text in various English translations

[Swieten:]
By frost cemented stands the lake,
arrested is the stream in his course,
and in his precipitous fall o'er the cliff
there stopt and dumb the torrent hangs.

[English Decca:]
A crystal pavement lies the pool,
the bick'ring stream arrested stands;
and o'er the beetling cliff, the dumb cascade
its idle torrent pendent throws.

[Van Camp:]
The lake is frozen hard with ice,
the stream no longer flows in its course.
The once bold sparkling waterfall now hangs,
a frozen statue, white and mute.

[Novello/G. Schirmer:]
A crystal pavement lies the lake;
Arrested stands the rapid stream;
And o'er the lofty cliff the torrent hangs
with idle threat and seeming roar.

[Parker/Pyle:]
By icy chains the sea is held,
the rushing stream is stopp'ed in its course.
The torrent that falls down the mountain hangs,
now white and cold and motionless.

Table 9.2: Structural Outline of *The Creation*

Nr	Title	Theme	Forces/Style	Key	Tempo	Neukomm's M.M.
PART I						
1.	Introd: The Representation of Chaos	(*Gen. 1:1-4*; heaven, earth, light)	Orch/fantasia	c-C	Largo ¢	♩ = 54
	"In the beginning God created..."		Raphael/RA	i-III		
	"And the spirit of God"		Chorus/RA	III-I		
	"And God saw the light"		Uriel/RA	I		
2.	"Now vanish before the holy beams"	(*comment*; light, fallen angels)	Uriel/aria	A:I	Andante ¢	♩ = 112
	"Despairing, cursing rage"		Chorus/fugato	iii		
	"A new created world"		Uriel, Chorus	I	Allegro mod.	♩ = 84
3.	"And God made the firmament"	(*Gen. 1:6-7*; div. of the waters)	Raphael/RA	:	Allegro assai	♩ = 152
4.	"The marv'lous work beholds amaz'd"	(*comment*; storms, floods)	Gabriel, Chorus	C	Allegro ¢	♩ = 88
		(*praise*; the heavenly host)				
5.	"And God said"	(*Gen. 1:9-10*; seas, earth)	Raphael/RS	:		
6.	"Rolling in foaming billows"	(*comment*; seas, rivers, streams)	Raphael/aria	d-D	Allegro assai ¢	♩ = 138
7.	"And God said: Let the earth"	(*Gen. 1:11*; grass, trees)	Gabriel/RS	:		
8.	"With verdure clad"	(*comment*; grass, flowers, plants)	Gabriel/aria	B♭	Andante 6/8	♪ = 120
9.	"And the heavenly host"		Uriel/RS	:		
10.	"Awake the harp"	(*praise*; the heavenly host)	Chorus	D	Vivace ¢	♩ = 104
11.	"And God said: Let there be light"	(*Gen. 1:14-16*; lights in firmament)	Uriel/RS	:		
12.	"In splendour bright"	(*comment*; sun, moon, stars)	Uriel/RA	D-C	Andante ¢	♩ = 100; ♩ = 64
13.	"The heavens are telling"	(*praise*; the heavenly host)	Tutti	C	Allegro ¢	♩ = 88; ♩ = 108

PART II

14. "And God said: Let the waters"	(*Gen. 1:20*; fish, birds)	Gabriel/RA	:	Moderato ¢	♪=126
15. "On mighty pens"	(*comment*; eagle, lark, et al.)	Gabriel/aria	F	Poco adagio ¢	♪=116
16. "And God created great whales"	(*Gen. 1:21-22*; whales, "multiply")	Raphael/RS, RA	d		
17. "And the angels"	(*praise, commentary*; by the archangels [hills, water, birds, fish])	Raphael/RS	:		
18. "Most beautyfull appear"		Trio	A	Moderato 2/4	♪=116
19. "The Lord is great"	(*praise*; archangels and h. host)	Trio, Chorus	A	Vivace ¢	♩=116
20. "And God said: Let the earth"	(*Gen. 1:24*; beasts)	Raphael/RS	:		
21. "Strait opening her fertile womb"	(*comment*; lion, tiger, stag et al.)	Raphael/RA	:	Presto ¢ et al.	♩=92; ♩=116; ♪=132; ♩=58
22. "Now heav'n in fullest glory shone"	(*comment*; birds, fish, et al., but creation still incomplete)	Raphael/aria	D	Maestoso 3/4	♩=100
23. "And God created man"	(*Gen. 1:26*; man)	Uriel/RS	:		
24. "In native worth and honour clad"	(*comment*; man, woman)	Uriel/aria	C	Andante ¢	♩=108
25. "And God saw ev'ry thing"	(*Gen. 1:31*; survey of creation)	Raphael/RS	:		
26. "Achieved is the glorious work"	(*praise*; the heavenly host)	Chorus	B♭	Vivace ¢	♩=104
27. "To thee each living soul"	"	Trio	B♭	Poco Adagio 3/4	♪=112
28. "Achieved is the glorious work"	"	Chorus	B♭	Vivace ¢	♩=104

PART III

29. "In rosy mantle"	(narrative introd to 30.)	Uriel/RA	E:C	Largo 3/4	♪=80
30. "By thee with bliss"	(*praise* for the Creation)	Duet, Chorus	C	Adagio ¢ / Allegretto 2/4	♩=56 / ♩=92
31. "Our duty we performed now"	(introd. to 32.)	Adam/RS	:		
32. "Graceful consort"	(love duet of Adam and Eve)	Duet	B♭	Adagio 3/4	♪=112
33. "O happy pair"	(suggests the fall from grace)	Uriel/RS	:	Allegro 2/4	♩=112
34. "Sing the Lord, ye voices all!"	(*praise* and thanksgiving)	Tutti	B♭	Andante ¢ / Allegro ¢	♪=108 / ♩=120

Example 9.1: Haydn *The Creation*, 21, mm. 33-66

Example 9.2: Haydn *The Creation*, 1, mm. 72-86

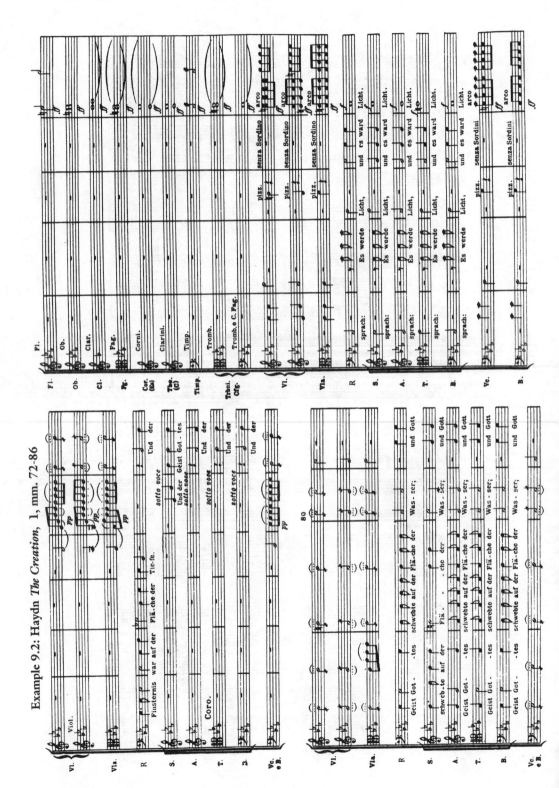

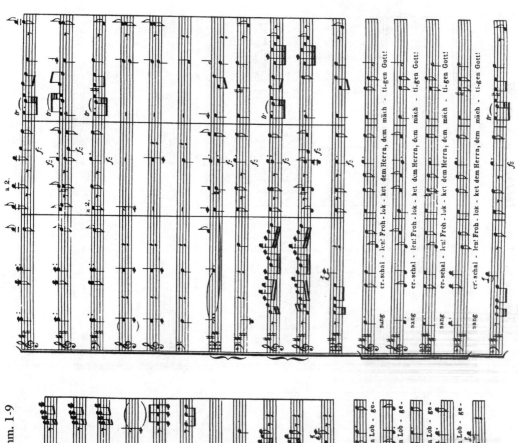

Example 9.3: Haydn *The Creation*, 10, mm. 1-9

Example 9.7: Haydn *The Creation*, 2, mm. 97-106

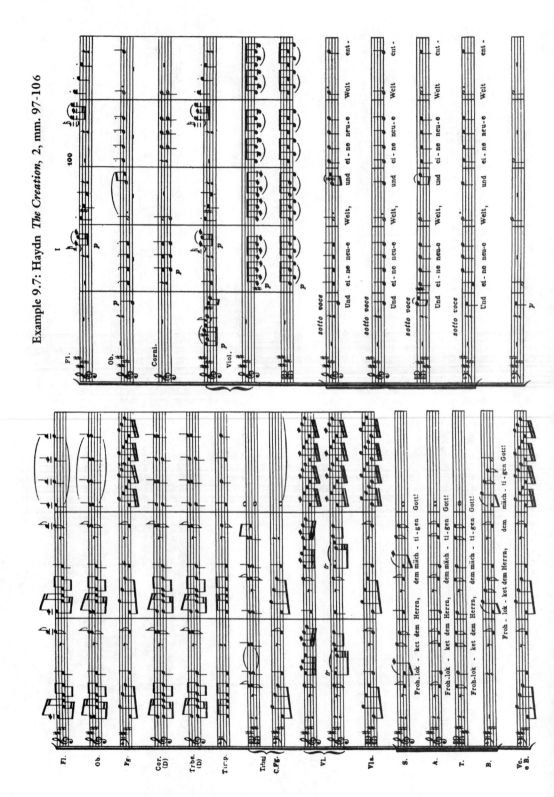

Example 9.8: Haydn *The Creation*, 2, mm. 145-151

Example 9.10: Haydn *The Seasons*, 44, mm. 1-17

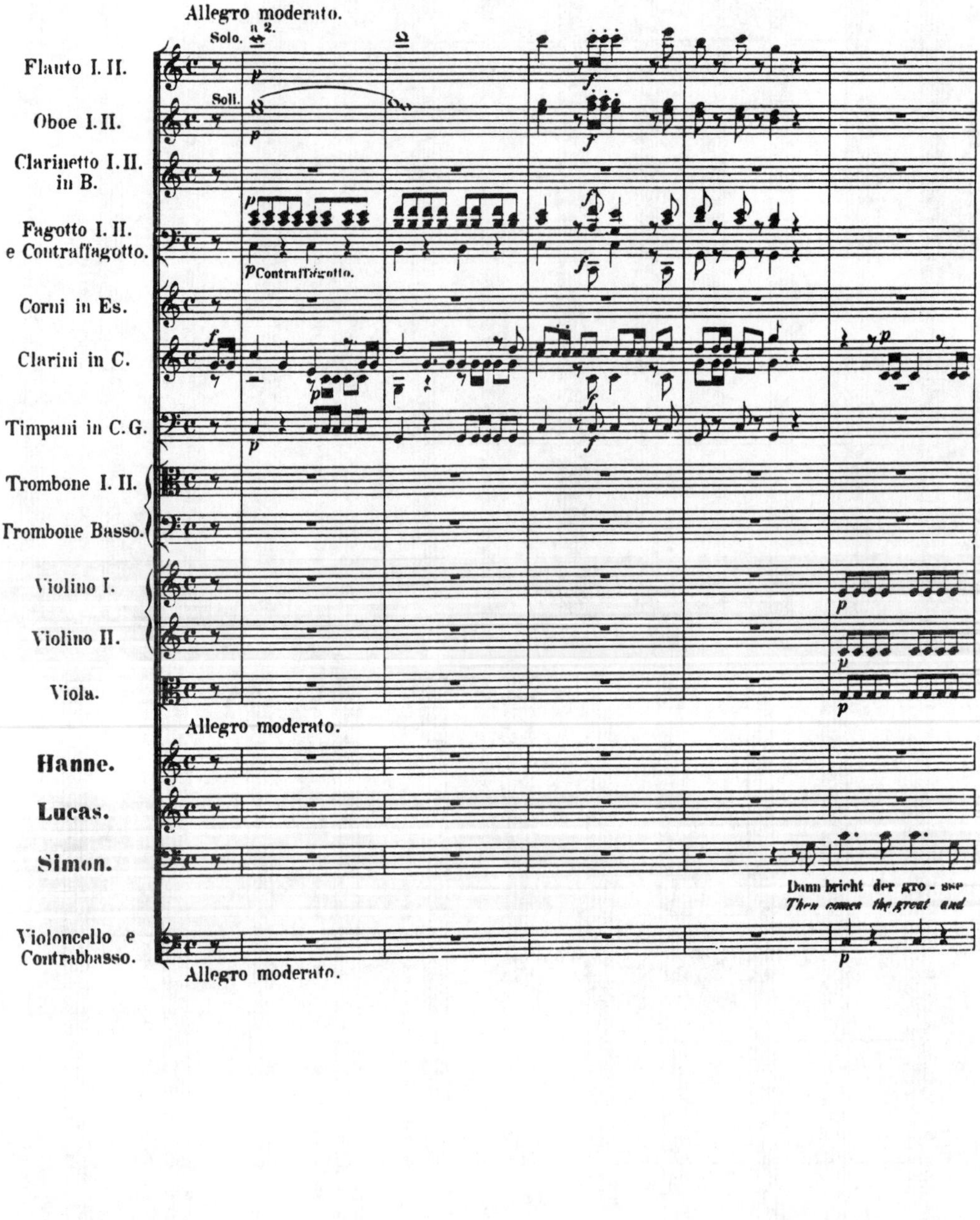

PERFORMANCE

10

PERFORMANCE PRACTICES

Everything depends on good execution. . . . Many a would-be composer is thrilled with delight and plumes himself anew when he hears his musical Galimatias played by good performers who know how to produce the effect (of which he himself never dreamed) in the right place; and how to vary the character (which never occurred to him) as much as it is humanly possible to do so, and who therefore know how to make the whole miserable scribble bearable to the ears of the listeners by means of good performance. And to whom, on the other hand, is it not known that the best composition is often played so wretchedly that the composer himself has great difficulty in recognizing his own work?[1]

SINGERS AND THEIR TECHNIQUE

In general, singers in Haydn's time continued to be trained in the Baroque traditions of Tosi and Mancini, and they passed these practices on to their students. Haydn himself learned something of the art of *bel canto* from the aged Porpora, and was in turn expected to coach the singers at Esterháza, taking care that the female vocalists in particular "may not again forget (when staying in the country) that which they have been taught with much effort and at great expense in Vienna."[2] What were the basics of this style?

In his *Histoire de la Musique* of 1725, Le Cerf de la Viéville made a concise note of the requirements for Baroque singing:

---

[1] Leopold Mozart, in his *Violinschule* (3), 215.

[2] Detail of Haydn's original contract of 1761 with Prince Paul Anton Esterházy, quoted in Landon *HCW* 1, 351.

A perfect voice should be sonorous, extensive, sweet, neat, lively, flexible. These six qualities[,] which nature assembles but once in a century, are usually found bestowed by halves.[3]

Charles Burney, writing nearly fifty years later, could only echo La Viéville in describing the best singers he heard abroad:

> She sings from G to E in *altissimo*, with the greatest ease and force, and both her *portamento di voce*, and her volubility are, in my opinion, unrivalled . . . nothing was too difficult to her execution, which was easy and neat.
>
> [Of another:] Her voice was sweetly toned, and she sang perfectly well in tune. She has an excellent shake, a good expression, and facility of executing and articulating rapid and difficult divisions, that is astonishing . . . she was by no means lavish of graces, but those she used, were perfectly suited to the style of the music, and idea of the poet.
>
> [Of another:] Her execution was articulate and brilliant. She had a fluent tongue for pronouncing words rapidly and distinctly, and a flexible throat for divisions, with so beautiful and quick a shake, that she could put it in motion upon short notice, just when she would. The passage might be smooth, or by leaps, or consist of iterations of the same tone, their execution was equally easy to her, as to any instrument whatever.[4]

We shall use these brief descriptions of Baroque singing as a starting point for defining *bel canto* technique in the eighteenth century.

"Sweetly toned"

In particular the ideal of sweetness in vocal tone connoted rich but compact sound (i.e., one which did not impede the execution of rapid passagework) and an absolute prohibition of stridency:

> A beautiful tone . . . should not be harsh at even the highest degree of loudness.[5]

> Each singing voice, the higher it goes, should be produced increasingly temperately and lightly.[6]

> Let him take care . . . that the higher the Notes, the more it is necessary to touch them with Softness.[7]

---

[3] Quoted and trans. in Donington *Interpretation*, 517.

[4] *The Present State of Music in Germany*, 108, 111, 188.

[5] Türk *Klavierschule* (2), 354.

[6] Mattheson *Capellmeister* (2), 266.

For male voices, this sweetness was maintained in the upper range through a greater employment of falsetto than is common today. The tenor's heroic, ringing high B♭ or C was not heard until the 1830s and did not win widespread approval for some time after that.[8] In Haydn's Esterházy cantatas, also in the early Masses, we find numerous instances that call for tenor singing equal to coloratura soprano in technique and range. As late as *The Creation*, this tendency still surfaces from time to time, as in No. 19, "The Lord is great," where the tenor soloist's lines patently echo the soprano's (see Ex. 10.60). This excerpt also suggests that period instruments, with their inherently narrower range of dynamics, must have aided the tenor in projecting such a passage over the *fortissimo* chorus, orchestra, and soloists.

"A flexible throat for divisions"

We have only to open the pages of nearly any Baroque or Classic masterwork to see the dizzying succession of scales, arpeggios, and other figures—*passaggi*—the singer was called upon to perform. Basic Baroque style demanded flexibility and speed. According to Quantz, the eighteenth century recognized two means of producing vocal runs:

> A singer who articulates all fast passage-work from the chest can hardly produce it as quickly as one who produces it in the throat, although the former method, because of its distinctness, is always superior to the latter, particularly in large places.[9]

That Quantz favored a combination of fluidity and articulation in vocal passagework may be inferred from the following:

> [The singer] must perform the Allegro in a lively, brilliant, and easy manner. He must produce the passage-work roundly, neither attacking it too harshly nor slurring it in a lame and lazy manner.[10]

---

[7] Tosi *Opinioni* (3), 19.

[8] The negative comments of Garcia and Rossini are noted in, among many other sources, Shrock "Aspects," iv.

[9] Quantz *Versuch* (2), [XVII, vii, 52] 287.

[10] Quantz *Versuch* (2), [XVIII, 11] 301. In another passage, he criticized provincial German choirs for not yet having mastered the modern Italian approach to *passaggi*: "Their disagreeable, forced, and exceedingly noisy chest attacks, in which they make vigorous use of the faculty of the Germans for pronouncing the *h*, singing ha-ha-ha-ha for each note, make all the passage-work sound hacked up, and are far removed from the Italian manner of executing passage-work with the chest voice"[i.e., with vigorous involvement from the breath-support mechanism]; [XVIII, 80n] 336.

"An excellent shake"

In his *The Singers Preceptor* of 1810, Domenico Corri called the shake (i.e., trill) an "elegant and important ornament of the vocal art, without which melody would often languish."[11] Yet the ability to execute this ornament is often missing from singers' techniques today. "From the instructions I received from my Preceptor Porpora, and from my own observation of almost all the best Singers Europe has produced within these last 50 years," wrote Corri,

> I find that the qualifications necessary to form a perfect Shake are
> EQUALITY OF NOTES DISTINCTLY MARKED EASY AND MODERATELY QUICK.
> Also that the Note which bears the Shake ought to be the most predominant, being the Note belonging to the Melody, and if the auxiliary Note is to closely blended, the principal cannot be sufficiently distinguished, by which means the Melody must suffer and the Harmony become perplexed. . . .
> The long Shake should begin with the Note on which the Shake is to be made. The short Shake should begin with the upper Note.[12]

"Portamento di voce"

According to Corri,

> *Portamento di voce* is the perfection of vocal music; it consists in the swell and dying of the voice, the sliding and blending one note into another with delicacy and expression—and expression comprehends every charm which music can produce; the Portamento di voce may justly be compared to the highest degree of refinement in elegant pronunciation in speaking. . . .
> [Nevertheless, bear] in mind that as too much Honey will be apt to cloy, so too much of the Italian Taste of dragging Notes as if from the very bottom of the Stomach, may too much resemble that retrograde motion it is sometimes subject to, and which would be indelicate to express in broader terms.[13]

In condensing the wisdom of countless vocal masters, Robert Donington wrote that the *portamento di voce* "is always *practised* as if on definite notes: chromatic if the interval bridged is less than about a fifth; diatonic if it is more. It is . . . *sung* by almost running the

---

[11] Corri *Preceptor*, 7.

[12] Corri *Preceptor*, 30.

[13] Corri *Preceptor*, 3, 63. From the context it is clear that Corri primarily regards the *portamento di voce* as an enhancer of text delivery and wishes to see it used, not in an indiscriminant manner, but as guided by the affects found in the words.

notes together, but is still distinctly heard as notes, and not as a mere *glissando* scoop."[14] The device was essential, but so were proper technique and good taste in its execution.

Phrasing; The "messa di voce"

Central to a singer's musicianship was the ability to apply subtle gradations of dynamics to every line. The *messa di voce*, a smooth crescendo and diminuendo on a single pitch, was employed both as a basic exercise for dynamic control and as an expressive device on held notes within arias. When this technique was fully mastered, it was to be carried into every phrase in music, as Corri's "Third Requisite" (Table 10.1) makes clear. The *messa di voce* was as important to vocal phrasing as was the "small softness" at the beginning of a bow and die-away at the end of the bow for string players (see below).[15]

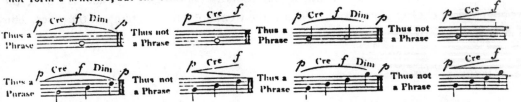

THIRD REQUISITE.

A Phrase in Music is like a sentence in Language, with this difference, that one word will not form a sentence, but one Note can form a Phrase in Music.

and so on of any number of Notes that form a passage, wherever the Voice falls by a diminuendo.

Some sentences containing many words may be uttered in one breath; indeed a sentence is seldom or ever broke in the midst by taking breath; whereas, in a musical Phrase you are frequently compelled to do so, from the length of some Notes, and the slow movement of the Music but when the Singer finds it necessary to take breath, he should always contrive to do so by a dying or diminuendo of the Voice, because the break will then be less perceived; this does not produce any defect in Vocal Music, on the contrary it is sometimes productive of happy effect, as it serves to separate words which when conjoined might lose their true and precise meaning.

Table 10.1[16]

---

[14] Donington *Interpretation*, 522.

[15] Nevertheless it is possible to misapply the *messa di voce*, especially in choral textures. It would sound anachronistic, for example, in the *stile antico* counterpoint of Haydn's *Non nobis Domine*, and by extension in most contrapuntal passages. An appropriate—and notated—choral usage can be found in the first few bars of the *Nelsonmesse* Sanctus.

[16] Corri *Preceptor*, 65.

Vibrato

However we interpret the various definitions attached to words like *vibrato* and *tremolo* in the old treatises, it is impossible to escape the message that a pronounced or extreme vibrato was frowned upon in eighteenth-century music. Wolfgang Mozart wrote to his father in 1778 that the singer

> Meis[s]ner, as you know, has the bad habit of making his voice tremble at times, turning a note that should be sustained into distinct crochets, or even quavers— and this I never could endure in him. And really it is a detestable habit and one which is quite contrary to nature. The human voice trembles naturally—but in its own way—and only to such a degree that the effect is beautiful. . . . But the moment the proper limit is overstepped, it is no longer beautiful—because it is contrary to nature.[17]

A pronounced vibrato/tremolo was either considered an ornament (see instrumental discussion below) or a technical deficiency. In the first case, it was limited to appropriate moments in a piece; in the second, it was roundly condemned. As late as 1894, the younger Manuel Garcia remarked, "What is the tremolo? The trembling of the voice. This intolerable fault ruins every style of singing."[18]

Taste and style

The question of when and how often to introduce "graces" was often discussed (see also *Free Ornaments*, below). Corri wrote:

> Ornaments should ever be in subordination to the character and design of the composition, and introduced only on words which will admit of decoration, without destroying the sentiment; nor, indeed, should they ever be introduced, but by singers capable of executing them with precision and effect; when used properly, and with moderation, they are no doubt brilliant concomitants to the vocal art; but, at present, no one thinks of singing a song without flourishing on every note, as is now the general practice and manner of our first performers, whereas, would they content themselves with singing according to their ability, observing the character and meaning of the composition, to give to each its true expression, though their performance be not ornamented, they may be entitled to as much admiration, as sometimes is excited by a display of superfluous decoration.[19]

---

[17] Anderson *Letters of Mozart*, 552.

[18] Garcia *Hints*, 18.

[19] Corri *Preceptor*, 3.

That singers continued, well into the nineteenth century, to ornament their parts with considerable freedom is borne out not only by Corri's comments but by many others.[20] Yet toward the end of his lifetime, Haydn helped establish a newer manner of singing in Vienna, one which relied less on ornamentation and more on vocal power. The young soprano Anna Milder, who would later become Beethoven's first Leonore in *Fidelio*, came to Vienna at the age of fourteen and sang for the old composer. "My dear child," said Haydn, "you've got a voice like a house." Subsequently he entrusted her to his pupil Sigismund Neukomm, who trained her in the "Haydn manner of singing" for three years. After her debut in 1803, Griesinger said that "her voice sounds—and that's rarely the case—like the purest metal and she gives us, since she's studied with Neukomm from the Haydn school, long, powerful notes without arabesques and exaggerated ornaments."[21]

INSTRUMENTS, INSTRUMENTAL TECHNIQUES, AND TIMBRE

In compiling this brief review of Haydn's instruments, we have been mindful that our readers will probably resort to modern instruments for their Haydn performances. Likewise those who regularly use period instruments will probably know more about their nature and history than we have space for here. So our remarks are confined to introducing these instruments with a view to showing their (sometimes profound) influence on Haydn's choral music.

We are fortunate to live in a time which has seen a burgeoning revival of the old instruments and their technique. Early-music specialists have extended their domain from Bach into Haydn, Mozart, Beethoven, and even Berlioz and Brahms in the last few years; this advance is likely to continue as the twentieth century itself becomes history. And why not? The relatedness of authentic phrasing, balances, ornamentation, and tempo often only becomes clear when period instruments and their techniques are used. Every one of us can learn from the revivalists' experience, even if we never do more with old instruments than hear them played.

But since there are now in a number of American cities skilled groups of these players, people who make a living from the Baroque and post-Baroque repertoire, we hope our readers will do more than merely listen. We hope they will collaborate. By plunging into choral performance with period instruments, conductors reward not only themselves but their audiences with more of the real sound of eighteenth-century cantatas, Masses, and oratorios.

---

[20] Christoph Mahling cited a report in the *Allgemeine Musikalische Zeitung* from 1824 in which the critic reviewing a performance of *Die Zauberflöte* in Berlin noted that *at long last* Sarastro's aria "In diesen heil'gen Hallen" had not been ornamented, and the singer had added no embellishments; Larsen *Haydn Studies*, 195.

[21] Landon *HCW* 4, 499, quoting Pohl *Haydn* 3, 155f., and others.

Strings

The body of the violin underwent gradual and relatively minor changes from around 1730 to 1830, which is not to say it came to resemble today's instrument in every particular. Early in the eighteenth century, its fingerboard and neck were often shorter and more nearly parallel to the body, supporting somewhat less string tension. The bridge was lower, making double stops easier but mitigating against the most forceful playing (which would have created *unwanted* double stops). Wire-wound lower strings and gut upper strings were customary. Modern authorities often describe the sound of these violins as "luminous" (i.e., transparent yet rich in overtones).[22]

As the century progressed, the main body of the violin remained unchanged, but the bridge was gradually transformed into a thinner, higher form, so that the strings could be held at a greater tension. The fingerboard had to be correspondingly elevated, which meant morticing the neck (now thinner, to faciliate fingerwork) into the block at an angle. Bass bar, soundpost, and fingerboard were also strengthened or otherwise altered in order to support the added tension and new techniques. Taken together with the contemporary, and much more substantial, transformation of the bow, the effect was to heighten the violin's tonal power and brilliance at the expense of luminosity.[23]

It is the changes in bow design that are most clearly reflected in Haydn's music. The pre-1730 Baroque bow had a convex stick which curved away from the hair. It was somewhat shorter and lighter than its modern counterpart, and its hair tension could not be adjusted. The modern bow, following the innovations of Tourte and Viotti, was perfected around 1785. It was longer, heavier, and stronger, with a wider ribbon of hair. Its stick was concave, its hair tension adjustable from a screw nut at the frog. Between the old bow and the new, many transitional forms were used. Nevertheless they all had a concave stick and many had adjustable hair. David Boyden has summarized these bows' various technical capabilities in this way:

> In eighteenth-century bows, when the bow hair is brought in contact with the string, it yields more under the pressure of the player's hand than is the case with the modern bow hair. The yielding hair of these early bows requires a small "take-up" or "give" before the tone emerges—what Leopold Mozart called a "small softness."[24] By contrast, the concave stick of the modern bow makes the hair tighter and less yielding, producing the tone practically at once. The modern bow can produce a good *sforzando* easily, even a true biting *martelé*, and so can the

---

[22] Donington *Interpretation*, 531-533. It is important to note that this violin was not identical with the pre-1730 Baroque violin, either. It may perhaps be thought of as a transitional instrument. Melkus called it the "Classical" violin and noted that both Mozart's concert violin preserved at the Salzburg Mozarteum and the Paganini violin in Genoa share its characteristics. See Melkus "Development."

[23] Stowell *Violin Technique*, 23-27, 31.

[24] See n.76 in this Chapter.

transitional bow (to a lesser extent). Both *sf* and *martelé* are much more difficult to produce with an old bow. Hence it is not surprising that *sf* is uncommon in music written before 1750.

In the old bow, the "small softness" and the relatively light head combine to produce a basic non-legato stroke which, in turn, is the basis of a brilliantly clear articulation in rapid passage-work and string crossing, especially in the upper third of the bow. The action of the transitional bow is partway between the old bow and the modern bow. While it lacks the strength and tension of the modern bow, it seems to produce a *piano* or *pianissimo* of good or even luminous quality more easily than the modern bow. It also produces double stops without scratching, and nuances of tone or delicate changes of bow strokes demanded by mixed bowings more easily.[25]

The proliferation of *sforzandi* and other accents (>, ^, etc.) after 1780 in the string parts of Haydn's choral music is proof of the newer bows' power and of their acceptance by the foremost composers. We can also more easily find places that call for true *spiccato* and *martelé*.[26] On the other hand, it is wise to limit the range of bowing styles in the earliest Haydn choral works to a "sprung" *détaché* for passagework, a basic *cantabile* for slower tempos, and of course the "small softness."[27] (Violinists using modern instruments will find it easier to approximate a "take-up" or "give" in their attack by avoiding the lower third of the bow.) These few devices complement the simplicity of works like the E-major *Salve Regina* and yet bring out their deeply expressive nature.

The sounds of contemporary violas, cellos, and basses were also less opaque, more transparent and "stringy." Some disagreement exists about the relative size and strength of eighteenth-century violas.[28] This was a transitional period when the large tenor violas of the previous century may still have been in use, but were increasingly displaced by the more violin-sized alto violas. The popularity of the trio sonata (and the adoption of its two-violins-plus-basso texture by other genres) had caused a downturn in the manufacture and use of all violas. When the viola was employed, it was generally played by a violinist doubling for the moment; naturally these players wanted something more like their primary instrument under their fingers. Some went so far as to restring and retune violins to play viola parts, although the sound of these makeshift instruments was far from ideal. By

---

[25] Boyden "Evolution," 223-224.

[26] For example see, respectively, Exs. 10.20 and 10.17.

[27] Limit bowing styles, but not articulations! See the section on phrasing. The "sprung" *détaché* is a relaxed and easy alternation of bow strokes in which the bow eases its pressure on the string between each note by its own natural "springy" resilience without actually leaving the string, thus halfway between *détaché* and *spiccato*. See Donington *Interpretation*, 538-539.

[28] Eduard Melkus described the Classical viola as "much smaller than the modern viola . . . just a second instrument for the violinist." But Nikolaus Harnoncourt has cited evidence that in the second half of the eighteenth century, as earlier, orchestral players employed mainly "very large violas . . . these had a powerful, ringing sound." Melkus quoted in discussion, Larsen *Haydn Studies*, 226. Cf. Harnoncourt *Dialog* (2), 123-124.

the beginning of the nineteenth century, composers and conductors were complaining widely about the viola's inadequacy to cope with the demands of the new music. Numerous experimenters tinkered with viola design, hoping to arrive at an easily playable instrument with a bigger, clearer sound.[29]

Haydn's neglect of the viola in his early choral music only reflects its position in musical life at the time. But the important role Haydn assigned the viola in his late Masses and oratorios shows his anticipation of nineteenth-century demands for a stronger instrument. Whether he had such violas or not, he must certainly have wished for them.[30]

Our knowledge of Haydn's double bass, and especially of double-bass tunings in eighteenth-century Austria, has been clouded by modern misinterpretation of the historical evidence. Leopold Mozart's remarks may serve as a convenient focal point, since they have been widely disseminated and misconstrued:

> The Great-Bass or the Violon . . . is also made in various sizes, but the tuning remains the same. . . . Because the Violon is much bigger than the Violoncello, it is tuned a whole octave lower. Usually it has four strings [at times only three], but the larger ones may have five.[31]

With these few words, Mozart implied that the contemporary "Violon" duplicated the tuning of the cello an octave lower, thus C_1-G_1-D-A. In fact, only the French and Italians commonly used tuning by fifths, and they were more apt to employ three-stringed basses. The Viennese cultivated the five-string bass in particular, but its customary tuning was F_1-A_1-D-F$\sharp$-A. Neither three-, nor four-, nor five-string basses in Haydn's time extended downward in range to a 16-foot C. Although many of Haydn's works apparently demand such a downward extension, we should assume that his players coped by transposing those lowest pitches up an octave in performance. It is certainly a mistake to consider the historical Viennese five-string bass the ancestor of those modern basses that *can* supply C_1. And thus it follows that using such modern instruments is hardly necessary to ensure a correct or authentic performance; the opposite may be true.[32]

---

[29] Riley *Viola*, 218-240.

[30] Archival records of an instrument by Nicolo Amati, plus a surviving viola now in the Burgenländisches Landesmuseum, imply that the Esterházy orchestra owned some of the larger violas. Landon *HCW* 2, 89-90.

[31] Mozart *Violinschule* (3), 11. The bracketed material was added for the 1787 edition; Italian influence accounted for the rise of the three-string bass, and many older five-string models were restrung with four or even three strings in the nineteenth century.

[32] See Meier *Kontrabass*, 26-32, for an authoritative and detailed explanation of double-bass tuning in the eighteenth century. Landon *Symphonies*, 126, apparently confuses the capabilities of the old and modern five-string instruments.

Winds and Percussion

Thirty years ago H. C. Robbins Landon prefaced his comments on performing the Haydn symphonies with this conventional wisdom: "No one will want to perform Haydn's music with natural trumpets and ancient woodwind instruments when our modern counterparts are in most cases so far superior in every way."[33] Today we more often recognize the degree to which Classical music depended on the unique colors and powers of those older winds to make its points. Modern wind instruments are not what Haydn had in mind when he was scoring his music. Not only in solo lines, but in doublings and balances, the period instruments can be surprisingly more effective. Even if we cannot employ "natural trumpets and ancient woodwinds," we must become sufficiently aware of their qualities to compensate properly for them in modern performances. (That does not always mean a one-to-one substitution of the new instrument for the old.)

In general, the sound of the woodwind section in Haydn's concerted choral music is apt to be somewhat "reedy" and penetrating. Until the 1790s, Haydn preferred oboes and bassoons to flutes or clarinets (the clarinet being a notably late bloomer in Haydn's palette), so the conductor should work to project that color distinction in performance. The case of the bassoon is critical. Often used to double the bass line (see below), its ability to complement—i.e., strengthen—the sound of a cello section was taken for granted. Yet today's wonderfully refined Heckel (German) bassoons tend to get lost among the cellos; at most they add a bit of dark mahogany color. With a modern-instrument ensemble, it may be better to use a French bassoon, the engineering of which has changed little since the seventeenth century.[34] At any rate, if a bassoonist playing in a modern ensemble wants to emulate her forebears, she had better strive for a stringy/reedy tone that will enliven the bass line with upper partials.

All woodwind players, whether playing old or modern instruments, should be expected to match string phrasing and articulation by using combinations of slurring and tonguing. Eighteenth-century woodwind players employed a variety of articulation syllables to create distinctions in phrasing: Quantz, for example, considered the "tongue-stroke" *ti* best for "short, equal, lively, and quick notes," whereas for "slow and sustained (*nourrisantes*) notes, the stroke must not be firm," and the syllable *di* was preferable. Combination syllables like *tiri, diri* (Italianate *r*) or *did'll* were suggested for specific rhythms and subtler

---

[33] Landon *Symphonies*, 110.

[34] Recommended in Donington *Interpretation*, 559, which also quotes Jean-Laurent de Béthizy, 1754/64: "The sounds of [the bassoon] are strong and brusque. A clever man nevertheless knows how to draw from it very sweet, very gracious and very tender sounds." As a sound reference, we recommend the properly dulcet tones made by Milan Turkovic on various recordings by Trevor Pinnock's English Concert: Mr. Turkovic plays a four-key instrument made by M. Deper, Vienna, ca. 1720.

effects.[35] Naturally syllables would also have been used to bring out the varieties of staccato and legato marked or implied in players' parts (on the subject of markings, see *Phrasing and Articulation*, below).

The sound of eighteenth-century brasses was, like that of woodwinds, less dark yet more colorful. Natural (i.e., unvalved) trumpets were substantially longer than their modern descendants, making their sound richer in overtones. But because of their small, steeply flared bells and thinner tubing, they produced a brilliant sound even at a medium *forte*. The great majority of their appearances in mid-Classical music demand this brassy blare. Whereas the virtuoso trumpeters of the Baroque Era had taken pride in their versatility, imitating every nuance of the human voice, trumpeters in concerted music after 1750 increasingly found themselves limited to stereotypically martial, heroic, or triumphant strains. Because the heroic *Affekt* was but one mood of the many that found voice in a Classical work, the trumpeters now had to count far more measures of rests.[36] Later, the invention of valved instruments and other technical refinements would again render the brass more versatile. But Nikolaus Harnoncourt, so well-versed in both early and "modern" music, was right to remind us that, with Mozart and Haydn,

> Every *forte*-entrance of the brass together with the timpani (played as they customarily were then with wooden beaters) should have the effect of a sharp thrust: heroic or aggressive or triumphal, but never a mere color-note in the overall sound, as it is in today's orchestra.[37]

Indeed one of the saddest things to observe in performances of Classical music today is the trumpet section politely holding back so as not to overpower the others. Let the brass ring forth! If old instruments are used, they will not overpower. With modern instruments, balance problems can be somewhat moderated by increasing the size of the string and choral complements to competitive levels, and by seating the brass and percussion players at a higher level, so that their entrances will be prominent (by issuing from a slightly different acoustic space) but less likely to drown out their fellows.[38] A caveat: true *clarino* parts are

---

[35] Quantz *Versuch* (2), 71-85; cf. Tromlitz *Unterricht* (2), 150-211, which greatly expands upon Quantz's directions, and Mahaut *Nouvelle Méthode* (2), 21, which does not, urging the student instead to approach articulation creatively and not to "worry too much about syllables." Although we most frequently encounter instruction on articulation syllables in flute treatises, some sources imply that the techniques could be transferred to oboe and bassoon; see Quantz *Versuch* (2), 85.

[36] Tarr *Trumpet*, 138, 144-145. Tarr's chapter on trumpet playing in the time of Haydn is entitled "The Trumpet in an Era of Decline."

[37] Harnoncourt *Dialog* (2), 121-122. This chapter, from which we have drawn freely in our own discussion, offers a colorful overview of the issues of instrumental timbre and balance in the Classical (Mozart) orchestra.

[38] Cf. Haydn's seating plans for the original performances of *The Creation*, given as Table 10.3.

rare in Haydn. In most cases, the flute-like sound of the valved "Baroque" or piccolo trumpet is less appropriate than that of common B♭ or C trumpets handled well.[39]

As for the kettledrum tattoos that invariably accompany brass statements, one can present a more authentic sound-picture and avoid balance problems by using the smaller, less resonant timpani common to the Classic era. Incidentally, the notation of timpani rolls (i.e., fast unmeasured beating with alternating mallets) was not standardized at the time. It is probable that most occurrences of 𝄐 in the timpani parts to Haydn's choral music are meant to designate a roll. Viennese tradition supports this practice.[40]

The trombone is less of a problem in Haydn's choral music. That is partly because it has undergone fewer fundamental changes and partly because Haydn employed it less often. Aside from *Il ritorno di Tobia*, *The Seven Last Words*, *The Storm*, and the late oratorios, he did not call for trombones in his original scores. It is true that a number of contemporary manuscript copies include trombone parts, but these are generally unauthorized "improvements" reflecting local (especially Viennese) performance traditions.[41] In particular we must note that Haydn did not follow the Mozartian custom of doubling voice lines with trombones. For these reasons, modern alto, tenor, and bass trombones work fairly well in, say, *The Creation*.[42]

As with the Viennese trombones, spurious horn parts exist for some of the early choral music (e.g., *Lauda* 2). The horn was more basic to Haydn's orchestral texture, however, and is an authentic component of many choral works from the time of his Esterházy appointment onward. At times Haydn employed horns as trumpet substitutes in his scoring, which implies much about their timbre and penetration (hand-stopped notes were rare). The Esterházy band included skilled horn players; their virtuosity was notably called upon in a number of symphonies and other instrumental works Haydn composed between 1761 and 1776. In the choral works of this period we find horns in all the so-called "Esterházy

---

[39] Or especially the slightly older, and longer-tubed, F trumpet if it can be obtained.

[40] As in the *Paukenmesse* Kyrie introduction or the first movement of *The Creation*. Landon *HCW* 4, 396-397. But Brown shows that the parts Haydn himself used for large-scale performances of *The Creation* are ambiguous and possibly contradictory on this point; see *Performing*, 67-70.

[41] An interesting example is the set of trombone parts for Haydn's second *Te Deum*. Only the performance materials from the Hofburgkapelle (the Empress's chapel) contain trombone parts; all the other authentic contemporary sources lack them. Moreover, of the Hofburgkapelle parts, only the alto and tenor trombone parts were made at the same time as the other performance materials. The bass trombone part appears to have been added later. That would square with what we know of contemporary Viennese practice, in which only alto and tenor trombones were used in church music and oratorios. Thus the evidence points to the trombones parts for this *Te Deum* as reflecting less the composer's wish than Viennese tradition, a tradition that continued to evolve in the early nineteenth century to include the bass trombone (as encouraged by Haydn in *The Creation* and *The Seasons*). See Landon *HCW* 4, 606, and Mac Intyre *Mass*, 104.

[42] It is also difficult to acquire authentic late-eighteenth-century trombones or copies of them. I am told that many early-music groups make use of seventeenth- or even sixteenth-century replicas, which can hardly contribute a Haydnesque sound to the ensemble.

cantatas," the *Applausus* cantata, the *Grosse Orgelmesse*, and the *Nicolaimesse*. However, none of these pieces present horn players with the bravura technical demands seen in Haydn's purely instrumental works from that time. Nor is there any real question of whether *alto* or *basso* horns should be used (the only parts subject to that issue—in three of the cantatas—can be presumed to be C *basso*).

In Haydn's late works the horns are also prominent, now more often filling dual roles as brass- and woodwind-choir members. Without question the C and B♭ parts in the late Masses are intended for *basso* horns. But in *The Creation*, a Viennese tradition going back to Haydn's day dictates that arias in B♭ major are to be performed with *alto* horns, the trumpets-and-drums choruses with *basso* ones. And Haydn specified three horns in C *alto*, plus three C trumpets, for the finale of *The Seasons*.[43]

With the advent of the modern double horn combining F and B♭ *alto* tubings, it is now possible to play a very broad range of Haydn's parts more easily. Nevertheless the single F horn is to be preferred, even at the expense of some security of execution: its length gives it a richer sonority much more like that of its ancestors.

Keyboard Instruments

At various times and for various genres, Haydn employed organ, harpsichord, and fortepiano as the accompanying keyboard instrument in his choral music. In general, the organ would have been customary for church music, the harpsichord for secular or concert works before the London trips, and the fortepiano for such works composed in London or thereafter.

The organs at which Haydn sat were essentially Baroque instruments. To anyone who has heard today's many reconstructions or new models designed along historical lines, their basic sound should be familiar. The central features of that sound are vivid color contrasts and clean, forward voicing. Although the sheer number of stops may be limited, these little organs are often rich in mixtures and mutations. Everything needed in Haydn's choral works, from the early works' simple continuo to the defiant snarls of the *Nelsonmesse*, can be obtained from them.

In Austria, the basic Baroque organ was indeed usually a *Kleinorgel* type with limited pedalboard (twelve notes, short octave) and one or two manuals (also with short octaves). Since organ builders were often also fortepiano builders, the same aesthetic that saw to the development of the Hammerflügel's quickly rebounding action was also at work on the mechanics of the organ. Likewise the musical style of the solos in Haydn's *Orgelsolo* Masses, with their highly ornamented single melody lines, is quite similar to that of other contemporary keyboard music.

---

[43] For more background on Haydn's horns, and esp. on the *alto* vs. *basso* issue, see Landon *Symphonies*, 121-125; Bryan "Horn"; and Bryan "Alto."

Especially in his later scores, Haydn customarily indicated changes in registration and/or manuals as the dynamic and the size of the accompanied body changed. Thus *Solo* and *Tutti* are written in solo (also choral *piano*) and choral *forte* sections, respectively. *Tasto solo* means to play only the bass line (as at the beginning of fugal passages, or in *all' unisono* patches); it is customarily followed by *Organo*, meaning that the harmonic texture can again be filled out in continuo fashion. When *Organo* occurs in conjunction with *forte* or with the term *Pleno*, it then indicates the fullest possible sound. Otherwise the organ continuo player can be guided by this advice from Petri's *Anleitung* (1782):

> The organist [when accompanying] takes the chords short; [avoids reeds, mixtures, and mutations; with a small church and organ, draws only] one eight-foot Gedackt, or, if this is too softly voiced, two eight-foot stops in the manual, and in the pedal a sixteen-foot or two at most, and again an eight-foot principal for the forte, and for the loudest forte a four-foot, which however is better absent. And yet, when the singer comes in and the piano arrives, the [extra] eight-foot stop must be taken out, so that the bass does not overwhelm the piano of the violins and flutes. Moreover the notes must be taken off short.[44]

One finds similar warnings—against sustaining the chords ("take the chords short") and in favor of overarticulation, especially in recitative ("when the singer comes in . . . the notes must be taken off short")—in many other contemporary treatises.[45] The idea was to preserve transparency of texture while sidestepping intonation conflicts between the organ and other instruments. This practice also mitigated against dragging the tempo, the cardinal sin in most recitative accompaniment.

Some Rococo organs were capable of a wider variety of colorings, including bird calls and orchestral effects. The genial and intimate organ obbligati in Haydn's "Orgelsolo" Masses hardly call for such sounds, and they are better off avoided. Likewise the swell pedal, although introduced on some instruments early in the eighteenth century, is really a creature of the Romantic era and should be left untouched in Haydn. Nor is it necessary (or even possible on the *Kleinorgel*) to play the continuo bass on the pedals; that line is well brought out by the other instruments.

Eighteenth-century organists were accustomed to improvising a great deal of music in the course of a church service.[46] That tradition, as we know from Bach's heritage, relied heavily on use of the old hymns and, for Austrian Catholics, Gregorian chant. This, along

---

[44] Petri *Anleitung* (2), 17.

[45] See, for example, Bach *Versuch* (3), 422, which reminds the keyboardist that "even if the score expresses tied white notes, the sharply detached execution [implicit in all faster-moving recitative] is retained," and "in recitatives with sustained accompanying instruments, the organ holds only the bass, the chords being quitted soon after they are struck." Incidentally, *Versuch* (3), 420-425, makes a good primer on the art of recitative accompaniment, an important subject that lies beyond the scope of the present text.

[46] See Freeman "Role."

with a contemporary trend toward harmonizing and "adapting" chant, suggests that the organist probably also harmonized accompaniments for plainsong, including the occasional *incipit* that prefaced a concerted Mass movement (e.g., the Gloria and Credo of the *Grosse Orgelmesse*).

Table 10.2 shows the disposition of the organ built by Johann Gottfried Mallek in 1778 for the Cathedral Church of St. Martin at Eisenstadt.[47] This is the instrument upon which Haydn played the organ obbligato at the first performance of the *Nelsonmesse*. The organ at the Bergkirche, which Haydn played for the first performances of the last three Masses, was also built by Mallek, in 1797, and is very similarly configured.

"Manual" (Hauptwerk)		Positiv	Pedal
Prinzipal 8'	Fugara 4'	Copula 8'	Subbass 16'
Gedackt 8'	Quint 3'	Prinzipal 4'	Prinzipalbass 8'
Quintadena 8'	Octav 2'	Copula 4'	Gedackt 8'
Octav 4'	Mixtur 4 fach	Octav 2'	Octav 4'
Flöte 4'		Mixtur 2 fach	Posaune 16' (zugefügt)

Table 10.2: Organ, Martinskirche, Eisenstadt (Mallek, 1778)

The harpsichords at Eisenstadt and Esterháza upon which Haydn played, for example, the elaborate obbligati of the cantatas *Qual dubbio omai* and *Da qual gioja improviso* were fairly simple Italian or Italian-derived instruments. They usually had one manual and two eight-foot stops (often coupled together). Thus his accompaniments, and even the obbligati mentioned above, were unlikely to have gotten changes of registration during the course of a performance. Playing any of Haydn's harpsichord continuo accompaniments with varied use of stops, etc., as is possible on a more elaborate French double-manual instrument, will run contrary to their affects as well as to historical evidence.[48]

From 1784 on, the word *fortepiano* occasionally appears on Haydn's manuscripts in place of the earlier *cembalo*, etc. We may assume that his acquaintance with the instrument goes back a few years before that.[49] Haydn's use of the fortepiano for keyboard continuo at his London symphonic concerts is fairly well documented, as is his continuing to use it in Vienna, for example at the performances of *The Creation* and *The Seasons*. But one may well question the extent to which this keyboard was actually employed in the old continuo style by that time. Just because Haydn or Salieri or Wiegl sat at the fortepiano does not mean that any of them realized an accompaniment from the figured bass throughout the performance; at most, the pianist may have added appropriate extemporizations for secco

---

[47] From Mertin "Orgelinstrumenten," 74.

[48] Cf. Landon "Foreword" to the full score of *Qual dubbio omai* by Joseph Haydn (Diletto Musicale 200; Doblinger, Vienna 1982).

[49] Walter "Keyboard," 214; for a fuller discussion see Walter "Klaviere."

recitatives and played enough during tutti passages to "conduct" the ensemble. The music had long since become full-textured enough that it no longer required constant harmonic support.[50] Modern performers should bear this in mind and use keyboard accompaniment with discrimination. That will also have the very desirable result of varying the sonorities in the performance.

On the same subject, we should note that the sound of the eighteenth-century fortepiano—small, colorful, clear, with bell-like attack but quick decay—was closer in many ways to the harpsichord than to the modern piano. Use of a Steinway or a Bösendorfer as a continuo instrument in *The Creation* will evoke the Vienna of Richard Strauss, not Joseph Haydn. If a fortepiano is not available, it is better to use a harpsichord.

Regarding instrument substitution, we have evidence implying that Haydn himself was no stranger to it. For example, there is Count Zinzendorf's diary entry describing a concert of February 15, 1799, at the Lobkowitz Palace: "Musique de Hayd'n et ennui. Messe bruyante [a noisy Mass] . . ."[51] What continuo instrument, if any, did Haydn use for that performance? There was no organ at the palace.

Pitch

In the late twentieth century we have become accustomed to hearing early-music groups perform Baroque music at an "old" pitch of a^1 = 415 Hz, that is, a half-step lower than the modern standard of a^1 = 440 Hz. Some groups performing late-eighteenth- and early-nineteenth-century music have been using a^1 = 430 Hz.[52] But if we wanted to prepare a performance that recreated in every manner the conditions under which Haydn performed his choral music, we would beware of these "old" pitches. They represent a compromise, a generalization of seventeenth- and eighteenth-century conditions that has been agreed to by the period-instrument community.

When we examine the evidence, which is incomplete, confusing, and contradictory, we find that an astonishing variety of pitch standards was in use during the eighteenth century.[53] Even if this evidence is restricted to that which immediately applies to the original

---

[50] See the lively discussion on the subject of continuo accompaniment in late Haydn in Larsen *Haydn Studies*, 194-197. Temperley *Creation*, 113, offers a more conservative viewpoint and cites contemporary keyboard realizations for *The Creation* published by Neukomm and Clementi.

[51] Quoted in Olleson, "Haydn in the Diaries of Count Karl von Zinzendorf," *Haydn Yearbook* 2 (1963-64), 55.

[52] This latter pitch standard is presumably based upon the accepted notion that throughout Europe, a slight general rise in pitch occurred around the end of the eighteenth century; see Stowell *Violin Technique*, 23-26 *passim*, and esp. 241-245, which admirably recaps the contemporary evidence and provides a fuller précis of Mendel *Pitch* than our own (see next n.).

[53] See Mendel *Pitch*, esp. 73-93, from which we have abstracted the following brief summary, for a detailed explanation of the incredibly complex European pitch picture in the eighteenth century. Mendel took pains to correct many of the assumptions upon which the modern standards for "old" pitch were established.

pitch of Haydn's choral music, we must grapple with two different Baroque "standards," *Chor-Ton* and *Cammerthon*. *Chor-Ton* (choir-tone) was the pitch at which the local organ was tuned and thus the pitch to which the choir sang. In many German and Austrian churches, this tone was one or two half-steps higher than the modern equivalent: for example, during Mozart's time the a^1 of the big organ in the Cathedral at Salzburg was about 454 Hz. *Cammerthon* (chamber-tone), on the other hand, was the pitch to which orchestras and other ensembles tuned, and it was often significantly lower. The "A-Kammerton" of Quantz and Agricola appears to have been about a half-step below $a^1 = 440$ Hz; after about 1720 a number of organs in England and Germany were also pitched in that vicinity.

These two pitch standards (and it should be understood that they too are generalized concepts) have practical implications for Haydn's choral music. His sacred works must often have been performed at *Chor-Ton*, meaning that the low-ranging choral bass parts in the F-major *Missa brevis* or the *Cäcilienmesse* did not plumb quite so deeply then as they do today.[54] But Haydn's Esterházy cantatas were more likely performed at *Cammerthon*, which means that high notes in the solo soprano and tenor parts will have been slightly less daunting to his singers than they are to ours.

Given this internal evidence, it is tempting to believe that Haydn took differing pitch standards into account. Yet we have no way of knowing exactly how his groups were pitched. Two strong recommendations can still be made: *1)* performance of the choral sacred music at today's "old" pitches is often impracticable because of the low Fs and E♭s in the choral bass parts, and furthermore cannot be justified on the grounds of historical veracity; *2)* Haydn's other choral music can and should be performed at whatever pitch renders the music most practicable. In the case of the works with coloratura vocal parts, that will often be *at least* a half step lower than $a^1 = 440$. On no account should violin parts be transposed upward or downward, since this practice can alter the sound of an entire composition. It is much better simply to retune the instruments or to use instruments already strung and tuned to a different pitch standard.

HAYDN'S CHOIRS

The so-called symphonic choir and choral society as we know them did not exist in Haydn's time. The choral instrument he used to perform his own cantatas, Masses, and oratorios differed in size, timbre, and training from the groups most often brought to bear on such works today. True, these massive amateur groups were waiting in the wings his-

---

[54] I have examined dozens of eighteenth-century organ parts to Haydn works from a number of Austrian monasteries without once encountering a transposed part or, conversely, transposed string and wind parts. Yet the pitch standards for organs at these monasteries varied and were often in the old *Chor-Ton* territory. It is, of course, likely that in some cases the performers transposed their parts on the spot.

torically—Haydn was so impressed by the large choirs he heard at the Westminster Abbey Handel concerts that he determined to reproduce this effect in the public performances of his own late oratorios. But it was the generation following Beethoven and Schubert that saw the rise of singing societies and an outpouring of oratorios (by Mendelssohn, Spohr, Berlioz, and others) to meet their needs.

Like the Classical orchestra, the late-eighteenth-century choir had its roots in Baroque ensembles. And like that orchestra, it was apt to be small and relatively well trained. The question of the chorus's capabilities can almost be reduced to the question of the typical singer's capabilities. In a sense, every chorister was a professional, even the choirboy who received daily instruction in music as part of his tuition. These singers knew how to count, how to trill and execute other ornaments, and how to "measure the voice." With minimal preparation, they could sing concerted music and plainsong at a number of services and other functions every week. The distinction between soloists and ripienists was not as great as it is today; vocal soloists—the concertante quartet of Viennese Classicism—could join in the choral sections as well, especially for climactic passages. Soloists and chorus members stood together and often shared music.

The typical well-founded church choir numbered between ten and twelve singers. Such a choir would have had an S/A/T/B division of approximately 3/2/1/2 or 4/3/2/2. More treble singers were used for two reasons: 1) the soprano carried the melody and hence deserved prominence (preeminence); 2) boys were used for the soprano and alto lines, and their smaller voices recommended greater numbers for the sake of balance. Haydn's own experience at St. Stephen's is one handy example of this practice; we also can point to the evidence of surviving performance materials at various Austrian monasteries, consisting of an average of two soprano parts to each alto, tenor, or bass part. Assuming that two or three singers shared a part, that would have meant a choir of between eight and fifteen singers. That may in fact be a rather generous estimate, if the embarrassing situation at the Eisenstadt Castle Chapel in the 1780s was common.[55] Some court and concert ensembles will have had larger choirs, as Marpurg's contemporary survey of various ensembles shows:

> [1754:] Gotha, chamber and chapel: . . . two female singers; one male soprano, one male alto, one tenor, two basses; six violins, one double-bass (violon), [plus winds and keyboards].

> Breslau, Bishop's Chapel: five male singers (incl. two sopranos and one alto); seven violins . . . one viola, one double bass, [winds and keyboards].

> [1755:] Paris, Concerts Spirituels; . . . four female and four male solo singers, choir of six female and six male sopranos, six male altos, seven tenors, five high

---

[55] See the letters from Eleonora Jäger and P. Rahier in Chapter 6.

basses, eight low basses; orchestra of sixteen violins, two violas, six cellos, two double basses, [plus winds].[56]

[1756:] Dresden, King's chapel and chamber music: . . . five female and six male sopranos, one female and three male altos, three tenors, four basses, . . . [strings 8/8/4/4/2, plus winds].

Mannheim: . . . three female and three male sopranos, two male altos, three tenor, two basses; [strings 10/10/4/4/2, winds].

[1757:] Salzburg, archbishop's music: . . . solo singers, five male sopranos (three vacant), three tenors, two basses, with additions from the choir; fifteen boy singers . . . three male altos, nine tenors, nine basses (*Chorherren*) and one male alto, three tenors, four basses (*Choralisten*—four of these can play double bass). [Plus Capellmeister, Vice-Capellmeister, three court composers, including Leopold Mozart; strings 5/5/2/2/2, winds, three organists, etc. etc.][57]

That large-choir performance, even of oratorios, was hardly the norm in Vienna is shown by the surviving accounts of oratorio performances in which Mozart played a role:

Vienna 26 February 1788. On this day and on 4 March Ramler's cantata *Die Auferstehung und Himmelfahrt Christi*, in the excellent composition of the incomparable Hamburg *Bach*, was performed at Count *Johann Esterhazy's*, with the unanimous approbation of all the nobility present, by an orchestra of 86 persons in the presence and under the direction of that great connoisseur of the art of music, Baron *von Swieten*. The I. & R. Capellmeister Herr *Mozart* beat time and had the score, and the I. & R. Capellmeister Herr Umlauff was at the keyboard. The performance was the more excellent because it had been preceded by two general rehearsals. . . . Among the singers were Mme. *Lange*, the tenor *Adamberger*, the bass *Saale*, 30 choristers, &c.

[Handel's *Messiah*, in Mozart's orchestration (K. 572), was] Excellently performed on 6 March 1789 at Count Johann Esterhazy's — Mozart directed the orchestra, Umlauf the vocalists. Madam Lange, Mad^elle Altomonte, Herr Saal and Herr Adamberger sang in it, with 12 choristers.[58]

---

[56] Not all of these musicians may be have been used at once. But note that the proportions remain consistent with those of smaller groups.

[57] As with the *Concerts Spirituels*, it may be assumed that this aggregate—more a court ensemble than a church group—seldom performed en masse, but was employed in part as required. Friedrich Wilhelm Marpurg, *Historisch-kritische Beyträge* (Berlin, 1754 etc.), cited and trans. in Donington *Interpretation*, 589-590.

[58] Ramler was a poet not unknown to Haydn; see Chapter 7. The "incomparable Hamburg Bach" was, of course, Carl Phillip Emanuel. Count Johann Esterházy, "of the middle line *zu Frakno*," was Privy Councillor in the Royal Siebenbürgen Court, Master of a Masonic Lodge in Vienna, and an oboe player; he took a leading role in Viennese musical life. The first quotation is from Forkel's *Musikalischer Almanach* . . . (Leipzig), the second a hand-

If we consider these lists in terms of their proportions, we see that courts and concert organizations employed anywhere from one-and-a-half to four times as many players as singers. Not all the players would have taken part in a typical choral performance, but even so we have to accept the fact of orchestral dominance in numbers. How could balance be achieved with these proportions? Writing to his father from Mannheim in 1777, the young Mozart indicated that it was no easy task:

> Now I must tell you about the music here. On Saturday, All Saints' Day, I was at High Mass in the Capelle. The orchestra is excellent and very strong. On either side there are ten or eleven violins, four violas, two oboes, two flutes and two clarinets, two horns, four violoncellos, four bassoons and four double basses, also trumpets and drums. They can produce fine music, but I should not care to have one of my Masses performed here. Why? On account of their shortness? No, everything must be short here too. Because a different style of composition is required? Not at all. But because, as things are at present, you must write principally for the instruments, as you cannot imagine anything worse than the voices here. Six sopranos, six altos, six tenors and six basses against twenty violins and twelve basses is just like zero to one.[59]

Nevertheless, at least three factors may have helped mitigate such imbalances: *1)* singers stood at the front of the ensemble (see Fig. 10.7 and 10.8); *2)* professional singers were used, and a small number of these would project better than a larger number of amateurs; *3)* the softer, more transparent sound and the gentler attacks of period instruments would have interfered less with the choral projection of text, especially those initial consonants so important to understanding. Listeners may not always have heard vocal sound predominant, but they nearly always heard the text. To these we must add other, related factors: the smaller, more acoustically "live" rooms in which the music was performed, and the timbre advantage enjoyed by a smaller vocal ensemble. Such a group will sound brighter and also richer in the overtones of individual voices. On the other hand, a chorus twice as large (like a string section doubled) will not sound twice as loud; rather there will be more weight or "refinement" to the sound and a corresponding loss of brilliance.

And how were these groups led? In various places in this chapter the common Baroque practice of beating time with a roll of paper, when necessary, is mentioned. Otherwise, eye contact on the performance platform was an important way of maintaining ensemble (see below). The Capellmeister will have held rehearsals of his vocal ensembles while seated at the keyboard, thus further shifting the responsibility for musical independence (i.e., self-reliance) and ensemble unity to the individual members of the group—not a bad strategy.

---

written note on the title-page of a textbook from the *Messiah* performance; both quoted in Deutsch *Mozart*, 310 and 335.

[59] Anderson *Letters of Mozart*, 355-356 (L. 235).

HAYDN'S ORCHESTRAS

Throughout our chronological survey of Haydn's choral works and the events which occasioned them, we have included data on the original performing forces when that was available. Here it remains only to make general remarks about the nature of orchestras and orchestral playing in Haydn's time and the development of what might be called Haydn's choral orchestra.

Although much has been made of the occasional contemporary performance of a Mozart symphony or Handel oratorio with gargantuan forces, it is clear that the daily round of concerts, operas, and church music in Haydn's time depended on rather small ensembles. These ensembles did not evolve in smooth step with the development of the Viennese Classical style. Rather, the size of an eighteenth-century orchestra continued to be more related to its social origin than to intrinsic musical factors: thus a private orchestra in the household of a wealthy person might have six violinists, a church orchestra eleven, a court orchestra twelve, an opera orchestra sixteen, and a concert orchestra nineteen, with the other instruments distributed in proportion to these. Neal Zaslaw, who along with Christoph-Hellmut Mahling has done the major research in this area, noted that 18th-century musicians preferred a relatively heavy bass line—the basso continuo was shared by cellos, double basses, and bassoons—and a light viola part.[60] Winds were employed singly or in pairs, but nearly always in greater proportion to the number of string players than is customary today. If more than twenty or twenty-five strings were used, the woodwinds, and sometimes the brass, were doubled. When wind instruments were used, at least one bassoon also doubled the bass line if there was no specific bassoon part.[61]

A number of theorists took the trouble to set down their ideas about properly balanced string sections in ensembles ranging from 4 to 74 members. Table 10.3 gives a comparative sampling of their recommendations for middle-sized string sections.

	Vln I	Vln II	Vla	Cello	Bass	Total
Quant *Versuch* (1752)	4	4	2	2	2	14
Petri *Anleitung* (1767)	5-6	4-5	2	1-2	2	13-16
Petri *Anleitung* (1782)	7	5	3	4-5	2	21-22
Galeazzi *Elementi* (1791)	5-6	4-6	[3]	2	2	16-19
(ranging up to:)	24-26	23-26	10	6	6	69-74
Koch *Lexikon* (1802)	5	5	3	3	2	18

Table 10.3: Orchestral String Proportions from the Treatises

---

[60] Figures used here are adapted from Zaslaw "Size," 187, and Zaslaw "Orchestra," 170-184; see also Mahling "Orchesterpraxis Haydn" and Mahling *Orchester*. But cf. Haydn, in his *Applausus* letter of March 1768: "I would ask you to use two players on the viola part throughout, for the inner parts sometimes need to be heard more than the upper parts." Of course this admonition is also a tacit recognition of the prevailing tendency to slight the viola.

[61] Zaslaw "Orchestra," 181.

We must remember that these writers' views encompassed a wide range of times, places, and aesthetics, from the mid-century treble domination of the *galant* school to the richer, more evenly balanced textures of mature Classicism. On viola strength, Quantz's words somewhat betray his *galant* outlook:

> Since one viola, if a good and strong instrument, is sufficient against four or even six violins, the violist must moderate the strength of his tone if only two or three violins play with him, so that he does not cover the others. . . . The middle parts, which, considered in themselves, provide the listener with the least pleasure, must never be heard as strongly as the principal parts.[62]

On the other hand, Galeazzi remarked, "I am of the opinion that it would always produce the best effect if the violas were one-third the number of violins, and I have always censured the scarcity of violas in our orchestras."[63] Quantz was probably writing with the old, large Baroque viola in mind, of course, whereas Galeazzi may have been influenced by the newer, smaller instruments (see above).

Haydn's instrumental scoring of a choral work was always tailored to the situation in which it would be performed. Thus as early as 1766, with the *Cäcilienmesse*, he departed from the use of the church trio when he knew that he would have a large orchestra at his disposal, either in Vienna or Mariazell or both. And as late as 1775 he reverted to the trio format for the *Kleine Orgelmesse*, which had to be performed in more modest circumstances. Thus there is little point in attempting to trace an artistic "development" in these accompaniments taken by themselves.

Nor is there much point in attempting to reconstruct orchestral parts that seem to be missing. This issue is most often broached in connection with the viola. "Should Haydn's sacred works omitting the viola parts be performed without violas today, or should a viola part be added?" asked Karl Geiringer in 1975.[64] The tacit assumption behind this question was that viola players were available in all of Haydn's ensembles. Not so. He could draw upon one or more of the violinists in his *Cammermusik* to play viola, but the Castle Chapel instrumentalists could not be so divided; there simply weren't enough of them. As we have seen earlier in this study, Baroque trio texture—two violins and basso—lingered long in Austrian church music. Haydn used it for most of his early church works. When he began to add viola (as in the *Mariazellermesse* or the *Nicolaimesse*), he sometimes used it to reinforce the bass an octave higher and sometimes gave it an independent line.[65] By the

---

[62] *Versuch*, 239.

[63] *Elementi* 1, 215n; quoted in Zaslaw "Orchestra," 180n.

[64] Geiringer "Remarks," 204.

[65] A special case is presented by the *Nicolaimesse*, in which the Et incarnatus est and the Benedictus both got an independent viola part that is otherwise absent from Haydn's scoring. Robbins Landon noted that the part reverted to doubling the bass at the Osanna; from this he concluded that it must also have been present, and doubling the bass, in the (typically) identical Osanna at the end of the Sanctus and, furthermore, that it must have been

1780s, the development of the orchestra and the independence of the viola part in Haydn's church and choral works were fully established. That does not mean we need to return to, say, the little F-major Mass and give it a *colla parte* viola line.[66]

Within the smallish ensembles that accompanied choral music, as many as a third to a half of the players may have been competent soloists, the rest mere tutti players (reflecting the old concertino-ripieno division of labors). We know from the Esterházy chronicles—and from Haydn's early symphonies with *concerto grosso* features—that Haydn's band was constituted in this way. Not only the soloistic passages, but also any soft, chromatic, or contrapuntal patches in Haydn's music could have been left to the more expert players only. Places exist throughout the choral works that would benefit from this approach.

It was the soloists who ultimately gave the music whatever personal interpretations were possible. No interpretive conductor, at least in the sense of a Szell or Bernstein, was present. Haydn led his groups from the keyboard with the assistance of his concertmaster Tomasini.[67] Since the ensemble was small, the music based mainly on dance or march rhythms, and its style already in the blood of each player or singer, there was little need for conducting at all. The old choral tradition of a leader who beat the *tactus* with a rolled-up scroll of music probably remained in effect for grand events (see the descriptions above and in Chapter 9 of various oratorio performances). But such practices are not to be confused with actual interpretive conducting: can anyone imagine a twentieth-century critic soberly informing us, à la Forkel, that "Mr. Giulini beat time and had the score"?

Forkel's commentary on the first Mozart *Messiah* (see above) reminds us of an unpleasant fact of eighteenth-century musical life: rehearsal time was scant. One rehearsal was typical, two a luxury; church musicians often dispensed with rehearsals altogether. That Haydn did not readily accept this state of affairs can be seen from his remarks in the *Applausus* letter and his meticulous behavior at other times.[68] Musical discipline stayed on a relatively high level in Haydn's groups.

And there was need for it, given the chaotic state of much eighteenth-century performance. Robert Bremner (d. 1789), an English pupil of Geminiani, offered this guide to correct orchestral behavior, implying that it was often more honored in the breach:

---

doubling the bass everywhere else in the Mass except in the specially written parts. Therefore he has reconstructed a complete viola part for the Faber/G. Schirmer edition; *HCW* 2, 251. Because of the haste in which the Mass was composed and copied, this is an acceptable theory, but it cannot provide a paradigm for interpretation of the scoring in other Haydn choral works.

[66] See, besides Zaslaw and others, Fellerer "Remarks."

[67] This method of divided leadership was Italian. Galeazzi wrote that if the ensemble became shaky during performance, the concertmaster was expected to stamp his feet; likewise harpsichordists sometimes had to pound their instruments to bring things together; see Zaslaw "Orchestra," 163.

[68] "On 30th March 1795 I was invited by Dr. Arnold and his associates to a grand concert in Free Maisons Hall: one of my big symphonies was to have been given under my direction, but since they wouldn't have any rehearsal, I refused to cooperate and did not appear." From Haydn's London notebooks, quoted and trans. in Landon *HCW* 3, 299.

The concert, or orchestra player . . . is only a member of that whole by which a united effect is to be produced; and if there be more than one to a part, he becomes no more than a part of a part; therefore his performance, with that of those who play the same part, must, like the unisons of an organ or harpsichord, coincide so as to pass for one entire sound, whether loud or soft. . . .

From what has been observed above, it must follow, that when gentlemen are performing in concert, should they, instead of considering themselves as relative parts of one great whole, assume each of them the discretional power of applying tremolos, shakes, beats, appoggiaturas, together with some of them slurring, while others are articulating, the same notes; or, in other words, carrying all their different solo-playing powers into an orchestra performance; a concert thus rebellious cannot be productive of any noble effect.[69]

Beyond Bremner's simple call for orchestral discipline, four things should be noted about his remarks: *1)* he implies that soloists were free to add all manner of ornaments and *manieri* to a part; *2)* he further implies that many ripienists did the same thing; in other words, that a performance with reckless ripieno embellishments might be, in a sense, authentic without being a good thing at all; *3)* he does not censure, or even address, *composers* who indicate non-uniform slurring, articulation, ornaments, etc., only *orchestral players* who depart from composer-dictated unity; *4)* among the embellishments he would ban in orchestral playing is the *tremolo.* That is what we would call today *vibrato* and would consider nearly essential to good string tone. Nevertheless, vibrato must have had little place in Classical orchestral playing.[70] All of these issues are amplified elsewhere in this chapter, with conclusions and admonitions similar to Bremner's.

Heinrich Koch's *Musikalisches Lexikon* (1802) contains a long article on seating and placement.[71] Koch recommended that, for church performance (i.e., in the organ loft), singers be grouped at the front and the principal violinist, cellist, and double bassist be brought as close as possible to the organist. For concerts, Koch likewise urged that the singers (or the string players if there were no singers) be placed in front, since they had the most important musical lines; next forward should be the weaker instruments. Stronger instruments would move toward the back; never were weak instruments to be placed next to strong ones (e.g., flutes next to trumpets). It would be best if the leader of the singers and leader of the orchestra were visible to each member of their respective groups and the two leaders visible to each other. The whole orchestra should be on a raised platform, not too wide and shallow. The principal performers should be placed in the center of the plat-

---

[69] Quoted in Zaslaw "Compleat," 50, 52. Bremner added in a footnote, "Choruses, the most awful of all musical entertainments, are too often performed in this undisciplined manner; not intentionally, but from ill-judged ambition, which fires the breasts of many singers with a desire of excelling their neighbours in skill and vociferation."

[70] This point is echoed by Geminiani, Galeazzi, Spohr, and others, who also state or imply that vibrato is a soloist's ornament. See Zaslaw "Compleat," 52, for a summary of their comments.

[71] "Stellung," col. 1435-1438; summarized in Zaslaw "Orchestra," 163-165.

form, with the leaders of the first and second violins on either side of them. The rest of the violins should fan out behind their leaders, forming a semicircle along the front. Solo singers or instrumentalists should stand in the center of this semicircle where they can lead.

The seating plans Haydn used for his London concerts of 1791-93, and later for oratorio performances in Vienna, adhere fairly closely to Koch's prescriptions and were widely influential. They are given at the end of this chapter as Figures 10.7 and 10.8.

PHRASING AND ARTICULATION

Seldom is the gradual emergence of Classical style in Haydn's music more apparent to the performer than when the variety of its phrasing and articulation are considered. The very hallmark of Viennese Classicism is its remarkable synthesis of *galant* phrase structure with other traditions, providing a richness of gesture that has no equal in Western music. We can savor this growth in Haydn's powers almost on a work-to-work basis in the chronicle created by his choral music.

But in no way does our wonder at the composer's increasing control of (*invention* of) a style simplify the practical issues involved in performing his music. Quite the contrary—in Haydn's choral works we are confronted not only with a chronological shift of expression but also with conscious archaisms, introduced as the composer moved from one genre to another. Thus the Baroque mentality of *Il ritorno di Tobia* (1774-5, rev. 1784) will raise somewhat different performance questions than the Masses of 1772-82 and their more progressive elements.

Fortunately for us, Haydn was among the most modern composers of his time in attempting to develop a precise, simple, didactic notation, one that strangers could readily interpret. Especially from about 1780 on (after he had made contact with Artaria and other publishers), Haydn's manuscripts and correspondence began to show an interest in the preparation of genuine editions, i.e., scores that specified performance details the composer himself would formerly have set in rehearsal (or, far less often, entrusted to the individual players).[72]

So it is in the works before 1780 that more ambiguities abound and more guidance is needed. Even the experienced early-music specialist will have to take pains here, for the Baroque traditions in which Haydn was raised were not always those of Corelli or Vivaldi or Bach. Not all of our specialists' treasured repertory of free articulations, extra ornaments, rhythmic alterations, and the like will find a place in "authentic" Haydn performance. And the converse is also true: nonspecialists must note that markings considered most precise and simple in Haydn's time may have since acquired new meanings, or no

---

[72] Somfai "Notation" provides a brief discussion, with tables, of broad notational changes throughout Haydn's career.

meaning. Thus do today's "urtext" editions, with their clean, authoritative surfaces, sometimes mislead us into mechanical "urtext" performances. Restraint is in order at one end of the spectrum, but creativity (re-creativity?) still needed at the other.

Proper phrasing lies at the heart of any Haydn performance. And *phrasing* necessarily connotes a constellation of elements extending well beyond simple articulation: dynamics above all, rhythmic flexibility, even the choice and combination of instruments. If the discussion here begins with matters of articulation, that is only in order to provide a foundation for equally important other matters.

Conductors seeking a thorough introduction to early-Classic articulation, especially in Haydn, would do well to read certain chapters in Leopold Mozart's *Violinschule* and then vow to reread them once a year. Mozart *père* was, after all, from the same South-German/Austrian school of the Baroque that nurtured young Haydn; his treatise appeared shortly after the birth of his son Wolfgang Amadeus, was immediately and highly successful (more so than Quantz's or Emanuel Bach's), was enlarged and reprinted in 1769 and 1787, and was consulted well into the nineteenth century. As a practical violinist writing for his colleagues, Leopold avoided both the precious particulars of genre style (which filled many contemporary keyboard treatises) and undue emphasis on virtuosity.[73] Instead he focused on basics, exhorting his readers always to strive for the effect of fine singing. In fact, string players and singers can profit almost equally from his advice.

For reasons of space we give here only the most basic principles set forth in Mozart's treatise, dealing with basic bowings and variations on them.[74] Composers often simply assumed players' acquaintance with these principles and marked little in the music unless they desired a deviation from custom. Today the conductor preparing parts will have to mark a few more things or a great many more, depending on their performers.

Basic bowings

i) The first note of each measure should be taken as a downbow, "even if two downstrokes should follow each other." After rests that begin a beat, use an upbow:

ii) In rapid tempos, some modifications may be needed, but continue to take care that the first note of ea. measure is a downbow:

---

[73] Perhaps because C.P.E. Bach's *Versuch* is just such a genre-specific treatise, Haydn made only limited use of it in developing his own notation of ornaments, etc., despite having known it from his earliest years.

[74] See [L.] Mozart *Violinschule* (3), 73-95, 103-131.

In the first measure, the two Es are taken in one stroke, but the bow is lifted so that they are clearly separated. (Note Mozart's marking for this articulation; it will appear again below and is similar to modern usage.)

iii) When two quick notes follow a slow one, a slur is customary:

But Mozart alludes to many exceptions, either for the sake of "special flavors" or to maintain basic bowing routine.

iv) A corollary and general rule: If the first of two quick notes is played upbow, then both are taken in the same bow. But if the first note is a downbow, then each gets a separate stroke.

v) In common time, the note after a half-note gets a downbow:

(This can often be used effectively in fugal passages to provide phrase articulations.)

vi) In "divided" (i.e., syncopated) figures, the bow "is drawn up and down according to the notes before your eyes, and without regard to the rules given hitherto":

(But note the example is written so that in at least every other bar, the first beat gets a downbow.)

vii) For dotted figures that occupy one beat or less: if the figure is long-short, each note is played separately; if short-long, note pairs are slurred.

viii) Music in triple time presents difficulties, since one cannot continue to observe the downbeat/downbow rule without bowing two or more notes together. Mozart shows the beginner how to do that with "good taste and sound judgement" even when "the composer has forgotten to mark the slurs." In so demonstrating, he states the fundamental principle of Classic articulation: "Notes at close intervals should usually be slurred, but notes far apart should be played with separate strokes and in particular be arranged to give a pleasant variety."[75]

(Note that his examples show two-note bowings both slurred and detached, plus a great deal of "pleasant variety"!)

---

[75] In agreement with this fundamental principal, but established apart from it, is Mozart's rule for appoggiaturas: "The appoggiatura is never separated from its main note, but is taken at all times in the same stroke." See the discussion on fixed ornaments which follows herein.

Variations on the bowings

i) We are now ready for Mozart's more artistic advice, the aesthetic meat on the bones of his up- and down-strokes. "Every figure can be varied in many ways by means of bowings, even if it consists of but few notes. These variations are usually indicated by a sensible composer."

The basic figure above, which can certainly be performed with each note receiving its own separate stroke, can also be bowed in a great variety of other ways:

ii) And furthermore:

> It is not enough to play such figures [see above] just as they stand, according to the bowings indicated; they must also be so performed that the variation *strikes the ear at once* [italics added]. . . . Now if in a musical composition two, three, four, and even more notes be bound together by the half circle, so that one recognizes therefrom that the composer wishes the notes not to be separated but played singingly in one slur, the first of such united notes must be somewhat more strongly stressed, but the remainder slurred on to it quite smoothly and more and more quietly. Let it be tried in the foregoing examples. It will be seen that the stress falls now on the first, now on the second, or third beat, yea, frequently even on the second half of the first, second, or third beat. Now this changes indisputably the whole style of performance."[76]

---

[76] Mozart *Violinschule* (3), 123-124. Mozart had a great deal more to say about the role of dynamics in shaping the phrase. "Every tone, even the strongest attack, has a small . . . softness at the beginning of the stroke; . . . this same softness must be heard also at the end of each stroke." (Ch. 5 § 3 [97]) Thus each bow stroke had an audible dynamic arch (*pf* → dim. → *p*) giving it further definition as a unit. Elsewhere Leopold speaks of unwritten dynamics to be applied *within* the phrase: "one must know [also] how to change from *piano* to *forte* without directions and of one's own accord, each at the right time; for this means, in the well-known phraseology of the

(Well into the nineteenth century, the importance of clearly articulated phrasing was similarly advocated for singers by Manuel Garcia: "Where notes are united in groups, the last note of the group must be quitted as soon as intonated."[77])

What Leopold was driving at is that the rhythmic qualities of a passage become significantly altered in its bowing—whether marked by the composer or, failing that, added by the performer—and these rhythms must be forcefully expressed through dynamics (and also perhaps occasional rubato, since "stress" can be a matter of durations as well).[78] Four sixteenths take on the feeling of two eighths, or a dotted eighth and a sixteenth, or something else again. When we pass from the treatise to a bit of real music, as in Example 10.1, the effect is of course even more striking:

Example 10.1a: Haydn *Ave Regina*, i, mm. 1-11; Melk MS.

Example 10.1b: same passage bowed according to Leopold Mozart's principles

painters, Light and Shade [i.e., *chiaroscuro*]. The notes raised by a ♯ and ♮ should always be played rather more strongly, the tone then diminishing again . . . [likewise for] a sudden lowering of a note by a ♭ and ♮." (Ch. 12 § 8 [218-19]). Harnoncourt suggested that the word *tenuto* (or *ten.*) was applied by Classic-era composers to indicate when a note or phrase should be exempt from these rules of dynamic arch and chiaroscuro (*Dialog* (2), 153). That would be in line with Marpurg: "If certain notes should be held for their full value [i.e., not "phrased" dynamically or otherwise], *ten*, or *tenuto* is written above them"; *Anleitung*, 28-29. Cf. Haydn's *Paukenmesse*/Benedictus, mm. 9-11.

[77] *Hints*, 31.

[78] See Harnoncourt *Dialog* (2) 149-158, for an interesting interpretation of this maxim as applied to W. A. Mozart's music.

Although Haydn seldom marked vocal parts as thoroughly, he certainly intended singers to observe similar ideals of phrasing. Here is a section of soprano melisma from one of the Esterházy cantatas, showing the composer's careful indications and, in brackets, the customary articulations unwritten but understood by composer and performer:

pu gna

Example 10.2: Haydn *Qual dubbio*, II, mm. 90-98

iii) Leopold devotes an entire chapter to triplets, mainly emphasizing correct rhythmic execution and—again—the great variety of articulations possible with these figures. In this regard we need only mention here a related problem, the interpretation of so-called "flying" slurs[79] associated with triplet notation:

Example 10.3a: Haydn *Heiligmesse* Credo, mm. 189-193, as in *JHW*

Example 10.3b: same passage as it should be bowed

---

[79] Somfai "Notation," 27.

In the autograph, one can see that the slurs of measures 191-192 are actually a manuscript shorthand associated with triplet figures and are not necessarily intended as bowing instructions. The character of this passage dictates vigorous separate bows on each note.

iv) Elsewhere Mozart emphasizes the importance of a basic cantabile:

> Not a little is added to evenness and purity of tone if you know how to fit much into one stroke. Yea, it goes against nature if you are constantly interrupting and changing. . . . The human voice glides quite easily from one note to another; and a sensible singer will never make a break unless some special kind of expression, or the divisions or rests of the phrase demand one. . . . You must therefore take pains where the Cantilena of the piece demands no break, not only to leave the bow on the violin when changing the stroke, in order to connect one stroke with another, but also to play many notes in one stroke, and in such fashion that the notes which belong together shall run into each other, and are only differentiated in some degree by means of *forte* and *piano*.[80]

Those words, taken together with the variations quoted above, should refute those who still believe that the unphrased sewing-machine rattles once mistaken for Baroque "purity" should for some reason also be carried into performances of early Mozart or Haydn.

To summarize the argument thus far: Phrasing is the most important element in building an expressive Haydn performance. The essence of correct Haydn phrasing can be derived from late-Baroque violin bowing (extended, by analogy, to tonguing and slurring in wind instruments) as described in Leopold Mozart's *Violinschule*. Its fundamental principle is to slur "notes at close intervals" (i.e., seconds and thirds) and to separate "notes far apart" so as to create a "pleasant variety" in the phrases. Such "pleasant variety" should be immediately perceptible to the listener through an adroit *Gestalt* of performance that includes dynamic and rhythmic nuances. Notwithstanding all this, performers should hold fast to the general ideal of a seamless legato—the effortless sound of good singing.

Haydn took increasing care to mark the phrasing he wished, particularly after 1780. But there are many places in his music, both early and late, in which articulation marks are not present; the performer was expected to supply appropriate phrasing based on custom and the character of the passage. Several such instances are quoted within this chapter.

Before going on, we must add a caveat for the conductor approaching the very earliest Haydn. It must be admitted that, in works like the F-major Mass, often the string writing is so mechanical that any thoroughgoing attempt to give it a "pleasant variety" of phrases is doomed to failure, and is antithetical to the music in the bargain. Part of the charm of that piece (also of the first *Te Deum*) is its naiveté, which would be spoiled by an overapplication of Leopold's rules. Anyway, one can hardly find a moment for such phrasing in passagework like this:

---

[80] Mozart *Violinschule* (3), 101-102.

Example 10.4: Haydn *Missa brevis* in F, Gloria, mm. 11-14, violins

The most that can be done is to see that the downbows come out right and that occasional simple patterns are brought out (Haydn has marked most of those already). To strain for further effects only emphasizes the awkwardness of the writing.

Single-note articulations

In his autograph scores, Haydn generally indicated articulations of individual notes by means of a thin perpendicular stroke directly above or below the notehead (Ex. 10.5a; cf. Ex. 4.12). Less often we can also find staccato-dots above noteheads (Ex. 10.5b), plus a number of intermediate, but hardly indeterminate, scratches of the quill (Ex. 10.5c).

Example 10.5a: Haydn *Mariazellermesse*, Kyrie, mm. 9-12, soprano and upper strings

Example 10.5b: Haydn *Mariazellermesse*, Kyrie, mm. 53-54, as above

Example 10.5c: Haydn *Mariazellermesse,* Kyrie, mm. 21-23[81]

These markings have been taken over into printed editions with varying degrees of accuracy.[82] Oftentimes, even in current scholarly offerings, Haydn's strokes have been rendered either as wedges (') or as dots (˙). Since these wedges and dots have different meanings to us and had still other meanings in Haydn's time, a natural confusion has arisen over how they should be performed. The question is not really what Haydn wanted; his hand was capable of rather fine distinctions. The question has become what we should do with those wedges and dots in *JHW* and other editions.

First, a bit of history.[83] In Haydn's time, stroke and wedge were virtually interchangeable. Probably they originated as visual analogues to the sharp downward stroke the bow makes when a violinist accents and detaches a note. After 1750 they acquired a more general meaning when certain Viennese publishers (Torricella, Artaria) refined the wedge and chose to use it as their only staccato-mark. Only in the nineteenth century did the wedge again take on a specialized meaning, at that point to denote an especially sharp staccato (very short, with an accent) used primarily in keyboard music. The use of the wedge in modern editions of Haydn's choral music no doubt stems from a desire to approximate Haydn's own marking (the vertical stroke) while giving a nod to printers' tradition (the wedge as an easier-to-see vertical stroke).

In eighteenth-century music, the staccato-dot appears more often over groups of notes than over single tones. It makes notes lighter, just as a dotted line gives a lighter appearance than an unbroken one. Its effect is therefore contrary to that of the wedge or stroke. We find many examples of this usage in Mozart,[84] fewer in Haydn. When staccato-dots are present in a modern Haydn edition, they may have been placed there by the editor as substitutes for the vertical strokes that can be seen in the autograph. Perhaps the editor has determined that a routined modern performer will be less likely to misinterpret those familiar dots.

Other than by consulting the autograph in every case, the safest way to interpret wedges and dots is via their individual context: examine tempo, dynamics, affect, and function. In the opening measures of the *Nelsonmesse* (Ex. 8.6), the *allegro* marking, the

---

[81] Facsimiles by kind permission of the Staatsbibliothek zu Berlin - Preußischer Kulturbesitz, Musikabteilung (Mus.ms.autogr. Jos. Haydn 58).

[82] The editions issued so far by *JHW* have generally achieved a high standard of faithfulness within the limitations of conventional printed notation.

[83] Gratefully drawn from Hermann Keller's excellent essay in Albrecht *Bedeutung,* 7-21.

[84] See Harnoncourt *Dialog* (2), 156-158.

forte, and the firm downward stride of the D-minor motive tell us that these notes should indeed be accented and rather heavy (therefore not too short). But consider Example 10.40 (also the *Nelsonmesse*). Here the *piano* dynamic, the stepwise motion, and the function—accompaniment for a soprano solo right before an outburst from the whole band—dictate an almost playful tiptoe, quite light and short. Another accompaniment figure is shown in Example 10.42. Considering the text, the sustained character of the other parts, and the general dynamic, these sixteenths should also be light but rather more lyric than clipped. Two further points on 10.42: Haydn actually did write staccato-dots in the autograph here (cf. Ex. 10.5b), and of course the staccato character of the first-violin part should continue into the following measures. It was not customary for the composer to waste time and ink repeating the obvious.

We close this meditation on wedges, strokes, and dots with one more scrap from the *Nelsonmesse* (Ex. 10.41). What is the real character of the sixteenths in measure 38? And why are there no articulation marks in measures 36-37? The second question is more easily answered: repeated eighths and sixteenths automatically imply separated execution, and—given this very Haydnesque martial rhythm—there can be no denying them a vigorous treatment.[85] In measure 38, the role of custom must also be taken into account. If Haydn had *not* marked the articulation, his players might well have felt free to slur the notes into groups of two or four. He must have wanted something else, presumably in order to enhance the rhythmic drive, perhaps also to help the concertmaster preserve ensemble while "settling" the tempo (anticipating the soprano's entrance and the dynamic change).[86] All these things are more readily accomplished with separate strokes; *détaché* is the goal of Haydn's marking here and not necessarily a true staccato, which would be less manageable and less in character anyway.

Non-uniform articulations [87]

One aspect of phrasing and articulation in Haydn that announces itself immediately is a lack of uniform phrasing, both simultaneous (vertical) and consecutive (horizontal). The conductor is continually confronted with pitches, rhythms, bowings, and more that don't quite match, or have been left unmarked, in a lower or later part. How is one to reconcile all these discrepancies?

---

[85] The quarter-notes in m. 37, like *every other* unslurred quarter-note in this movement, share the qualities of m. 1 (Ex. 10.17), hence are also an implied *marcato*.

[86] Cf. the *Cäcilienmesse* Kyrie, mm. 86-87, with its similarly marked transitional figure. See also the section following in this book on tempo and tempo modification.

[87] Here we lump together for discussion all manner of variant phrasings, including differences in articulation, pitch, and rhythm; to deal with them separately would disadvantage the reader, since they form a *Gestalt* in Haydn's style. The problem of non-uniform notation for fixed ornaments is of a different order and will be discussed later.

The short answer is that one had better not.[88] Ours is an age that prizes unity of design and execution: our Bauhaus-influenced architecture, our scientific world view, our culture of mass production have all conditioned us to look askance at irregularities in the surface. The aesthetic of Haydn's time was far different. One only has to enter a Baroque church in Austria, with its typical rows (or clumps) of paintings, plaster cherubs, chandeliers, drapery, and gilded altarpieces, to realize this. There is no way such an assortment of artifacts could pass muster with Mies van der Rohe, yet it can impart—in the best cases—power as well as charm. The very profusion of different media, colors, shapes, and gestures overwhelms us, the clutter becomes glorious. And so it is with the varied nuances embedded in Haydn's phrasing: they can be seen as a kind of aural complement to the visual *abbellimenti* among which the composer lived.

Several examples given at the end of this chapter show typical uses of vertical non-unity in Haydn's choral music. Often the text setting will dictate a non-uniform articulation of otherwise identical lines (Exx. 10.39, 10.43). And Example 10.38, from the *Paukenmesse*, demonstrates Haydn's skill at foregrounding the melody via contrasting articulations. But most of this vertical non-unity can be traced to considerations of idiom: *1)* strings, especially the violins, had the most flexible, well-developed techniques; they could play more notes, in a wider range, with more complex articulations, than any other instruments; *2)* voices and woodwinds filled an intermediate category; vocal soloists were expected to be nearly as versatile as violinists, choirs much less so; the woodwind writing in the late Masses and oratorios can be quite sophisticated, but throughout his life Haydn also employed woodwinds and choruses as species of continuo, giving them blocks of harmony to play or declaim upon while the violins danced above;[89] *3)* trumpets and drums were generally confined to playing formulas; the horns wandered stylistically between woodwind and trumpet camps but were seldom asked to do much in the way of articulation.

As much or more of the non-unity is a matter of basic style. One beautiful example of Haydn's skill at transforming consecutive related phrases via changes in articulation can be seen in the first part of the *Paukenmesse*'s nativity scene (Ex. 10.44). The unison strings' first articulation anticipates the more cantabile vocal solo (a common strategy in Haydn "cantata" introductions), but before the solo begins, this first period is capped by a marcato transformation of its dotted figure. Here changes of dynamic, scoring, and octave parallel the implied change of articulation. After the bass soloist enters, the dotted figure is

---

[88] Naturally, there are various long answers too. Some discrepancies are a matter of notation, not actual sound; see the section below on fixed ornaments describing a number of different signs, etc., which dictate identical or near-identical execution. Proof that non-uniform articulations in Haydn and others should be interpreted as marked is purportedly offered in a rigorously limited study by Dene Barnett ("Slurring"). Herein we prefer to approach the problem from the viewpoint of culture and internal stylistic evidence, both of which provide far more ample, and applicable, demonstrations on the matter.

[89] In the autograph scores, one occasionally finds evidence (scratched-out or erased notes) implying that Haydn simplified choral lines for the sake of easier execution without altering the doubling instrumental lines. That is the case, for example, in the *Nelsonmesse* Credo, m. 143.

continued, but again transformed into a delicately traced violin accompaniment that shadows (and counters) the main tune's upward stride. One idea, three articulations. We offer this not so much as a performance problem (the passage strongly resists misinterpretation) but as a reminder of Haydn's basic sense of the language.

It will be, in fact, the smallest things that give pause to the performer. Should the soprano soloist in Example 10.39 borrow the first violin's turn (m. 74)? Should the bass soloist of Example 10.44 be coached to coordinate his pickup with the first violin's (going into m. 44)? Under the common rules of eighteenth-century musicianship they would not be forbidden to make such adjustments. In the first case violin and soprano share the same line, and an adjustment could easily be accommodated within the singer's technique. But in the second, the bass and violin lines have different characters and functions; it would be inappropriate for the singer to adopt the violin's rhythm, and possibly difficult to match its articulation. Better for the bass to take the opposing tack, by slightly anticipating his G (or delaying his C), making a fat "German" eighth and maintaining legato. Once again, context and common sense provide a great deal of help in applying historical principles.

One final example of non-uniform articulations and unmarked phrasing in Haydn, this one more typical of what the conductor faces in preparing a pre-1780 work, is given as Example 10.45. Most of the measures left unmarked are simple continuations of the main idea (as we would expect, a Baroque unity of affect and gesture is more apparent here). These bars can be marked by analogy with others, which is what editor H. C. Robbins Landon suggested (see broken slurs).[90] But other articulations are possible too, for instance separate bows for the first violin in measures 44 and 48.

In summary, two rules: *1)* Do not change firm bowings, slurs, or other marks of articulation. Celebrate and emphasize their variety. *2)* In unmarked passages, determine whether the notes in question are meant as a repetition of a gesture or as a departure from that gesture. Recall what the customary articulation would be. Then phrase accordingly, keeping in mind Leopold Mozart's call for "pleasant variety." Only rarely does one find a transformed gesture that is not heralded as such—if not by slurs and dots, then by changes of dynamics, tessitura, scoring, and more.

Metric and other accentuations

Every child begins his or her musical education with a basic indoctrination in metric emphasis. We are all supposed to know that in a measure of common time, the first beat gets the most weight, the third beat the next-most, the second beat the most after that, and the fourth beat the least—and so on for every meter. That these basic rules were also explained in the eighteenth-century treatises thus comes as no great shock. But we cannot help being surprised by the vehemence and length which writers expended on the subject:

---

[90] Doblinger Ed. 46 006 (Vienna, 1964).

everyone from Türk to Leopold Mozart to Jean-Jacques Rousseau went on and on about "good and bad parts," "ruling or strong beats," "how to play [the] notes with respect to their different weight," and so forth. The reason for their pains should be obvious: to the eighteenth century, meter and its emphases were of much greater importance for stylish execution of music than they have become to us. Eighteenth-century music was built on dance rhythms; its motoric schemes depended on unfailing arrival at a strong downbeat. We have since suffered the Romantic era, which gave us far less vital, varied rhythms and consequently taught us to avoid the "tyranny of the bar line." Who among us has not had the experience of turning on the radio—to a classical station, of course—and hearing an orchestra deftly articulate a rhythm in a way that gave nary a clue to its meter? (Precise ensemble for large groups, it would seem, is highly dependent on lessening such imprecise things as metric accent.)

For Haydn's choral music, proper performance depends upon metric accentuation. It is part of the miniaturized, subtle art of phrasing that has occupied so much space in this chapter. We must take care to let the music dance.[91]

FIXED ORNAMENTS[92]

Long appoggiaturas

By far the most common fixed ornaments in Haydn's choral music are trills, turns (the so-called Haydn-ornament, ∿) and single appoggiaturas. These (and all fixed ornaments generally) have the common function of introducing and resolving a dissonance. That function is most easily seen in the *single appoggiatura*, a small, uncancelled sixteenth, eighth, or quarter note (the dissonance) placed immediately to the left of the principal note (consonance), to which it usually resolves downward. It must be performed on the beat and slurred into the principal note. Dynamic enhancement of this phrasing (i.e., $f \rightarrow p$) is also a part of proper style. Most of these appoggiaturas are "long," that is, they take half the value of the principal note. If the principal note is dotted, the appoggiatura

---

[91] A specific study of metric accentuation in Haydn's choral music is Trott "Accentuation," a portion of which appeared in *The Choral Journal* as Trott "Emphasis." See also Shrock "Aspects," which provides an admirable summary of the treatises regarding metric accentuation.

[92] In the following discussion of fixed ornaments, we have relied in the main on two eighteenth-century treatises, those of Leopold Mozart (see above) and Carl Philipp Emanuel Bach. These two works are closest to Haydn chronologically and also in terms of reflecting or influencing his usages. "Of the making of books there is no end," and the same was certainly true of the music tutors, who in an era of changing tastes could disagree on innumerable fine points of performance. Mozart and Bach serve our purposes here quite well without introducing more confusion and argument than we have space to address. References to other treatises and to modern commentaries are noted as they occur.

takes the value of the principal note less the dot, whose value is assigned to the principal note.[93] Here are some examples from Haydn:

Simple. Example 10.6: Haydn *Mariazellermesse*, Gloria, mm. 50-55 (See also Ex. 10.x.)

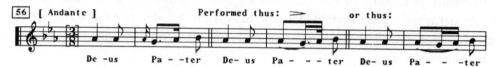

Dotted. Example 10.7: Haydn *Grosse Orgelmesse*, "Gratias," mm. 56-57

Dotted. Example 10.8: Haydn *Cäcilienmesse*, Gloria, mm. 176-77

In Ex. 10.8, the first interpretation suggested is preferable, because it preserves the dotted feeling through an inexact division of time-values.[94]

Single-note appoggiaturas are often added to certain figures, mimicking a turn (⌁ or ∾) or a trill figure (the *Nachschlag* need not be written out):

Example 10.9: Haydn *Grosse Orgelmesse*, Credo, m. 1, 7

The rhythmic difference introduced in measure 7 is another instance of the subtle changes in phrasing that add freshness and charm throughout a movement.

---

[93] In the case of appoggiature to a half-note, the small note takes three-quarters of the time, according to Mozart. This is a rare ornament in Haydn, but see Ex. 10.22.

[94] As in Mozart's *Violinschule* Ch. 9 § 4 (168-169). Landon cited one place in Haydn's choral music where this interpretation is particularly necessary: the *Heiligmesse* Benedictus, m. 32, in which *a)* first- and second-violin appoggiature must congrue rhythmically and *b)* consistent ♪ ♪ patterns undergird the entire movement. *Symphonies*, 141.

Another version of the long appoggiatura is found in vocal recitatives; Haydn discusses it in his *Applausus* letter (see the Appendix). This practice can also be used to good effect in arias,[95] but it does not apply to similar figures in instrumental parts.

Short appoggiaturas

"Now there be also," wrote Mozart, "short appoggiature with which the stress falls not on the appoggiatura but on the principal note. The short appoggiatura is made as rapidly as possible and is not attacked strongly, but quite softly."[96] Far fewer short appoggiaturas than long occur in Haydn's choral music, but the rules for recognizing them seem far more numerous and conflicting—a sign that this ornament was becoming increasingly important. The short appoggiatura was usually notated as a sixteenth- or thirty-second note. Here are some of the ways it could be used (remember, this is the short list!):

i) Before (groups of) quick notes
ii Before long notes, either unrepeated or (more often) repeated
iii Whenever "a melody ascends a second and then returns" (Bach)
iv) Before triplets, to keep the rhythm clear
v) As a substitute for a cadential trill
vi) To avoid obscuring imitative passages in polyphony
vii) To avoid offensive harmonies (i.e., voice-leading)
viii) When "the resolving tone of a melody must be quitted abruptly" (Bach)
ix) "In an allegro or other playful tempo, [between] notes [that] descend in consecutive degrees or even in thirds" (Mozart)

To these rules from Bach and Mozart may be appended three more that represent later eighteenth-century practices.[97] Many examples in Haydn indicate that he observed these rules by using short appoggiaturas in the following situations:

x) Before figures of four notes (e.g., four sixteenths), *and*
xi) When appoggiaturas resolve by leap, *but*
xii) *Not* before a note which is followed by two of shorter duration (See Ex. 10.33a; such appoggiaturas are played "long")

We can see already that distinguishing between long and short appoggiaturas will sometimes be difficult. Distinguishing further, between onbeat short appoggiaturas and anticipatory short appoggiaturas, will in performance often be nearly impossible. Although all the short-appoggiatura types listed above were considered onbeat ornaments, conduc-

---

[95] See the discussion of the *Grosse Orgelmesse* "Et incarnatus est" below in *Free Ornaments.*

[96] *Violinschule* (3), Ch. 9 § 9, 171.

[97] These are taken from Johann Friedrich Schubert's *Neue Singe-Schule* (ca. 1805), 52, 54; cited in Landon *Symphonies,* 147-149.

tors will find that many are heard as coming before the beat (and therefore may as well be played that way). Robbins Landon[98] offered performers three manageable categories in which anticipatory appoggiaturas may be made:

xiii) Before triplets (i.e., rule *iv* made practical)
xiv) Before groups [or multiples] of four (rule *x* made practical)
xv) Before passages which would be distorted rhythmically or harmonically

Here is a sampling of certifiable short appoggiaturas from Haydn's choral works, plus a special case or two. The appoggiaturas are shown below as cancelled notes whenever that rendering has been given them by twentieth-century editors.

Ex. 10.10: Haydn *Paukenmesse*, Sanctus, m. 1 (Rule *iii* applies.)

Ex. 10.11: Haydn *Paukenmesse*, Benedictus, mm. 56-57 (rule *viii*)

Ex. 10.12: Haydn Salve Regina in G minor, III, mm. 38-41 (rule *xi*)

Ex. 10.13: Haydn *The Seasons*, 2, mm. 1-4 (rule *xiii*, then rule *iii*)

Ex. 10.14: Haydn *Grosse Orgelmesse*, Gloria, mm. 4-5 soprano)

---

[98] *Symphonies*, 149-152.

Does rule *ix* apply here? No, because neither the tempo, texture (sustained choral chords and murmuring violins), nor text ("Et in terra pax") are "playful." Performance with long appoggiaturas is correct. See also the recommended execution of Ex. 10.50, in which the short appoggiatura is substituted for a notated trill.

We may consider the multiple-note *appoggiatura* (*Schleifer*, stepwise, and *Arpeggio*, skipwise; see Table 10.4) a cousin of the single-note short appoggiatura. The actual speed of its execution will vary according to tempo and affect, but it is most important that it be performed on the beat. Example 10.46 (end of chapter) shows a Haydn *Schleifer* in context. Note the motivic relationship between measures 14-17 and the actual *Schleifer* of measure 26; an anticipatory execution of the appoggiatura would weaken that.

And here are two *Arpeggii*:

Ex. 10.15: *Grosse Orgelmesse*, Benedictus, mm. 10-11

Ex. 10.16: *Mariazellermesse*, Gloria, mm. 1-2

One function of the *Arpeggio* is to enrich—in a unique *settecento* manner—the accent and sonority of the chord it decorates. For that reason, the ornament should never anticipate the beat, nor should it necessarily be hurried.[99]

Trills

It is possible that during Haydn's lifetime the nineteenth century's garden-variety trill (i.e., that which begins on the principal note) had begun to make inroads with performers. But the treatises of the age seldom mention it. They almost invariably instruct players to

---

[99] Cf. Harnoncourt *Dialog* (2), 161-162.

begin a trill *1) on the beat* and *2) with the upper auxiliary*, i.e., the dissonance.[100] Where Haydn is concerned, this approach proves very effective in the great majority of cases.

A trill may be taken at various speeds, according to the spirit and tempo of the music and the acoustic of the room.[101] The first note (i.e., dissonance) of the trill may be slightly accented or prolonged, depending on the affect and tempo.[102] And it may end in several ways: *i)* "One closes it thus most frequently and naturally," according to Leopold, as in Example 10.17; or *ii)* with an afterbeat (*Nachschlag*) (Ex. 10.18). Mozart's example (*a*) features a slight pause before the afterbeat is made. Bach (*b*) preferred no pause, and often this latter execution is implied in Haydn's music; or *iii)* with a more elaborate embellishment (Ex. 10.19).

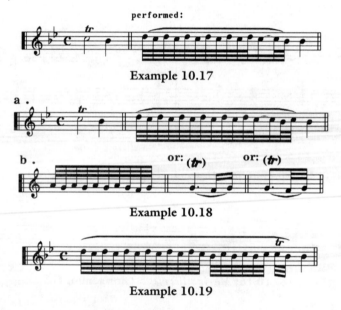

Example 10.17

Example 10.18

Example 10.19

If possible, short trills (those lasting one beat or less) should be played with an afterbeat; otherwise they lack both fire and grace. There is also evidence that the afterbeat gradually became a convention with all trills in the second half of the eighteenth century.[103]

Haydn often wrote out the afterbeat (or some other ending) to the trill. In those cases it would be superfluous to add another. In Example 10.20, the execution of the trills should be identical.

---

[100] Cf. Mozart *Violinschule* (3), 186-188; Bach *Versuch* (3), 99-101; Türk *Klavierschule* (2), 245-246.

[101] A cadential trill may also *change* speeds (i.e., accelerate or decelerate).

[102] Cf. Leopold Mozart's "quick appoggiatura," *Violinschule* (3), Ch. 10 § 6 (188).

[103] Donington *Interpretation*, 257-259. Robbins Landon, citing Bach, also prescribed the afterbeat ("suffix") for all trills except "when there is no time for it" or "when some kind of substitute . . . appears." Cf. Bach *Versuch* (3), 100ff.; *Symphonies*, 153-154.

Example 10.20: Haydn *Nicolaimesse*, Kyrie, mm. 7-8

Ex. 10.21: Haydn *Cäcilienmesse*, Kyrie, mm. 70-71

When the trill is combined with a (long) appoggiatura, the first note can be considerably lengthened, although this rule needs flexible interpretation; see Examples 10.22 and 10.23. In both these examples (and there are many similar ones!) the performer must stop short of giving full value to the appoggiatura, in order not to emphasize the parallel fifths with the immediately lower voice.[104]

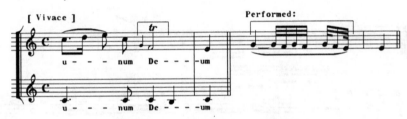

Ex. 10.22: Haydn *Cäcilienmesse*, Credo, m. 2

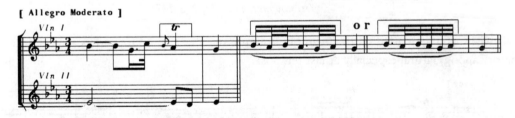

Ex. 10.23: Haydn *Grosse Orgelmesse*, Kyrie, m. 3

Some trills, because of their shortness and the speed with which they must be played, may need practical solutions that are implied but not always given outright in the treatises. These stopgap or hybrid measures are especially convenient when one is dealing with modern instruments and limited rehearsal time. Following are suggestions for coping with such spots in Haydn.

---

[104] It must be emphasized, however, that Baroque musicians probably felt no such qualms; to them the "progression" was acceptable. Cf. Donington *Interpretation*, 637-638, which cites Telemann and Michel de Saint-Lambert on the matter.

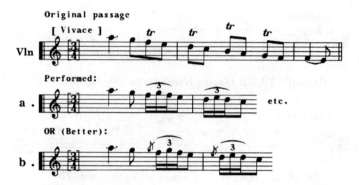

Ex. 10.24a, b: Haydn *Paukenmesse*, Gloria, mm. 33-36

A succession of quick trills in a descending passage can easily turn to mud. In Example 10.24 one could substitute (a) half trills or (b) half-trills with short appoggiaturas.[105] It is important that clarity be preserved, so that listeners can more easily sense the relationship of this passage to later variations on it:

Ex. 10.24c, d: Haydn *Paukenmesse*, Gloria, mm. 38-40, 284-287
(see also mm. 111-113, 235-237)

Likewise a trill appended to an already-busy figure may have to be treated as a short antici-patory appoggiatura, especially at fast tempos:

Ex. 10.25: Haydn *Cäcilienmesse*, Credo, mm. 50-51

---

[105] Substitute (a) is the *Pralltriller* or *Schneller*, sometimes also called a "Spanish" trill. See Bach *Versuch* (3), 110-112; also Mozart *Violinschule* (3), Ch. 10 § 16-17 (193).

Another solution would be to substitute a turn for the trill:[106]

Ex. 10.26: Haydn *Cäcilienmesse*, Kyrie, mm. 18-19

In all such cases, performers must make it their first priority to enhance the poise and élan of the music.

Another special case is the choral trill. These are usually indicated only for the upper voices; they can make a fine effect when executed by a small, well-trained section. But since the conductor is often likely to encounter a larger section and/or one containing many singers who cannot trill, substitute ornaments may need to be devised. Example 10.27a shows a cadential choral trill from the Kyrie of the F-Major *Missa brevis*. To properly close this vibrant *allegro* movement, the substitute ornament should have some rhythmic snap, as in Examples 10.27b and c. Example 10.27d shows choral trills in a contrasting setting, the more gentle *allegro moderato* of the *Grosse Orgelmesse* Kyrie. Here the suggested substitutes (Ex. 10.27e, f) can be similarly graceful.

Example 10.27a-c: Haydn *Missa brevis* in F, Kyrie, mm. 20-21;
Example 10.27d-f: *Grosse Orgelmesse*, Kyrie, mm. 15-19

---

[106] As Türk recommended for keyboard players in similar passages; *Klavierschule* (2), Ch 4 § 75 [273-274].

Turns (Doppelschlagen)

Emanuel Bach said it best: "This lovely ornament is almost too obliging. It fits almost everywhere and consequently is often abused. . . . Hence its correct use must be carefully investigated."[107] The turn can be especially confusing in Haydn's music because of the varied ways in which it is notated. We are grateful to Dr. László Somfai for having compiled a table of Haydn's common onbeat ornaments (given here as Table 10.4) along with a further table devoted solely to the different species of *Doppelschlag* (Table 10.5).[108] These two tables furnish a sense of the relationships among various ornaments and can also serve as a reference point for our discussion of a few examples.

	with small notes	with diacritic mark	suggested execution	
Haydn - ornament, *Doppelschlag*				
mordent				
Pralltriller	—			not a three-note *Schneller*( )!
trill	—		etc.	
			etc.	
			etc.	
		—	or:? etc. etc.	
geschnellter *Doppelschlag*		—	or:	
Schneller [very rare!]		—		
prallender *Doppelschlag*	—			
Schleifer		—		slower, singing performance
Anschlag		—	(p f)	onbeat beginning but accented main note
Arpeggio		—		

Table 10.4: Haydn's most common *onbeat position* ornaments

---

[107] Bach *Versuch* (3), 114.

[108] Somfai "Notation," 29-30.

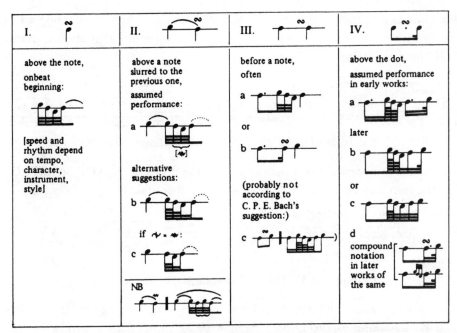

Table 10.5: Haydn-ornament or *Doppelschlag*—Four typical positions

The following must be borne in mind: *i)* Like appoggiaturas and trills, turns serve to introduce a dissonance; their execution likewise implies a slur into the principal note (consonance). *ii)* Both "vertical" and "horizontal" non-uniformity of notation are common. But unlike the situation with non-uniform articulations, most variant notations of turns imply an identical execution (cf. Ex. 10.28, 10.29):

Example 10.28: Haydn *Paukenmesse*, Gloria, mm. 148-151

Example 10.29: Haydn *Grosse Orgelmesse*, Kyrie, m. 3

iii) One must take special care to play or sing all Category I turns, including written-out turns, as onbeat ornaments. Otherwise an implied relationship with another motive (see Ex. 10.30) may be obscured.

Ex. 10.30: Haydn *Paukenmesse*, Gloria, mm. 202-203

iv) If the turn-sign occurs above a note slurred to the previous one (Dr. Somfai's Category II), then the turn may be said to have begun on that first note:

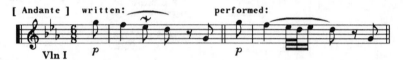

Example 10.31: Haydn *Paukenmesse*, Benedictus, m. 7

v) Haydn usually wrote out the turn-between-two-notes (Category III) so that there would be no mistaking its execution. Example 10.32 shows such a turn, followed by yet another turn type (IV). This delicate line is from the introduction to the recitative "Welcome now, ye shady groves" in *The Seasons*. It is variously doubled or scored in Italian thirds for flute, two bassoons, and the violins, so ensemble precision is critical.

Example 10.32: Haydn *The Seasons*, 16, mm. 1-2

vi) Here is the Category IV turn again, this time notated in its "early" form:

Example 10.33: Haydn *Nelsonmesse*, Credo, m. 104

vii) Single appoggiaturas can also appear together with the turn; the resulting ornament is similar to the appoggiatura-trill combination (and can be considered a subclass of Dr. Somfai's Category II):

Example 10.34: Haydn *Kleine Orgelmesse*, Kyrie, mm. 1-2

The organ solo in the Benedictus of the *Kleine Orgelmesse* provides a gold mine of turns and trills, well worth study simply for its complex of ornamentation.

FREE ORNAMENTS

Free embellishment is the addition, in performance, of ornaments not specified by the composer. But eighteenth-century free embellishment typically went beyond the use of conventional ornamentation (e.g., trills, appoggiaturas) to include a considerable amount of melodic improvisation. Thus the contour, if not the character, of a passage or a piece might be altered almost beyond recognition. In the hands of a master performer the results were welcomed, as contemporary accounts bear out. With less talented musicians, free embellishment was more likely to be considered an abuse.

Because Haydn's choral music covers a broad range of styles and a wide swath of time, the degree of free embellishment proper to each work will vary greatly. Only one absolute should be observed: free embellishment is the prerogative of the soloist, not the ensemble member.[109] Otherwise, one can gain a notion of the extent to which free embellishment should be be applied by considering the balance of style, chronology, genre, and other factors. Since free embellishment developed and flourished in Italian Baroque opera, we can expect that Haydn's choral music most influenced by it will contain the most opportunities for such embellishment (see Table 10.6).

---

[109] See Spitzer/Zaslaw "Ornamentation," esp. 525-529, and also Zaslaw "Compleat" for summaries of the prevailing attitudes of the authorites. The players and singers themselves, as both articles make clear, were apt to transgress frequently in this regard; thus free embellishment in choirs and orchestras was both "authentic" and frowned upon.

Example 10.35: Haydn *Ave Regina*, III, mm. 205ff

Just as in recitative, soloists also had to watch out for places where appoggiaturas were needed. Example 10.47 (end of chapter) demonstrates a number of such instances. After the florid buildup of measure 8, the simple cadence formula of measure 9 seems inappropriate. The soloist probably added to it, just as he would have added to measure 15—without destroying its chromatic affect, we hope. In measures 11 and 12, appoggiaturas can be added to increase the expressivity and variety of the phrases, which are quite recitative-like. The tenor solo in the *Cäcilienmesse* on this text reveals similar places where such embellishment is helpful.

By the time of *The Creation* and *The Seasons*, Haydn's wishes regarding free embellishment had changed. He praised Mademoiselle Fischer, the Gabriel of the first *Creation* performances, for having "sung her part with the utmost grace and so truly that she allowed herself not the least unsuitable addition."[111] Haydn's early biographer Carpani, who witnessed the first performances of these works, wrote regarding *The Creation*: "This music needs to be executed with simplicity, exactness, expression, and deportment, but without ornaments."[112] Carpani's remarks should not, of course, be interpreted in a literal or absolute way; considering historical context, the true meaning of *without ornaments* is probably closer to *without unsuitable additions* (cf. Haydn's praise for Mlle. Fischer). Small-scale ornaments and/or ornaments specified by the composer would have been permitted and expected; in fact, the surviving materials from Haydn's own performances show that mod-

---

[111] Dies *Nachrichten* (3), 180.

[112] *Haydine*, 182.

est embellishments were added. By examining them, we can arrive at general rules for free embellishment in Haydn's late works as a whole.[113]

One general rule for the late works is that Haydn more often wrote in the embellishments desired. In so doing, he established careful balances that should not be upset by the addition of more ornaments. For example, in the bass aria No. 6 of *The Creation*, the second strophe of "Leise rauschend gleitet fort" is melodically embellished and also receives a brief cadenza at the fermata in measure 111 (see Ex. 10.36, below). If the first strophe were to be ornamented by the performer, the impact of Haydn's delicate alterations would be stolen. And the folk-like quality of this number (like many in *The Creation*) can bear little embellishment beyond what the composer eventually gives it, so further ornaments in the second strophe would also have negative results.

Ex. 10.36: Haydn *The Creation*, 6, mm. 73-79, 94-99, 106-113

When we turn to the soprano arias, we find more embellishment in the old *seria* vein, especially in the two arias, Nos. 8 and 15, cast in *seria* types. Brown noted that these added ornaments, etc., essentially have three musical functions: they provide *1)* small-dimension activity—turns, trills, etc., *2)* greater weight for the main cadences—i.e., cadenzas; and *3)* localized definition to the brief tonal meanderings of the central episodic section.[114] Example 10.37, below, shows the difference in weight given to two successive cadenzas in No. 32 (cadenzas taken from the so-called Tonkünstler Parts[115]). Conductors planning a performance of the work will want to consult the many other evidences of authentic vocal embellishment presented in Brown's study as well.

---

[113] As one of its most valuable features, Brown *Performing* includes copious musical examples of the added embellishments from these Vienna parts. The examples used in this discussion are gratefully drawn from that much more exhaustive treatment.

[114] Brown *Performing*, 50.

[115] Regarding the Tonkünstler and Estate parts and scores, see Chapter 9.

Example 10.37: Haydn *The Creation*, 30, mm. 113-220

TEMPO AND RHYTHM

Tempo

Little direct evidence can be found of Haydn's own tempos in performance. Although he died a few years before Mälzel's metronome became generally available, two of his associates, Antonio Salieri and Sigismund Neukomm, eventually went on record with "authentic" metronome markings for *The Creation*. Their claims were the subject of a study by Nicholas Temperley;[116] it reveals a couple of general truths about past and present Haydn performance that can be summarized here as an introduction to our topic.

If the metronome markings of Neukomm are accepted as closest to Haydn's own tempos, then a three-stage approach to Haydn tempos can be traced since the early nineteenth century: in the first, or Romantic, stage, tempos adopted were considerably slower than Haydn's; in the second stage—mid-twentieth-century "traditional" performances—slow tempos still tended to be slower than Haydn's, although less slow than the Romantics', but moderate and fast tempos were slightly faster than Haydn's; in the third stage, consisting of conductors influenced by the early-music movement, nearly all tempos were somewhat faster than Haydn's, with moderate and fast tempos being much faster. Table 9.2 includes Neukomm's metronome markings.

In the end, such studies as Temperley's may tell us more about the history of Haydn performance than they do about Haydn in his time. Since our present task is to discover principles of execution that can be judiciously applied to a broad range of Haydn's choral music, we will make more headway by first exploring the basic elements of eighteenth-century doctrine regarding tempo.

(i. General Guidelines) Tempo in Haydn's choral music can usually be determined by its affect (cf. *content* in the quotation below), by tempo indications and meter signatures,

---

[116] Temperley "Tempo."

and especially by the rhythms and note values of the individual movement. Bach's summary remarks on tempo can serve as a guide:

> The pace of a composition, which is usually indicated by several well-known Italian expressions, is based on its general content as well as on the fastest notes and passages contained in it. Due consideration of these factors will prevent an allegro from being rushed and an adagio from being dragged.[117]

One may also infer from Bach's words that tempo can be determined from the character of the articulations in the music, whether they be marked or merely implied:

> In general the briskness of allegros is expressed by detached notes and the tenderness of adagios by broad, slurred notes. The performer must keep in mind that these characteristic features of allegros and adagios are to be given consideration even when a composition is not so marked, as well as when the performer has not yet gained an adequate understanding of the affect of a work.[118]

(*ii. Tempo Classes*) Other treatises divide Bach's *allegro* and *adagio* into further categories. For Quantz, pieces in common time can be placed in one of four classes:

> (1) The *Allegro assai*, (2) the *Allegretto*, (3) the *Adagio cantabile*, (4) the *Adagio assai*. In the first class I include: the Allegro di molti, the Presto, &c. In the second: the Allegro ma non tanto, non troppo, non presto, moderato, &c. In the third class I count: the Cantabile, Arioso, Larghetto, Soave, Dolce, Poco Andante, Affetuoso, Pomposo, Maestoso, Alla Siciliana, Adagio spiritoso, &c. To the fourth belong: the Adagio pesante, Lento, Largo assai, Mesto, Grave, &c. Each of these titles, to be sure, has an individual meaning of its own, but *it refers more to the expression of the dominant passions in each piece than to the tempo proper* [italics added].[119]

Like Bach, Quantz notes the importance of "the fastest notes and passages" in fixing proper tempo:

> In the Allegro assai the passagework consists of sixteenth-notes or eighth-note triplets, and in the Allegretto, of thirty-second-notes or sixteenth-note triplets. Since, however, the passagework just cited must usually be played at the same speed whether it is in sixteenths or thirty-seconds, it follows that notes of the same value in the one are twice as fast as in the other. In alla breve [i.e., ¢] time . . . the situation is the same, except that all the notes in it are taken twice as fast as in common time. Fast passagework in the Allegro assai is therefore written in eighths in this meter, and played like the passagework in sixteenths in the Allegro assai in

---

[117] Bach *Versuch* (3), 151.

[118] Bach *Versuch* (3), 149.

[119] Quantz *Versuch* (2), Ch. XVII, VII, §49, 284.

common time. . . . [He goes on to apply this principal to triple meters:] For example, if in three-four time only eighths occur . . . the piece is in the fastest tempo.[120]

Adjustment of tempos to the prevailing passagework is an obvious, common-sense measure. Nothing can more quickly muddy the expressive intent of a Baroque or Classic work than failure to observe this principle.

Note also, in the Quantz passage above, the passing allusion to *alla breve*. It is simply to be interpreted as indicating a tempo twice as fast, or—more to the musical point—a pulse on the note half the value of the note that would otherwise bear it. Thus an *allegretto* commonly taken at ♩ = MM 80 in common time would be taken at ♪ = MM 80 in *alla breve* (or in 2/4; see below). An *adagio* ¢ will have a quarter-note pulse, never an eighth-note pulse.

(iii. Absolute Measures and Their Limitations) Quantz also set absolute measures for his tempo classes, using as his guide "the pulse beat at the hand of a healthy person" (in pre-aerobic Europe, that was evidently about eighty beats per minute).

> Since no more than eight very fast notes [!] can be executed in the time of a pulse beat . . . it follows that there is
> In common time:
> In an Allegro assai, the time of a pulse beat for each half note. [♩ = MM 160]
> In an Allegretto, a pulse beat for each quarter note. [♩ = MM 80]
> In an Adagio cantabile, a pulse beat for each eighth note. [♩ = MM 40]
> And in an Adagio assai, two pulse beats for each quaver. [♪ = MM 40]
> [In alla breve time, these speeds are doubled.]
> [Also] there is, particularly in common time, a kind of moderate Allegro, which is approximately the mean between the Allegro assai and the Allegretto [i.e., ♩ = MM 120]. It occurs frequently in vocal pieces . . . [and] is usually indicated with the words Poco Allegro, Vivace [!] or, most of all, simply with Allegro alone.[121]

Quantz's absolute tempo measures should be interpreted with caution; they cannot be considered to represent Haydn's views on tempo nor even taken to reflect all mid-18th-century music. Bach, Quantz's fellow musician at the court of Frederick the Great, allowed that in Berlin, "adagio is far slower and allegro far faster than is customary elsewhere."[122] We shall find evidence that insofar as Haydn was concerned, a kind of moderating Austrian *Gemütlichkeit* worked to bring his music—especially his choral music—into more comfortable ranges of speed.

---

[120] Quantz *Versuch* (2), Ch. XVII, VII, §50, 284-285.

[121] Quantz *Versuch* (2), Ch. XVII, VII, §51, 285-286.

[122] Bach *Versuch* (3), 414.

(iv. Haydn's Allegros) Yet Haydn's choral music contains more *allegro* indications than any other kind, plus nearly as many again of *allegro molto, allegro con spirito, vivace, or presto.* Haydn liked brisk tempos.[123] In spite of the restraining influence of both vocal and sacred genres on speed in the Classical era,[124] we find that in Haydn's Masses the Gloria (esp. opening and concluding sections) and more jubilant parts of the Credo ("Et resurrexit," "Et vitam venturi") are often to be taken *allegro molto, con spirito,* or *vivace;* the "Dona nobis pacem," that merry (and thus much maligned) finale to the symphonic Mass, is usually also marked like the above, or even with *presto.*

Two of the best places to find Quantz's "moderate Allegro" in Haydn's choral music are at the beginning of his Kyries and Credos. That is as much a matter of overall pacing as of the inherent (text-related) affect. The Kyrie and Gloria were performed back-to-back in the service, usually as its first concerted music. Likewise the Credo's position in the liturgy isolates it musically from the rest of the Mass Ordinary. The composer naturally wished to begin with a flourish but to reserve the most spirited music for the conclusions of these musical units. (See, for examples, the tempo sequences listed elsewhere for Reutter's *Missa Sancti Caroli* [Table 1.1] or for Haydn's *Paukenmesse* [Table 8.1].) The conductor considering tempo in a Haydn sacred work should first make an overview of the tempo markings, keeping in mind the influence of the texts plus any liturgical functions that would have occasioned long intervals between movements.

The rhythmic style of a Kyrie and other lively movements in common time or in 3/4 is fairly consistent throughout Haydn. Voices and winds move in quarters and eighths, with occasional half notes; violins are often assigned passagework in sixteenths or even thirty-seconds. The quickest *allegri* will show fewer of these smallest notes. Instead, most of their ornamental notes will be eighths, as in the "Et resurrexit" of the *Paukenmesse.* The conductor must be alert to other style factors too: a 3/4 allegro with "drum bass" will be faster, an *allegro* in minuet style (e.g., the "Et resurrexit" of the *Heiligmesse*) more deliberate.

Two of the more problematic areas here center around *1)* the tempo implication of 3/8 meter and *2)* the meaning of *vivace;* the first area is trickier. An *allegro* in 6/8 means two beats to the bar; a 3/8 *allegro* cannot be so easily categorized. We are told that in the Baroque era, triple time-signatures generally connoted faster speeds.[125] Leopold Mozart implied that the 3/8 *allegro* might as well be considered an inferior variant of 12/8 (i.e., a compound meter conducted in four), and later evidence points to its speed as well.[126] But

---

[123] Brown cited Haydn's practice of increasing the speed whenever he saw fit to change a movement's tempo indication. This practice held true for all genres, but especially for the many Italian operas he prepared in the 1780s. Brown *Performance*, 71, based on Bartha/Somfai *Opernkapellmeister.*

[124] Cf. Quantz *Versuch* (2), Ch. XVII, VII, §52-53, 287.

[125] See Donington *Interpretation*, 414-417.

[126] Mozart *Violinschule* (3), Ch. I/ii, §4, 31-32: "For in 12/8 time-measure, a quicker melody is more suitable than one in 3/8 time as, in a rapid tempo, the latter cannot be beaten without moving the spectators to laughter."

Haydn uses 3/8 sparingly and nearly as often for *andante* as for *allegro*. It is clear from examining any one of these movements that, for him, 3/8 is a meter of convenience for music that may cross traditional genre lines. The complexities of the 3/8 *aria particolare* in Haydn's mature style are well illustrated by the "Gratias" from the *Mariazellermesse* of 1782 (Ex. 10.48, end of chapter).

The tune itself would be a perfect *siciliano* (i.e., 12/8 taken four-to-a-bar), were it not for an asymmetrical phrase structure that grows more irregular as the movement progresses (mm. 74-109 go approx. 4 + 3 + 4 + 2 + 4 + 5 + 4 + 6 + 4!). The walking bass also undercuts any pastoral or *siciliano* feeling, while not quite giving us a minuet (i.e., three-to-the-bar) in return. And then there are outbursts of *Sturm und Drang* (mm. 99, 109-111, etc.) on the way to the choral "Qui tollis," also full of lightning and shadows, that ends the movement. Can one tempo unite these stylistic meanderings?

It can, but the performers should use different metric sensibilities within it in order to highlight the abrupt changes of affect. At the outset, a one-to-the-bar lilt will help the soprano and violins/winds establish *cantabile;* this pulse should shift to a three-feeling whenever the instrumentalists join the bass in three unslurred eighths, or six sixteenths, to a bar (i.e., mm. 85-86, 90, 94-95, 98-99). Yet another level of metric sensibility, a very heavy emphasis on the eighth-note pulse, will predominate whenever a loud dynamic coincides with the three-feeling. The *allegro* marking, then, is mostly a warning not to set a sleepy pace for this music—its opening bars are deceptively serene. Within the *allegro*, the changing affect should be underscored by shifts more of pulse than of tempo.

Vivace is one term that seems to have undergone a sea change during the lifetime that Haydn used it. In his late Masses, we see it in places obviously meant to be faster-paced as well as more lively, for example the "Et vitam venturi" fugues of the *Heiligmesse* and *Paukenmesse*. But in earlier works this intent is not so obvious. There Quantz's notion of *vivace* (see above) can well be applied. An example is the Credo of the *Cäcilienmesse* (Ex. 10.49, end of chapter), in which the variegated ornamental figures, including many thirty-second-note runs, make performances at more than $\lrcorner$ = MM 100 a dubious venture. This *vivace* can and should be lively but not especially fast.

(v. Haydn's Adagios) One can generalize that in earlier pieces, *allegros* will be less quick and *adagios* less slow. To put it the other way around, we find few extremely fast or slow tempos until we get to the late Masses and oratorios. Even then, *presto* and *largo* will not be what they were to Berlioz or Brahms.

An examination of *adagio* and *largo* in Haydn's choral music bears this out. *Adagio* is by far the most common slow-tempo indication in the Haydn Masses; it is used with **C**, 3/4, even **¢**, and must be considered more basic to Haydn's sacred choral style than *andante, moderato,* or *allegretto*.[127] There are relatively fast *adagios*, such as the Agnus Dei of

---

Robbins Landon (*Symphonies,* 130) also cited an anonymous pamphlet (Leipzig, 1792): "The tempo of an Allegro in 3/8 time is quicker than an Allegro in 2/4."

[127] These tempos are used more often, and with greater specificity, in the two late oratorios.

the *Grosse Orgelmesse* (Ex. 10.50, e.o.c.), which should move rather more quickly than Quantz's *Adagio cantabile*, perhaps even to ♩ = MM 50 or so. Then there are "slower" *adagios* (cf. Ex. 10.51, e.o.c.), which would nevertheless feel very draggy at Quantz's ♪ = MM 40. Note that our "fast" example was in 3/4 meter from an early work, the "slower" example in C from a late work. The reader shouldn't infer too much from that. *Adagio* is not a ponderous tempo anywhere in Haydn's choral music. Most of his *adagios* in common or 3/4 time can be felt, and conducted, with a quarter-note pulse. In fact pulse, not speed, should again be the governing factor in interpretation of these movements. The slower *adagio* may actually need to move at about the same speed as a fast one, but the conductor may find that intrinsic musical factors (cf. Ex. 10.51, m. 3) make it preferable to indicate an eighth-note pulse or to subdivide at times.

The first, best thing to do with any *adagio* is to try the quarter-note pulse. Even a florid movement like the *Cäcilienmesse* Sanctus benefits from this approach (Ex. 10.52, e.o.c.). Incidentally, the transition from *adagio* to *allegro* in Example 10.52 works very well with a proportional interpretation, that is, if the ♪ of the "Sanctus" becomes the ♩ of the "Pleni." This is another sign that Quantz's absolute tempo measures (cf. ♪ = MM 80 in *adagio*, ♩ = MM 120 in *allegro*) touched on extremes seldom met with in contemporary Austrian practice.

Is *largo* appreciably slower than *adagio*? (This seems to be the dominant issue for slow tempos in Haydn.) Quantz and the other tutors, up through that anonymous Leipzig pamphleteer of 1792, thought so. But it is difficult to reconcile their rigid schemes with the *largos* we find in Haydn's choral music. More often the difference between *adagio* and *largo* is a matter of weight, not tempo. In the Masses, we often find *largo* used to indicate the affect of the "Et incarnatus est," an emotion-laden section of the Credo tracing Christ's life on earth from birth to crucifixion, death, and burial. Yet, based on their musical content alone, these sections so marked can seldom justify tempos slower than a generic *adagio*. If anything, some should move faster, like Haydn's 1768 setting of the "Et incarnatus est" (Ex. 4.15c).

A quarter-note pulse is strongly dictated by the string accompaniment; the soloist's short phrases and mixture of florid (ornamented) and plain (unornamented) lines also speak in favor of forward motion. Not least of the arguments for a *poco adagio* is the choral "Crucifixus" into which the movement flows without break (m. 18). It is a lengthy fugal passage in quarters and eighths that would be unbearable if taken at a pace much slower than ♩ = MM 60. Yet Haydn indicated no tempo change here, implying that the pace of the first part was not far removed from that of this concluding chorus.

The internal evidence on *largo* is more variable in the late works but generally supports the notion of slower tempos. The *Nelsonmesse* of 1798 contains a 3/4 "Et incarnatus est" of great emotional weight; readers can gain a good idea of the expressive difference between *largo* and *adagio* by comparing this movement with the same Mass's 3/4 "Qui tollis." The *adagio* "Qui tollis" moves to a steady eighth-note accompaniment: a drum bass is reinforced by the upper string voices and by chanted choral responses to the soloists. The dynamic scheme consists mainly of simple, consistent alternations of *piano* and *forte*. Everything moves forward. By contrast, the *largo* "Et incarnatus est" is shot through with varied rhythms, gestures, and interruptions; these are matched by a complex of dynamics that match every nuance. A slower execution, subdivided at times if not actually taken in six, may be helpful in shaping and imparting the tremendous depth of feeling that Haydn has encoded here.

Two final examples from *The Seasons* show the variety of expression that *largo* could encompass, even in very late Haydn. The trio and chorus No. 12, "The sun ascends," (Ex. 10.53, e.o.c.) is an obvious sequel to *The Creation's* "and there was light." The approach to the choral entrance and "sunburst" of measure 7 is much more exciting if we can feel a moderate eighth-note pulse from the beginning—each syllable comes weighted with suspense (note also the thirty-second-note figuration scattered throughout).[128] More surprising is the *largo* of No. 34, "Light and life in sadness languish" (Ex. 10.54, e.o.c.). It also reminds us of the importance of *alla breve* in Haydn's thinking. Confronted by this dreary text ("After sullen, heavy days follow long and dismal nights."), he must have decided to have a little fun. With sly humor he set the whole patch as a gavotte, albeit a gavotte in dirge time. Quarter-note gets the beat (the ¢ signature effectively warning us away from an eighth-note pulse).[129] Poor Jane must limp along to the end in a parody of a light, elegant court dance: the combination of *largo* and ¢ establishes just the right heaviness.

In the end it is better to infer that Haydn's markings became more specific, not simply more extreme, as time went on. In *The Seasons* we find only four indications of *adagio*, but four more of *poco adagio*, one of *adagio ma non troppo*, and five of *largo*. Even if we allow for the fact that this work's text and length differ from those of the Masses referred to above, this sampling implies that in the late works Haydn's tempo indications became more subtle (not necessarily the tempos themselves, which were always as varied as the affects they expressed).

(vi. Haydn's Moderatos) This brings us to a final issue related to Haydn's tempos, the implied *moderato*. We pointed out earlier that *andante, allegretto, moderato*, and other medium tempos seemed to take third place to the *allegros* and *adagios* in Haydn's choral music. But there are a number of moderate tempos in Haydn disguised as something else. These fall into two categories: *1)* the *adagio* or *allegro* which is really not; and *2)* the *allegretto* with misleading time-signature.

The *allegro*-which-is-not has been touched upon above (see Ex. 10.49 e.o.c). An *adagio*-which-is-not can be seen in the *Paukenmesse* Sanctus (Ex. 10.55, e.o.c.). It is really an *allegretto* in which the eighth-note gets the pulse (beat); this is established especially by the

---

[128] Similarly an eighth-note pulse is implied in No. 13, "Dem Druck erlieget die Natur"; here the doleful text and the chromaticism make a pulse choice even more obvious.

[129] As it likewise should in the first movement of *The Creation*. Cf. Brown *Performing*, 72-73.

afterbeats to the steady staccato eighths. The affect is similar to that of the famous second movement in Haydn's Symphony No. 101 (the "Clock"). Isn't that rather playful for a Sanctus? Indeed, but consider the *gigue* that Haydn fashioned for the Sanctus in the *Kleine Orgelmesse*.

Allegretto tempi with misleading time signatures are legion in Haydn, but they find particularly congenial nesting places in the Benedictus movements of his Masses. Consider Example 10.56 (e.o.c.), from the *Cäcilienmesse*. What are we to make of an *andante* in ¢? Not until measure 13 arrives, with its sixteenth-notes "a la Reutter," does a proper tempo suggest itself. As always, the best thing is to accommodate the ornamental note values. Thus the movement goes in a moderate four, not two. And *andante*? It is to be interpreted in the old manner, as a "walking" tempo well suited to this deliberate but flowing music.

Haydn wrote a number of later Benedictus movements in 2/4 with *allegretto* indicated. In these the affect and presence of ornamental thirty-second notes dictate a moderate-to-lively tempo with an eighth-note pulse, not the quarter-note pulse otherwise implied by the time signature (see Ex. 10.57, e.o.c.).

(*vii. Tempo Fluctuations in Haydn*) Basic tempos aside, one might well ask to what extent tempo fluctuations (e.g., *ritardando, stringendo,* etc.) are part of proper performing style in Haydn's choral music. The composer indicated no such fluctuations. We also know from contemporary accounts that conductors accustomed to changing tempo within a movement as part of their interpretive privilege were not yet present, had not yet been invented. The authors of the various performance treatises treated tempo fluctuation as a very special case. Here is what Türk had to say:

> Even when the composer has indicated the proper manner of expression as well as he can—in general and for specific parts—and the player has appropriately made use of all the means discussed . . . there still remain special cases for which the expression can be heightened by *extraordinary* means. Among these I include particularly the following: *1)* playing without keeping steady time; *2)* quickening and hesitating; *3)* the so-called tempo rubato. These three resources *when used sparingly and at the right time* can be of great effect [italics original].[130]

We must further bear in mind that Türk, like most of his colleagues, was writing primarily for the soloist. Before describing specific cases in which tempo fluctuation could be employed, he specially noted, "I assume . . . that the means which I am about to describe will only be used when one is playing alone or with a very attentive accompanist."

That would seem to leave no basis for tempo fluctuation in a typical eighteenth-century ensemble. But we may as well admit that since the advent of the interpretive conductor in the late nineteenth century, the entire orchestra and chorus have long since become one

---

[130] Türk *Klavierschule* (2), [6/5/§63] 359.

"very attentive accompanist." And when the music demands that the tempo vacillate, it may be self-defeating to avoid interpretive conducting as a means of obtaining that vacillation.

If we decide there is no good reason *not* to conduct interpretively, then the question becomes, When does the music demand it? Türk suggests three main instances for *accelerando: 1)* in "the most forceful passages" of compositions "whose character is vehemence, anger, rage, fury, and the like," *2)* for "certain thoughts which are repeated in a more intensified manner (generally higher)," and *3)* sometimes "when gentle feelings are interrupted by a lively passage." Contrariwise, "an increasing hesitation" can be employed *1)* "for extraordinarily tender, longing, or melancholy passages," *2)* "for tones before certain fermatas as if their powers were gradually being exhausted," and *3)* for "passages toward the end of a composition (or part of a composition) which are marked diminuendo, diluendo, smorzando, and the like." Also: "a tenderly moving passage between two lively and fiery thoughts . . . can be executed in a somewhat hesitating manner; but in this case, the tempo is not taken gradually slower, but *immediately* a little slower (however, only a *little*)."[italics original][131]

A practicable example of this last instance would be the setting of "mortuorum" in the *Paukenmesse* Credo (Ex. 10.58, e.o.c.). Besides being a "tenderly moving passage [etc.]," it is free of faster-moving accompanimental figures that would complicate its being executed by an ensemble as a moderate *ritenuto*.

Should the moments before the final cadence of a movement or a work be retarded? This is a time-honored practice confirmed by many eighteenth-century authorities, but it is best to keep C. P. E. Bach's admonition in mind: "In general, the retard is better suited to slow or comparatively moderate tempos than to very rapid ones."[132] The energy of many a fiery finish has been foolishly dampened by the conductor's *rallentando*.

Rhythm

A few very important lines in the old treatises indicate that eighteenth-century composers were not always meticulous about rhythmic notation, especially as it concerned dotted notes. Musicians were aware of these lapses (conventions) and customarily corrected (observed) them in performance. Leopold Mozart spoke toward this practice in the section of his *Violinschule* dealing with the elements of music:

> There are certain passages in slow pieces where the dot must be held rather longer than the [rule of half-value] demands if the performance is not to sound too sleepy. . . . the time taken up by the extended value must be, so to speak, stolen from the note standing after the dot. . . .

---

[131] *Klavierschule* (2), [6/5/§66-68] 360-361.

[132] *Versuch* (3), 160 [1/3/28].

The dot should in fact be held at all times [italics added] somewhat longer than its value. Not only is the performance thereby enlivened, but hurrying—that almost universal fault—is thereby checked. . . . It would be a good thing if this long retention of the dot were insisted on, and set down as a rule.[133]

We have no intention here of joining the scholarly battle over interpretation of passages like the one above. Luckily for us Haydn notated rhythms precisely, from the very beginning to the end of his career. When he wanted double-dotting, he wrote it in.[134]

That is not to state categorically that he never used various "shorthand" notational conventions; he may have. Robbins Landon pointed to a situation in the Benedictus of the *Mariazellermesse* which seems to call for continuation of a dotted pattern established in the opening measures (given e.o.c. as Ex. 10.57a). The music goes on, but in the notation shown in Example 10.57b. "It is quite clear," wrote Landon in the Preface to his edition, "that the dotted rhythm must be continued [in the viola part], and also added to the vocal parts."[135] But is it quite clear? We find it significant that the dotted pattern in the viola is dropped from the very moment it begins to double the tenor line. Also in measure 19 (and 20) the instrumental and vocal lines agree in (undotted) notation. Only in measure 18 is there a non-uniformity. Interestingly enough, when this passage is later repeated (mm. 79ff), the measure in question has been completely purged of dotted rhythms as well. It is possible that Haydn was reluctant to notate dotted-sixteenth rhythms for a choir he did not know and would not be present to rehearse.[136] Such rhythms would have been uncommon in choral parts in Haydn's time; he may have softened them to ensure ease of execution and good ensemble. All this may be yet another instance of the various non-uniformities so often encountered in Haydn's scores (see above). Conductors should feel free to play or sing the parts exactly as written.

Yet there are places where one can well apply the suggestion to overdot "if the performance is not to sound too sleepy." Overdotting works best with solo lines (instrumental or vocal) in simple textures at slow-to-moderate tempos. In Haydn's choral music one finds these combinations most often in the early works (see Ex. 2.12b).

DYNAMICS

There can be no doubt that the range of dynamics used in the late eighteenth century was narrower than our own. Only an extraordinary instance—the depiction of an earth-

---

[133] Mozart *Violinschule*, Ch 1/iii, §11, 41-42.

[134] Cf. the 1756 *Salve Regina*/iii, with its dotted sixteenth-rests and thirty-second-note pairs, etc. Or *The Creation*'s "Chaos," mm. 31-37 and later.

[135] Bärenreiter TP 96, [reprinted from *JHW* 23/2], vi.

[136] See our discussion of the *Mariazellermesse* in Chapter 4.

quake—provoked Haydn into finally using a *fortississimo* marking (in *The Seven Last Words*). The use of period instruments also dictates, as we have seen, a softer sound from the ensemble, without negating the possibility of a brilliant, brassy tutti.

The trouble is that when we attempt to carry this reduced range into performances with modern instruments and large choirs, we often create a music-box world in which no real climaxes are permitted. Everything becomes gently rounded off, beautifully shaped, and ultimately dead. That is a disservice to the powerful music Haydn gave us. It is far better to allow, at the right times, the big sounds that our singers and players have been trained to provide. That will not prevent us from teaching everyone also to make the true *piano* and *pianissimo* sounds called for in Haydn's scores.

One special case in Haydn's dynamic world is the *forzando* (*sf* or *fz*). These markings must not be rigidly interpreted. Sometimes the musical context demands a quick < > swell with warmth, not fire, at the dynamic peak. That is the case, for example, at the beginning of Part III of *The Creation* (Ex. 10.59, e.o.c.). But *fz* markings such as those in the Kyrie of the *Nelsonmesse* need no such refinement. They should sting.

DICTION

It has lately become fashionable for American singers to pronounce the Latin of Bach, Mozart, Haydn, and Beethoven as do singers from German-speaking lands. Germanic Latin diction makes sense when we realize that pronunciations such as (in IPA) [ma 'gni fi kat], with its added percussive emphasis on the second syllable, were what those composers probably heard, both in performance and in their minds' ears.

Learning yet another Latin diction may seem at first glance like a Sisyphean task, but in the present case it is rather easily accomplished: Austro-German Latin is pronounced much as if it were German. Thus "Gratias agimus tibi propter magnam" becomes ['gra tsi as 'a gi mus 'ti bɪ 'prop tɛr 'ma gnam]. "Benedictus qui venit in nomine Domini" becomes [be ne 'di ktus kvi 've nit in 'no mi nɛ 'do mɪ ni]. The distinction in German between open and closed *e* and *o* should be observed, especially with stressed vowels (e.g., [mi zɛ 're rɛ]). A few special cases exist: *c* is rendered as [ts] before *e* or *i*, *ae* or *oe,* making *coeli* sound as ['tse li]. In all positions, *g* is "hard" [g]; *s* is usually voiced [z] before a vowel; *qu* becomes [kv]; a clean break is made before initial vowels. One or two listening sessions with any appropriate recording by, say, the choir of Vienna's Augustinerkirche should provide the nuances needed to imitate such groups' diction successfully. For those who wish to explore further subtleties, an excellent published guide to singing in Continental Latin is now also available.[137]

---

[137] From which the preceding summary is drawn; see the thoroughly researched and engagingly presented Copeman *Singing,* esp. 214-225, 235-236, 297-298.

Whether Haydn and his singers used this Latin can be questioned. The Italian influence was particularly strong in Vienna during the eighteenth century among both ecclesiastics and musicians. Did such *echt* Viennese as Antonio Salieri and Nicola Porpora really teach their students to sing Germanic Latin? Did such Haydn charges as Barbara Benvenuti, Luigia Polzelli, and Benedetto Bianchi really spit out ['saŋk tʊm kvo kve pɑ rɑ 'kle tʊm 'spi ri tʊm] when pressed into singing a *Te Deum* for their Prince? It seems unlikely. Although there can be little doubt that provincial choirs sang Germanic Latin then as now (and probably with the same execrably pinched nasal vowels), we may reasonably assume that, in many cases, Haydn heard Italianate Latin from his singers. Perhaps that also explains why, in Haydn's Latin works, it is difficult to find passages whose musical rhetoric shows any evidence of having been shaped by Germanic Latin diction. Conductors have little reason to revert to such usage with modern English-speaking choirs.

Figure 10.7: Orchestral Seating Plan, Haydn-Salomon Concerts, 1791-93

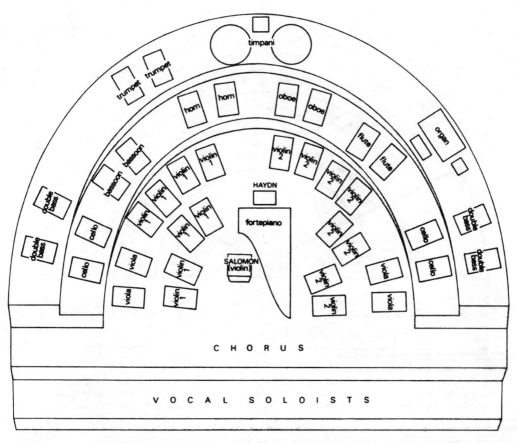

Hypothetical reconstruction by Neal Zaslaw of the amphitheater placement used at the Haydn-Salomon concerts in London, 1791-93. Based upon descriptions in Charlotte Papendiek, *Court and Private Life in the Time of Queen Charlotte* (London, 1887), 294-955; and in the *Berliner Musikzeitung* (March 18 and July 6, 1793). Reproduced with permission of Professor Zaslaw and Stanley Sadie, editor of *The New Grove Dictionary of Musical Instruments* (London, 1984), where this illustration appears in volume II on page 829.

Example 10.38: Haydn *Paukenmesse,* Benedictus, mm. 1-5

Reprinted from Carus-Verlag 40.607. This Carus Verlag reproduction is made with the express consent of Carus Verlag of Stuttgart and Mark Foster Music Company, Inc., of Champaign, Illinois, Sole U. S. Selling Agent, in accordance with the provisions of the United States Copyright Law.

Figure 10.8: Orchestral Seating Plan for *The Creation*, Vienna, 1799

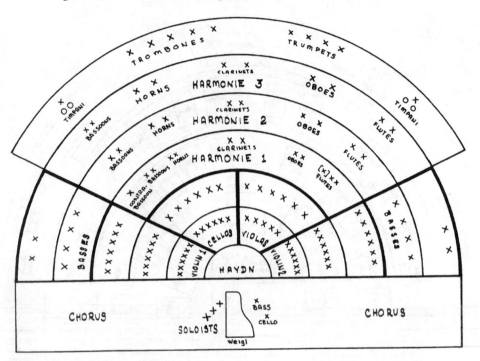

Attempted reconstruction by A. Peter Brown of the seating plan for the performance of *The Creation* at the Burgtheater, Vienna, on 19 March 1799, based on contemporary descriptions. This illustration appears on page 30 of *Performing Haydn's* The Creation: *Reconstructing the Earliest Renditions* (Bloomington, 1986) and is reproduced with permission of Professor Brown and the Indiana University Press.

Example 10.39: Haydn *Heiligmesse*, Gloria, mm. 69-77

Reprinted from Henle HN 5572 (*JHW* 23/2). © 1958 G. Henle, Munich; used by permission.

Example 10.40: Haydn *Nelsonmesse,* Gloria, mm. 1-4

Example 10.41: Haydn *Nelsonmesse,* Kyrie, mm. 36-41

Example 10.42: Haydn *Mariazellermesse*, Gloria, mm. 169-177

Example 10.43: Haydn *Heiligmesse*, Benedictus, mm. 13-20

Example 10.44: Haydn *Paukenmesse*, Credo, mm. 34-46

Reprinted from Henle HN 5572 (*JHW* 23/2). © 1958 G. Henle, Munich; used by permission.

Example 10.45: Haydn *Salve Regina* in G minor, II, mm. 42-53

Ex. 10.46: Haydn *Salve Regina* in E, III, mm. 14-28

Example 10.47: Haydn *Grosse Orgelmesse,* "Et incarnatus est," mm. 7-15; original solo line plus suggested ornaments

Example 10.48: Haydn *Mariazellermesse*, Gloria, mm. 50-57

Example 10.49: Haydn *Cäcilienmesse*, Credo, mm. 9-11

Example 10.50: Haydn *Grosse Orgelmesse*, Agnus Dei, mm. 1-6

Example 10.51: Haydn *The Seasons*, 9, mm. 1-6

Example 10.52: Haydn *Cäcilienmesse*, Sanctus, mm. 7-8

Reprinted from Henle HN 5562 (*JHW* 23/1a). © 1992 G. Henle, Munich; used by permission.

Example 10.53: Haydn *The Seasons*, 12, mm. 1-7

Example 10.54: Haydn *The Seasons*, 34, mm. 1-13

Example 10.55: Haydn *Paukenmesse*, Sanctus, mm. 1-3

Example 10.56: Haydn *Cäcilienmesse*, Benedictus, mm. 1-15

Example 10.57a: Haydn *Mariazellermesse*, Benedictus, mm. 1-6

Example 10.57b: Haydn *Mariazellermesse*, Benedictus, mm. 14-19

Exx. 10.57a and b reprinted from Carus-Verlag 40.606. This Carus Verlag reproduction is made with the express consent of Carus Verlag of Stuttgart and Mark Foster Music Company, Inc., of Champaign, Illinois, Sole U. S. Selling Agent, in accordance with the provisions of the United States Copyright Law.

Example 10.58: Haydn *Paukenmesse*, Credo, mm. 173-182

Example 10.59: Haydn *The Creation*, 29, mm. 1-10

Example 10.60: Haydn *The Creation*, 19, mm. 55-59

11

GENERAL WORKLIST

This general listing of Haydn's choral music presents concise, performance-related information about works discussed elsewhere in detail. It is organized by genre into four major sections:

I.   Masses
II. Oratorios and Cantatas
III. Smaller Sacred Works
IV. Secular Works

Within each section, the works are arranged alphabetically. Each work is described using the following scheme:

> **Title** (Alternate Title[s]) (key) (Hoboken #) (*New Grove* #) (date)
> > Soli; choral voicing if not SATB; instrumentation; # of mvts.; timing. Description by mvt. Brief stylistic comment. **Practical Considerations:** [difficulty, range and tessitura, unusual instrumental needs, etc.]
> > Publisher[s] & catalog # [usu. vocal score]. Language[s]. Editor. Date; comment (title of edition, if different) (type of performance materials available).
> > *Bibliography:* [most significant references to this work in dissertations, published literature]

NB: Abbreviations and symbols are listed in a table at the end of the chapter. The given catalog number given refers to piano/vocal score and paper binding whenever available. But the reader should check the parenthetical material following date and comments for each publication to see if a piano/vocal score (voc sc) is in fact available; sometimes it is not. Carus-Verlag catalog numbers are listed here without the [/##] suffix used by that publisher to denote specific items of performance material, including piano/vocal score.

In other areas, the general scheme has also been changed if a variation fit the situation better. Thus if a category was inapplicable or superfluous (e.g., key listing for an Esterházy cantata), it was omitted. Common sense and the nature of the material dictated other omissions as well; for example, because so much of this choral music is homophonic with moderate ranges and difficulty, only exceptions to, or paradigms of, that style were noted.

Likewise the comments on "Practical Considerations" were limited, since beyond the basics, every performer's concerns will be different. It is hoped that the repertoire lists in Chapter 12 suggested for various age groups or types of organization will prove to be of further practical help.

The list of published editions is selective. It does not include excerpts, arrangements, or every possible reprint of the old "standard" editions. In several cases I have listed publications with outdated or less-than-ideal editorial standards. The particular nature of an edition, including its shortcomings, is indicated wherever possible. Readers should take special note of these sources of reliable texts: 1) the three attempts made in this century at scholarly complete editions of Haydn's music, especially the ongoing work of the Cologne Haydn Institute; these editions are listed as M, HS, and JHW in the catalog below. Publications of the Cologne Haydn Institute (JHW) are available as separate cloth-bound volumes from Henle; many have also been issued in practical performing editions by Bärenreiter. A separate listing of the complete JHW series, present and projected, is given in Chapter 12. 2) a series of works, edited by H. C. Robbins Landon and published by Doblinger and others, generally adhering to high standards of scholarship and making a number of little-known works available for the first time. 3) a new series of Haydn Masses edited by various scholars and published by Carus-Verlag of Stuttgart. Each Mass so far issued has included a foreword and critical report and, at reasonable prices, complete performing materials: vocal scores, choral scores, instrumental parts, and so forth.

Finally, a word about the bibliographies attached to each work. These too are selective, being confined to major, usually recent, contributions on the piece. The reader can obtain further citations by several means: 1) the more exhaustive bibliography included at the end of this book, 2) the work-specific bibliographies in the *Kritischer Bericht* issued by the Cologne Haydn Institute for each volume in its series, and 3) the comprehensive Haydn bibliographies that have appeared in *Haydn-Studien*—see Brown "Bibliography" and Walter "Haydn-Bibliographie" in this book's bibliography.

I. Masses

Cäcilienmesse: see *Missa Cellensis in honorem* . . .

"Creation" Mass: see *Missa*

Dreiviertelmesse: see *Missa Sancti Nicolai*

"Great" Organ Mass, Grosse Orgelmesse: see *Missa in honorem . . .*

Harmoniemesse: see *Missa (Harmoniemesse . . .)*

Heiligmesse: see *Missa Sancti Bernardi von Offida*

Imperial Mass: see *Missa in angustiis*

Jugendmesse: see *Missa brevis [in F]*

Kleine Orgelmesse: see *Missa brevis Sti. Joannis de Deo*

"Little" Organ Mass: see *Missa brevis Sti. Joannis de Deo*

Mariazellermesse: see *Missa Cellensis*

Mass in Time of War: see *Missa in tempore belli*

Missa (*Harmoniemesse*; *"Wind-Band" Mass*) (B♭) (XXII:14) (A 14) (1802)
SATB; 2ob 2cl 2bn 2hn 2tp timp str org vc/cb; X (Gloria, Credo sectional); 55'. Last to be composed of Haydn's six late Masses; see *Missa Sancti Bernardi von Offida.* Longest and most richly scored of these works. Many beautiful passages for winds, as in "Et incarnatus est." *Poco adagio* Kyrie ("exalted, but also filled with . . . nostalgia"—Landon) unusual for Haydn; *Allegro molto e pianissimo* Benedictus just unusual. Elsewhere the musical style pointedly recalls earlier works. **Practical Considerations:** Larger wind group may require larger ch.
Bärenreiter 4659a. Lat. F. Lippmann. 1978 (voc sc, ips BA 4659, min sc TP 97).
Carus 40.612. Lat. (sc, voc sc, ch sc, ips).
Henle HN 5602 (*JHW* 23/5, cloth; HN 539, paper). Lat. F. Lippmann. 1966 (sc; for voc sc, min sc, perf mat see Bärenreiter).
Kalmus 6225. Lat. (sc, voc sc, ips).
Peters P3538. Lat. (voc sc, ipr).
G. Schirmer ED2613. Lat. W. Herrmann. (voc sc, ipr).
Bibliography: Becker-Glauch "Remarks"; Brand *Messen* 451-510; Landon *HCW* 5 242-251.

Missa (*Schöpfungsmesse*; *"Creation" Mass*) (B♭) (XXII:13) (A 13) (1801)
SATB; fl 1ob 2cl 2bn 2hn 2tp timp str org vc/cb; X (Gloria, Credo divide); 46'. Fifth to be composed of Haydn's six late Masses; see *Missa Sancti Bernardi von Offida.* Considered by composer's contemporaries to be among his greatest works. Written on larger scale with expanded instr, shows absolute command of symphonic form. Many sophisticated touches: Kyrie in 6/8 *allegro* is both lively and serious; Credo renews Baroque text-painting; Agnus/Dona filled with harmonic, dynamic surprises. **Practical Considerations:** "Et incarnatus est" requires org obbligato. Solo ensemble singing predominates, incl spot of SSATTB; crucial that solo voices be well-matched, lyric, flexible. Ch S to b♭² (important); B briefly to F.
Bärenreiter BA 4656a. Lat. I. Becker-Glauch. 1967 (sc, voc sc, ipr BA 4656).
Anton Böhm und Sohn. Lat. F. Habel. Contains full (i.e., rev) Mass text (sc, cps, ips).
Carus 40.611. Lat. V. Kalisch. 1984 (voc sc, sc, ch sc, ips).
Henle HN 3202. Lat. Wilhelm Virneisel. 1959 (facsimile of autograph sc).

Henle HN 5592 (*JHW* 23/4, cloth; HN 536, paper). Lat. I. Becker-Glauch. 1967; incl alteration of Gloria made for Empress Marie Therese (sc).

Kalmus 6238. Lat. (sc, voc sc, ips).

G. Schirmer ED2943. Lat. H. C. Robbins Landon. 1973 (voc sc, ipr).

Bibliography: Becker-Glauch "Remarks"; Brand *Messen* 407-450; Landon *HCW* 5 199-212.

Missa (*Theresienmesse*; *"Theresa" Mass*) (B♭) (XXII:12) (A 12) (1799)

SATB; 2cl bn* 2tp timp str org vc/cb; X (Gloria, Credo divide); 43'. Fourth to be composed of Haydn's six late Masses; see *Missa Sancti Bernardi von Offida*. Like *Missa in angustiis*, features reduced wind instr and org obbligato. Full of novel ideas, incl French-overture Kyrie; beautiful vocal quartet and ch fugal writing. Unjustly neglected. **Practical Considerations:** Soloists nearly equal in importance, with S having the edge. Ch parts med to med-dif.

Bärenreiter BA 4661a. Lat. G. Thomas. 1969 (voc sc, ips BA 4661, min sc TP 99).

Anton Böhm und Sohn. Lat. C. Rouland. Contains full (i.e., rev) Mass text (sc, cps, ips).

Carus 40.610. Lat. (sc, voc sc, ch sc, ips).

Henle HN 5582 (*JHW* 23/3, cloth). Lat. G. Thomas. 1965; incl sc of *Missa in angustiis* (sc; for voc sc, min sc, perf mat see Bärenreiter).

Kalmus 6243. Lat. (sc, voc sc, ips).

Novello. Lat. (voc sc, ipr).

G. Schirmer ED2820. Lat. W. Herrmann. (voc sc, ipr).

Bibliography: Becker-Glauch "Remarks"; Brand *Messen* 354-407; Landon *HCW* 4 524-537; Webb "Analysis."

Universal PH 121 (min sc). Lat.

Missa brevis [in F] (*... a due Soprani*; *Jugendmesse*) (F) (XXII:1) (A 2) (c. 1749)

SS; 2vl org vc/cb; VI; 12'. Possibly Haydn's first Mass setting (see also *Missa Rorate coeli*). Each mvt contains concertante S duets (florid, dif) plus features typical of Viennese church music: ch hom, busy vls, overlapping texts in Gloria and Credo (*Missa-brevis* texture), a Benedictus wholly given over to soloists. Haydn may have intended solos for himself and brother Michael; in any case they highlight this youthful-sounding, energetic work. **Practical Considerations:** Solo S I has higher tess than solo S II; mezzo could sing S II. Variety of rhythmic figures in vl parts may cause some awkwardness. Haydn doubled vl I & II in all *forte* passages, enabling work to be played with very small str contingent.

Arista AE 510. Lat. Repr of *HS* (sc, voc sc, ips).

Carus 40.601. Lat. W. Schulze. 1979 (sc, voc sc, ch sc, ips).

Doblinger 46 009. Lat. R. Moder. 1955; incl corrected partwriting borrowed from Brand; arr for liturgical use (i.e., rev text underlay and/or repeated musical sections in Gloria, Credo); otherwise sim *HS* (sc, cps, ips).

Henle HN 5562 (*JHW* 23/1a, cloth). Lat. J. Dack, G. Feder. 1994; incl sc of *Missa Cellensis in hon. B.V.M.* (sc).

HS XXIII/I. Lat. C. M. Brand. 1951 (sc).

Bibliography: Brand *Messen* 6-16; Gilbert "First"; McCaldin "First"; Landon *HCW* 1 145-147.

Missa [brevis] Rorate coeli desuper (G) (XXII:3/ii,73) (A 1b) (c. 1749)

2vl org vc/cb; VI; 5'. Of questionable authenticity. May be a youthful work heavily infl by Reutter and Arbesser (Haydn's teachers at St. Stephen's) or a minor work by one of them. *Missa brevis* with radically telescoped Gloria text; overall concision typical of 18th-c. Austrian Advent Mass.

Not without crude voice-leading, awkward doublings, and floundering harmonic progressions, all possible indications of its composer's inexperience. **Practical Considerations:** Text overlap makes precision, projection dif; use small ch and solo instr.

Carus 40.602. Lat. W. Schulze. 1982 (sc, voc sc, ch sc, ips).

Haydn-Mozart Press (Universal Ed.) HMP 21. Lat. H. C. Robbins Landon. 1957 (sc HMP 23, cps HMP 22A-D, ips).

Bibliography: Becker-Glauch "Neue Forschungen" 172; Landon "Aufgefundene"; Landon "Haydniana"; Landon *HCW* 1 139-144; Hofer "Beiden Reutter"; Schenk "Göttweiger Rorate-Messe."

Missa brevis Sancti Joannis de Deo (*Kleine Orgelmesse, "Little" Organ Mass*) (B♭) (XXII:7) (A 7) (c. 1775)

S; 2vl org vc/cb; VI; 15'. Very popular. Musical high point is Benedictus, a solo mvt for org obbligato (no pedals, florid), S solo (med, florid, high B♭). Elsewhere Haydn's by-now polished *Missa-brevis* manner deals efficiently, but not always sensitively, with limited resources: 30-m. Gloria seems especially abrupt. **Practical Considerations:** Skilled organist required, but not a large org or instr group.

Bärenreiter BA 4653a. Lat. H. C. Robbins Landon et al. (see Henle). 1962 (voc sc, ipr BA 4653, min sc TP 95).

Anton Böhm und Sohn Ausgabe A. Lat. Arr. F. Habel. Repeats sections of Gloria, Credo to enhance text presentation (sc, cps, ips) (also available arr. for SSA [Ausgabe C] and for male choir [Ausgabe B]).

Carus 40.079. Lat. W. Schulze. 1980 (sc, voc sc, ips).

Henle HN 5572 (*JHW* 23/2, cloth). Lat. H. C. Robbins Landon, K. H. Füssl, C. Landon. 1958; incl sc of 3 other Haydn Masses plus Michael Haydn's lengthened adaptation of Gloria (sc; for voc sc, min sc, perf mat see Bärenreiter).

Kalmus 6240. Lat. (voc sc, ips, ipr)

G. Schirmer ED2923. Lat. H. C. Robbins Landon. (voc sc).

Bibliography: Brand *Messen* 131-143; Landon *HCW* 2 554.

Missa Cellensis (*Mariazellermesse*) (C) (XXII:8) (A 8) (1782)

SATB; 2ob 2bn 2tp timp str org vc/cb; X (Gloria, Credo sectional); 29'. This Mass "made for Herr Liebe von Kreutzner" seems to stand midway between Haydn's earlier styles and that of his late Masses. New goals of unity, simplicity, energy are forcefully achieved through cyclic repetition of motives and textures, reliance on drum bass, and popular-sounding melodies. But several solo sections are still arias, with ancestors in *Grosse Orgelmesse* or *Cäcilienmesse*. **Practical Considerations:** ST soli med dif, AB soli concertante & med; ch easy-med. Ideal for high-school or amateur church ch performance.

Bärenreiter BA 4654a. Lat. H. C. Robbins Landon, K. H. Füssl (see Henle). 1962; incl ornamentation found in contemporary perf mat (voc sc, ipr BA 4654, min sc TP 96).

Anton Böhm und Sohn. Lat. P. R. Johandl. Music arranged and repeated to avoid text overlap in Credo (sc, cps, ips).

Carus 40.606. Lat. A. Ballstaedt, V. Kalisch. 1986 (sc, min sc, voc sc, ch sc, ips).

Henle HN 5572 (*JHW* 23/2, cloth). Lat. H. C. Robbins Landon, K. H. Füssl. 1958; incl sc of 3 other Haydn Masses (sc; for voc sc, min sc, perf mat see Bärenreiter).

Kalmus 6244. Lat. (voc sc, ips).

Bibliography: Brand *Messen* 143-183; Landon *Essays* 72, *HCW* 2 555-560, *Symphonies* 395.

Missa Cellensis in honorem Beatissimae Virginis Mariae (*Missa Sanctae Caecilia*; *Cäcilienmesse*) (C) (XXII:5) (A 3) (1766-c.73/4)

SATB; 2ob 2bn 2hn* 2tp timp str org vc/cb; XVII; 70'. Lengthy "cantata" Mass, sim to Mozart K. 427, Bach BWV 232, Caldara *Missa dolorosa*. Juxtaposes conservative and operatic styles; probably composed over period of several years. Several great fugues. Later sections contain wider variety of moods, techniques: pathos, stormy interruptions, experiments. **Practical Considerations:** S, B soli dif; A, T soli med dif; S soli often ornate or w/ very dif coloratura ("Laudamus te," "Quoniam"). B solo tess often quite low (secure F mandatory); "Domine Deus" contains huge leaps (e.g., E-d'). Ch med dif (ranges, some melismatic passages). Exposed and ornate vl writing in several mvts.

Carus-Verlag 40.604. Lat. (sc, voc sc, ch sc, ips).

Haydn-Mozart Press (Universal Ed.) HMP 14/15. Lat. C.M. Brand. 1952; based on *HS* (voc sc, ipr).

Henle HN 5562 (*JHW* 23/1a, cloth). Lat. J. Dack, G. Feder. 1992; incl sc of *Missa brevis* [in F] (sc).

HS XXIII/I. Lat. C. M. Brand. 1951 (sc).

Bibliography: Brand *Messen* 51-99; Dack "Dating"; Landon *HCW* 2 228-232, "Autograph."

Missa in angustiis (*Nelsonmesse*; *Imperial Mass*) (d) (XXII:11) (A 11) (1798)

SATB; 3tp timp str org vc/cb; X (Gloria, Credo divide); 45'. Third to be composed of Haydn's six late Masses; see *Missa Sancti Bernardi von Offida*. Title refers to "the narrow," possibly meaning danger or affliction. Composed at height of Napoleonic wars, work is extremely dramatic. D-minor Kyrie sets tone with riveting tp calls, tightly constructed Allegro. Benedictus also explosive, but D-major Gloria, Credo provide relief. Although two later versions with added winds exist, many will find original stark instr most effective. **Practical Considerations:** original orch requires org obbligato. S solo (to b♭^{2}) dif, requires power and flexibility; B solo needs ringing tone to G. Ch S to b^2; ch parts med-dif to dif (power, flexibility).

Bärenreiter BA 4660a. Lat. G. Thomas. 1979; incl Fuchs' wind parts as option (voc sc, ips BA 4660, min sc TP 98).

Anton Böhm und Sohn. Lat. Contains full (i.e., rev) Mass text (sc, ips, cps).

Carus 40.609. Lat. (sc, voc sc, ch sc, ips).

Dover 28108-6 Pa. Lat. Repr of Peters; incl sc of *Missa in tempore belli* (sc).

Eulenburg 995 (min sc). Lat. H. C. Robbins Landon. 1963 (for voc sc, perf mat see Schott).

Henle HN 5582 (*JHW* 23/3, cloth). Lat. G. Thomas. 1965; incl sc of *Theresienmesse* (sc; for voc sc, min sc, perf mat see Bärenreiter).

Kalmus 6241. Lat. Repr of Peters (voc sc, ips).

Peters P4351. Lat. W. Weissman. 1931; based not on autograph but on first Breitkopf edition, incl Breitkopf wind scoring; numerous inaccuracies (voc sc, ips P4372).

G. Schirmer ED409. Lat. (voc sc, ipr).

Schott 10808. Lat. H. C. Robbins Landon. 1963; based on autograph sc and authentic parts w/out extra wind parts (voc sc, ipr).

Bibliography: Becker-Glauch "Remarks"; Brand *Messen* 307-353; Landon *HCW* 4 427-444; Schenbeck "Missa"; Schmid "Bemerkungen"; Town "Missa."

Missa in honorem Beatissimae Virginis Mariae (*Great Organ Mass, Grosse Orgelmesse*) (E♭) (XXII:4) (A 5) (c. 1768-9)

SATB; 2ehn 2hn 2tp* timp* str bn org vc/cb; X (Gloria, Credo divide); 40'. Nickname comes from elaborate solo org part which Haydn presumably played himself. Like others of this period, work is a stylistic mixture and considered uneven by some critics. Great fugues end Gloria and Credo; Sanctus monumental; Dona fugue and its org solo may seem frivolous by comparison. **Practical Considerations:** Dif, rather high E♭ tp parts apparently date (as do timp parts) from a second authentic version made around 1775. Since ehn parts extend slightly below range of modern insts, Robbins Landon included ossia readings for these passages in his edition.

Carus 40.603. Lat. (sc, voc sc, ch sc, ips).

Doblinger. Lat. A. Straßl. 1955 (sc, voc sc, ips; *basso* part has been simplified, and edition shows no evidence of collation with autograph fragment).

HS XXIII/I. Lat. C. M. Brand. 1951 (sc; prepared from three secondary manuscripts—requires rev).

University College Cardiff Press. Lat. H. C. Robbins Landon. 1983 (sc, ipr).

Bibliography: Brand *Messen* 36; Feder "Source"; Landon "Autograph"; Landon *HCW* 2 243-244.

Missa in tempore belli (*Paukenmesse; Mass in Time of War*) (C) (XXII:9) (A 10) (1796)

SATB; fl* 2ob 2cl 2bn 2hn 2tp timp str org vc/cb; X (Gloria, Credo divide); 40'. Second to be composed of Haydn's six late Masses; see *Missa Sancti Bernardi von Offida*. Very popular work, owing to its festive orch setting and to drama of Agnus Dei. In that mvt, "the words . . . are performed in singular fashion with timpani accompaniment, 'as though one heard the enemy coming in the distance.' At the following words, 'dona nobis pacem' he has all the instruments enter in a very striking way." (Haydn's contemporary Griesinger) **Practical Considerations:** S solo florid, med dif; B (or baritone) solo "Qui tollis" has important 'cello obbligato (thus *divisi* cellos required). Fl part probably inauthentic. Ch occasionally florid; ch S regularly to a^2, ch B once to E.

Bärenreiter BA 4652a. Lat. H. C. Robbins Landon et al. (see Henle). 1962; min sc incl supplementary cl parts (voc sc, ips BA 4652, min sc TP 94).

Anton Böhm und Sohn. Lat. F. Habel. Contains full (i.e., rev) Mass text.

Carus 40.607. Lat. (sc, voc sc, ch sc, ips).

Dover 28108-6 Pa. Lat. Eng. A. Hoboken. 1944; incl sc of *Missa in angustiis* (sc).

Henle HN 5572 (*JHW* 23/2, cloth). Lat. H. C. Robbins Landon, K. H. Füssl, C. Landon. 1958; incl sc of 3 other Haydn Masses (sc; for voc sc, min sc, perf mat see Bärenreiter).

Kalmus L389. Lat. (sc, voc sc, ips).

G. Schirmer 2600. Lat. M. Miller. (voc sc, ipr).

Bibliography: Becker-Glauch "Remarks"; Biba "Pflege"; Brand *Messen* 217-260; Landon *HCW* 4 162-180; Ricks "Tempo."

Missa Sanctae Caecilia: see *Missa Cellensis in honorem . . .*

Missa Sancti Bernardi von Offida (*Heiligmesse*) (B♭) (XXII:10) (A 9) (1796)

SATB; 2ob 2cl 2bn 2hn* 2tp timp str org vc/cb; X (Gloria, Credo divide); 50'. First to be composed of Haydn's six late Masses. All are masterpieces, all share certain characteristics: symphonic form and scope plied with new flexibility; varied, skillful instrumentation; counterpoint renewed by encounter with Handel's art in London; inclusion of folk-like tunes, humor, and other popular elements; preference for solo quartet over aria. Notwithstanding their origin in Catholic liturgy, they can rightly be called Haydn's final set of symphonies. Of these, *Heiligmesse* is distinguished by warmth and grace that is a product of several factors—its key; its use of agreeably "popular" melodies often in triple meter; its reliance on ch or quartet textures. **Practical Considerations:** Soloists used less often in this Mass than in any other of the late six. But solo ensembles important: at one point SSATBB required. Moderate ranges and med dif of ch parts make this good choice for high school or amateur performance.

Bärenreiter BA 4651a. Lat. H. C. Robbins Landon et al. (see Henle) 1962 (voc sc, ipr BA 4651, min sc TP 93).

Anton Böhm und Sohn. Lat. C. Rouland. Contains full (i.e., rev) Mass text (sc, ips, cps).

Carus 40.608. Lat. (voc sc, ch sc, ips).

Henle HN 5572 (*JHW* 23/2, cloth). Lat. H. C. Robbins Landon, K. H. Füssl, C. Landon. 1958; incl sc of 3 other Haydn Masses (sc; for voc sc, min sc, perf mat see Bärenreiter).

Peters P1372. Lat. (voc sc, ipr).

Kalmus 6246. Lat. (sc, voc sc, ips).

G. Schirmer 2885. Lat. H. C. Robbins Landon (ipr).

Bibliography: Becker-Glauch "Remarks"; Brand *Messen* 261-306; Landon *HCW* 4 124-137 (late Masses), 138-161 (Missa Sti. Bernardi).

Missa Sancti Nicolai (*Dreiviertelmesse; Nikolausmesse*) (G) (XXII:6) (A 6) (1772)
SATB; 2ob bn* 2hn str org vc/cb; VI; 26'. In spite of its telescoped Credo text, this is more a *Missa ruralis* than a *brevis* Mass; its lilting folklike Kyrie/Dona tune, use of parallel thirds, and woodwind scoring must have delighted namesake Prince Nicolaus, who was fond of the countryside. Title, style, length make this an ideal work for Christmas season. **Practical Considerations:** Ch med dif (some melismas; S will need an effortless a^2, occasional b^2; B part also wide-ranged); soli med dif. Comparatively simple, straightforward instr accomp.

Arista AE 460. Lat. Repr of *HS* (voc sc, ips).

Anton Böhm und Sohn. Lat. C. Rouland. Incl 2tp* timp*, full (i.e., rev) Mass text (sc, cps, ips).

Carus 40.605. Lat. V. Kalisch. 1982 (sc, voc sc, ch sc, ips).

Eulenburg (min sc). Lat. H. C. Robbins Landon.

Faber/G. Schirmer F50177X. Lat. H. C. Robbins Landon. 1969 (voc sc, sc F507220, ipr).

HS XXIII/1. Lat. C. M. Brand. 1951; edited without Eisenstadt or St. Florian sources (sc).

Kalmus 6242. Lat. "St. Nicholas Mass" (sc, voc sc, ips, ipr).

Bibliography: Brand *Messen* 100-131; Landon *HCW* 2 251-252; McCaldin "Missa."

Missa Sunt bona mixta malis (d) (XXII:2) (A 4) (c. 1767-69)
Org vc/cb*; II; 6'. Only Kyrie and first mvt of Gloria survive; these were recovered in 1983. Fragment is in *stile antico* with appropriately heavy reliance on formal counterpoint, especially in Kyrie. Org has several perfunctory interludes.

Éditions Mario Bois (Presser) 312-41654. Lat. H. C. Robbins Landon, D. Wyn Jones. 1993 (sc incl separate vc/cb part).

Bibliography: Landon/Jones *Haydn*, 142-143; Landon *HCW* 2 291-295; Landon "Lost."

"Nelson" Mass, Nelsonmesse: see *Missa in angustiis*

Nikolausmesse: see *Missa Sancti Nicolai*

Paukenmesse: see *Missa in tempore belli*

Schöpfungsmesse: see *Missa (Schöpfungsmesse . . .)*

"Theresa" Mass, Theresienmesse: see *Missa*

"Wind-Band" Mass: see *Missa*

II. ORATORIOS AND CANTATAS

Applausus (XXIVa:6) (C 2) (1768)

SATBB; 2ob bn 2hn 2tp timp str(incl solo vl) kb(incl solo) vc/cb; XVI; 90'. Although filled with beautiful parts, cantata seems on the whole overlong and overly abstract. Text is allegory in which four Cardinal Virtues and a fifth Virtue, Theology, discuss merits of monastic life. Haydn manages to inject considerable variety into *accompagnato* recitatives' instrumental interludes, and each aria abounds in lovely details of scoring. But lack of dramatic impetus is fatal. Even final ch, one of Haydn's 3/4 Allegros, offers tempered festivity at best. Cf. sacred contrafacta of individual numbers, which are more programmable: "Dictamina mea/Alleluia," "O Jesu, te invocamus."
Practical Considerations: Extremely dif vocal solo parts, esp coloratura T. Double cadenzas for vl solo, harpsichord in T arias. Tp parts are *clarino*, range extending to c^3.

Doblinger DM 500. Lat. H. C. Robbins Landon. 1969 (sc, voc sc, ch sc, ips).

Henle HN 5792 (*JHW* 27/2, cloth). Lat. Wiens, Becker-Glauch. 1969 (sc).

Bibliography: Landon *HCW* 2 236-238; Nowak *Haydn* 206; Pohl *Haydn* 2 39.

Creation, The (*Die Schöpfung*) (XXI:2) (C 5) (1796-8)

STB; 3fl 2ob 2cl 2bn cbn 2hn 2tp 3tn timp str kb vc/cb; 34; full. Haydn's great masterwork in this genre. Text after Genesis and Milton's *Paradise Lost*, music greatly influenced by London Handel experience. Structure built mainly on series of scripture-commentary-praise units set to recit-aria-ch, sim *Messiah* or Bach's *Matthew Passion*. Thus many opportunities for ch music within a balanced dramatic and musical framework. Part I: first four days of Creation. II: days five and six culminating in creation of Man. III: Garden of Eden before the Fall. Soloists portray angels in Parts I, II; in III S and B become Adam and Eve. Ch generally represents Heavenly Host.
Practical Considerations: See esp. Brown *Performing*, Franz *Schöpfung*.

Breitkopf & Härtel. Ger. E. Mandyczewski. 1924; issued originally as *M* 16/V; based on authentic first edition only.

Dover 26411-4 (sc). Eng, Ger. Repr of Peters sc.

Eulenburg 955 (min sc). Ger. Based on Mandyczewski ed.

Kalmus 6236. Eng. (sc, voc sc, ips).

Lawson-Gould 51595. Eng (Shaw, Parker). 1957; voc sc repr Peters P66 (voc sc, ipr).

Novello. Eng. V. Novello. 1847, 1858, c.1900 (voc sc, sc on rental).

Oxford University Press. Eng, Ger. A. Peter Brown. 1990; based on authentic perf mat (sc, voc sc, ipr).

Peters Edition (London). Eng. N. Temperley. 2nd ed 1989; based on Peters P66 with rev, suggestions for perf practice; contains rev English text based on 18th-c. London wordbooks (sc, voc sc available through English retailers only).

Peters P66. Eng, Ger. (voc sc, ipr). Based on Mandyczewski ed.

G. Schirmer 190. Eng. c,1890; based on Novello. (voc sc, ch sections only 1511, ipr).

Bibliography: Biba "Beispiele"; Brown "Chaos," "Options," *Performing*; Chailley "Création"; Franz *Schöpfung*; Gotwals "Creation"; Landon *Creation*, *HCW* 4 118-119, 342-426; Levarie "Closing"; Lucas "Analysis"; Mandyczewski *Schöpfung*; Olleson "Origin"; Pohl *Haydn* 3 355-362; Schenker "Schöpfung"; Smither *History* 3 488-511; Temperley *Creation*, "New light," "Tempos"; Tovey *Essays* 5 114-146, (2) 349-381.

Da qual gioja improviso (C) (XXIVa:3) (D 4) (1764)

S; SSTB; 2fl 2ob bn 2hn str kb vc/cb; II. I: Allegro di molto; lengthy ritornello followed by accomp recit for S II: Moderato; ch or solo quartet (med-dif) and extensive kb solo. Cantata celebrating Nicolaus's return from Frankfurt Coronation. Text is Italian, spouting fulsome praise of "il nostro Prence." Mvt I quite symphonic in scope, while II, thanks to its alternation of vocal and kb solo sections, has concerto-like qualities. **Practical Considerations:** Skilled harpsichordist needed; likewise ch may be better handled by soloists or some combination of ch and soli (cf. contrafactum of II, "Plausus honores date," which assigns such roles).
Bibliography: Landon *HCW* 1 474-485; Pohl *Haydn* 1 242.

Destatevi, o miei fidi (XXIVa:2) (D 2) (1763)

SST; 2ob 2hn str kb vc/cb; VI. I: Allegro; lengthy ritornello followed by accomp recit for S II: Allegro; duet for ST (very dif) III: secco recit for S IV: Allegretto; duet for SS (dif) V: Allegro di molto; aria for S VI: Allegro; ch (easy). Cantata celebrating name-day of Prince Nicolaus. II is pompous, V in heroic *Sturm und Drang* manner, IV a simpler cantabile (parodied in Duetto "Jam Cordi"—see section I). **Practical Considerations:** Ch style of last mvt quasi opera finale, can be done by soloists.
Bibliography: Becker-Glauch "Neue Forschungen" 183-184; Landon *HCW* 1 463-474; Pohl *Haydn* 1 242.

Qual dubbio omai (XXIVa:4) (D 3) (1764)

S [brief SATB 4tet in IV]; 2ob 2hn str vc/cb kb; IV; 16'. I: Allegro; grand orch ritornello leading to accomp recit II: Allegro; long da capo aria with extensive harpsichord obbligato (S florid, high, dif; kb dif) III: short recit IV: Allegro; ch tutti (melismas, med to dif). Only one of Haydn's several cantatas for Esterházy family in print so far. Interesting and musically worthy. S solo in high *opera seria* style is centerpiece; its difficulties, sim to Mozart's Queen of the Night arias, will not deter ambitious singers. Orch music and final ch are lively and brilliantly scored. Kb obbligato, which Haydn undoubtedly played, is as important as S solo and almost as dif. **Practical Considerations:** Requires professional forces.
Doblinger DM 200. H. C. Robbins Landon. 1982 (sc, voc sc, ch sc, ips).
Bibliography: Landon *HCW* 1 485-494; Pohl *Haydn* 1 242.

ritorno di Tobia, Il (XXI:1) (C 3) (1775, rev 1784)

SSATB; 2fl 2ob 2ehn 2bn 2hn 2tp timp str kb vc/cb (rev version incl 4hn 2tb); 17; full. Italian oratorio on a Metastasian libretto; story from Book of Tobias in Apocrypha. Although battles, miracles, and murders occur, focus of onstage "drama" is moralizing reflection on these events. Rich, varied orch; outstanding ch mvts. Rev form musically tighter, contains more ch music: "Ah, gran Dio" has counterpoint sim to late oratorios; "Svanisce in un momento" powerful D-minor mvt (cf. contrafactum "Insanae et vanae curae"). **Practical Considerations:** Large orch, incl full str section, important for weight, color.
Bärenreiter BA 4657. It. E. F. Schmid. (all perf mat rental).

Henle HN 5812/5815 (*JHW* 28/1-2, cloth; HN 5814, paper 2nd vol). It. E. F. Schmid. 1963 (sc; for perf mat see Bärenreiter).

Bibliography: Edelmann "Haydns *Il ritorno*"; Landon *HCW* 2 259-262; Michel "Tobias-Dramen"; Pohl *Haydn* 2 68, 84, 86, 201, 338; Schmid "Haydns Oratorium"; Smither "Haydns *ritorno*," *History* 3 160-181.

Seasons, The (*Die Jahreszeiten*) (XXI:3) (C 6) (1799-1801)
STB; 2fl 2ob 2cl 2bn cbn 4hn 3tp 3tb timp perc str kb vc/cb; 44; full. Libretto after Thomson and others. Four parts, "Spring," "Summer," "Autumn," and "Winter" with no overarching literary or musical theme; thus effect is more like four related cantatas. Quaint Rococo nature scenes enlivened by Haydn's text painting, skill at orch and ch writing. Three soloists portray Simon, a farmer, Jane (Hanne), his daughter, and Lucas, a country boy. Ch at times is given a role (e.g., "Girls and Lads") but often comments, praises God, etc. from outside the picture-frame. **Practical Considerations:** May be more effective if only one or two "seasons" are done. Large wind section must be balanced by adequate str. Likewise many ch *divisi* sections (SSAA, TTBB, et al.) demand a large, skilled ch.

Breitkopf & Härtel Wiesbaden PB-4382. Eng, Ger, Fr. E. Mandyczewski. Issued originally as *M* 16/VI-VII, 1922; based on authentic first edition (sc, voc sc, ips). *Revisionsbericht* (in *M* sc only) incl material later cut by Haydn.

Eulenburg 987 (min sc). Ger. Based on Mandyczewski.

Dover 25022-9 (sc). Ger. Repr of Peters sc.

Kalmus 6237. Eng, Ger, Fr. (sc, voc sc, ips).

Laudamus Press (1810 S. Broadway, St. Louis MO 63104). Eng. L. Van Camp. Abridged to 90' (voc sc, cassette).

Lawson-Gould 51747. Eng (Parker, Pyle). R. Shaw. 1973 (voc sc, ipr).

Peters P67. Eng, Ger. (voc sc, sc 659, ipr). Based on Mandyczewski.

G. Schirmer ED44. Eng. (voc sc, ipr).

G. Schirmer. H. C. Robbins Landon. 1973; orch concert mat only: overture (i.e., introduction to "Spring") plus uncut introductions to "Autumn," "Winter" (sc, ipr).

Schott ETP 987 (min sc).

Bibliography: Biba "Beispiele"; Feder "Jahreszeiten," "Korrekturen"; Heartz "Hunting"; Landon *HCW* 5 93-199; Mandyczewski *Jahreszeiten*; Pohl *Haydn* 3 363-372; Smither *History* 3 511-513; Tovey *Essays* 5 146-161, (2) 381-396.

Seven Last Words, The (*Die sieben letzten Worte unseres Erlösers am Kreuze*) (XX:2) (C 4) (1795-6)
SATB; 2fl 2ob 2cl 2bn cbn 2hn 2tp 2tb timp str org vc/cb; 10; 60'. Began life as series of orch adagios to be played in Good Friday service between homilies on each of the Seven Words. Later rev, with added mvts, appropriate text, and freshened instr, for ch perf. In this ver each Sonata is prefaced by an a cappella ch declamation of the Word. Sonatas themselves provide personalized explications of that Word, sim aria in Baroque Passion setting. Instr introduction, interlude for wind band, and final "earthquake" help frame work. **Practical Considerations:** Ch parts med dif. Greatest problems are unrelenting slow tempi and mawkish text. Makes strongest effect in proper ecclesiastical and seasonal context, perhaps with brief meditations interspersed as originally intended.

Bärenreiter BA 4655a. Ger. H. Unverricht. (voc sc, ipr).

Breitkopf & Härtel Wiesbaden EB-1235. Ger. (voc sc, ipr).

Eulenburg 10098 (min sc). Ger. A. Fodor.

Henle HN 5822 (*JHW* 28/2, cloth). Ger. H. Unverricht. 1961 (sc; for perf mat see Bärenreiter).
Kalmus 6239. Eng. "The Last Words..." (sc, voc sc, ips).
Peters P1371. Ger. (voc sc, ipr).
Novello. Eng. ("The Passion") (voc sc, ipr).
G. Schirmer ED2302. Eng. (voc sc, ipr).
 Bibliography: Bartha "Sieben Worte"; Barrett-Ayres "Words"; Drury "Words"; Hailparn "Words";
  Landon *HCW* 3 615-621, *HCW* 4 180-183; Saam "'sieben Worte'"; Unverricht *Bericht/Sieben*,
  "Haydns *Worte*," "Vorwort 1."

Stabat Mater (XXbis) (C 1) (1767)
  SATB; 2ob/ehn str vc/cb org; 13; 80'. Monumental Baroque oratorio treatment of this text; has
  not aged well. Length, no. of slow mvts, somewhat conventional approach are obstacles to modern appreciation. Florid, rhythmically mercurial vocal lines display a Rococo aesthetic distinct
  from Haydn's later vocal works. Although some sections (e.g., ch "Virgo virginum") show simpler *galant* contours and masterful ch writing, more often piece is symptomatic of bygone tastes
  (e.g., elaborate S solo that interrupts last mvt's ch fugue). Fine B solo, "Flammis orci." **Practical
  Considerations:** Ch parts have wide ranges; some dif solo sections. Instr parts require execution
  of manneristic rhythms notated in small values and thus may need coaching to make intended
  rhetoric convincing.
Breitkopf & Härtel Wiesbaden. Lat. (sc, voc sc, ips).
Faber/G. Schirmer F505007. Lat. H. C. Robbins Landon. 1977 (voc sc, sc F505201, ipr).
Henle HN 5532 (*JHW* 22/1, cloth; HN 5531, paper). Lat. M. Helms, F. Stoltzfus. 1993 (sc; incl
  Sigismund Neukomm's expanded instr).
Kalmus 6248. Lat. (voc sc, ips).
 Bibliography: Becker-Glauch "Neue Forschungen" 199; Berkenstock "Smaller Sacred Composi-
  tions" 125-141; Landon *HCW* 2 234-236, *HCW* 3 58, *HCW* 5 268; Schenk "Genese."

III. SMALLER SACRED WORKS

Alleluia (G) (XXIIIc:3) (B 9) (c. 1768-69)
  SA; str org vc/cb; 1'. In MS copies always linked with, and following, duetto from *Applausus*
  "Dictamina mea" (see below); its 50 bars of 6/8 *presto* are too brief to stand alone. Lively, forth-
  right, balanced ABA with complete recapitulation.
 Bibliography: Becker-Glauch "Neue Forschungen" 208-210; Berkenstock "Smaller Sacred Compo-
  sitions" 142-148; Geiringer "Small Sacred Works" 463; Landon *HCW* 2 236.

Animae Deo gratae (*Agite properate ad aras*) (C) (XXIIIa:2) (B 7) (c. 1761-9)
  2ob 2tp timp 2vl vc/cb org; 5'. Festive offertory sim to final ch of "Applausus."
 Bibliography: Becker-Glauch "Neue Forschungen" 211-213; Berkenstock "Smaller Sacred Compositions" 149-151; Geiringer "Small Sacred Works" 467; Landon *HCW* 2 245-246.

Ave Regina (A) (XXIIIb:3) (B 2) (c. 1755)
  S; 2vl org vc/cb; III; 10'. I: Andante; long, florid solo II: Allegro; ch III: Adagio; solo & ch.
  Flow of warm, ornate melody reveals young Haydn's debt to Porpora, his teacher in Italian vocal

style. Small orch handled well, provides added interest. Cf. *Salve Regina* in E. **Practical Considerations:** S solo dif; ch parts easy.

Anton Böhm und Sohn. Lat. F. Schroeder. 1970; incl suggested cadenzas (sc, cps, ipa).

Bibliography: Becker-Glauch "*Ave Regina*," "Neue Forschungen" 175-176; Berkenstock "Smaller Sacred Compositions" 62-69; Landon *HCW* 1 166-168.

Dictamina mea (C) (—) (App.B.1 3) (1768)

SA; no ch; bn 2hn str(incl divisi va) org vc/cb; 4'. Duetto from *Applausus* which appears as a sacred contrafactum in MS copies; always linked with ch *Alleluia* in G (see above), hence its inclusion in this listing. Pairing may have been used at Epiphany Vespers for Gradual/Alleluia. Virtuosic solo style.

Bibliography: Berkenstock "Smaller Sacred Compositions" 142-148; Landon *HCW* 2 237.

Duetto ("Jam cordi") & Chorus ("Sit laus plena") (D) (XXIVa:2c, *deest*) (—) (c. 1763, 1755)

ST; 2ob 2tp 2hn timp str vc/cb org; II; 5'. I: Allegretto; florid ST duet (dif) II: Allegro molto; ch with florid AB concertante soloists. Contrafacta of an Esterházy cantata duet (see II. "Destatevi, o miei fidi") and a ch from (possibly) an early Haydn *Singspiel*. Short ch is of greater interest, because it shows young Haydn reveling in bold strokes and primary colors needed for effective theater music. Ch text from *Lauda Sion*. **Practical Considerations:** Easy ch parts, dif but brilliant orch writing.

Doblinger. Lat. H. C. Robbins Landon. 1990 (sc, voc sc, ips).

Bibliography: Landon *HCW* 1 169-179.

English Psalms (keys below) (ii, 181) (B 17-22) (1794)

SAB ch; VI; titles, timings below. On his second English visit, Haydn was asked to contribute to an edition of psalm tunes with metric English texts. These 6 charming, accessible settings resulted. Mainly hom and strophic, but extended, imitative Ps. 41 has a spirit reminiscent of "The heavens are telling." Ps. 50 heroic too; others triple-meter, more *gemütlich*. **Practical Considerations:** easy.

Bärenreiter BA 6232. Eng/Ger. Ulrich W. Zimmer. In open score (*Sechs Psalmen/Six Psalms*).

Broude Bros. Ltd. Eng. H. C. Robbins Landon. 1980. Published separately:

    CR 13 *Blest be the name of Jacob's God* (Ps. 31) (E♭) (2')

    CR 1 *How oft, instinct with warmth divine* (Ps. 26) (F) (3')

    CR 15 *Long life shall Israel's king behold* (Ps. 61) (E♭) (2')

    CR 14 *Lord, th'Almighty Monarch, spake, The* (Ps. 50) (C) (3')

    CR 2 *Maker of all! be Thou my guard* (Ps. 41) (D) (2')

    CR 16 *O let me in th'accepted hour* (Ps. 69) (A) (3')

Bibliography: Becker-Glauch "Neue Forschungen" 229-233; Berkenstock "Smaller Sacred Compositions" 174-183; Landon *HCW* 3 364-370.

Ens aeternum ("Walte gnädig") (G) (XXIIIa:3) (B 6) (c. 1761-9)

Str org vc/cb; 5'. May have been composed, like *Kleine Orgelmesse*, for Eisenstadt chapel of Barmherzige Brüdern. Later copies contain (unauthenticated) parts for winds and timpani. Geiringer, having in mind the expanded version, called it a "monumental chorus in *da capo* form. . . a solemn, powerful piece [combining] elegance of structure with textural solidity."

Breitkopf & Härtel. Lat, Ger. 1813; with additional instrs (sc).

Doblinger. Lat. H. C. Robbins Landon. (sc, ch sc, ips).

Bibliography: Becker-Glauch "Neue Forschungen" 210-211; Berkenstock "Smaller Sacred Compositions" 90-93; Geiringer "Small Sacred Works" 467; Landon *HCW* 2 245-246.

Hymnus de Venerabili (*Lauda Sion; Responsoria da Venerabili*) (B♭/d/A/E♭) (XXIIIc:4a-d) (B 8) (c. 1767)

2vl 2hn* org vc/cb; IV; 23'. Haydn's mature setting of text from Thomas Aquinas's great hymn for Feast of Corpus Christi. All 4 mvts feature slow tempi, simple ch textures, tutti accomp. Within these parameters, remarkable variety is achieved, so that celebration mingles with feelings of mystery and strength. Cf. *Motetto de Venerabili.*

Henle HN 302. Lat. I. Becker-Glauch. 1964; an "advance impression" from *JHW* 22/2 (voc sc, sc HN 184, ips HN 303-308).

Bibliography: Becker-Glauch "Neue Forschungen" 204-207, "Remarks" 207; Berkenstock "Smaller Sacred Compositions" 80-90; Geiringer "Small Sacred Works" 467; Landon *HCW* 2 245-246.

Il ritorno di Tobia: see *ritorno di Tobia, Il* under ORATORIOS AND CANTATAS.

Insanae et vanae curae ("Distraught with care") (d) (—) (B.1 4) (before 1798)

Fl 2ob 2bn 2tp 2hn 2tb timp str kb vc/cb; 6'. Contrafactum of "Svanisce in un momento" from *Il ritorno di Tobia*; D-hn parts given to high tps, timp added. Sections of Verdi-like ch declamation and chromaticism alternate with cantabile D-maj parts. Although this "motet" became one of Haydn's most popular sacred works, it is perhaps better suited to concert than service use.

Henle HN 5814 (*JHW* 28/1/II, cloth). Lat. E. F. Schmid. 1963 (sc of Second Part, *Il ritorno di Tobia*).

Novello 29 0214 01. Lat. "The accomp. arr. for the organ by J. Barnby"; (voc sc, ipr).

Bibliography: see *Il ritorno di Tobia;* also Becker-Glauch "Neue Forschungen" 233-235; Geiringer "Small Sacred Works" 464; Landon *HCW* 4 82-84.

Lauda Sion: see *Hymnus de Venerabili* and *Motetto de Venerabili Sacramento*

Libera me, Domine (d) (XXIIb:1) (B 16) (c. 1790)

T; 2vl* org vc/cb; 3'. Responsory of absolution from Catholic burial service. Stark ch declamation alternates with plainchant (T solo). Composed (? perhaps copied from another source) for an Esterházy court funeral. Landon felt this work could "form an apt conclusion for future liturgical performances of Mozart's *Requiem*," which lacks a setting of "Libera." Cf. "Non nobis, Domine." **Practical Considerations:** Instr parts double voices; easy.

Broude Bros. Ltd. CR 18. Lat/Eng. H. C. Robbins Landon.

Haydn-Mozart Presse (Universal Ed.) HMP 211. Lat. H. C. Robbins Landon. (ips HMP 212, cps HMP 213)

Bibliography: Becker-Glauch "Neue Forschungen" 222-224; Berkenstock "Smaller Sacred Compositions" 161-167; Landon *HCW* 2 738, "'Responsorium'"; Pohl *Haydn* 2 192.

Motetto de Venerabili Sacramento (*Lauda Sion*) (C) (XXIIIc:5) (B 1) (c. 1750-55)

SAB; 2ob 2tp str org vc/cb; IV; 11'. All 4 mvts are in C, 3/4 meter, and marked *Vivace*. An early setting of Corpus Christi music. Strong, simple ch hom predominates—Haydn's first embrace of Austrian popular church style. Solo passages brief, easy; orch often brilliant. Devotion in a very extroverted form. Cf. *Hymnus de Venerabili.* **Practical Considerations:** Ch T line low tess; good for festival or other large-choir presentations.

Doblinger 46 064. Lat. H. C. Robbins Landon. 1988 (sc, ch sc, ips).

Bibliography: Becker-Glauch "Neue Forschungen"172-174; Berkenstock "Smaller Sacred Compositions" 36-50; Landon *HCW* 1 147-157.

Motetto di Sancta Thecla ("Quis stellae radius") (F, C) (XXIIIa:4) (B 4) (c. 1762)
S; str org vc/cb; II; 9'. I: Allegro; recit. and long da capo aria with coloratura, high tess, cadenza (dif) II: Allegro; short declamatory ch (easy). Possibly a contrafactum of a cantata for Prince Nicolaus. As with those works (see II: "Qual dubbio omai"), emphasis is on S soloist's coloratura, which is at least as demanding as in Mozart's "Exultate, Jubilate." Concluding ch of 32 m is properly jubilant. **Practical Considerations:** Becker-Glauch suggested that Haydn's overture-like Symphony No. 9 may have served to introduce cantata; that would still make an interesting program.
Doblinger. Lat. H. C. Robbins Landon. 1989 (sc, voc sc, ips).
Bibliography: Becker-Glauch "Neue Forschungen" 178-183, "Version"; Geiringer "Small Sacred Works" 467; Landon *HCW* 1 495-503.

Non nobis, Domine (d) (XXIIIa:1) (B 15) (c. 1795, rev. c. 1802)
Org vc/cb; 4'. Offertory in *stile antico* (i.e., quasi-Renaissance polyphony), which continued in usage throughout 18th century. Builds to fine climax complete with pedal point, after careful imitative working out of theme. Text is Ps. 115, v. 1.
Anton Böhm und Sohn. Lat. A. M. Müller. Early version (sc, cps).
Concordia 98-1515. Lat/Eng. Karl Geiringer. Early version ("We Seek Not, God our Lord, for Glory").
Doblinger 45 300. Lat. H. C. Robbins Landon. Both versions.
Bibliography: Becker-Glauch "Neue Forschungen" 224-228; Berkenstock "Smaller Sacred Compositions" 167-173; Geiringer "Small Sacred Works" 460-467; Landon *HCW* 4, 77-84.

O coelitum beati (G/C) (XXIIIa:G9) (—) (c. 1765)
SAT; 2fl* 2tp str org vc/cb; II; 13'. I: Andante; contrafactum of an aria from a (lost) Haydn opera. Ornate da capo S solo with high C; str accomp II: Andante; festive "Alleluia" ch, untaxing SAT concertante solos; orch adds high tp. Not only a pleasing work but (in I) an interesting record of Haydn's operatic style. Discovered in 1983.
University College Cardiff Press (Cardiff, Wales) [sc with piano red]. Lat. H. C. Robbins Landon.
Bibliography: Landon/Jones *Haydn*, 59.

O Jesu, te invocamus ("Allmächt'ger, Preis dir und Ehre!") (C) (—) (B.1 6) (after 1768)
2ob 2tp str timp org vc/cb; 6'. Contrafactum of "O caelites, vos invocamus" from *Applausus.* Another monumental da capo ch, this one a spirited 3/4 Allegro. Ch largely hom but does not lack textural variety. Orch scoring is conventionally festive; Landon speaks of its "rather cool brilliance."
Anton Böhm und Sohn. Lat. A. M. Müller (sc, cps, ips).
Henle HN 5792 (*JHW* 27/2, cloth). Lat. H. Wiens & I. Becker-Glauch. 1969; sc of *Applausus.*
Bibliography: see *Applausus;* also Becker-Glauch "Neue Forschungen" 207; Geiringer "Small Sacred Works" 461-462.

Plausus honores date (C) (—) (B.1 7) (after 1764)

SSTB soli or ch; 2fl 2ob bn 2hn str kb vc/cb; I. Contrafactum of Esterházy Cantata *Da qual gioja improviso*, mvt II.

Quis stellae radius: see *Motetto di Sta. Thecla*

Salve Regina (E) (XXIIIb:1) (B 3) (c. 1756)

S; 2vl org vc/cb; V; 15'. I: Adagio; long florid solo (dif) II: Allegro-Adagio; ch sections framing shorter, simpler solo III: Allegro moderato; extended solo IV: Adagio; ch with dotted accomp (cf. Mozart C-Minor Mass "Qui tollis") V: Andante un poco; alternating ch and solo. The great sacred masterwork of Haydn's earliest years. In it he unites Italian vocal grace (cf. *Ave Regina*), Germanic structural and symphonic command, and newfound emotional depth. Apprenticeship with Porpora had improved Haydn's craftsmanship; deep affection for this antiphon spurred his imagination.

Doblinger 16 468. Lat. H. C. Robbins Landon. 1988 (sc, ips).

Bibliography: Badura-Skoda "Comoedie-Arien" 62; Becker-Glauch "Neue Forschungen" 174-176; Berkenstock "Smaller Sacred Compositions" 50-62; Brand *Messen* 16-29; Landon *HCW* 1 158-166; Mayeda "Porpora" 54-58; Schenk "Genese."

Salve Regina "a quattro voci ma Soli" (g) (XXIIIb:2) (B 11) (1771)

SATB [see below]; str org vc/cb; III; 18'. I: Adagio; extensive org solo (cf. *Little Organ Mass*), vocal tutti II: Allegro; vocal parts become only slightly more concertante III: Largo-Allegretto; T solo succeeded by vocal tutti sim to II. Haydn's original intent was "chamber music" for four soloists and a skilled organist. Assigning some vocal parts to a choir does not constitute a felony, however, and is provided for in Doblinger edition. This setting is roughly contemporary with Haydn's *Sturm und Drang* symphonies, experimental Op. 20 quartets, and deeply serious *Stabat Mater* (also in g). Like those works, it draws upon rich vocabulary of chromaticism, rhythmic displacement, and strong contrasts.

Associated Music Publishers AMP A489 [same as Doblinger edition].

Doblinger 46 006. Lat. H. C. Robbins Landon. 1965 (sc, voc sc, ips)

Bibliography: Becker-Glauch "Neue Forschungen" 215-218; Berkenstock "Smaller Sacred Compositions" 152-158; Geiringer "Small Sacred Works" 465; Landon *HCW* 2 249-251; Larsen *HÜb* 63, 171.

Sit laus plena: see *Duetto ("Jam cordi")*

Six English Psalms: see *English Psalms*

Te Deum [for Prince Nicolaus Esterházy] (C) (XXIIIc:1) (B 5) (c. 1762-4)

SATB; 2ob* 2tp timp 2vl org vc/cb; III; 7' (mvts linked by half-cadences). I: Allegro moderato; tutti succeeded by T solo II: Adagio; brief, chromatic, quiet tutti III: Allegro; SAB concertante soli, tutti; short fugue on "In te Domine speravi." One can hear Fux, Reutter, and other earlier Austrian masters in these measures. In outer mvts, vls scurry around with a truly Baroque variety of 16ths, 32nds, and triplets (cf. *Missa "Rorate coeli desuper"*). **Practical Considerations:** Solo parts easy. Younger or less-experienced choirs will find sturdy choral lines easy to negotiate; they are almost free of melismas. Ch T lies low, crossing B at times. Vls unison in *forte* passages, aiding performance by small orch.

Doblinger 46 003. Lat. H. C. Robbins Landon. 1967 (sc, voc sc, ips).

Universal Ed. Philharmonia 455 (min sc). Lat. H. C. Robbins Landon.

Bibliography: Becker-Glauch "Neue Forschungen" 192-194; Berkenstock "Smaller Sacred Compositions" 118-125; Brand *Messen* 31-36; Landon *HCW* 1 494-495; Pohl *Haydn* 1 242.

Te Deum [for Marie Therese] (C) (XXIIIc:2) (B 23) (1800)

Fl 2ob 2bn 3tp 2hn 3 tb* timp str org vc/cb; III; 10' (no breaks between mvts). Chronologically and artistically most mature of Haydn's short sacred works. Mastery of every musical element—melody, rhythm, texture, form, orchestration—displayed as readily here as in "London" symphonies, late Masses, or *The Creation*. Within its 194 measures one encounters Eighth Psalm Tone, deft use of sonata structure, infinitely supple choral textures, operatic sense of drama, and a magnificent double fugue. Med to dif.

Doblinger 46 001. Lat. H. C. Robbins Landon. 1959 (sc, voc sc, ips)

Kalmus 6247. Lat. (sc, voc sc, ips).

Novello. Lat. (voc sc, ipr).

Oxford Univ. Press 46.124. Lat/Eng. Ivor Atkins. 1932 (voc sc, ipr).

Oxford Univ. Press. Lat. Denis McCaldin. 1992. (sc, org continuo).

Associated/G. Schirmer AMP A488. Repr of Doblinger (voc sc, ipr).

Universal Ed. Philharmonia 454 (min sc). Lat. H. C. Robbins Landon.

Bibliography: Becker-Glauch "Neue Forschungen" 236-237, "Te Deum"; Berkenstock "Smaller Sacred Compositions" 183-192; Landon *HCW* 4 604-615.

Ten Commandments, The: see *Canons* under SECULAR WORKS.

IV. SECULAR WORKS

Abendlied zu Gott: see *Partsongs*

Alfred, König der Angelsachsen (XXX:5) (E 25a-c) (1796)

STT; STB; 2ob 2cl 2bn 2tp 2hn timp str vc/cb ?harp; III. I: ch "Triumph dir, Haldane" II: S aria with speaker "Ausgesandt vom Strahlenthrone" III: TT duet "Der Morgen graut." Fragments of incidental music to play performed for name-day festivities of Princess Marie Hermenegild. Ch "stirring and really warlike" (Landon), in 6/8 with prominent tp & timp (cf. *Missa in tempore belli*). Other numbers also effective in dramatic context.

Haydn-Mozart Press (Universal Ed.)(aria only). Ger. H. C. Robbins Landon. (vol *Haydn Arias for Soprano* incl "Arie des Schutzgeistes") (sc, voc sc, ips).

Bibliography: Landon *HCW* 4 106-108, 183-187.

Alles hat seine Zeit: see *Partsongs*

L'anima del filosofo (*Orfeo ed Euridice*) (XXVIII:13) (E 24) (1791)

SSTB; SATB (but see below); 2fl 2ob 2cl 2ehn 2bn 2hn 2tp 2tb timp harp str kb vc/cb; full. Several fine ch are part of this *opera seria* composed for Haydn's first London visit in 1791. Rosemary Hughes found the opera "hopelessly undramatic" but glimpsed Haydn's future achievements in Mass and oratorio in its "ominous C-minor opening chorus, the deceptive gaiety of the women's chorus at the wedding, the warm and tender funeral dirge, and in the choruses of the spirits of the underworld." In addition to SATB or SSBB numbers, opera includes 2-part men's and women's ch. One ch for women, "Finché circola il vigore," also arr by Haydn for STB and performed in London as "Su cantiamo, su beviamo." **Practical Considerations:** Easy ch parts nevertheless require mature voices if full orch used (see esp. female ch Act IV).

Henle HN 5752 (*JHW* 25/13, cloth; HN 5751, paper). It. H. Wirth. 1974 (sc).

Haydn-Mozart Presse (Universal Ed.). It. H. C. Robbins Landon. (sc, perf mat).

Bibliography: Landon *HCW* 3 323-354; Hughes *Haydn* 200-201.

Augenblick, Der: see *Partsongs*

Beredsamkeit, Die: see *Partsongs*

Betrachtung des Todes: see *Partsongs*

Canons (XXVII) (I) (c. 1791-9)

For equal voices 2-8 pts. Great majority of Haydn's canons are set to German texts and reflect their composer's distinctive attitudes toward life. Thus his setting of Ninth Commandment ("Thou shalt not covet thy neighbor's wife"), for example, is rather more sprightly and sly than otherwise. But these works cannot be dismissed as playful trifles; their span of emotion includes great feeling as well as wit and irony. Contrapuntal intricacies often demand careful rehearsal and strong musicianship. Following complete edition, several octavo selections are listed with brief descriptions of their contents.

Henle HN 5882 (*JHW* 31, cloth). Ger, Eng, Lat, It. Otto Erich Deutsch. 1959 (sc).

Oxford Univ. Press. W. G. Whittaker. Eng. (*[56] Rounds and Canons by Haydn*).

Peters Ed. 6999. Eng. W. Weismann. Incl *Ten Commandments* and 14 others; Eng versions by Jean Lunn (*24 Canons*).

Presser 352-00010. Eng/Ger. Paul Boepple. For 3-5 eq v. (*The Holy Ten Commandments*)

G. Schirmer LG 51812. Eng. Bird, L. Van Camp. TTBB (*Three Canons*).

Bibliography: Deutsch "Kanons"; Heer "Kanons"; Landon *HCW* 3 357-360; Mies "Singkanons."

Danklied zu Gott: see *Partsongs*

Da qual gioja improviso: see under *ORATORIOS AND CANTATAS*

Daphnens einziger Fehler: see *Partsongs*

Destatevi, o miei fidi: see under *ORATORIOS AND CANTATAS*

Dr. Harington's Compliment (A) (XXVIb:3) ((H 3) (1794)

S; SSTB ch or soli; kb; 6'. Written for performance in home of one of Haydn's English friends, this is a lovely but curious amalgam of song, piano variations, and ch. **Practical Considerations:** Singer and pianist are allotted most attention; conceivably short ch could be repeated at end. Would fit easily into a *Liederabend* program with comparable works by Haydn, Mozart, Beethoven, Schubert, or even Brahms. Kb dif, solo med.

Broude Bros. Ltd. H. C. Robbins Landon.

Bibliography: Landon *HCW* 3 403-404.

L'anima del filosofo See *anima* ...

Feuersbrunst, Die (XXIXb:A) (E 16b) (c. 1775-8)

S 5T B; 2fl 2ob 2cl 2bn 2hn 2tp timp str kb vc/cb; 27; full. Two simple ch conclude Acts I and II of this marionette *Singspiel*. Plot, characters derive from Venetian *commedia dell'arte*. Comedy and some *Sturm-und-Drang* moments in music. Cf. *Philemon und Baucis*.

Henle HN 5626 (*JHW* 24/3, cloth). Ger. 1992 (sc).

Schott (London) 10779. Ger, Eng. H. C. Robbins Landon. 1963 (voc sc, ipr).

Bibliography: Landon *HCW* 2 517-522, "Marionette."

Frauen, An die: see *Partsongs*

Greis, Der: see *Partsongs*

Harmonie in der Ehe, Die: see *Partsongs*

Mare Clausum (F/D) (XXIVa:9) (D 9) (c. 1794)

B; fl 2ob 2cl 2bn 2hn 2tp timp str; II; 15'. Fragment of an incomplete cantata or oratorio. I: B solo with full orch II: Festive D-maj ch sim those in "Nelson" Mass, late oratorios. Easy ch parts, interesting and fresh program material. Quaint text is allegory of England as maritime power.

Doblinger DM 90. Eng. H. C. Robbins Landon. 1990 (sc, cps, ips).

Bibliography: Landon *HCW* 3 356.

Mehrstimmige Gesänge: see *Partsongs*

Nor can I think/Thy great endeavors: see *Mare Clausum*

Partsongs ("Aus des Ramlers Lyrischer Blumenlese") (XXVc:1-13) (H 6-18) (1796-9)

3- and 4-pt mixed voicings—see below; kb vc*; 13; 3-6' ea. "Written *con amore* in happy hours, not commissioned," Haydn told Griesinger, and results bear him out. Intimate, somewhat "unbuttoned" pieces that rank with finest partsongs of Schubert or Brahms. Although subject matter usually earthy and treated with wit, some fine sacred texts included. Vocal parts (easy to med) can be sung by soloists or ch; vc can generally be omitted, and org can substitute for kb where necessary.

Bärenreiter BA 901. Ger. Bernhard Paumgartner. 1951; in series *Concerto vocale* (*Die drei- und vierstimmigen Gesänge*).

Henle HN 5872 (*JHW* 30, cloth). Ger. Paul Mies. 1958 (*Mehrstimmige Gesänge*) (sc).

[Separate titles, with issues by various publishers:]

Abendlied zu Gott (SATB)
Arista AE 137. Eng. (*Evening Song to God*)
G. Schirmer LG 51067. Eng/Ger. (*Evensong*)

Alles hat seine Zeit (SATB)
Arista AE 132. Eng. (*Everything in its Place*)

Augenblick, Der (SATB)
Arista AE 134. Eng. (*The Moment*)

Beredsamkeit, Die (SATB)
Arista AE 131. Eng. (*Eloquence*)
Elkan-Vogel 1133. Eng/Ger. (*Eloquence*)
B. Schotts Söhne C 37 674. Ger.

Betrachtung des Todes (STB)

Aus dem Danklied zu Gott (SATB)
    Arista AE 136. Eng. (*Thanksgiving Song to God*)
    Bärenreiter BA 6237. Ger. (*Danklied*)
    Anton Böhm und Sohn. Lat. (*Tui sunt coeli*) (sc, cps, ips)
    Doblinger. Ger.
    Presser 352-00084. Eng. (*Tis Thou to Whom All Honor*)
Daphnens einziger Fehler (TTB)
Frauen, An die (TTB)
Greis, Der (SATB)
    Arista AE 138. Eng. (*The Old Man*)
    Broude International RM 2024. Eng/Ger. (*The Old Man*)
    B. Schotts Söhne CHB 271. Ger.
Harmonie in der Ehe, Die (SATB)
    Arista AE 133. Eng. (*Harmony in Marriage*)
    B. Schotts Söhne C 38 152. Ger.
Vetter, An den (SAT)
Warnung, Die (SATB)
    Arista AE 135. Eng. (*An Admonition*)
Wider den Übermut (SATB)
    Arista AE 139. Eng. (*Invocation*)
Bibliography: Landon *HCW* 4 189-193; Lunn "Quest"; Mies "Textdichter."

Philemon und Baucis (XXIXb:2) (E 12) (1773, rev c. 1776)
    2S 2T 2 speaking roles; 2fl 2ob 2bn 2hn 2tp timp str kb vc/cb; 8; one act. Marionette opera (1773) in *Singspiel* form (1776). Besides fine D-minor overture and some pleasant arias, contains two extended ch scenes that could stand alone in concert or be performed as part of a selection from the opera. Opening ch is "Thunderstorm" painted with broad brushstrokes, well suited to fairy-tale action. Ch style generally hom declamation, although alternating unison men's and women's voices are also used effectively. **Practical Considerations:** Ch parts easy but need mature voices for projection.
Bärenreiter. Ger. H. C. Robbins Landon. 1776 version (sc, voc sc)
 Henle HN 5612 (*JHW* 24/1, cloth; HN 5611, paper). Ger. J. Braun. 1971; reconstruction of 1773 version (sc).
T. Presser. Eng ver Cecil Adkins. (sc, voc sc, ipr).
 Bibliography: Becker-Glauch "Neue Forschungen" 221; Landon *HCW* 2 257-259, "Marionette," *Symphonies* 276, 315.

Qual dubbio omai: see under *ORATORIOS AND CANTATAS*

Storm, The (*Der Sturm*) (d-D) (XXIVa:8) (D 8a,b) (1792, rev 1793)
    SATB; 2fl 2ob 2cl* 2bn 2tp 2hn 2tb* timp str; 14. Construction sim "Insanae et vanae curae," with alternating turbulent and peaceful sections. So impressed the English that Haydn was urged from all sides to create a Handelian oratorio. Vienna success in rev version equally impressed Swieten, Haydn's future collaborator [* in this listing shows instruments added in 1793].
Breitkopf & Härtel (Wiesbaden). Ger, It. Sc based on 1793 rev. (*Der Sturm*)
Doblinger DM 316a. Ger. F. Burkhart. 1958; sc based on 1793 rev. (*Der Sturm*) (sc DM 316, ch sc, ips).

Editio Musica (Budapest)/Doblinger. Eng. F. Szekeres. Sc based on autograph of 1792, and thus incomplete (sc, voc sc, ips).
Bibliography: Landon *HCW* 3 354-356; Olleson "Griesinger" 37.

Su cantiamo, su beviamo (A) (ii, 433) (D 7) (c. 1791)
STB; STB ch; fl 2ob 2tp 2hn timp str vc/cb; 8'. Rev number from *L'anima del filosofo,* Act II. Haydn's ch writing in this opera is varied and colorful; happy ch of (originally) "Amorini divini" appeals immediately. **Practical Considerations:** Suitable for young or amateur singers. Concertante solo parts can be assigned to ch members.
Doblinger. It. H. C. Robbins Landon. ("Su, cantiamo") (sc, voc sc, ips)
Bibliography: Landon *HCW* 3 356-357.

Triumph dir, Haldane see *Alfred, König der Angelsachsen*

Twelve Sentimental Catches and Glees (XXXIc:16) (App. H 1-12) (c. 1794)
3 eq v; kb; 12'. Haydn's friend Willoughby Bertie, Earl of Abingdon, induced him to write "Harp or Piano-Forte" accompaniments to these insignificant but pleasant pieces, for which the Earl himself had written melodies. Catches are sung in manner of a round, while glees are hom. **Practical Considerations:** Voc parts, accomp both undemanding.
Bibliography: Landon *HCW* 3 361-364.

Vetter, An den: see *Partsongs*

Warnung, Die: see *Partsongs*

Wider den Übermut: see *Partsongs*

ABBREVIATIONS AND SYMBOLS

Pitch classification used in this catalog:

$$C_2 \qquad C_1 \qquad C \qquad c \qquad c^1 \qquad c^2 \qquad c^3$$

(The form of the name changes with each C, proceeding upward.)

*	optional instrument(s)
accomp	accompaniment, accompanied
bn	bassoon
cbn	contrabassoon
ch	choir, chorus, choral
ch sc	choral score on sale
cl	clarinet
cps	individual choral parts (S, A, T, B) on sale
dif	difficult or difficulty
ehn	English horn
Eng	English
fl	flute
Fr	French
Ger	German
hn	horn
hom	homophonic texture
HS	Haydn-Society *Gesamt-Ausgabe*, ed. Brand et al. 4 vols. Boston, 1951.
JHW	*J. Haydn: Werke*, ed. J. Haydn-Institut. 50 vols. Cologne, 1958- .
instr(s)	instrument(s), instrumentation
ipr	full score and instrumental parts on rental
ips	instrumental parts on sale
It	Italian
kb	harpsichord or piano
M	*J. Haydns Werke*, ed. E. Mandyczewski et al. 10 vols. Leipzig, 1907-33.
med	medium
ob	oboe
orch	orchestra, orchestral
org	organ
perf mat	performance material
red	reduction
repr	reprint
rev	revised, revision
sc	full score on sale
sim	similar (to)
str	2vl, 1va
tb	trombone
tess	tessitura
tp	trumpet
timp	timpani
va	viola
vc/cb	cello doubled by bass
vl	violin
voc sc	vocal score on sale

12

SPECIALIZED WORKLISTS

This chapter is designed mainly for those seeking materials suited to a particular kind of performing group or situation. It is divided into eight major sections:

I.	Equal Voices and/or Younger Choirs
II.	Changing Voices
III.	High School Choirs
IV.	College and Professional Choirs
V.	Women's Choirs
VI.	Men's Choirs
VII.	Seasons, Services, or Occasions in the Church Year
VIII.	Choral Music in Volumes of the Cologne Haydn Institute

The comprehensive performance-related information given in Chapter 11 for each work is not repeated here. However, unlike Chapter 11, this chapter does include selected excerpts and arrangements in its listings. In the case of excerpts and arrangements, no evaluation or endorsement of their editorial procedures is implied by their inclusion here.

The new complete edition of Joseph Haydn's works (*JHW*) is published by the Joseph Haydn-Institute of Cologne under the direction of Georg Feder. Volumes in the series, generally cloth-bound, are available individually from G. Henle Verlag. In many cases, performing materials have also been issued (see Chapter 11). In the outline of the series given below, all present and projected volumes of interest to the choral conductor (i.e., containing significant choral music) are listed, with an asterisk placed beside those now (1995) available.

I. EQUAL VOICES AND/OR YOUNGER CHOIRS
    24 Canons (Eng. ver. Jean Lunn)

II. CHANGING VOICES
    24 Canons (Eng. ver. Jean Lunn)
    Vetter, An den (see *Partsongs*)
    Su cantiamo, su beviamo

III. HIGH SCHOOL CHOIRS
    Abendlied zu Gott (see *Partsongs*)
    Alles hat seine Zeit (see *Partsongs*)
    Augenblick, Der (see *Partsongs*)
    Ave Regina
    Beredsamkeit, Die (see *Partsongs*)
    Danklied zu Gott (see *Partsongs*)
    English Psalms
    Ens aeternum
    Greis, Der (see *Partsongs*)
    Harmonie in der Ehe, Die (see *Partsongs*)
    Hymnus de Venerabili
    Missa (*Theresienmesse*)
    Missa brevis in F Major
    Missa brevis Sancti Joannis de Deo
    Missa Cellensis (*Mariazellermesse*)
    Missa Sancti Bernardi von Offida (*Heiligmesse*)
    Motetto de Venerabili Sacramento
    Non nobis, Domine
    Salve Regina in E Major
    Te Deum for Prince Nicolaus Esterházy
    Warnung, Die (see *Partsongs*)
    Wider den Übermut (see *Partsongs*)

IV. COLLEGE AND PROFESSIONAL CHOIRS
    Creation, The
    Insanae et vanae curae
    Missa (*Harmoniemesse*)
    Missa (*Schöpfungsmesse*)
    Missa Cellensis in honorem B.V.M. (*Cäcilienmesse*)
    Missa in angustiis (*Nelsonmesse*)
    Missa in honorem B.V.M. (*Grosse Orgelmesse*)
    Missa in tempore belli (*Paukenmesse*)
    Missa Sancti Nicolai
    Philemon und Baucis
    Qual dubbio omai
    Seasons, The
    Salve Regina in G Minor
    Storm, The
    Te Deum for Empress Marie Therese

V. WOMEN'S CHOIRS
    24 *Canons* (Eng. ver. Jean Lunn)
    Finché circola il vigore (see *L'anima del filosofo*)
    Holy Ten Commandments, The (ed. Boepple)
    Missa brevis Sancti Joannis de Deo (arr. Habel)

VI. MEN'S CHOIRS
    24 *Canons* (Eng. ver. Jean Lunn)
    Daphnens einziger Fehler (see *Partsongs*)
    Frauen, An die (see *Partsongs*)
    Holy Ten Commandments, The (ed. Boepple)
    Missa brevis Sancti Joannis de Deo (arr. Habel)
    Three Canons (ed. Bird & Van Camp)

VII.   SEASONS, SERVICES, OR OCCASIONS IN THE CHURCH YEAR
    Christmas:
        Missa Sancti Nicolai
    Lent:
        Seven Last Words, The
        Stabat Mater
    Feast of Corpus Christi:
        Hymnus de Venerabili
        Motetto de Venerabili Sacramento
    Feasts of Our Lady:
        Ave Regina
        Missa Cellensis in hon. B.V.M. (*Cäcilienmesse*)
        Missa in hon. B.V.M. (*Grosse Orgelmesse*)
        Salve Regina in E Major
        Salve Regina in G Minor
    Funerals and Memorial Services:
        Libera me, Domine
        Missa Sunt bona mixta malis

VIII. CHORAL VOLUMES IN THE COLOGNE HAYDN-INSTITUTE SERIES

Reihe XXII
    Band 1: *Stabat Mater**
    Band 2: Church Music, 1st set of smaller works
    Band 3: Church Music, 2nd set of smaller works

Reihe XXIII
    Band 1: Masses No. 1-4*
    Band 2: Masses No. 5-8*
    Band 3: Masses No. 9-10*
    Band 4: Mass No. 11*
    Band 5: Mass No. 12*

Reihe XXIV
    Band 1: *Philemon und Baucis**
    Band 2: *Die Feuersbrunst*

Reihe XXV
    Band 13: *L'anima del filosofo ossia Orfeo ed Euridice**

Reihe XXVII
    Band 1: Early Cantatas
    Band 2: *Appplausus**
    Band 3: Cantatas, Choruses, and Theatre Music

Reihe XXVIII
    Band 1: *Il ritorno di Tobia**
    Band 2: *The Seven Last Words* (choral version)*
    Band 3: *The Creation*
    Band 4: *The Seasons* (I, II)

Reihe XXX
    Mehrstimmige Gesänge*

Reihe XXXI
    Canons*

Reihe XXXIII
    Arrangements and Sketches

Reihe XXXIV
    Supplement
    Band 1: *The Seven Last Words* (arrangement by Joseph Friebert)

APPENDIX

HAYDN'S *APPLAUSUS* LETTER

[Undated: but written c. March 1768]

Since I cannot be present myself at this *Applaus* [*sic : Applausus*], I have found it necessary to provide one or two explanations concerning its execution, *viz.*:

First, I would ask you to observe strictly the tempi of all the arias and recitatives, and since the whole text applauds, I would rather have the allegros taken a bit more quickly than usual, especially in the very first ritornello and in one or two of the recitatives; but no less in the two bass arias.

Secondly: for the overture all you need to play is an allegro and an andante, for the opening ritornello takes the place of the final allegro. If I knew the day of the performance, I might perhaps send you a new overture by that time.

Thirdly: in the accompanied recitatives, you must observe that the accompaniment should not enter until the singer has quite finished his text, even though the score often shows the contrary. For instance, at the beginning where the word "metamorphosis" is repeated, and the orchestra comes in at "-phosis", you must nevertheless wait until the last syllable is finished and then enter quickly; for it would be ridiculous if you would fiddle away the word from the singer's mouth, and understand only the words "quae metamo...". But I leave this to the harpsichord player, and all the others must follow him. N.B.: our scholars in Eisenstadt—and there are very few—disputed a great deal over the word "metamorphosis"; one wanted the penultimate syllable short, the other long; and despite the fact that in Italian one says "metamorfosi," I have always heard it pronounced "metamorphosis" in Latin; should I have made a mistake, the error can be easily corrected.

Fourthly: that the fortes and pianos are written correctly throughout, and should be observed exactly; for there is a very great difference between *piano* and *pianissimo, forte,* and *fortiss[imo]*, between *crescendo* and *forzando*, and so forth. It should be noted, too, when in the score the one or the other *forte* or *piano* is not marked throughout all the parts, that the copyist should rectify this when preparing the performance material.

Fifthly: I have often been annoyed at certain violinists in various concerts, who absolutely ruined the so-called ties—which are among the most beautiful things in music—in that they bounced the bows off the tied note, which should have been joined to the preceding note. And so I would point out to the first violinist that it would be silly to play the following (as found in bar 47)

in which the first two notes are to be taken on one bow—in such a disagreeable and mistaken way as

all staccato, and as if there were no ties present.

Sixthly: I would ask you to use two players on the viola part throughout, for the inner parts sometimes need to be heard more than the upper parts, and you will find in all my compositions that the viola rarely doubles the bass.

Seventhly: if you have to copy two sets of violin parts, the copyist should see that they do not turn their pages at the same time, because this takes away a great deal of strength from an orchestra with only a few musicians. The copyist should also see that the *da capo* signs ss are written in one of the violins parts as in the score, but in the other he can put the *da capo* a couple of bars after the sign ss, and then write the sign in its proper place.

Eighthly: I suggest that the two boys [soloists] in particular have a clear pronunciation, singing slowly in recitatives so that one can understand every syllable; and likewise they should follow the method of singing the recitation whereby, for example

quae me-ta- mor - pho - sis

must be sung

quae me-ta- mor - pho - sis

and not

quae me-ta- mor - pho - sis

The penultimate note 'g' drops out entirely, and this applies to all similar cases. I rely on the skill of the tenor, who will explain such things to the boys.

Ninthly: I hope for at least three or four rehearsals for the entire work.

Tenthly: in the soprano aria the bassoon can be omitted if absolutely necessary, but I would rather have it present, at least when the bass is *obbligato* throughout. And I prefer a band with 3 bass instruments—'cello, bassoon and double bass—to one with 6 double basses and 3 'celli, because certain passages stand our better that way.

Finally I ask everyone, and especially the musicians, for the sake of my reputation as well as their own, to be as diligent as possible: if I have perhaps not guessed the taste of these gentlemen, I am not to be blamed for it, for I know neither the persons nor the place, and that fact that they were concealed from me really made my work very difficult. For the rest, I hope that this *Applausus* will please the poet, the worthy musicians, and the honourable reverend *Auditorio*, all of whom I greet with profound respect, and for whom I remain

Your most obedient servant,
Giuseppe Haydn.
Maestro di Cap: di Sua Alt:
Sere: Prencipe d'Estorhazy.

As quoted and translated in H. C. Robbins Landon, *Haydn: Chronicle and Works.* Vol. 2, *Haydn at Eszterháza 1766-1790* (Bloomington and London, 1978), 146-148. See also Haydn *CCLN,* 9-11. Used by permission of the translator and Indiana University Press.

ARIA "QUANDO MI DONA"
from *Il ritorno di Tobia*

Tenor Carl Friberth, the son of a lower-Austrian schoolteacher, studied with Vienna court composer Giuseppe Bonno, thereby absorbing the finer points of Italian singing style from one of its masters. He was one of Haydn's favorite artists and is mentioned in his letter regarding the *Stabat Mater* performance in Vienna of 1768 (see Chapter 5). The title role of *Il ritorno di Tobia* (1775) was written with his talents in mind. Among the surviving performance materials for *Tobia* is a short score of the aria "Quando mi dona" with the vocal line richly ornamented; it may or may not be an autograph, but it is undoubtedly a contemporary copy. E. F. Schmid, who edited the oratorio for *JHW*, suggested that Haydn could have prepared it for the ill-fated 1784 remounting in Vienna. That occasion was to have featured the tenor Valentin Adamberger, who apparently did not possess Friberth's skill at free embellishment—and in the event, pulled out of the performances (again, see Chapter 5).

If Haydn caused this short score to be made, he could well have been remembering Friberth's earlier performances of the role. The ornamented version is, at the very least, an 18th-century realization of the aria using widely accepted practices. This excerpt—not quite half the aria, plus the cadenzas—is reprinted, with portions translated, from E. F. Schmid, "Joseph Haydn und die vokale Zierpraxis seiner Zeit, dargestellt an einer Arie seines Tobias-Oratoriums," in Bence Szabolcsi and Dénes Bartha, eds., *Bericht über die Internationale Konferenz zum Andenken Joseph Haydns. Budapest, 17.-22. September 1959* (Budapest, 1961), 122-129. The ornamented version of the aria is also given in *JHW* 28/1.

BIBLIOGRAPHY

This general bibliography comprises all known works of scholarship and criticism pertaining to the choral music of Joseph Haydn in some way. Works to which the present volume refers are listed first, in *alphabetical* order according to their short citations. Any remaining works by the same author are listed after that, in *chronological* order beginning with the most recent.

Abraham, Gerald, ed. *The Age of Humanism 1540-1630* [*NOH* 4]. Vol. 4 of *The New Oxford History of Music*. London, 1968.

Albrecht *Bedeutung* Albrecht, Hans, ed. *Die Bedeutung der Zeichen Keil, Strich und Punkt bei Mozart*. Kassel, 1957.

Anderson *Letters of Mozart* Anderson, Emily, ed. *The Letters of Mozart and His Family*. 3 vols. London, 1938.

Arndt, E. M. *Reisen durch einen Theil Teutschlands, Ungarns, Italiens und Frankreichs in den Jahren 1798 und 1799*. 2nd ed. 4 vols. Leipzig, 1804.

Arnold, Denis. "Haydn's Counterpoint and Fux's Gradus." *Monthly Musical Record* 87/980 (March-April 1957), 52-58.

Aull, Otto. *Eisenstadt. Ein Führer durch seine Geschichte und Kunst*. Eisenstadt, 1931.

Bach *Versuch* Bach, Carl Philipp Emanuel. *Versuch über die wahre Art das Clavier zu spielen*. . . . 2 vols. Berlin, 1753-62. (2) Facs. ed. L. Hoffmann-Erbrecht. Leipzig, 1957. (3) Eng. trans. William J. Mitchell as *Essay on the True Art of Keyboard Playing*. . . . New York, 1949.

Bach, Hans-Elmar. "Die Chorwerke hielten Haydns Andenken lebendig. Zum 250. Geburtstag des Komponisten." *Lied und Chor. Zeitschrift für das Chorwesen* 74/5 (1982), 108.

Badura-Skoda "Comoedie-Arien" Badura-Skoda, Eva. "'Teutsche Comoedie-Arien' und Joseph Haydn." In Schwarz *junge Haydn*, 59-73.

Badura-Skoda *Proceedings* _____, ed. *Proceedings of the International Joseph Haydn Congress*. Munich, 1986.

_____. "The Influence of the Viennese Popular Comedy on Haydn and Mozart." *Proceedings of the Royal Musical Association* 100 (1974), 185-199.

Badura-Skoda, Eva, and Paul Badura-Skoda. *Interpreting Mozart on the Keyboard*. Trans. L. Black. London, 1962.

Badura-Skoda, Paul. "On Ornamentation in Haydn." Trans. by F. E. Kirby of "Beiträge." *Piano Quarterly* 34/135 (1986), 38-48.

_____. "Beiträge zu Haydns Ornamentik." *Musica* 36/5 (1982), 409-418. Corrections added 36/6 (1982), 575. [Eng. trans. see "On Ornamentation."]

_____. "Über Mozarts Tempi." *Österreichische Musikzeitschrift* 9 (1954), 347-351.

Barea *Vienna*   Barea, Ilsa. *Vienna*. New York, 1966.

Barnett "Slurring"   Barnett, Dene. "Non-uniform Slurring in 18th Century Music: Accident or Design?" *The Haydn Yearbook* 10 (1978), 179-199.

Barrett-Ayres "Words"   Barrett-Ayres, Reginald. "Haydn's 'Seven Last Words.'" *The Musical Times* 108/1494 (August 1967), 699-700.

Bartha "Repertory"   Bartha, Dénes. "Haydn's Italian Opera Repertory at Esterháza Palace." In *New Looks at Italian Opera. Essays in Honor of Donald J. Grout*. Wm. W. Austin, ed. Ithaca (NY), 1968.

Bartha "'Sieben Worte'"   _____. "A 'Sieben Worte' Változatainak Keletkezése az Esterhazy-Gyüjtemény Kéziratainak Tükrében." *Zenetudományi Tanulmányok* 8 (1960), 107ff. [Joseph Friebert's vocal version of *The Seven Words*.]

Bartha/Somfai   Bartha, Dénes and László Somfai. *Haydn als Opernkapellmeister. Die Haydn-*
Opernkapellmeister   *Documente der Esterházy-Opernsammlung*. Budapest, 1960.

Baumgärtner, Paul. "Gottfried van Swieten als Textdichter von Haydns Oratorien." Diss., University of Vienna, 1930.

Bayer, Friedrich. "Über den Gebrauch der Instrumente in den Kirchen- und Instrumentalwerken von Wolfgang Amadeus Mozart." *Studien zur Musikwissenschaft* 14 (1927), 33-74.

Becker-Glauch "*Ave*   Becker-Glauch, Irmgard. "Joseph Haydn's *Ave Regina* in A." In Lan-
Regina."   don/Chapman *Studies*, 68-75.

Becker-Glauch "Neue   _____. "Neue Forschungen zu Haydns Kirchenmusik." *Haydn-Studien*
Forschungen"   2/3 (May 1970), 167-241.

Becker-Glauch   _____. "Remarks on the Late Church Music." In Larsen *Haydn Studies*,
"Remarks"   206-207.

Becker-Glauch   _____. "Joseph Haydns 'Te Deum' für die Kaiserin. Eine Quellenstudie."
"Te Deum"   In *Colloquium Amicorum Joseph Schmidt-Görg zum 70. Geburtstag*, 1-10. Ed. Siegfried Kross and Hans Schmidt. Bonn, 1967.

Becker-Glauch "Version"   _____. "The Apparently Authentic Version of the Motetto de Sancta Thecla (Hob. XXIIIa:4)." In Larsen *Haydn Studies*, 82-84.

_____. "Haydn, Franz Joseph." In *International Musicological Society - International Association of Music Libraries. RISM* A/i/4 (1974), 140-279. Kassel, 1974.

_____. "Die Kirchenmusik des jungen Haydn." In Schwarz *junge Haydn*, 74-85.

_____. *Kritischer Bericht. Messe Nr. 11.* 23/4 of Haydn *JHW*. 1969.

_____. "Vorwort." In *Messe Nr. 11*, vi-ix. 23/4 of Haydn *JHW*. 1967.

_____. "Wiederaufgefundene Kirchenmusikwerke Joseph Haydns." *Die Musikforschung* 17/4 (October-December 1964), 413-414.

Becker-Glauch/Wiens "Vorwort" *Applausus* — Becker-Glauch, I., and Wiens, Heinrich. "Vorwort." In *Applausus*, vii-x. 27/2 of Haydn *JHW*. 1969.

Benyovszky, Karl. "Johann Nepomuk Hummel und Eisenstadt." *Burgenländische Heimatblätter* (Eisenstadt) 6/3 (September 1937), 41-52.

Bergmann, Alfred. "Kleinere Mitteilungen. Haydns 42 Canons." *Jahrbuch der Sammlung Kippenberg* (Leipzig) 6 (1926), 299-306.

Berkenstock "Smaller Sacred Compositions" — Berkenstock, James Turner. "The smaller sacred compositions of Joseph Haydn." 2 vols. Ph. D. diss., Northwestern University, 1975.

Bernhardt, Reinhold. "Aus der Umwelt der Wiener Klassiker. Freiherr Gottfried van Swieten (1734-1803)." *Der Bär. Jahrbuch von Breitkopf & Härtel* 6/9 (1929-30), 74-164.

_____. "'Der für die Sünden der Welt gemarterte Jesus.' Eine Händel-Partitur aus Joseph Haydns Besitz." *Die Musik* 21/4 (January 1929), 249-252.

Biba "Beispiele" — Biba, Otto. "Beispiele für die Besetzungsverhältnisse bei Aufführungen von Haydns Oratorien in Wien zwischen 1784 und 1808." *Haydn-Studien* 4 (1978), 94.

Biba "Pflege" — _____. "Die Pflege der Kirchenmusik in der Piaristenkirche." In *Festschrift 250 Jahr Piaristenkirche Maria Treu*, 45ff. Vienna, 1969.

Biba "Werke" — _____. "Die kirchenmusikalischen Werke Haydns." In Mraz *Haydn in seiner Zeit*, 142-151.

_____. "Der falsche Haydn." *Singende Kirche. Zeitschrift für katholische Kirchenmusik* 29/6 (1981-82), 281-282.

_____. "Instrumentale Kirchenmusik rund um Joseph Haydn." *Singende Kirche. Zeitschrift für katholische Kirchenmusik* 29/5 (1981-82), 227-229.

_____. "Wofür Haydn seine kirchenmusikalischen Werke geschrieben hat." *Singende Kirche. Zeitschrift für katholische Kirchenmusik* 29/4 (1981-82), 172-175. Eng. trans. in *Sacred Music* 109/4 (1982), 7-10.

_____. "Joseph Haydns kirchenmusikalische Werke—heute aufgeführt." *Singende Kirche. Zeitschrift für katholische Kirchenmusik* 29/3 (1981-82), 111-114.

_____. "Die Wiener Kirchenmusik um 1783." In *Beiträge zur Musikgeschichte des 18. Jahrhunderts*, 7-79. Gerda Mraz, ed. [*Jahrbuch für österreichische Kulturgeschichte* 1/2.] Eisenstadt, 1971.

Bittel, Hermann. "Joseph Haydn als Kirchenmusiker." *Musik und Altar* 12/1 (July 1959), 3-5.

Blakeney, Edward H., ed. *Twenty-Four Hymns of the Western Church.* London, 1930.

Bogati, A. "Gregor Joseph Werner. Biographisches über den Vorgänger Haydns in Kapellmeister-Amt zu Eisenstadt," *Burgenländische Heimat-Blätter* (Eisenstadt) 5/1 (March 1936), 2-4.

Bouyer, Louis. *Life and Liturgy.* London and New York, 1956.

Boyden "Evolution"   Boyden, David D. "The Evolution of the Bow During Haydn's Lifetime." In Larsen *Haydn Studies*, 222-224.

_____. "Der Geigenbogen von Corelli bis Tourte." In *Violinspiel und Violinmusik in Geschichte und Gegenwart: Bericht über den Internationalen Kongress am Institut für Aufführungspraxis der Hochschule für Musik und darstellende Kunst in Graz, vom 25. Juni bis 2. Juli 1972,* 295-310. Beiträge zur Aufführungspraxis, 3. Vera Schwarz, ed. Vienna, c.1975.

Brand *Messen*   Brand, Carl Maria. *Die Messen von Joseph Haydn.* (Musik und Geistesgeschichte Berliner Studien zur Musikwissenschaft, II). Würzburg, 1941. [Ph.D. diss., University of Berlin, 1939.]

_____. "Revisionsbericht." In *Masses 1-4,* 331-404. 23/1 of *JH-HS.* 1951.

Branscombe, P. "Music in the Viennese Popular Theatre of the Eighteenth and Nineteenth Centuries." *Proceedings of the Royal Musical Association* 98(1971-2).

Braun, Jürgen. *Kritischer Bericht. Philemon und Baucis oder Jupiters Reise auf die Erde.* 24/1 of Haydn *JHW.* 1971.

_____. "Vorwort." In *Philemon und Baucis oder Jupiters Reise auf die Erde,* vii-ix. 24/1 of Haydn *JHW.* 1971.

Brenet, Michel [pseud.] "Les oratorios de Haydn." *La Vie Musicale* 2/2 (October 1 1908), 21-24.

Brichta, S. "Haydns Kirchenmusik." *Signale für die musikalische Welt* 92/22-23 (May 30 1934), 350-351.

Britt, Dom Matthew, O.S.B., ed. *The Hymns of the Breviary and Missal.* Rev. ed. New York, 1955.

Brook, Barry S. "Sturm und Drang and the Romantic Period in Music." *Studies in Romanticism* 9/4 (Fall 1970), 269-284.

Brown "Bibliography"   Brown, A. Peter, J. T. Berkenstock and C. V. Brown. "Joseph Haydn in Literature: A Bibliography." *Haydn-Studien* 3/3-4 (1974), 173-352.

Brown "'Chaos'"   Brown, A. Peter. "Haydn's 'Chaos': Genesis and Genre." *The Musical Quarterly* 73/1 (1989), 18-59.

Brown "Influence"   _____. "Haydn and C. P. E. Bach: The Question of Influence." In Larsen *Haydn Studies,* 158-164.

Brown "Marianna ————. "Marianna Martines' Autobiography as a New Source for Haydn's
Martines" Biography During the 1750's." *Haydn-Studien* 6/1 (December 1986), 68-70.

Brown "Options" ————. "Options: authentic, allowable and possible in performing Haydn's *The Creation*." *The Musical Times* 131 (1990), 73-76.

Brown *Performing* ————. *Performing Haydn's* The Creation: *Reconstructing the Earliest Renditions.* Bloomington, 1986.

————. "Zur profanen Vokalmusik Joseph Haydns." In Mraz *Haydn in seiner Zeit*, 283-290.

————. "Approaching Musical Classicism: Understanding Styles and Style Change in Eighteenth-century Instrumental Music." *College Music Symposium* 20/1 (Spring 1980), 7-48.

Brown, A. Peter, with J. T. Berkenstock and C. V. Brown, "Joseph Haydn in Literature: A Survey." *Notes* 31 (1974-75), 530.

Bryan "Alto" Bryan, Paul. "Haydn's Alto Horns: Their Effect and the Question of Authenticity." In Larsen *Haydn Studies*, 190-192.

Bryan "Horn" ————. "The Horn in the Works of Mozart and Haydn: Some Observations and Comparisons." *The Haydn Yearbook* 9 (1975), 189-255.

Bukofzer *Baroque* Bukofzer, Manfred G. *Music in the Baroque Era.* New York, 1947.

Burney *State* Burney, Charles. *The Present State of Music in Germany, the Netherlands and United Provinces.* 2nd ed., corrected. 2 vols. London, 1775. Facs. repr. New York, 1969.

————. *A General History of Music from the Earliest Ages to the Present Period, to Which is Prefixed a Dissertation on the Music of the Ancients.* 4 vols. London, 1776-89. [Haydn: Vol. 4, 599-602.] (2) Modern ed. by Frank Mercer. New York, 1935. Repr. 196-.

Buschbeck *Austria* Buschbeck, Ernest H. *Austria.* London, 1949.

Cadenbach, Rainer, and Helmut Loos, eds. *Beiträge zur Geschichte des Oratoriums seit Händel. Festschrift Günther Massenkeil zum 60. Geburtstag.* Bonn, 1986.

Carpani *Haydine* Carpani, Giuseppe. *Le Haydine.* Milan, 1812.

Carse, Adam. *The Orchestra in the XVIIIth Century.* Cambridge, 1940. Facs. repr. New York, 1969.

Chailley "Création" Chailley, Jacques. "La 'Création' de Haydn, oratorio Biblique et Maçonnique." *L'Education Musicale* 35/246 and 248 (1978), 203-206 and 295-297.

Chew, Geoffrey. "The Night-Watchman's Song Quoted by Haydn and Its Implications," *Haydn-Studien* 3/2 (1974), 106-124.

Chop, Max. *Joseph Haydn: Die Jahreszeiten. Oratorium. Geschichtlich, szenisch und musikalisch analysiert, mit zahlreichen Notenbeispielen.* (Universal Bibliothek 5857). Leipzig, ca. 1916.

_____. *Haydns Schöpfung.* (Universal Bibliothek 5407). Leipzig, 1912.

Chusid "Liturgy" Chusid, Martin. "Some Observations on Liturgy, Text, and Structure in Haydn's Late Masses." In Landon/Chapman *Studies*, 125-135.

Clewing, C. *Musik und Jägerei.* Kassel, 1937.

Coar, Birchard. *The Masters of the Classical Period as Conductors.* Dekalb (IA.), 1949.

Cohen, R. *The Art of Discrimination: Thomson's "The Seasons" and the Language of Criticism.* Baltimore (Md.), 1964.

_____. *The Unfolding of "The Seasons": A Study of Thomson's Poem.* Baltimore (Md.), 1970.

Connelly, Joseph. *Hymns of the Roman Liturgy.* Westminster (Md.), 1957.

Copeman *Singing* Copeman, Harold. *Singing in Latin, or, Pronunciation explor'd.* Oxford [by the author], 1990.

Corri *Preceptor* Corri, Domenico. *The Singers Preceptor, or Corri's Treatise on Vocal Music.* 2 vols. London, 1810. (2) Facs. ed. by Edward Foreman as part of *The Porpora Tradition*, n.p., 1968.

Craig, D. Millar. "When Haydn Met Nelson." *The Musical Times* 80/1156 (June 1939), 416-417.

Cramer, Carl Friedrich. "Über die Schönheiten und den Ausdruck der Leidenschaft in einer Cantate von J. Haydn." *[Cramers] Magazin der Musik* 1 (November 10 1783), 1073-1115.

Crankshaw *Habsburgs* Crankshaw, Edward. *The Habsburgs: Portrait of a Dynasty.* New York, 1971.

Crankshaw, Geoffrey. "Haydn's Masses." *The Monthly Musical Record* 80/918 (July-August 1950), 148-152.

Croll, G. "Mitteilungen über die 'Schöpfung' und die 'Jahreszeiten' aus dem Schwarzenberg-Archiv." *Haydn-Studien* 3/2 (1974), 85-92.

Crosse *Account* Crosse, J. *An Account of the Grand Musical Festival, held in September 1823, in the Cathedral Church of York . . ..* York, 1825.

Crotch *Substance* Crotch, William. *Substance of Several Courses of Lectures on Music.* London, 1831. Repr. Clarabricken, Co. Kilkenny, Ireland, 1986.

Crutchfield, Will. "The Prosodic Appoggiatura in the Music of Mozart and his Contemporaries." *Journal of the American Musicological Society* 42/2 (1989), 229-274.

Csatkai, André. "Die Beziehungen Gregor Josef Werners, Joseph Haydns und der fürstlichen Musiker zur Eisenstädter Pfarrkirche." *Burgenländische Heimatblätter* (Eisenstadt) 1/1 (April 1932), 13-17.

_____. "Beiträge zur Geschichte der Musikkultur in Eisenstadt." *Mitteilungen des Burgenländischen Heimat- und Naturschutzvereines* (Eisenstadt) 5/2 (April-June 1931), 21-27.

Dack "Dating"   Dack, James. "The Dating of Haydn's Missa Cellensis in Honorem Beatissimae Virginis Mariae: an Interim Discussion." *The Haydn Yearbook* 13 (1983), 97-112.

Dack "Origins"   _____. "The Origins and Development of the Esterházy Kapelle in Eisenstadt until 1790." 2 vols. Diss., University of Liverpool, 1976.

Dennerlein, Hans. "Zum Orgelgebrauch in Mozarts Messen." *Mozart-Jahrbuch* 1955, 113-116.

Dent "Italian Opera"   Dent, Edward J. "Italian Opera in the Eighteenth Century, and Its Influence on the Music of the Classical Period." In *Twentieth-Century Views of Music History*, 262-274. William Hays, ed. New York, 1972. [Orig. in *Sammelbände der Internationalen Musikgesellschaft* 14 (1912-1913), 500-509.]

Derfler, A. "Gottesdienst; Kirchenmusik." *Mitteilungen des Burgenländischen Heimat- und Naturschutzvereines* (Eisenstadt) 4/1-3 (January-September 1930), 27-28.

Deutsch *Nelson und Haydn*   Deutsch, Otto Erich. *Admiral Nelson und Joseph Haydn. Ein britisch-österreichisches Gipfeltreffen.* Gitta Deutsch and Rudolf Klein, eds. Vienna, 1982.

Deutsch "Kanons"   _____. "Haydns Kanons." *Zeitschrift für Musikwissenschaft* 15 (1932-33), 112-124, 172.

Deutsch *Mozart*   _____. *Mozart: A Documentary Biography.* Trans. Eric Blom et al. London and Stanford (CA), 1965.

_____. "Haydn und Nelson." *Die Musik* 24/6 (March 1932), 436-440. Repr. *Österreichische Musikzeitschrift* 23/1 (January 1968), 13-17.

_____. *Kritischer Bericht. Kanons.* 31 of Haydn *JHW.* 1965.

_____. "Vorwort." In *Kanons.* 31 of Haydn *JHW.* 1959.

_____. "Haydn's Hymn and Burney's Translation." *The Music Review* 4/3 (August 1943), 157-162.

_____. "Zelter und Goethe über Haydn." *Österreichische Kunst* 3/5 (May 1932), 19-21.

_____. "Zwei Scherzkanons von Mozart und Haydn." *Die Musik* 24/1 (October 1931), 44-45.

Deutsch, Walter. "'Volkstümliche' Wirkungen in der Musik Joseph Haydns." *Musikerziehung* [Vienna] 14 (1960), 88-92.

Dies *Nachrichten*   Dies, Albert Christoph. *Biographische Nachrichten von Joseph Haydn.* Vienna, 1810. (2) Modern ed. Horst Seeger. Berlin, 1959. (3) Eng. trans. see Gotwals *Contemporary.*

Dimpfl, A. A. "Die Pastoralmesse." Diss., University of Erlangen, 1945.

Dittersdorf, Karl Ditters von. *Lebensbeschreibung: Seinem Sohne in die Feder diktirt.* Leipzig, 1801. (2) Eng. trans. 1896 [reprint 1970].

Donington *Interpretation*   Donington, Robert. *The Interpretation of Early Music.* New Version. London, 1974.

Dreo, Harald. "Die Musiktradition der ehemaligen Stadtpfarrkirche zu Eisenstadt." In Mraz *Haydn in seiner Zeit*, 134-141.

Drury "Words"   Drury, J. D. "Haydn's Seven Last Words: an Historical and Critical Study." Diss., University of Illinois, 1975.

Eaton, Thomas Damant. "Remarks of Haydn's 'Creation'." In *Musical Criticism and Biography: From the Published and Unpublished Writings of Thomas Damant Eaton*, 44-64. Edited "by his sons." London, 1872. [orig. pub. in 1849 for a Norwich perf.]

Eby, John. "A New Missa Brevis Attributed to 'Heyden'." *studies in music from the university of western ontario* 3 (1978), 127-156.

Edelmann "Haydns *Il ritorno*"   Edelmann, Bernd. "Haydns *Il ritorno di Tobia* und der Wandel des 'Geschmacks' in Wien nach 1780." In Feder *Tradition*, 189-214.

————. "Händel-Einflüss in Haydns vokalen Spätwerk." Ph.D. diss., University of Munich, 1986.

Eichborn, Hermann. "Die Clarintrompeterei." *Musikalisches Wochenblatt* 16 (1885), 622-624, 638-639.

Einstein, Alfred. "Haydn, Mozart, and English Sea-Heroes." *The Monthly Musical Record* 64/762 (December 1934), 217-218.

Ekdahl, Richard W. "The Influence of Handel on the Oratorios of Haydn and Mendelssohn." Master's thesis, Boston University, 1954.

Engel, Hans. "Probleme der Aufführungspraxis." *Mozart-Jahrbuch* 1955, 56-65.

F. "Genesis der Schöpfung von Joseph Haydn." *Wiener Allgemeine Theater-Zeitung* 43/220 (September 15 1850), 878.

Feder "Jahreszeiten"   Feder, Georg. "Die Jahreszeiten nach Thomson, In Musik gesezt von Joseph Haydn." In Cadenbach *Beiträge*, 185-202.

Feder "Korrekturen"   ————. "Haydns Korrekturen zum Klavierauszug der 'Jahreszeiten'." In *Festschrift Georg von Dadelsen zum 60. Geburtstag*, 101-12. T. Kohlhase and V. Scherliess, eds. Stuttgart, 1978.

Feder "Manuscript Sources"   ————. "Manuscript Sources of Haydn's Works and Their Distribution." Trans. Eugene Hartzell *The Haydn Yearbook* 4 (1968), 102-39. [Trans. of "Die Überlieferung und Verbreitung der handschriftlichen Quellen zu Haydns Werken (Erste Folge)."]

Feder "Quellen"   ————. "Die Überlieferung und Verbreitung der handschriftlichen Quellen zu Haydns Werken (Erste Folge)." *Haydn-Studien* 1/1 (1965), 3-42.

Feder "Similarities"   ————. "Similarities in the Works of Haydn." In Landon/Chapman *Studies*, 186-197.

Feder "Source"   ————. "A Newly Found Authentic Source for Joseph Haydn's *Missa in honorem B.V.M.*" In *Music in the Classic Period: Essays in Honor of Barry S. Brook*, 61-65. Allan W. Atlas, ed. New York, 1985.

Feder *Tradition* _____, H. Hüschen, and U. Tank, eds. *Joseph Haydn: Tradition und Rezeption. Bericht über die Jahrestagung der Gesellschaft für Musikforschung, Köln 1982.* Regensburg, 1985.

  _____. "Haydn und das Libretto." *FUSA. Journal für Kenner & Liebhaber von Kunst - Literatur - Musik* Heft 10 (Köln: Fusa Verlag GmbH, 1982), 9-20.

  _____. "A Special Feature of Neapolitan Opera Tradition in Haydn's Vocal Works." In Larsen *Haydn Studies*, 367-371.

  _____. "Ein Kanon-Autograph von J. Haydn in Leningrad." *Haydn-Studien* 4/1 (1976), 52-55.

  _____. "Haydn und Eisenstadt." *Österreichische Musikzeitschrift* 25/4 (April 1970), 213-221.

  _____. "Zur Datierung Haydnscher Werke." In *Anthony von Hoboken. Festschrift zum 75. Geburtstag*, 50-54. J. Schmidt-Görg, ed. Mainz, 1962.

Federhofer, Hellmut. "Johann Joseph Fux und Joseph Haydn." *Musica* 14/5 (May 1960), 269-273.

Fellerer "Altklassische Polyphonie" Fellerer, Karl Gustav. "Die vokale Kirchenmusik des 17./18. Jahrhunderts und die altklassische Polyphonie." *Zeitschrift für Musikwissenschaft* 11 (1928-29), 354-364.

Fellerer "Liturgical Basis" _____. "The Liturgical Basis of Haydn's Masses." In Larsen *Haydn Studies*, 164-168. [Cf. "Liturgische Grundlage der Kirchenmusik Mozarts," in *Festschrift Walter Senn*, 64. Munich and Salzburg, 1975.]

Fellerer "Remarks" _____. "Remarks on the Viola in Haydn's Church Music." In Larsen *Haydn Studies*, 205-206.

Fellerer *Soziologie* _____. *Soziologie der Kirchenmusik.* Cologne, 1963.

  _____. *Die Kirchenmusik W. A. Mozarts.* Laaber, 1985.

  _____. "Text and Music in Mozart's and Haydn's Masses." In Larsen *Haydn Studies*, 416-419.

  _____. "Joseph Haydns Messen." In Szabolcsi *Konferenz Budapest*, 41-48.

Feuchtmüller, R., F. Hadamowsky and L. Nowak. *Joseph Haydn und seine Zeit: Ausstellung Schloss Petronell (N. Ö) Mai bis Oktober 1959.* Vienna, 1959.

Fitzpatrick, H. *The Horn and Horn-playing, and the Austro-Bohemian Tradition 1680-1830.* London, 1970.

Fogle, James C. B. "Elements of expression in selected Masses by Johann Michael Haydn, Franz Joseph Haydn, and Wolfgang Amadeus Mozart." Master's thesis, University of North Carolina, 1973.

Franz *Schöpfung* Franz, Helmut. *Joseph Haydn. Die Schöpfung* (Praxis der Chorprobe). Frankfurt, 1977.

Freeman "Melk" Freeman, Robert N. "The Practice of Music at Melk Monastery in the Eighteenth Century." Ph.D. diss., University of California at Los Angeles, 1971.

Freeman "Role"   _____. "The Role of Organ Improvisation in Haydn's Church Music." In Larsen *Haydn Studies*, 192-194.

_____. "The Function of Haydn's Instrumental Compositions in the Abbeys." In Larsen *Haydn Studies*, 199-201.

_____. "Zwei Melker Musik-Kataloge aus der zweiten Hälfte des 18. Jahrhunderts." *Die Musikforschung* 23 (1970), 176-184.

Freunschlag "Predieri"   Freunschlag, Heinrich. "Luca Antonio Predieri als Kirchenkomponist." Ph.D. diss., University of Vienna, 1927.

Friedländer, Max. "Van Swieten und das Textbuch zu Haydns 'Jahreszeiten'." *Jahrbuch der Musikbibliothek Peters* 16 (1905), 47-56.

Fux *Gradus*   Fux, Johann Joseph. *Gradus ad Parnassum, sive manuductio ad compositionem musicae regularem, methodo nova*. . . Vienna, 1725. Facs. repr. New York, 1966. (2) Modern ed. by Alfred Mann in Fux *Sämtliche Werke* 7/1. Kassel, 1967. (3) *Gradus ad Parnassum oder Anführung zur regelmässigen musikalischen Composition*. Trans. Lorenz Christoph Mizler. Leipzig, 1742. (4) excerpt: *The Study of Counterpoint*. . . Trans. Alfred Mann. New York, 1943.

Galeazzi *Elementi 1*   Galeazzi, Francesco. *Elementi teorico-pratici di musica con un saggio sopra l'arte di suonare il violino analizzata, ed a dimostrabili principi ridotta*. . . . [Vol. 1.] Rome, 1791.

Garcia *Hints*   Garcia, Manuel. *Hints on Singing*. Trans. from Fr. by B. Garcia. London and New York, 1894. Repr. Canoga Park (CA), 1970.

Gardiner, William. *Music and Friends; or, Pleasant Recollections of a Dilettante*. 3 vols. London, 1838-53.

Gárdonyi, Zoltán. "Haydn oratórium-formálása." ["Formal structure in the oratorios of Haydn."] In Szabolcsi *Haydn Emlékére*, 95-106. [German summary, 105-106.]

Gathy, August. "Haydns Schöpfung in Paris. Ein Rückblick." *Monatsschrift für Theater und Musik* [Vienna] 1 (1855), 412-420.

Gebauer, Alfred. "Haydn als Dirigent." *Cäcilia* (Breslau) 17/5 (1905), 35-38.

Geck, Martin. "Haydn in London." *Neue Zeitschrift für Musik* 126/4 (April 1965), 157-158.

Geiringer *Haydn*   Geiringer, Karl, and Irene Geiringer. *Haydn, A Creative Life in Music*. 3rd ed., rev. & enl. Berkeley and Los Angeles, 1982.

Geiringer "Remarks"   Geiringer, Karl. "Remarks on the Early Masses." In Larsen *Haydn Studies*, 204-205.

Geiringer "Small Sacred Works"   _____. "The Small Sacred Works by Haydn in the Esterházy Archives at Eisenstadt." *The Musical Quarterly* 45/4 (October 1959), 460-72. [trans. of "Joseph Haydn als Kirchenmusiker. Die kleinen geistlichen Werke des Meisters im Eisenstädter Schloss."

————. "Stylistic Change in Haydn's Oratorios: Il Ritorno di Tobia and The Creation." In Larsen *Haydn Studies*, 392-393.

————. "Sidelights on Haydn's Activities in the Field of Sacred Music." In Szabolcsi *Konferenz Budapest*, 49-56. [NB: content essentially same as Geiringer "Small Sacred Works."]

————. "Joseph Haydn als Kirchenmusiker. Die kleinen geistlichen Werke des Meisters im Eisenstädter Schloss." *Kirchenmusikalisches Jahrbuch* 44 (1960), 54-61. [Eng. trans. see "Small Sacred Works."]

————. "The Cantatas and Oratorios of Haydn's Youth." Trans. H. B. Weiner. *Musical Opinion* 61/726 (March 1938), 497-498.

————. "Haydn's Sketches for 'The Creation'." Trans. M. M. Marble. *The Musical Quarterly* 18/2 (April 1932) 299-308.

Gerber *Lexikon*   Gerber, Ernst Ludwig. *Neues historisch-biographisches Lexikon der Tonkünstler.* 4 vols. Leipzig, 1812-14. (2) Facs. ed. by O. Wessely. Graz, 1966.

Gerlach, S. "Haydns Orchester-Musiker von 1761 bis 1774." *Haydn-Studien* 4 (1976), 35-48.

Gianturco *Mozart*   Gianturco, Carolyn. *Mozart's Early Operas.* London, 1981.

Gibbs, T. J. "A Study of Form in the Late Masses of Joseph Haydn." Diss., University of Texas, 1973.

Gilbert "First"   Gilbert, Nina. "Haydn's First Mass: A Practical Introduction to His Style." *The Choral Journal* 25/9 (May 1985), 19-23.

Glöggl, Franz Xaver. *Kirchen-Musik-Ordnung: Erklärendes Handbuch des musikalischen Gottesdienst.* Vienna, 1828.

Goethe, Johann Wolfgang von. [Essay on "The Creation", orig. in *Über Kunst und Altertum* (Aug. 1826).]

Göller, Gottfried. "Liturgische Aspekte der Rezeption kirchenmusikalischer Werke Beethovens und Haydns in der Domkapelle zu Köln unter Carl Leibl." In Gesellschaft für Musikforschung. *Bericht über den Internationalen Musikwissenschaftlichen Kongress Bonn 1970*, 408-410. Carl Dahlhaus, Hans Joachim Marx, Magda Marx-Weber, and Günther Massenkeil, eds. Kassel, [1973].

Gotwals *Contemporary*   Gotwals, Vernon, ed. *Haydn: Two Contemporary Portraits.* Madison (WI), 1968. [Ed. & trans. of Griesinger *Notizen* and Dies *Nachrichten*]

Gotwals "'Creation'"   ————. "'The Creation' by Joseph Haydn." *American Guild of Organists Quarterly* 12/2 (April 1967), 47-60; 12/3 (July 1967), 95-98.

————. "Haydn's 'Creation' Revisited: An Introductory Essay." In *Studies in Music History. Essays for Oliver Strunk*, 429-442. Harold Powers, ed. Princeton, 1968.

————. "Haydn in London again." *The Music Review* 22/3 (1961), 189-194.

Gradwohl, Karl. "Musikkultur in Eisenstadt." In *Eisenstadt: 300 Jahre Freistadt*, 43-51. Landesmuseum and Landesarchiv with the Volksbildungswerk für das Burgenland, ed. Vienna, 1948.

Grasberger, Franz. *Die Hymnen Österreichs*. Tutzing, 1968.

Griesbacher, P. "Neue Akten zu Kontrafakten." *Monatshefte für katholische Kirchenmusik* (Essen) 10/5 (May 1928), 113-19.

Griesinger *Notizen*   Griesinger, Georg August. *Biographische Notizen über Joseph Haydn*. Leipzig, 1810. (2) Modern ed. Franz Grasberger. Vienna, 1954. (3) English trans. see Gotwals *Contemporary*.

Gruber, Genot. "Musikalische Rhetorik und barocke Bildlichkeit in Kompositionen des jungen Haydn." In Schwarz *junge Haydn*, 168-191.

Haas "Stegreifkomödie"   Haas, R. "Die Musik in der Wiener deutschen Stegreifkomödie." *Studien zur Musikwissenschaft* 12 (1925), 3-64.

_____. *Aufführungspraxis der Musik*. Potsdam, 1931.

Haid, Gerlinde. "Volksmusik um den jungen Haydn." In Badura-Skoda *Proceedings*, 232-238.

Hailparn "Words"   Hailparn, Lydia. "Haydn: The Seven Last Words. A new Look at an old Masterpiece." *The Music Review* 34/1 (1973), 1-21.

Hanslick, Eduard. *Geschichte des Concertwesens in Wien*. Vienna, 1869; repr New York, 1979.

Hárich, Janos. "Beethoven in Eisenstadt." *Burgenländische Heimatblätter* 21/2 [special supplement]. Eisenstadt, 1959.

Hárich "Orchester"   Hárich, Janos. "Das Haydn-Orchester im Jahr 1780." *The Haydn Yearbook* 7 (1970), 5-46.

Hárich "Repertoire"   _____. "Das Repertoire des Opernkapellmeisters Haydn in Eszterházá (1780-1790)." *The Haydn Yearbook* 1 (1962), 9-110.

Harnoncourt *Dialog*   Harnoncourt, Nikolaus. *Der musikalische Dialog. Gedanken zu Monteverdi, Bach und Mozart*. Salzburg and Vienna, 1984. (2) Repr. Munich and Kassel, 1987. (3) Trans. Mary O'Neill as *The Musical Dialogue: Thoughts on Monteverdi, Bach and Mozart*. Portland (OR), 1989.

[Haydn] *CCLN*   Haydn, Franz Joseph. *The Collected Correspondence and London Notebooks of Joseph Haydn*. H. C. Robbins Landon, ed. London, 1959.

Haydn *EK*   _____. [Entwurf-Katalog.] Berlin, Deutsche Staatsbibliothek, Mus. ms. Kat. 607.

Haydn *HS*   _____. *Kritische Gesamtausgabe*. J. P. Larsen, gen. ed. 4 vols. Boston, Leipzig, and Vienna, 1950-51.

Haydn *HV*   _____. "Verzeichniss aller derjenigen Compositionen welche ich mich beyläufig erinnere von meinem 18ten bis in das 73ste Jahr verfetiget zu haben." MS, copied by Johann Elssler; now lost. (2) Facs. repr. in Larsen, *Drei Haydn Kataloge*.

Haydn *JHW* _____. *Werke.* J. P. Larsen and G. Feder, gen. eds. 50+ vols. Cologne, 1958- .

Haydn *M* _____. *J. Haydns Werke.* E. Mandyczewski et al., eds. 10 vols. Leipzig, 1907-33.

_____. [A comprehensive list of Haydn's MS. catalogues, notebooks, letters, facsimile editions of autograph scores, catalog of the music collection of the National Széchényi Library of Budapest, and more can be found in "Haydn, F. J.", Bibliography, Landon *HCW* 5, 451ff.]

_____. *Schöpfungsmesse.* Facs. autograph score, Wilhelm Virneisel, ed. Munich-Duisburg, 1959.

Haydn-Zentenarfeier *Haydn-Zentenarfeier, III. Kongress der Internationalen Musikgesellschaft, Wien, 25. bis 29. Mai 1909. Bericht vorgelegt vom Wiener Kongressausschuss.* Vienna and Leipzig, 1909.

[Haydn "Teremtés"]. *Magyar Hirmondó* 22 [1800?], 370. ["A performance of Haydn's 'Creation' in Budapest." Concerning the March 8, 1800 perf. which H. conducted for Alexandra Pavlovna's birthday.]

Heartz "Hunting" Heartz, Daniel. "The Hunting Chorus in Haydn's Jahreszeiten and the 'Airs de chasse' in the Encyclopédie." *Eighteenth-century Studies* 9 (1976), 523-539.

Heartz "Opera" _____. "Opera and the Periodization of Eighteenth-century Music." In International Musicological Society. *Report of the Tenth Congress Ljubljana 1967*, 160-168. Dragotin Cvetko, ed. Kassel and Ljubljana, 1970.

Heer "Kanons" Heer, Josef. "Die Kanons von Haydn. Zum Ausklang des Haydn-Jahres." *Musik im Unterricht* 50/10 (October 1959), 300-303.

Heiling, Hans. "Orgeln um Joseph Haydn." *Singende Kirche* (Vienna), 8/2 (December 1960-February 1961), 69-71.

Hennerberg, Carl Fredrik. *Paul Struck, ein Wiener Komponist aus Haydns und Beethovens Tagan.* Stralsund, 1931. [The first performance of *The Creation* in Stockholm, 18-26.]

Hess, Willy. "Die amputierte 'Schöpfung' Haydns. Ein sinnloser Strich im Duett Adam-Eva." *Musica* 26/4 (1972), 379-380.

Hidaka, Junko. ["The Early Masses of Joseph Haydn."] Graduating thesis of the Master Course, Tokyo University of Arts, 1963. [In Japanese]

Hines, Robert S. "The Masses of Joseph Haydn." Master's thesis, University of Michigan, 1956.

Hirose, Hidemi. [Study of Haydn's Oratorio "Il ritorno di Tobia"]. M.A. thesis, Ochanomizu University, 1974. [In Japanese]

Hirshowitz, B. "The Old Testament in the works of Joseph Haydn." *Tatzlil (The Chord). Forum for Music Research and Bibliography* 17 (1977), 140-141. [Also in Hebrew.]

His, Marie E. "Zu Haydns 'Ein Mädchen, das auf Ehre hielt'." *Zeitschrift der Internationalen Musikgesellschaft* 12/6 (March 1911), 159-161.

Hoboken *Werkverzeichnis*   Hoboken, Anthony van. *Joseph Haydn: Thematische-bibliographisches Werkverzeichnis.* Vol I: Instrumentalwerke. Vol. II: Vokalwerke. Vol. III: Index. Mainz, 1957-78.

_____. "The First Thematic Catalog of Haydn's Works—Volume II." Trans. Neil Ratliff and Susana Herz. *Notes* 28/2 (December 1971), 209-211.

Hofer "beiden Reutter"   Hofer, P. Norbert. "Die beiden Reutter als Kirchenkomponisten." Ph.D. diss., University of Vienna, 1915.

Hogwood, Christopher. *Haydn's Visits to England.* London, 1980.

Hollis, Helen R. *The Musical Instruments of Joseph Haydn: an Introduction.* Smithsonian Studies in History and Technology 38. Washington, D. C., 1977.

Horányi, Mátyás. *The Magnificence of Eszterháza.* Trans. András Deák. Philadelphia, 1962. [Orig. Budapest, 1959.]

Horn, Hans-Jürgen. "FIAT LVX. Zum kunsttheoretischen Hintergrund der 'Erschaffung' des Lichtes in Haydns Schöpfung." *Haydn-Studien* 3/2 (1974), 65-84.

Höslinger "Standpunkt"   Höslinger, C. "Der überwundene Standpunkt: Joseph Haydn in der Wiener Musikkritik des 19. Jahrhunderts." In *Beiträge zur Musikgeschichte des 18. Jahrhunderts II: Joseph Haydn und seine Zeit,* 116-42. [*Jahrbuch für österreichische Kulturgeschichte* 1/2.] Eisenstadt, 1971/2.

HS   See Haydn *HS.*

Huemer, G. *Die Pflege der Musik im Stifte Kremsmünster.* Wels, 1877.

Hughes *Haydn*   Hughes, Rosemary. *Haydn.* Rev. (3rd) ed. London, 1970.

_____. "The Haydn Orchestra." *The Musical Times* 93 (1952), 299-301.

_____. "Two Haydn Masses." *The Musical Times* 91/1288 (June 1950), 213-218.

Hunter, M. "Haydn's Sonata-Form Arias," *Current Musicology* 37-38 (1984), 19-32.

Hurwitz "Freemasons"   Hurwitz, Joachim. "Haydn and the Freemasons." *The Haydn Yearbook* 16 (1985), 5-98.

Jackson, William. *Observations on the Present State of Music in London.* Dublin and London, 1791.

Jancik, Hans. "Joseph Haydn als Kirchenmusiker." *Singende Kirche* 6/3 (March-May 1959), 98-99.

Jesson, Ronald F. "An Analysis of 'The Seven Last Words of Christ' by Franz Joseph Haydn." Master's thesis, Eastman School of Music of the University of Rochester, 1949.

JHW   See Haydn *JHW.*

Jong, W. C. "De Paukenmesse van Joseph Haydn." *Ouverture* 4/9 (May 1970), 235-237.

Jungmann *Mass* Jungmann, Joseph A. *The Mass of the Roman Rite: Its Origins and Development (Missarum Sollemnia).* 2 vols. Trans. Francis A. Brunner. New York, 1951.

Kadotshnikov, Viktor P. ["The Oratorios of J. Haydn in the Context of the Epoch."] In *Tezisy III vserossijskoy nautshno-teoretitshkeskoj konferentsii aspirantov wuzow kul'tury i iskusstwa,* 113-115. Swerdlowsk, 1981. [In Russian]

————. ["The Path from the Symphonies to the Oratorios. The 'Nelson' Mass of J. Haydn."] In *Shanrovo-stilistitsheskije tendentsii klassitsheskoj i sovremennoj muzyki,* 37-51. Leningrad, 1980. [In Russian].

Kantner, Leopold M. "Das Messenschaffen Joseph Haydns und seiner italienischen Zeitgenossen—Ein Vergleich." In Feder *Tradition,* 145-159.

Karpf, Roswitha V. "Haydn und Carl Friberth: Marginalien zur Gesangskunst im 18. Jahrhundert." In Badura-Skoda *Proceedings,* 361-369.

Keller, Hermann. *Phrasing and Articulation.* Trans. L. Gerdine. New York, 1965.

————. "[Die Bedeutung der Zeichen Keil, Strich und Punkt bei Mozart]." In Albrecht *Bedeutung,* 7-21.

Kellner *Kremsmünster* Kellner, Altman. *Musikgeschichte des Stiftes Kremsmünster.* Kassel, 1956.

Kendall *Vivaldi* Kendall, Alan. *Vivaldi.* London, 1978.

Kirby "Impact" Kirby, Paul H. "The Impact of Haydn's Conducted Performances of *The Creation* on the Work and the History of Conducting." *Journal of the Conductors' Guild* 13/1 (Winter-Spring 1992), 7-22.

Kirkendale "New Roads" Kirkendale, Warren. "New Roads to Old Ideas in Beethoven's Missa Solemnis." *The Musical Quarterly* 56 (1970), 668-701.

————. "Beethovens Missa Solemnis und die Rhetorische Tradition." In *Sitzunsberichte der österreichischen Akademie der Wissenschaften. Philosophisch.-historische Klasse* Bd. 271 (Beethoven Number). Vienna, 1971. [Eng. trans. see "New Roads"]

Klein, Rudolf. "Der Applausus-Brief." *Österreichische Musikzeitschrift* 14/5-6 (May-June 1959), 198-200.

Kobald, Karl. "Die ersten Wiener Aufführungen von Haydns 'Schöpfung'." *Goethe- und Haydn-Almanach. Deutscher Sänger-Kalender* (1932), 178-183.

Koch *Lexikon* Koch, Heinrich Christoph. *Musikalisches Lexikon.* Frankfurt am Main, 1802. Repr. Hildesheim, 1964.

Köchel *Fux* Köchel, Ludwig Ritter von. *Johann Josef Fux.* Vienna, 1872. Repr. Hildesheim and New York, 1974.

Kohut, Adolph. "Die Erstaufführung von Joseph Haydns Jahreszeiten vor 100 Jahren." *Neue Musik-Zeitung* 22/9-11 (1901), 115, 122-123, 134.

Kosch, Franz. "Fl. L. Gassmann als Kirchenkomponist." *Studien zur Musikwissenschaft* 14 (1927), 213.

Koury, Daniel L. *Orchestral Performance Practices in the Nineteenth Century: Size, Proportions, and Seating.* Ann Arbor (MI), 1986.

Kramer, Lawrence. "Haydn's Chaos, Schenker's Order; or, Hermeneutics and Musical Analysis: Can They Mix?" *19th Century Music* 16 (Summer 1992), 3-17, 70-79.

Krehbiel, Henry Edward. *Music and Manners from Pergolesi to Beethoven.* London, 1898.

Kufferath, Maurice. "Les 'Saisons' de Haydn." *Le Guide Musical* (Brussels) 42/10 (March 8, 1896) 188-189.

Kumbier, William A. "A 'New Quickening': Haydn's *The Creation*, Wordsworth, and the Pictorialist Imagination." *Studies in Romanticism* 30 (Winter 1991), 535-563.

Kürzinger, Ignatz Franz Xaver. *Getreuer Unterricht zum Singen mit Manieren, und die Violin zu Spielen.* Augsburg, 1763.

[C.] Landon "Dokument"   Landon, Christa. "Ein Dokument zur Schöpfung." *Haydn-Studien* 4/2 (1978), 113.

Landon "aufgefundene"   Landon, H. C. Robbins. "Eine aufgefundene Haydn-Messe." *Österreichische Musikzeitschrift* 12/5 (May 1957), 183-185.

Landon "Autograph"   _____. "The newly discovered Autograph to Haydn's Missa Cellensis of 1776 (formerly known as the 'Missa Sanctae Caeciliae')." *The Haydn Yearbook* 9 (1975), 306-308.

Landon *Creation*   _____, ed. *The Creation and The Seasons. The complete authentic sources for the Word-Books.* Cardiff, 1985.

Landon *Essays*   _____. *Essays on the Viennese Classical Style.* London, 1970.

Landon "Haydniana"   _____. "Haydniana (I)." *The Haydn Yearbook* 4 (1968), 199-206.

Landon *HCW*   _____. *Haydn: Chronicle and Works* [*HCW*]. 5 vols. London, 1976-1980.

Landon "Lost"   _____. "A lost autograph re-discovered: Missa 'Sunt bona mixta malis.'" *The Haydn Yearbook* 14 (1983), 5-8.

Landon "Marionette"   _____. "Haydn's Marionette Operas." *Haydn Yearbook* 1 (1962), 111-199.

Landon "Preface" 1   _____. "Preface" [1] to Joseph Haydn, *Missa Sancti Nicolai.* London and New York, 1969.

Landon "'Responsorium'"   _____. "Haydn's Newly Discovered 'Responsorium ad absolutionem: Libera me, Domine'." *The Haydn Yearbook* 4 (1968), 140-147, 228-235. [Facs. & mod. ed., pp. 228-235.]

Landon *Symphonies*   _____. *The Symphonies of Joseph Haydn.* London, 1955; New York, 1956.

_____. "Haydn on record - 1. Symphonies and vocal music." *Early Music* 10/3 (1982), 351-360.

_____. *Haydn. A Documentary Study.* London, 1981.

_____. "The Haydn Masses on Records." *High Fidelity* 14/12 (December 1964), 105-107.

_____. "Einiges zur Aufführungspraxis von Haydn-Symphonies durch Liebhaber- und Schulorchester." *Das Liebhaberorchester* 12/3 (September 1964), 43-50.

_____. "Preface" [2] to Joseph Haydn, *Collected Symphonies, 1-49*. Vienna, 1962.

_____. "Problems of Authenticity in Eighteenth-Century Music." In *Instrumental Music: A Conference at Isham Memorial Library, May 4, 1957*, 31-56. David G. Hughes, ed. Cambridge (MA), 1959.

Landon/Chapman *Studies*   Landon, H. C. Robbins, and Roger E. Chapman, eds. *Studies in Eighteenth-Century Music. A Tribute to Karl Geiringer on His Seventieth Birthday*. New York, 1970.

Landon, H. C. Robbins, Karl Heinz Füssl, and Christa Landon. "Vorwort." In *Messen. Nr. 5-8*, vii-viii. 23/2 of Haydn *JHW*. 1958.

Landon/Jones *Haydn*   Landon, H. C. Robbins, and David Wyn Jones. *Haydn: His Life and Music*. Bloomington and Indianapolis, 1988.

Lang, Paul Henry. "The Symphonic Mass." *American Choral Review* 18/2 (April 1976), esp. 11-12.

_____. "Outlines of the Classical Choral Style." *American Choral Review* 17/2 (1975), 32-38.

Larsen *Drei Haydn Kataloge*   Larsen, Jens Peter, ed. *Drei Haydn Kataloge in Faksimile mit Einleitung und ergänzenden Themenverzeichnissen*. Copenhagen, 1941. (2) Repr in Eng. and Ger. as *Three Haydn Catalogues*. New York, 1979.

Larsen *Haydn Studies*   _____, Howard Serwer, and James Webster, eds. *Haydn Studies. Proceedings of the International Haydn Conference. Washington, D. C., 1975*. New York, 1981.

Larsen *HHV*   _____. *Handel, Haydn, and the Viennese Classical Style [HHV]*. Trans. Ulrich Krämer. Ann Arbor, 1988.

Larsen *Messiah*   _____. *Handel's Messiah: Origins, Composition, Sources*. 2nd ed. New York, 1972.

Larsen *New Grove Haydn*   _____, and Georg Feder. *The New Grove Haydn*. New York and London, 1983.

Larsen "Observations"   _____. "Some Observations on the Development and Characteristics of Viennese Classical Instrumental Music." *Studia Musicologica* 9/1-2 (1967) 115-139.

_____. "Haydn's Early Masses. Evolution of a Genre." *American Choral Review* 24/2-3 (1982), 48-60. (Special vol. entitled *From Schütz to Schubert. Essays on Choral Music. A Festschrift [for Alfred Mann]*) (Repr. in Larsen *HHV*, 137-148.)

_____. "Haydn im 20. Jahrhundert." In *Musik - Edition - Interpretation, Gedenkschrift Günter Henle*, 319-325. Munich, 1980.

_____. "Beethovens C-dur Messe und die Spätmessen Joseph Haydns." In *Beiträge '76-'78. Beethoven-Kolloquium 1977 Dokumentation umd Aufführungspraxis*, 12-19. R. Klein, ed. Kassel, 1978. (Repr. as "Beethoven's C-Major Mass and the Late Masses of Joseph Haydn," in Larsen *HHV*, 149-157.)

_____. "Händel und Haydn." In *Georg Friedrich Händel als Wegbereiter der Wiener Klassik. Wissenschaftliche Konferenz zu den 26. Händelfestspielen der DDR...*, 25-33. W. Siegmund-Schultze, ed. Halle, 1977. (Repr. *Händel-Jahrbuch* 28 (1982), 93-99.)

_____, et al. "Schlussdiskussion." In Schwarz *junge Haydn*, 259-264.

_____. "Towards an Understanding of the Development of the Viennese Classical Style." In *International Musicological Society. Report of the Eleventh Congress*, 23. Copenhagen, 1972. (Reprinted in Larsen *HHV*, 251-261.)

_____. "En Haydnsk gaadekanon." *Svensk Tidskrift för Musikforskning* 43 (1961), 215-226.

_____, and Nils Schiorring. "Haydns oratorier og deres musikalske forudsaetninger..." In *Festskrift udg. af Kobenhavns Universitet*, 228-232. (November 1959).

_____. *Die Haydn-Überlieferung*. Copenhagen, 1939. (2) New ed. "Mit einem Vorwort des Verfassers zur Neuausgabe." Munich, 1980. (Eng. trans. essential excerpts repr. Larsen *HHV*, 185-224.)

LaRue, Jan. "General Considerations in Performing Haydn and Mozart." *Bulletin of the American Choral Foundation* 2/4 (June 1960), 1-2.

Lawrence, V. B. "The earliest performances of The Creation in the United States." *Moravian Music Journal* (Winston-Salem, NC) 27/4 (1982), 90-91.

Leidinger, S. *900 Jahre Lambach*. Lambach, 1956.

Levarie "Closing"   Levarie, Siegmund. "The Closing Numbers of 'Die Schöpfung'." In Landon/Chapman *Studies*, 315-322.

Levysohn, S. "Die Pflege der Haydnschen Musik in Dänemark." In *Haydn-Zentenarfeier*, 529-530.

Lightwood, James T. "Joseph Haydn." *The Choir* 23/267 (March 1932), 47-50.

Lippmann, Friedrich. *Kritischer Bericht. Messe Nr. 12.* 23/5 of Haydn *JHW*. 1967.

_____. "Vorwort." In *Messe Nr. 12*, vi-vii. 23/5 of Haydn *JHW*. 1966.

Lorenz, Franz. *Haydns, Mozarts und Beethovens Kirchenmusik und ihre Katholischen und protestantischen Gegner*. Breslau, 1866.

Lowens, Irving. *Haydn in America*. Bibliographies in American Music 5. Detroit, 1979.

Lowinsky, Edward E. "On Mozart's Rhythm." *The Musical Quarterly* 42/2 (April 1956), 162-186. (Repr. *The Creative World of Mozart*, 31-55. Paul Henry Lang, ed. New York, 1963.)

Lucas "Analysis"   Lucas, James Arnold. "A Conductor's Analysis of *The Creation* by Franz Joseph Haydn." D.M.A. diss., University of Iowa, 1977.

Ludwig, V. O. *Klosterneuburg: Kulturgeschichte eines österreichischen Stiftes.* Vienna, 1951.

Luger, W. "Beitrage zur Musikgeschichte des Stiftes Lambach vom Mittelalter bis zum Barock." *Oberösterreichischer Heimatblätter* 15 (1961). 1, 102ff.

————. *Die Benediktinerabtei Lambach.* Linz, 1952.

Lunn "Quest"   Lunn, Jean. "The Quest of the Missing Poet." *The Haydn Yearbook* 4 (1968), 195-199.

Luoma, Robert G. "The function of dynamics in the music of Haydn, Mozart, and Beethoven: some implications for the performer." *College Music Symposium* 16 (Spring 1976), 32-41.

M   See Haydn *M*.

Mac Intyre "Doubtful"   Mac Intyre, Bruce C. "Haydn's Doubtful and Spurious Masses: An Attribution Update." *Haydn-Studien* 5 (1982), 42-54.

Mac Intyre *Mass*   ————. *The Viennese Concerted Mass of the Early Classic Period.* Ann Arbor, Michigan, 1986.

————. "Die Entwicklung der konzertierenden Messen Joseph Haydns und seiner Wiener Zeitgenossen." *Haydn-Studien* 6/2 (1988), 80-87.

————. "The City University of New York: An Unusual Haydn Seminar." *Current Musicology* 20 (1975), 42-49.

Mahaut *Nouvelle Méthode*   Mahaut, Antoine. *Nouvelle Méthode pour apprendre en peu de tems à jouer de a flûte traversière.* Paris, 1759. (2) Trans. and ed. Eileen Hadidian as *A New Method for Learning to Play the Transverse Flute.* Bloomington and Indianapolis, 1989.

Mahling *Orchester*   Mahling, Christoph-Hellmut. *Orchester und Orchestermusiker in Deutschland von 1700 bis 1850.* Habilitationsschrift, University of Saarbrücken, 1972.

Mahling "Orchesterpraxis Haydn"   ————. "Orchester, Orchesterpraxis und Orchestermusiker zur Zeit des jungen Haydn (1740-1770)." In Schwarz *junge Haydn*, 98-113.

————. "Mozart und die Orchesterpraxis seiner Zeit." *Mozart-Jahrbuch* (1967), 229-243.

Malherbe, Charles. "Joseph Haydn und 'Die Schöpfung'." *Musikalisches Wochenblatt* 40/16-18 (July 15-29, 1909), 229-232, 251-254.

Mandyczewski *Jahreszeiten*   Mandyczewski, Eusebius. "Vorwort" and "Revisionsbericht." *Die Jahreszeiten.* XVI/6-7 of Haydn *M*. n. d. iii-xi.

Mandyczewski *Schöpfung*   ————. "Vorwort" and "Revisionsbericht." In *Die Schöpfung*, iii-vi. 16/5 of Haydn *M*. n.d.

Mann "Critic"   Mann, Alfred. "Haydn as Student and Critic of Fux." In Landon/Chapman *Studies*, 323-332.

Mansfield "Bath"   Mansfield, Orlando. "Haydn at Bath." *Monthly Musical Record* 58 (1928), 201ff.

Marguerre, K. "Forte und Piano bei Mozart." *Neue Zeitschrift für Musik* 128 (1967), 153-160.

Marpurg *Anleitung*   Marpurg, Friedrich Wilhelm. *Anleitung zum Clavierspielen*. Berlin, 1765. Repr. New York, 1969.

Marshall, D. *Eighteenth-Century England*. In *A History of England*. 10 vols. Ed. W. N. Medlicott. London, 1962.

Marty, Jean-Pierre. *The Tempo Indications of Mozart*. New Haven, 1989.

Massenkeil, Günther. "Die Idylle in der Musik." In *Jahres- und Tagungsbericht der Görres-Gesellschaft 1979*, 34-44. Görres-Gesellschaft zur Pflege der Wissenschaft. Cologne, 1980.

Matteson *Capellmeister*   Mattheson, Johann. *Der vollkommene Capellmeister*. Hamburg, 1739. Facs. repr. ed. Margarete Reimann. Kassel, 1974. (2) English trans. Ernest C. Harriss. Ann Arbor, 1981.

Mayeda "Porpora"   Mayeda, Akio. "Nicola Antonio Porpora und der junge Haydn." In Schwarz *junge Haydn*, 41-58.

Mayer-Rosa, E. "The Creation in compositions from the 18th to the 20th centuries." *ISME* 7 (1980), 108ff.

McCaldin "First"   McCaldin, Denis. "Haydn's First and Last Work: The 'Missa Brevis' in F Major." *The Music Review* 28/3 (August 1967), 165-172.

McCaldin "'Missa'"   _____. "The 'Missa Sancti Nicolai': Haydn's Long 'Missa Brevis'." *Soundings* 3 (1973), 7-17.

_____. "Seeking Haydn. A Conductor's Guide to His Choral Music." *Organist's Review. Quarterly Record of the Incorporated Association of Organists* 68/1 (1983), 13-15.

McLean, Hugh J. "Mozart Parodies and Haydn Perplexities: new sources in Poland." *studies in music from the university of western ontario* 1 (1976), 1-7.

Mee, John Henry. *The Oldest Music Room in Europe; a Record of Eighteenth-Century Enterprise at Oxford*. London and New York, 1911.

Meier *Kontrabass*   Meier, Adolf. *Konzertante Musik für Kontrabass in der Wiener Klassik. Mit Beiträgen zur Geschichte des Kontrabaßbaues in Österreich*. (Bd. 4, Schriften zur Musik, ed. Walter Kolneder.) Giebing über Prien am Chiemsee, 1969.

Melkus "Development"   Melkus, Eduard. "The Development of the Violin during Haydn's Lifetime." In Larsen *Haydn Studies*, 224-225.

_____. "Die Entwicklung der freien Auszierung im 18. Jahrhundert." In Schwarz *junge Haydn*, 147-167.

_____. "Über die Ausführung der Stricharten in Mozarts Werken." *Mozart-Jahrbuch* (1967), 244-265.

Mendel *Pitch*   Mendel, Arthur. *Pitch in Western Music since 1500: A re-examination.* ["Sonderdruck aus *ACTA MUSICOLOGICA* 1978"] Kassel, 1979.

Menerth, Edward F. "Singing in Style: Classic." *Music Educator's Journal* 53/1 (September 1966), 64-66, 135-139.

Mertin   Mertin, Josef. "Zu den Orgelinstrumenten Joseph Haydns." In Badura-Skoda
"Orgelinstrumenten"   *Proceedings,* 72-75.

Meyer, Jürgen. "Raumakustik und Orchesterklang in den Konzertsälen Joseph Haydns." *Acustica. Internationale Akustische Zeitschrift* 41/3 (1978), 145-162.

MGG   *Die Musik in Geschichte und Gegenwart. Allgemeine Enzyklopädie der Musik.* 16 vols. Friedrich Blume, ed. Kassel, 1947-1979.

Michel, Walter. "Die Tobias-Dramen bis Haydns Oratorium 'Il ritorno di Tobia'." *Haydn-Studien* 5/3 (December 1984), 147-168.

Mies "Singkanons"   Mies, Paul. "Joseph Haydns Singkanons und ihre Grundidee." In Szabolcsi *Konferenz Budapest,* 93-94.

Mies "Textdichter"   _____. "Textdichter zu J. Haydns 'Mehrstimmigen Gesängen'." *The Haydn Yearbook* 1 (1962), 201.

_____. "Joseph Haydn und seine Singkanons." *Musica sacra* (Cologne) 80 (1960), 45-49.

_____. "Die Artikulationszeichen Strich und Punkt bei Wolfgang Amadeus Mozart." *Die Musikforschung* 11 (1958), 428-455.

_____. *Kritischer Bericht. Mehrstimmige Gesänge.* 30 of Haydn *JHW.* 1958.

_____. "Vorwort." In *Mehrstimmige Gesänge,* vi-ix. 30 of Haydn *JHW.* 1958.

_____. "Joseph Haydns geistliche Lieder für eine und mehrere Singstimmen mit Klavierbegleitung. Zu Geschichte und Ästhetik des Liedes bei J. Haydn." *Musica sacra* (Cologne) 77/4 (April 1957), 113-17.

Milde, Theodor. *Über das Leben und die Werke der beliebtesten deutschen Dichter und Tonsetzer.* 2 vols. Meissen, 1834.

Moder, Richard. "Gregor Joseph Werner, ein Meister des Ausgehenden musikalischen Barock in Eisenstadt." *Burgenländische Heimatblätter* (Eisenstadt) 21/2 (1959), 140-156.

Moe, Orin, Jr. "'Las Siete Ultimas Palabras' de Haydn: un análisis." *Revista Musical Chilena* 30/135-136 (1976), 22-38.

_____. "Structure in Haydn's 'The Seasons'." *The Haydn Yearbook* 9 (1975), 340-348.

Moissl, Franz. "Haydns Messen—'Klassische Kirchenmusik'?" *Gregorianische Rundschau* (Graz) 10/4-5 (April-May 1911), 49-51.

Mörner "Haydniana"   Mörner, C.-G. Stellan. "Haydniana aus Schweden um 1800." *Haydn-Studien* 2/1 (1969), 1-33.

Morrow, Mary Sue. *Concert Life in Haydn's Vienna: Aspects of a Developing Social Institution.* Sociology of Music Series No. 7. New York, 1989.

Mozart, J. C. W. A., et al. *Letters.* See Anderson *Letters of Mozart.*

Mozart *Violinschule* Mozart, Leopold. *Versuch einer gründlichen Violinschule.* Augsburg, 1756. 2nd ed. 1769/70; repr. 1787 as 3rd ed. (2) Facs. repr. ed. Hans Joachim Moser. Leipzig, 1956. (3) English trans. of 1756/1787 eds. by Edith Knocker as *A Treatise on the Fundamentals of Violin Playing.* 2nd ed. London, 1951.

Mraz *Haydn in seiner Zeit* Mraz, Gerda, Gottfried Mraz, and Gerald Schlag, eds. *Joseph Haydn in seiner Zeit. Eisenstadt, 20. Mai - 26. Oktober 1982.* [Ausstellung, veranstaltet von der Kulturabteilung des Amtes der Burgenländischen Landesregierung.] Eisenstadt[: Amt der Burgenländischen Landesregierung, Abt. 12/1], 1982.

Müller, Erich H. "Haydns Schöpfung und das Prager Konsistorium." *Signale für die musikalische Welt* 84/17 (1926), 663.

Müller, Theodor. "Grundsätzliches zur Interpretation der Violinwerke W. A. Mozarts." In *Wissenschaft und Praxis, eine Festschrift zum 70. Geburtstag von Bernhard Paumgartner,* 119-127. [Zürich, 1957.]

Müller *Hasse* Müller, Walther. *Johann Adolf Hasse als Kirchenkomponist.* Leipzig, 1910.

Münster, Joseph Joachim Benedicto. *Scala Jacob ascendendô, et descendô. Das ist: kürzlich, doch wohlgegründete Anleitung, und vollkommener Unterrich, die edle Choral-Music denen Regeln gemäss recht aus dem Fundament zu lernen.* Augsburg, 1743.

Murányi, R. Á. "Ein unbekanntes Manuskript der Missa Sancti Nicolai von Haydn." *Studia Musicologica* 8 (1966), 291-295.

Músiol, Rab. "Das Textbuch zur 'Schöpfung'." *Blätter für Haus- und Kirchenmusik* 3 (1899), 105-107.

Nafziger, Kenneth J. "The Masses of Haydn and Schubert: A Study in the Rise of Romanticism." D.M.A. thesis, University of Oregon, 1970.

Nakano, Hiroshi. ["J. Haydn as Composer for the Church."] *Philharmony* (Japan) 41 (May 1969), 16-20. [In Japanese]

Neumann, Frederick. *Ornamentation and Improvisation in Mozart.* Princeton (NJ), 1986.

New Catholic *New Catholic Encyclopedia.* 17 vols. New York, 1967.

New Grove *The New Grove Dictionary of Music and Musicians.* Stanley Sadie, ed. 20 vols. London, 1980.

Newman *Sonata* Newman, William S. *The Sonata in the Classic Era.* Chapel Hill, 1963. (2) 2nd ed. New York, 1972.

Nicolai *Beschreibung* Nicolai, Friedrich Christoph. *Beschreibung einer Reise durch Deutschland und die Schweiz, im Jahre 1781.* 4 vols. Berlin and Stettin, 1784.

Noé, G. von. "Die Fuge bei Joseph Haydn." Diss., University of Vienna, 1954.

NOH 4   See Abraham, Gerald, ed.

NOH 7   See Wellesz, Egon, and Frederick Sternfeld, eds.

Norton, M. D. Herter. "Haydn in America (before 1820)." *The Musical Quarterly* 18/2 (April 1932), 309-337.

Novello *Mozart Pilgrimage*   Novello, Vincent and Mary. *A Mozart Pilgrimage. Being the Travel Diaries of Vincent and Mary Novello in the Year 1829.* Transcr. and comp. Nerina Medici Di Marignano. Rosemary Hughes, ed. London, 1955.

Nowak *Haydn*   Nowak, Leopold. *Joseph Haydn: Leben, Bedeutung und Werk.* Zurich, 1951. (2) 3rd ed. 1966.

_____. "Joseph Haydn als Meister der Musica sacra." *Österreichische Musikzeitschrift* 14/5-6 (May-June 1959), 224-228.

Nützlader, Rudolf. "Salieri als Kirchenmusiker." *Studien zur Musikwissenschaft* 14 (1927), 160-178.

Nys, Carl de. "Mozart en Haydn in dienst van de heden- daagse liturgie?" *ADEM. Tweemaandelijks tijdschrift voor muziekcultuur* 18/4 (1982), 170-172. Fr. and Eng. summaries.

O'Douwes, Henk. "Johann Adolf Hasse en Joseph Haydn." *Mens en Melodie* 15/10 (October 1960), 294-295.

Ochs, Siegfried. *Der deutsche Gesangsverein für gemischten Chor.* 3 vols. (Hesses Musik-Handbücher, 78-81). Berlin, 1923-26.

Ohmiya, Akoto. "Text and Performance: The Treatment of Ossia Variants in Haydn Critical Scores." In Larsen *Haydn Studies*, 130-133.

Olleson "Diaries"   Olleson, D. Edward. "Haydn in the Diaries of Count Karl von Zinzendorf." *The Haydn Yearbook* 2 (1963-64), 45-63.

Olleson "Griesinger"   _____. "Georg August Griesinger's Correspondence with Breitkopf und Härtel." *The Haydn Yearbook* 3 (1965), 5-53.

Olleson "Origin"   _____. "The Origin and Libretto of Haydn's 'Creation'." *The Haydn Yearbook* 4 (1968), 148-168.

_____. "Gottfried, Baron van Swieten, and His Influence on Haydn and Mozart." Ph.D. diss., Oxford (Hertford), 1967.

_____. "Gottfried van Swieten, Patron of Haydn and Mozart." *Proceedings of the Royal Musical Association* 89 (1962-63), 63-74.

Pammler, Rudolf. "Eine Arie von Joseph Haydn im Unterricht." *Musik in der Schule* 8/6 (1957), 254-256.

Pannain, Guido. "Haydn e la 'Creazione'." *La Rassegna Musicale* 18/1 (January 1948), 1-8.

Pass "Josephinism"   Pass, Walter. "Josephinism and the Josephinian Reforms Concerning Haydn." In Larsen *Haydn Studies*, 168-171.

Pass "Melodic Construction"   _____. "Melodic Construction in Haydn's Two Salve Regina Settings." In Larsen *Haydn Studies*, 371-374.

_____. "Bemerkungen zu Werk- und Wirkungsgeschichte von Haydns Messen." In Badura-Skoda *Proceedings*, 476-479.

Pauly, Reinhard G. "The Reforms of Church Music under Joseph II." *The Musical Quarterly* 43/3 (July 1957), 372-382.

Payer, Otto. "Haydns Schöpfung eine Entweihung der Kirche." *Neue Musik-Zeitung* 15/13 (1894), 149-150.

Petri *Anleitung*   Petri, Johann Samuel. *Anleitung zur practischen Musik, vor neuangehende Sänger und Instrumentspieler.* Lauban, 1767. (2) 2nd ed. Leipzig, 1782.

Petzoldt, Richard. "Haydns Chorwerke." *Die Musik* 24/6 (March 1932), 408-412.

Pfannhauser, Karl. "Glossarien zu Haydns Kirchenmusik." In Badura-Skoda *Proceedings*, 496-501.

Philipp "Messenkomposition"   Philipp, Roland. "Die Messenkomposition der Wiener Vorklassiker G. M. Monn und G. Chr. Wagenseil." Ph.D. diss., University of Vienna, 1938.

Pohl *Haydn*   Pohl, C. F. *Joseph Haydn.* 3 vols. 1: Berlin, 1875 and Leipzig, 1878; 2: Leipzig, 1882; 3 ("weitergeführt von Hugo Botstiber"): Leipzig, 1927. (2) Facs. repr. Wiesbaden, 1970-71.

_____. "Haydn, Franz Joseph." In *Grove's Dictionary of Music and Musicians* 1, 702-22. Sir George Grove, ed. London, 1879. [In later eds., notes and additions by W. H. Hadow.]

_____. *Denkschrift aus Anlass des hunderthjährigen Bestehens der Tonkunstler-Societät, im Jahre 1862 reorganisirt als "Haydn." Witwen- und Waisen-Versorgungs-Verein der Tonkünstler in Wien.* Vienna, 1871.

_____. *Mozart und Haydn in London.* Vienna, 1867; repr. New York, 1970.

Preiss, C. "Die Musikpflege in Linz um die Wende des 18. Jahrhunderts." *Jahrbuch der Stadt Linz 1935* (1936), 104ff.

Prod'homme, J.-G. "Haydn and His Works in France." *The Chesterian* 13/102 (April-May 1932), 158-160.

Puttman, Max. "Joseph Haydn als Vokalkomponist." *Blätter fur Haus- und Kirchenmusik* 13/8-9 (May-June 1909), 117-121, 133-136.

Quantz *Versuch*   Quantz, Johann Joachim. *Versuch einer Anweisung die Flöte traversière zu spielen.* Berlin, 1752. (2) Eng. trans. Edward R. Reilly as *On Playing the Flute.* New York, 1966.

Quellmaly, Fred. "Haydns Kanons." *Zeitschrift für Musikwissenschaft* 15/4 (January 1933), 172-173.

Raby *History*   Raby, F. J. E. *A History of Christian-Latin Poetry from the Beginnings to the Close of the Middle Ages.* London, 1927.

Radant "Rosenbaum"   Radant, Else, ed. "Die Tagebücher von Joseph Carl Rosenbaum 1770-1829." *The Haydn Yearbook* 5 (1968), 7-159.

Rajeczky, Benjamin. "Zu Haydns späten Messen 'Kirchenstil' und Vortragsweise." In Badura-Skoda *Proceedings*, 479-482.

Ratner *Classic Music*   Ratner, Leonard. *Classic Music: Expression, Form, and Style*. New York, 1980.

_____. "Harmonic Aspects of Classic Form." *Journal of the American Musicological Society* 2/3 (1949), 159-168.

Ravizza, Victor. *Joseph Haydn. Die Schöpfung* (Meisterwerke der Musik. Werkmonographien zur Musikgeschichte 24). Munich, 1981.

Raynor, Henry. "Some Reflections on the Viennese Mass." *The Musical Times* 95 (November 1954), 592-596.

Redfern, Brian. *Haydn: A Biography, with a survey of books, editions, and recordings*. (The Concertgoer's Companions). London, 1970.

Reichardt, Johann Friedrich. *Vertraute Briefe geschrieben auf einer Reise nach Wien und den Österreichischen Staaten zu Ende des Jahres 1808 und zu Anfang 1809*. 2 vols. Amsterdam, 1810.

_____. *Über die Pflichten des Ripienviolinisten*. Berlin, 1776.

_____. *Briefe eines aufmerksamen Reisenden die Musik betreffend*. 2 vols. Frankfurt and Leipzig, 1774-76.

Ricks "Tempo"   Ricks, Robert. "Tempo Modification or Pacing/Dynamics." In Larsen *Haydn Studies*, 209-211.

Riedel *Hofe Karls VI*   Riedel, Friedrich W. *Kirchenmusik am Hofe Karls VI (1711-1740)*. Studien zur Landes- und Sozialgeschichte der Musik 1. Munich and Salzburg, 1977.

Reidel "Liturgie"   _____. "Liturgie und Kirchenmusik." In Mraz *Haydn in seiner Zeit*, 121-133.

_____. "Die Kirchenmusik im Benediktinerstift Göttweig." *Singende Kirche* 13 (1966), 196ff.

Riedel-Martiny, Anke. "Das Verhältnis von Text und Musik in Haydns Oratorien." *Haydn-Studien* 1/4 (April 1967), 205-240.

_____. "Die Oratorien Joseph Haydns. Ein Beitrag zum Problem der Textvertonung." Diss., University of Göttingen, 1965.

Riemer, Otto. "Realistisches Oratorium. Zur Phänomenologie von Haydns 'Schöpfung'." *Musica* 13/5 (May 1959), 283-286.

Riethmüller, Albrecht. "Die Vorstellung des Chaos in der Musik. Zu Joseph Haydns Oratorium 'Die Schöpfung'." In *Convivium Cosmologicum. Interdisziplinäre Studien. Helmut Hönl zum 70. Geburtstag*, 185-195. Anastasios Giannarás, ed. Basel, 1973.

Riley *Viola*   Riley, Maurice W. *The History of the Viola*. Ann Arbor, 1980.

Ringer "*Chasse*"   Ringer, A. L. "The *Chasse* as a Musical Topic of the 18th Century." *Journal of the American Musicological Society* 6/2 (1953), 148-159.

Roche "Caldara"   Roche, Elizabeth. "Caldara and the Mass." *The Musical Times* 111 (1970), 1101-1103.

Rosen *Style*   Rosen, Charles. *The Classical Style: Haydn, Mozart, Beethoven*. Rev. ed. (paperback). New York, 1972.

_____. *Sonata Forms*. New York and London, 1980.

Rosenbaum, Joseph Carl. [Diaries, 1797-1829]. (ms.) Österreichische Nationalbibliothek, s. n. 194-204. [See Radant "Rosenbaum."]

Rosser, Julie Glenn. "Haydn's 'Creation,' an Analysis and Appreciation." Master's thesis, Eastman School of Music of the University of Rochester, 1946.

Rothschild, F. *Musical Performance in the Times of Mozart and Beethoven*. London, 1961.

Runciman, John F. "Haydn and His 'Creation'." In *Old Scores and New Readings . . . Discussions on Music and Certain Musicians*, 85-92. London, 1899.

Runestad "Masses"   Runestad, Cornell Jesse. "The Masses of Joseph Haydn: A Stylistic Study." D.M.A. Thesis, University of Illinois, 1970.

Rushton, Julian. *Classical Music: A Concise History from Gluck to Beethoven*. London, 1986.

Rutz, Hans. *Österreichs grosse Musiker in Dokumenten der Zeit. Haydn, Mozart, Beethoven*. Österreichische Buchgemeinschaft 23. Vienna, 1949.

Saam "'sieben Worte'"   Saam, Josef. "'Die sieben Worte' von Haydn-Friebert." In *Humanistisches Gymnasium Passau*. Jahresbericht 1956-57, 79-83.

Sainsbury, John. "Haydn, Joseph." in *A Dictionary of Musicians from the Earliest Ages to the Present Time. Comprising the Most Important Biographical Contents of the Works of Gerber, Choron and Fayolle, Count Orloff, Dr. Burney, Sir John Hawkins, etc.* 1, 340-353. London, 1825. Repr. New York, 1966.

Saint-Saëns, Camille. "Joseph Haydn et les 'Sept Paroles'." In *École Buissonière. Notes et Souvenirs*, 189-97. Paris, [1913].

Sandberger, Adolf. "Zur Entstehungsgeschichte von Haydns 'Die Sieben Worten des Erlösers am Kreuze'." In *Jahrbuch der Musikbibliothek Peters* 10(1903), 47-59. Repr. Sandberger, *Ausgewählte Aufsätze zur Musikgeschichte* 1, 224-265. Munich, 1921.

Scacchi *Discorso*   Scacchi, Marco. *Breve discorso sopra la musica moderna*. Warsaw, 1649.

Schabasser, Josef. "Der kirchliche Volksgesang in Wien zur Zeit Maria Theresias und Josefs II. Aus den Handschriften der Wiener Augustinerkirche." *Singende Kirche* 27/3, 4 (1979-80), 124-127, 161-163.

Schandorfer, Erich. "Die drei Erzengel in Goethes 'Faust' und in Josef Haydns 'Schöpfung'." *Musica Divina* 25/5 (May 1937), 91-94.

Scheibe *Critischer*   Scheibe, Johann Adolph. *Critischer Musikus*. Leipzig, 1745. Repr. Hildesheim and Wiesbaden, 1970.

Schelp, Arend. "Het tekstboek van 'Die Schöpfung.' Baron van Swieten en Joseph Haydn." *Mens en Melodie* 23/5-6 (May-June 1968), 159-162.

Schenbeck "Baroque Influences"

Schenbeck, Lawrence. "Baroque Influences in Mozart's Masses." *American Choral Review* 20/1,4 (January, October 1978), 3-9, 3-16.

Schenbeck "Missa"

_____. "Missa in angustiis by Joseph Haydn." *The Choral Journal* 25/9 (May 1985), 19, 25-30.

Schenk "Genese"

Schenk, Erich. "Zur Genese der emphatischen None." In *Beiträge zur Musikdokumentation (Franz Grasberger zum 60. Geburtstag)*, 405-412. Günter Brosche, ed. Tutzing, 1975.

Schenk "Göttweiger Rorate-Messe"

_____. "Ist die Göttweiger Rorate-Messe ein Werk Joseph Haydns?" *Studien zur Musikwissenschaft* 24 (1960), 87-105.

_____. "Das Weltbild Joseph Haydns." In *Almanach. Österreichische Akademie der Wissenschaften* 109 (1959), 245-272. Repr. Schenk, *Ausgewählte Aufsätze, Reden und Vorträge*, 86-99. Graz, Vienna and Cologne, 1967.

_____. *Das Weltbild Joseph Haydns.* Vienna, 1960.

Schenker "Schöpfung"

Schenker, Heinrich. "Haydn: Die Schöpfung. Die Vorstellung des Chaos." In *Das Meisterwerk in der Musik* 2, 159-170. Munich, 1926.

_____. *Ein Beitrag zur Ornamentik. Als Einführung zu Ph. Em. Bachs Klavierwerken. Mitumfassend auch die Ornamentik Haydns, Mozarts und Beethovens etc.* Vienna, 1903. [2nd ed., 1908]

Schienerl "Bonno"

Schienerl, Alfred. "Giuseppe Bonnos Kirchenkompositionen." *Studien zur Musikwissenschaft* 15 (1928), 62-85.

Schmid "Bemerkungen"

Schmid, Ernst Fritz. "Bemerkungen zu Josef Haydns Nelson-Messe." *Neue Musik-Zeitung* 49/24 (1928), 770-775.

Schmid "Brüder"

_____. "Joseph Haydn und der Orden der Barmherzigen Brüder." In *Die Barmherzige Brüder*, 195-203. Friedrich Läufer, ed. Vienna, 1931.

Schmid *Haydn*

_____. *Joseph Haydn, Band I. Ein Buch von Vorfahren und Heimat des Meisters.* 2 vols. Kassel, 1934.

Schmid "Haydns Oratorium"

_____. "Haydns Oratorium 'Il ritorno di Tobia,' seine Entstehung und seine Schicksale." *Archiv für Musikwissenschaft* 16/3 (1959), 292-313.

Schmid "Jugendliebe"

_____. "Josef Haydns Jugendliebe." In *Festschrift Wilhelm Fischer*, 109-122. Innsbrücker Beiträge zur Kulturgeschichte, Sonderheft 3. Innsbruck, 1956.

_____. "Vorwort." In *Il Ritorno di Tobia. Oratorio*, vi-ix. 28/1 of Haydn *JHW*, 1963.

_____. "Joseph Haydn und die vokale Zierpraxis seiner Zeit, dargestellt an einer Arie seines Tobias-Oratoriums." In Szabolcsi *Konferenz Budapest*, 117-130. [See Appendix of this volume.]

_____. "Joseph Haydn in Eisenstadt. Ein Beitrag zur Biographie des Meisters." *Burgenländische Heimatblätter* (Eisenstadt) 1/1 (April 1932), 2-13.

_____. "Joseph Haydn und Carl Philipp Emanuel Bach." *Zeitschrift für Musikwissenschaft* 14/6 (March 1932), 299-312.

_____. "Zum Aufsatz Otto Ursprungs über Josef Haydns Requiem c-moll." *Musica Divina* 17/3 (March 1929), 53-55.

_____. "Ein neu-entdecktes Requiem Haydns." *Neue Musik-Zeitung* 49/2 (1928), 52-57. [Hob. XXIIa:c1]

Schmid, Manfred Hermann. *Die Musikaliensammlung der Erzabtei St. Peter in Salzburg. Katalog. Erster Teil: Leopold und Wolfgang Amadeus Mozart, Joseph und Michael Haydn.* (Schriftenreihe der Internationalen Stiftung Mozarts, 3-4). Salzburg, 1970.

Schmidt, Karl. "Die Sprache der Tonarten in Haydns 'Jahreszeiten'." *Musikerziehung. Zeitschrift der Musikerzieher Österreichs* 36/5 (1983), 211-214.

Schnerich "Chronologie"   Schnerich, Alfred. "Zur Chronologie der Messen Haydns." *Zeitschrift für Musikwissenschaft* 17/11 (November 1935), 472-474.

Schnerich *Messe*   _____. *Messe und Requiem seit Haydn und Mozart.* Vienna and Leipzig, 1909.

Schnerich "Versehen"   _____. "Die textlichen Versehen in den Messen Haydns und deren Korrektur." In *Haydn-Zentenarfeier*, 542-544.

_____. "Haydn und die Barmherzige Brüder." *Christliche Kunstblätter* (Linz) 73/4-6 (April-June 1932), 33-35.

_____. "Haydns Kirchenwerke." In *Goethe- und Haydn-Almanach. Deutscher Sänger-Kalendar* 1932, 209-213.

_____. "Die katholischen Glaubenssätze bei den Wiener Klassikern." *Zeitschrift für Musikwissenschaft* 8/4 (January 1926), 231-235.

_____. *Wiens Kirchen und Kapellen in kunst- und kulturgeschichtlicher Darstellung.* Zürich, Leipzig, and Vienna, 1921.

_____. "Haydns Messe. Zur ersten Gesamtaufführung in der Wiener Hofkapelle." *Neue Zeitschrift für Musik* 84/7 (February 15 1917), 53-55.

_____. "Zur Geschichte der späteren Messen Haydns." *Zeitschrift der Internationalen Musikgesellschaft* 15/12 (December 1914) 328-333.

_____. "Zur Geschichte der früheren Messen Haydns." *Zeitschrift der Internationalen Musikgesellschaft* 14/6 (June 1913), 169-170.

_____. "Haydns Maria Zeller Messe. Zur Errichtung des Haydn-Denkmals in Maria Zell." *Die Musik* 8/16 Bd. 31 (1908-09), 223-226.

_____. "Aufführungen von Kirchenwerken J. Haydns in Wien. Jänner bis Ende Juni 1909." In *Haydn-Zentenarfeier*, 683-684.

_____. "Die Haydn-Votivtafel für Mariazell." *Der Kirchenchor* (Bregenz) 39/6 (June 1909), 50-51.

_____. "Das hundertjährige Jubiläum von Haydns Theresienmesse." *Der Kirchenchor* (Bregenz) 29/11 (November 15 1899), 92-93, 101-102.

_____. "Zur Erinnerung an die erste Aufführung der Nelson-Messe von Josef Haydn von hundert Jahre (9. September 1898)." *Der Kirchenchor* (Bregenz) 28/11 (November 15 1898), 89-92.

Schnürl, Karl. "Haydns 'Schöpfung' als Messe." *Studien zur Musikwissenschaft (Festschrift für Erich Schenk)* 25 (1962), 463-474.

Schnyder von Wartensee, Joseph Xavier. *Ästhetische Betrachtungen über die Jahreszeiten und die Schöpfung von Joseph Haydn.* Frankfurt, 1861.

Schroeder, David P. "Haydn and Gellert: Parallels in Eighteenth-Century Music and Literature." *Current Musicology* 35 (1983), 7-18.

Schroeder, Hermann. "Die Messen Joseph Haydns." *Katholische Kirchenmusik. Zeitschrift für die Musik in der Liturgie* 107/2 (1982), 56-61.

Schubart *Ästhetik*   Schubart, Christian Friedr. Daniel. *Ideen zu eines Ästhetik der Tonkunst.* Ed. Ludwig Schubart. Vienna, 1806.

Schubert *Singe-Schule*   Schubert, Johann Friedrich. *Neue Singe-Schule oder gründliche und vollstaendige Anweisung zur Singkunst in drey Abtheilungen mit hinlänglichen Uebungsstücken.* Leipzig, [ca. 1805].

Schünemann, Georg, ed. "Franz Joseph Haydn, von Karl Friedrich Zelter." *Die Musikpflege. Monatschrift für Musikerziehung, Musikorganisation and Chorgesangwesen* (Leipzig) 3/2 (1932), 49-52.

Schwarz *junge Haydn*   Schwarz, Vera, ed. *Der junge Haydn. Wandel von Musikauffassung und Musikaufführung in der österreichischen Musik zwischen Barock und Klassik . . .* (Beiträge zur Aufführungspraxis, 1). Graz, 1972.

_____. "Die Rolle des Cembalos in Österreich nach 1760." In Schwarz *junge Haydn*, 249-258.

Scott, Marion M. "Haydn in England." *The Musical Quarterly* 18/2 (April 1932), 260-273.

_____. "Haydn: Relics and Reminiscences in England." *Music and Letters* 13/2 (April 1932), 126-136.

Sedlmayr "Reichsstil"   Sedlmayr, Hans. "Die politische Bedeutung des deutschen Barocks (Der Reichsstil)." In *Gesamtdeutsche Vergangenheit, Festgabe für Heinrich Ritter von Srbik zum 60. Geburtstag,* 126ff. Munich, 1938.

Seeger, Horst. "'Und eine neue Welt. . . ' Zur Bedeutung von Joseph Haydns Oratorium 'Die Schöpfung'." *Musik und Gesellschaft* 9/5 (May 1959) 15-19.

Sengstschmid, Walter. "Die Messkompositionen von Joseph Haydn. Übersicht über das Angebot der Musikverlage." *Singende Kirche. Zeitschrift für katholische Kirchenmusik* 29/4 (1981-82), 176-180.

Sherman, Charles H. "The Masses of Johann Michael Haydn: A Critical Survey of Sources." Ph.D. diss., University of Michigan, 1967.

Shrock "Aspects"   Shrock, Dennis. "Aspects of Performance Practice During the Classic Era." In *Essays on Choral Music in Honor of Howard Swan.* Stuyvesant (NY), 1990.

Shtorm, Georgii Petrovich. *Potaennyi Radishchev; votoraia zhyzn "Puteshestvie iz Peterburga v Moskva."* ["The mysterious Radishchev; from his biography 'A journey from St. Petersburg to Moscow.'"] Moscow, 1965.

Siegl, P. H. *Das Benediktinerstift Göttweig.* Göttweig, 1914.

Siegmund-Schultze, Walther. "Händel és Haydn: A händeli 'allegorikus-lírai' oratorium és hatása a klasszikus müvészetre, különösen Haydn Józsefre." ["The oratorios of Handel which are regarded as allegorical and their influence on the Classical period, esp. on Haydn."] In Szabolcsi *Haydn Emlékére*, 21-37. [Ger. summary, 31-37.]

Small, Barbara Mitchell. "A Proposed Librettist for Haydn's 'Creation': Benjamin Stillingfleet." M.A. thesis, University of Nevada, Reno, 1979.

Smith, Ruth M. "Intellectual Contexts of Handel's Oratorios." In *Music in Eighteenth-Century England: Essays in Memory of Charles Cudworth*, 115-133. C. Hogwood and R. Luckett, eds. Cambridge, 1983.

Smither "Haydns *ritorno*"   Smither, Howard E. "Haydns *Il ritorno di Tobia* und die Tradition des italienischen Oratoriums." In Feder *Tradition*, 160-188.

Smither *History*   _____. *A History of the Oratorio*. 4 vols. [Vol. 3: *The Oratorio in the Classical Era*] Chapel Hill (NC), 1977- .

Somerset, H. V. P. "Joseph Haydn in England." *Music and Letters* 13/3, 272ff.

Somfai "Notation"   Somfai, László. "How to Read and Understand Haydn's Notation in its Chronologically Changing Concepts." In Badura-Skoda *Proceedings*, 23-34.

_____. *Joseph Haydn: His Life in Contemporary Pictures*. Trans. and rev. Mari Kuttner and Karoly Ravasz. London and New York, 1969.

Sondheimer, Robert. "Art und Aufführungsstil vorklassischer Sinfonien." *Die Musik* 23 (1931), 344-350.

Sonneck, O. G. "The Haydn Centenary Festival at Vienna. Retrospective Impressions." *The New Music Review and Church Music Review* 8/96 (November 1909), 605-611.

Spazier, Johann Gottlieb Karl, ed. *Berlinische musikalische Zeitung*. Berlin, 1794.

Spitzer/Zaslaw "Ornamentation"   Spitzer, John, and Neal Zaslaw. "Improvised Ornamentation in Eighteenth-Century Orchestras." *Journal of the American Musicological Society* 39 (1986), 524-577.

Steglich, Rudolf. "Das Auszierungswesen in der Musik W. A. Mozarts." *Mozart-Jahrbuch* (1955), 181-237.

_____. "Das Tempo als Problem der Mozartinterpretation." In *Bericht über die musikwissenschaftliche Tagung der Internationalen Stiftung Mozarteum in Salzburg*, 172-179. E. Schenk, ed. Leipzig, 1932.

Steinpress, Boris. "Haydns Oratorien in Russland zu Lebzeiten des Komponisten." *Haydn-Studien* 2/2 (May 1969), 77-112.

Stekl, Konrad. "Joseph Haydn in Mariazell und Graz." *Mitteilungen des Steirischen Tonkünstlerbundes* 44 (April-June 1970), 7-10.

Stephens, Howard. "The 'Creation'." *Music Teacher* 58/1 (1979), 16-17.

Stern "Schöpfung"   Stern, Martin. "Haydns 'Schöpfung.' Geist und Herkunft des van Swieten-schen Librettos. Ein Beitrag zum Thema 'Säkularisation' im Zeitalter der Aufklärung." *Haydn-Studien* 1/3 (October 1966), 121-198.

Stewart, Gordon. "Haydn and Milton." *Royal College of Music Magazine* 72/1 (1976), 17-22.

Stolbrock "Reutter"   Stolbrock, L. "Leben und Wirken des K. K. Hofkapellmeisters und Hofkompositors Johann Georg Reutter jun." *Vierteljahrschrift für Musikwissenschaft* 8 (1892), 161-203, 289-306.

Stowell *Violin Technique*   Stowell, Robin. *Violin Technique and Performance Practice in the Late Eighteenth and Early Nineteenth Centuries.* Cambridge, 1985.

Stradner, Gerhard. "Zur Stimmtonhöhe der Blasinstrumente zur Zeit Joseph Haydns." In Badura-Skoda *Proceedings*, 81-86.

Strobl, August. "Kirchenmusikkomponisten um Joseph Haydn im Lichte des Notenarchivs der Stadtpfarrkirche zu Eisenstadt." *Musica Divina* 26/3; 11-12 (March; November-December 1938), 45-46; 191-193.

Sullivan, Michael J. "Brevis Technique in the Masses of Joseph Haydn." Master's paper, University of Chicago, 1969.

[Swieten, Gottfried van.] *The Creation and The Seasons: The Complete Authentic Sources for the Word-Books.* H. C. Robbins Landon, ed. Cardiff, Wales, 1988.

Szabolcsi, Bence. "Das Naturbild bei Händel und Haydn." In *Festschrift zur Händel-Ehrung der Deutschen Demokratischen Republik 1959*, 88-93. Leipzig, [1959].

Szabolcsi/Bartha *Haydn Emlékére*   Szabolcsi, Bence, and Dénes Bartha, eds. *Haydn Emlékére. Zenetudományi Tanulmányok* 8. Budapest, 1960.

Szabolcsi/Bartha *Konferenz Budapest*   _____, eds. *Bericht über die Internationale Konferenz zum Andenken Joseph Haydns. Budapest, 17.-22. September 1959.* Budapest, 1961.

Tank *Studien*   Tank, U. *Studien zur Esterházyschen Hofmusik von etwa 1620 bis 1790.* Regensburg, 1981.

_____. "Joseph Haydns geistliche Musik in der Anschauung des 19. Jahrhunderts." In Feder *Tradition*, 215-262.

Tarr *Trumpet*   Tarr, Edward. *The Trumpet.* Trans. S. E. Plank and E. Tarr. Portland (OR), 1988.

Tatnall, Anne. "The Use of Symphonic Forms in the Six Late Masses of Joseph Haydn." Master's thesis, Smith College, 1963.

Tattersall *Psalmody*   Tattersall, William Dechair, ed. *Improved Psalmody.* London, 1794.

Temperley *Creation*   Temperley, Nicholas. *Haydn: The Creation.* (Cambridge Music Handbooks.) Cambridge (UK), 1991.

Temperley "New light"   _____. "New light on the libretto of The Creation." In *Music in Eighteenth-Century England. Essays in memory of Charles Cudworth*, 189-211. Christopher Hogwood and Richard Luckett, eds. Cambridge, 1983.

Temperley "Tempos"   _____. "Haydn's Tempos in *The Creation.*" *Early Music* 19/2 (May 1991), 235-245.

Tenducci, Giusto Ferdinando. *Instruction of Mr. Tenducci to his Scholars.* [London, 1785].

Thomas, Günter. "Joseph Haydns Tanzmusik." In *Joseph Haydn und seine Zeit.* [Jahrbuch für Österreichisches Kulturgeschichte 2.] Eisenstadt, 1972.

_____. "Griesingers Briefe über Haydn: Aus seiner Korrespondenz mit Breitkopf & Härtel." *Haydn-Studien* 1 (1965-67), 49-114.

_____. "Vorwort." In *Messen Nr. 9-10,* vi-ix. 23/3 of Haydn *JHW.* 1965.

_____. *Kritischer Bericht. Messen Nr. 9-10.* 23/3 of Haydn *JHW.* 1971.

Tiersot, Julien. "Le Lied 'Ein Mädchen, das auf Ehre hielt' et ses prototypes français." *Zeitschrift der Internationalen Musikgesellschaft* 12/8-9 (May-June 1911), 222-26.

Timotheus. "Handel and Haydn Contrasted." *The Euterpeiad* (Boston), 1/30 (October 21 1820), 117-118.

Tittel, Ernst. *Österreichische Kirchenmusik.* Vienna, 1961.

_____. "Die Wiener Pastoralmesse." *Musica Divina* 23/12 (1935), 192-196.

Tolstoy, Christie. "The Identification and Interpretation of Sign Ornaments in Haydn's Instrumental Music." In Larsen *Haydn Studies,* 315-323.

Tosi *Opinioni*   Tosi, Pier Francesco. *Opinioni de' cantori antichi, e moderni.* Bologna, 1723. (2) Trans. and ed. J. E. Galliard as *Observations on the Florid Song.* London, 1742. (3) 2nd ed. of *Observations,* London, 1743. Many facs. repr. incl. London, 1926.

Tovey *Essays/Concertos*   Tovey, Sir Donald Francis. *Vocal Music.* Vol. V (5) of *Essays in Musical Analysis.* 7 vols. London, 1935-44. (2) Repr. in *Concertos and Choral Works.* London, 1981/9.

Town "Missa"   Town, Stephen. "Joseph Haydn's Missa in Angustiis: History, Analysis and Performance Suggestions." *Sacred Music* 110/2 (1983), 5-10.

Tromlitz *Unterricht*   Tromlitz, Johann George. *Ausführlicher und gründlicher Unterricht die Flöte zu spielen.* Leipzig, 1791. (2) Trans. and ed. Ardal Powell as *The Virtuoso Flute Player by Johann George Tromlitz.* Cambridge, 1991.

Trott "Accentuation"   Trott, Donald. "Patterns of Accentuation in the Classical Style as Supported by Primary Sources and as Illustrated in the Late Masses of Franz Joseph Haydn." D.M.A. document, University of Oklahoma, 1984.

Trott "Emphasis"   _____. "Patterns of Emphasis in Classical Music." *The Choral Journal* 28/2 (September 1987), 5-13.

Türk *Klavierschule*   Türk, Daniel Gottlob. *Klavierschule, oder Anweisung zum Klavierspielen für Lehrer und Lernende.* Leipzig and Halle, 1789. Facs. repr. ed. E. R. Jacobi. Kassel, 1962. 2nd ed. 1967. (2) *School of Clavier Playing, or Instructions in Playing the Clavier for Teachers & Students.* Trans. Raymond H. Haggh. Lincoln (NE) and London, 1982.

Turnbull, Robert. "Haydn and His 'Creation'." In *Musical Genius and Religion*, 36-49. London, 1907.

Unger, Max. "Haydn-Studien, I." *Musikalisches Wochenblatt* 40/24-25 (September 9-16 1909), 317-320, 333-334; 41/28 (October 13 1910), 297-300.

————. "Haydn-Studien, II." *Musikalisches Wochenblatt* 41/37-39 (December 15-22 1910), 413-415, 440-441.

Unverricht *Bericht/Sieben*   Unverricht, Hubert. *Kritischer Bericht. Die Sieben letzten Worte unseres Erlösers am Kreuze. Orchesterfassung.* 4 of Haydn *JHW.* 1963.

Unverricht "Haydns *Worte*"   Unverricht, Hubert. "Joseph Haydns *Die Sieben Worte Christi am Kreuze* in der Bearbeitung des Passauer Hofkapellmeisters Joseph Friebert." *Kirchenmusikalisches Jahrbuch* 65 (1981), 83-94.

Unverricht "Vorwort" 1   ————. "Vorwort." In *Die Sieben letzten Worte unseres Erlösers am Kreuze. Vokalfassung,* vi-ix. 28/2 of Haydn *JHW.* 1961.

Unverricht "Vorwort" 2   ————. "Vorwort." In *Die Sieben letzten Worte unseres Erlösers am Kreuze. Orchesterfassung (1785),* vii-ix. 4 of Haydn *JHW.* 1959.

Unverricht, H., and Alan Tyson. "[Letters to the editor:] Haydn's 'Seven Last Words'." *The Musical Times* 108/1498 (December 1967), 1116.

Ursprung *Kirchenmusik*   Ursprung, Otto. *Die katholische Kirchenmusik.* Potsdam, 1931.

————. "Die Echtheit des 'neu entdeckten' Requiems von Haydn." *Musica Divina* 16/11-12 (November-December 1928), 195-204.

V. M. "Haydn et sa musique religieuse." *Cäcilia. Organ der Diözesan-Cäcilien-Vereine* (Strassburg) 26/4 (April 1909), 52-57.

Van Camp, Leonard. "Haydn's *The Seasons*: An Unjustly Neglected Masterpiece." *American Choral Review* 30/3 (Summer 1988), 9-13.

Van der Meer, John Henry. "Die Verwendung der Blasinstrumente im Orchester bei Haydn und seinen Zeitgenossen." In Schwarz *junge Haydn,* 202-220.

[Varits, Karl.] *Geschichte des Calvarienberges und Wallfahrtsortes Maria-Eisenstadt. Von mehreren Priestern des Raaber Bisthums.* Györ, 1912.

Vignal, Marc. "L'interprétation de la musique de Haydn." In *L'interprétation de la musique classique de Haydn à Schubert. Colloque international, Evry, 13-15 Octobre 1977,* 57-65. Paris, 1980.

Vogel, Martin. "Drei Flöten in Haydns *Schöpfung.*" In Cadenbach *Beiträge,* 179-184.

Vogg "Tuma"   Vogg, Herbert. "Franz Tuma (1704-1774) als Instrumentalkomponist, nebst Beiträgen zur Wiener Musikgeschichte des 18. Jahrhunderts: Die Hofkapelle der Kaiserinwitwe Elisabeth Christine." Ph.D. diss., University of Vienna, 1951.

Walter "Haydn-   Walter, Horst. "Haydn-Bibliographie 1973-1983." *Haydn-Studien* 5/4
Bibliographie"   (1985), 205-306.

Walter "Keyboard"   _____. "Haydn's Keyboard Instruments." In Larsen *Haydn Studies*, 213-216.

Walter "Klaviere"   _____. "Haydns Klaviere." *Haydn-Studien* 2 (1969-70), 256-88.

Walter "Textbücher" _____. "Gottfried van Swietens handschriftliche Textbücher zu 'Schöpfung' und 'Jahreszeiten'." *Haydn-Studien* 1/4 (1967), 241-277.

                     _____. "Das Tasteninstrument beim jungen Haydn." In Schwarz *junge Haydn*, 237-248.

Walther *Lexicon*   Walther, Johann Gottfried. *Musicalisches Lexicon . . .* Leipzig, 1732. Facs. ed. Richard Schaal. Kassel, 1968.

                     Waninger, Edmund. "Zu Joseph Haydns 'Tenebrae factae sunt'." *Der Chor* 3/4 (April 1951), 72-73.

Webb "Analysis"   Webb, Brian Patrick. "A Conductor's Analysis of Haydn's Theresienmesse." D.M.A. diss., Indiana University, 1977.

                     Weber, J. F. "A Splendid Celebration of the Haydn Anniversary." *Fanfare. The Magazine for Serious Record Collectors* 6/1 (1982), 76-84, 504-505.

                     Weisen zu den Liedern der Kirche, aus den römischen Tagzeiten und Messbuche übersetzt. Vienna, 1773.

                     Wellesz, Egon, and Frederick Sternfeld, eds. *The Age of Enlightenment 1745-1790* [*NOH* 7]. Vol. 7 of *The New Oxford History of Music.* London, 1973.

                     Wessely, Othmar. "Linz und die Musik: von den Anfängen bis zum Beginn des 19. Jahrhunderts." *Jahrbuch der Stadt Linz* 1950 (1951), 96ff.

                     _____. *Musik in Oberösterreich.* Linz, 1951.

White List   *The White List of the Society of St. Gregory of America.* The Music Committee of the Society, ed. New York, 1951.

Wilson "Hasse"   Wilson, David J. "The Masses of Johann Adolf Hasse." 2 vols. D.M.A. thesis, University of Illinois, 1973.

                     Wöldike, Mogens. "Tempo." In Larsen *Haydn Studies*, 208-209.

                     [Wolf, Hugo.] "Hugo Wolf zu Haydns 'Schöpfung'." *Musik im Unterricht* 57/4 (April 1966), 132-133.

                     Worbs, Hans Christoph. "Anmerkungen zu Haydns Oratorien 'Die Schöpfung' und 'Die Jahreszeiten'." *FonoForum* 9/1982, 28-31.

                     Wutzel, O. *Das Chorherrenstift St. Florian.* Linz, 1971.

Zagiba, Franz. "Eine unbekannte Bearbeitung von Haydns Oratorium 'Die sieben Worte des Erlösers am Kreuz' aus dem Jahre 1844." *Anzeiger der österreichischen Akademie der Wissenschafte. Philosophisch-historische Klasse* 84/3 (1947), 5-8.

Zaslaw "Compleat" Zaslaw, Neal. "The Compleat Orchestral Musician." *Early Music* 7/1 (1979), 46-57.

Zaslaw "Orchestra" _____. "Toward the Revival of the Classical Orchestra." *Proceedings of the [Royal] Musical Association* 103 (1976-77), 158-187.

Zaslaw "Size" _____. "The Size and Composition of European Orchestras." In Larsen *Haydn Studies*, 186-188.

_____. "Mozart's tempo conventions." In *International Musicological Socety: Report of the Eleventh Congress, Copenhagen 1972*, 720-33. H. Glahn, S. Sorenson, and P. Ryom, eds. Copenhagen, 1974.

Zeman, H. "Das Textbuch Gottfried van Swietens zu Joseph Haydns 'Die Schöpfung'." In *Die österreichische Literatur. Ihr Profil an der Wende vom 18. zum 19. Jahrhundert*, 403-425. Graz, 1979. (2) Repr. in *Dichtung und Musik*. G. Schnitzler, ed. Stuttgart, 1979. (3) Short ver. in *Volk und Heimat. Zeitschrift für Kultur und Bildung* 37/3 (1982), 1-5.

INDEX OF WORKS BY HAYDN

Order of Categories: Masses, Oratorios and Cantatas, Smaller Sacred Works, Secular Works, Operas and Dramatic Works, Miscellaneous Vocal Works, Symphonic Works, Chamber and Keyboard Works.

MASSES

OPERAS AND DRAMATIC WORKS

MISCELLANEOUS VOCAL WORKS

SYMPHONIC WORKS

CHAMBER AND KEYBOARD WORKS

GENERAL INDEX

a cappella tradition, 7, 13, 23.
Abingdon, Lord. *See* Bertie, Willoughby.
Aboukir, 260.
Abraham a Sancta Clara, 4.
Academy of Antient Music, 232.
accents, metric, 385.
"Ach, du lieber Augustin," 5.
Adamberger, Valentin Joseph (singer), 184, 366.
afterbeat. *See* ornaments, fixed.
Agricola, Johann Friedrich, 364.
Albertarelli, Signor, 235.
Albrechtsberger, J. G., 100, 296, 312.
Alfred, oder der patriotische König, 257.
alla breve, 402, 403, 407.
Allgemeine Musikalische Zeitung, 234, 237 n.16, 300 n.22, 312 n.49.
Altomonte, Katharina von (singer), 366.
Alxinger, Johann Baptist von (poet).
    Die Vergötterung des Herkules, 295.
amateurs, 232, 233.
Anacreontics, 238.
Anglicans, 300.
anima, Jungian, 93.
Annus qui, 7, 14, 15.
Antient Concerts, 232.
Apocrypha, 182.
applausus, 92, 96, 99-106.
Applausus letter, 101, 370, 387, 459-461.
appoggiatura. *See* ornaments, fixed.
Arbesser, Ferdinand, 52, 53, 54, 55.
    Missa Nubes pluant justum, 54-56.
    Missa Rorate coeli, 54.
aria: binary, 31, 59, 62, 67; da capo, 67, 96-100, 104, 105; *di bravura,* 31; insertion, 135; motto, 31, 67; style in *The Creation,* 308-309.
arpeggio. *See* ornaments, fixed—appoggiatura.
Artaria (publishers), 142, 372, 381.
articulation, 349, 355, 357, 358, 361, 371-375, 378-380, 382-384, 395, 402; affected by instrumental idioms, 383; détaché, 355, 382; early-Classic, 373, 375; legato, 358, 379, 384; marcato, 382 n.85, 383; martelé, 355, 357; non-uniform, 382-384; single-note, 380; slurs, "flying," 378; spiccato, 355; staccato, 358, 380-382, 408; syllables, 357; in woodwind players, 357.

Bach, Carl Philipp Emanuel, 138, 212, 373, 394.
    Die Auferstehung und Himmelfahrt Christi, 366.
    Heilig, 25 n.77.
    Versuch über die wahre Art das Clavier zu spielen, 51, 394, 402, 403, 409.
    Württemberg Sonatas, 212.
Bach, Johann Sebastian, 135, 137, 295, 328-330, 353, 361, 411, 372.
    Cantata BWV 4, 30.
    Mass in B Minor, 135.
    Passions, 301, 306, 329.
    St. Matthew Passion, 30, 301.
Barmherzige Brüder, 50, 91, 146, 178, 210.
basso continuo. *See* continuo.
bassoon in Haydn's time, 309, 314, 322, 323, 325, 357; used to double bass line, 368.
Bath, England, 234-236.
Battle of the Nile, 260, 262.
Beethoven, Ludwig van, 264, 271, 274, 275, 296, 307, 326, 328, 331, 353, 365, 411.
    Die Ehre Gottes aus der Natur, 238.
    Fidelio, 5, 353.
    Mass in C, 275.
    Missa Solemnis, 271, 274.
    Piano Concerto No. 2, 296.
    Symphony No.6, "Pastoral," 307.
bel canto, 93, 347, 348.
Benvenuti, Barbara (singer), 412.
Berlioz, Hector, 69, 328, 353, 365, 405.
Bernardon. *See* Kurz.
Bertie, Willoughby, 235-236.
Berwald, Johan Fredrik (violinist), 313.
Betulia liberata, La, 182.
Bianchi, Benedetto (singer), 412.
Bible, Authorized Version, 300-303.
binary aria. *See* aria, binary.
Boccherini, Giovanni Gastone, 182.
Bon, Girolamo le, 98.
Bonno, Giuseppe, 28, 65.
Book of Common Prayer, 303.
bowing, 355, 373-377, 379, 382, 384; advanced, 376; basic, 373ff; rhythmic qualities of, 377.
Brahms, Johannes, 237, 353, 405.
Breitkopf & Härtel, 187, 216, 234, 236-238, 261, 263, 313, 324, 325.

This book was designed and typeset by the author using ITC Galliard® for both display and text fonts. Matthew Carter produced Galliard for Mergenthaler in 1978. It is modeled on the work of Robert Granjon, a 16th-century letter cutter whose type-faces are renowned for their beauty and legibility.

שיחבר-א בוריש
17